To The L... TAX

Edi... RS

JRL

OUTPUT, INPUT,
AND PRODUCTIVITY MEASUREMENT

NATIONAL BUREAU OF ECONOMIC RESEARCH

CONFERENCE ON RESEARCH IN INCOME AND WEALTH

Output, Input, and Productivity Measurement

STUDIES IN INCOME AND WEALTH
VOLUME TWENTY-FIVE
BY THE CONFERENCE ON RESEARCH
IN INCOME AND WEALTH

A REPORT OF THE
NATIONAL BUREAU OF ECONOMIC RESEARCH, INC.

PUBLISHED BY
PRINCETON UNIVERSITY PRESS, PRINCETON
1961

PRINTED IN THE UNITED STATES OF AMERICA

RELATION OF NATIONAL BUREAU DIRECTORS TO
PUBLICATIONS REPORTING CONFERENCE PROCEEDINGS

Since the present volume is a record of conference
proceedings, it has been exempted from the rules
governing submission of manuscripts to, and critical
review by, the Board of Directors of the National
Bureau. It has, however, been reviewed and accepted
for publication by the Director of Research.

*(Resolution adopted July 6, 1948 and revised
November 21, 1949)*

Prefatory Note

This volume of Studies in Income and Wealth is devoted to an appraisal of the measurement of output, input, and productivity. It contains the papers that were prepared for the Conference on Research in Income and Wealth held in October 1958 at the Carnegie Endowment International Center in New York City, together with the comments of participants. The Program Committee consisted of John W. Kendrick as chairman, Harold Barger, T. C. Schelling, and Irving H. Siegel; the Conference Editor was John W. Kendrick; the National Bureau Staff Reading Committee, in addition to Dr. Kendrick, was composed of Daniel M. Holland and G. Warren Nutter.

Contents

CONTENTS

PART II

The Estimation of Real Product in the Economy by Industries

PART III

The Estimation of Real Factor Inputs

CONTENTS

OUTPUT, INPUT,
AND PRODUCTIVITY MEASUREMENT

Introduction:
Productivity and National Income Accounting

JOHN W. KENDRICK

ALONG with the upsurge of interest in economic growth during the postwar period have come improvements in the measures of output, input, and productivity. Prior to World War II, most productivity measures were of the simple output-per-man-hour type. Useful though these measures are in showing changes in labor requirements per unit of output, they are obviously inadequate measures of changing productive efficiency as such because not all inputs are included. Since the war, substantial progress in the estimation of gross and net output and real capital stocks, as well as employment, in the economy and various industrial divisions has made possible the preparation of more comprehensive "total factor productivity" estimates.

Despite the care with which such estimates have been made, however, productivity remains one field in which economic statistics have run ahead of economic theory. Unaided by the theoretician with respect to the proper treatment of certain of the more difficult aspects of productivity measurement, especially the problem of measuring real-capital stock and input, the statistician has had to proceed using the most reasonable concepts and conventions he could devise. The results have been useful, but certainly current estimates are amenable to improvement, and both makers and users could profit by devoting more thought to their meaning and interpretation.

The Executive Committee of the conference decided it was time to pause and bring theoretician and statistician together in this important field to try to sharpen our concepts of output, input, and productivity, and to suggest needed improvements in methods of estimation and basic data. Refinement of productivity measures will make possible more meaningful analyses of dynamic economic processes and thus more effective policies in areas affected by productivity change.

The Relation of Productivity Measurement to the Economic Accounts

On first glance, the subject of productivity might appear to be somewhat tangential to the central focus of a Conference on Research in Income and Wealth. Actually, the national income accounts

3

provide an ideal framework for the measurement of productivity and of related variables on a consistent basis.

Productivity may be defined as a relation, frequently expressed in ratio form, between output and associated inputs in real terms. It is apparent that the current-value national product, "deflated" to eliminate the effects of price changes, provides a comprehensive measure of the physical volume of production of final goods and services for the economy as a whole. What is not as immediately apparent is that the national income, which represents the money costs of units of factor services, may also be deflated by appropriate factor price indexes in order to isolate changes in the physical volume of factor inputs, or "real-factor costs." In practice, it is more convenient to estimate the factor inputs directly, and to obtain the implicit factor price deflator as the quotient of national income and real-factor cost.

Since national income is defined and measured to equal the national product at factor cost, the real outputs and inputs are consistent, and equal in the base period, if the final goods and services are accorded unit-factor-cost weights. The constant dollar input series may be divided into the real product series to obtain productivity ratios through time.

The advantage of relating real product to the sum of associated factor inputs, human and material, is that the ratios indicate the *net* saving of inputs, and thus the change in productive efficiency; ratios of real product to single classes of input, such as labor, reflect the effect of factor substitutions as well. Further, the total factor productivity measures are consistent with the implicit product and factor price indexes. The product price index can be decomposed into unit factor costs of the various types, which, in turn, can be expressed as quotients of the corresponding factor price and partial productivity measures.

The national accounts framework can also be used to obtain industry estimates of real product, factor input, and productivity on a basis consistent with the national estimates. The industry approach is, in fact, a third method of obtaining national aggregates. Real product in the various industries may be estimated as the difference between the deflated values of output and of intermediate product purchases—the so-called "double deflation" method. The inter-industry or "input-output" matrix represents an elaboration of the industry production account, and is helpful in establishing weights for the price deflators of purchased goods.

In current values, industry product at factor cost, or net value added, is equal to the national income originating. Deflated national income, or real-factor cost, originating by industry represents a direct decomposition of the national aggregate, and is consistent with the industry real-product estimates. Industry productivity estimates, obtained as quotients of real-product and real-factor cost by industry, are thus consistent with the national productivity estimates. The industry unit value added and factor price indexes are likewise consistent with the national measures, and with one another.

Some of the conference papers reveal that substantial progress is being made toward the goal of a comprehensive set of real output, input, productivity, and price estimates for the economy and major sectors and industries in this country and others. A rich analytical harvest awaits the completion of this task; some of the analytical uses of productivity and related measures are illustrated in the papers.

It is interesting to recall that, at the first meetings of the Conference on Research in Income and Wealth, Morris Copeland recognized the potentialities of the national income accounts for productivity measurement.

> "Income derived from an area may be deflated to show changes in the physical volume of services of labor and wealth employed by the economic system from time to time. If we may neglect net income from abroad as relatively small, the deflated distributive shares may be compared with the deflated consumed and saved income to show changes in the efficiency of operation of the economic system."[1]

Recognition of the possibilities of estimation of productivity within the income and product framework is, however, a far cry from the realization of these possibilities; solutions to hundreds of specific conceptual and statistical problems lie in between. Many problems have already been solved in setting up the current value accounts, such as those relating to the scope of the estimates, the definition of "final" as contrasted with "intermediate" products, of consumption and investment, and so on. Even some of these solutions and conventions need re-examination from the viewpoint of requirements for productivity analysis, and alternative definitions, estimating methods, and rearrangements or extensions of the basic current value estimates may be required to give more satisfactory productivity results.

Beyond this, there are the specific problems involved in deflation of product and factor cost to separate price and quantity movements. Several papers given at earlier meetings of the conference have treated certain aspects of these problems, as can be seen from the Indexes to

[1] Morris A. Copeland, "Concepts of National Income," in *Studies in Income and Wealth*, Volume One, National Bureau of Economic Research, 1937, p. 31.

the twenty-five volumes of the "Studies in Income and Wealth" series at the end of this volume. There have been several papers on the deflation of the national product; the estimation of employment and the corresponding labor compensation has been touched on; and several sessions have been devoted to wealth estimates, which are a prerequisite to estimating the real services of capital stocks. But the problems of estimating real product and the associated factor inputs have not previously been systematically treated together from the integrating viewpoint of their use in productivity estimation and analysis.

The unifying theme of the meeting—productivity—was the subject of the first of the three conference sessions. The authors consider not only what we might ideally like to measure under this rubric but also the meaning of the actual measures that emerge from the national economic accounts. Both the statistical and theoretical requirements of meaningful measures are set forth, and the adequacy of basic data to implement the concepts is reviewed.

The second session was devoted to the concepts and problems of measuring real national product. Emphasis is given to the estimation of real product by industry, partly because the deflation of final expenditures by type of goods and services has received more emphasis in the past, but mainly because the alternative industry product approach makes possible the description of national productivity changes and relationships in terms of the component industry movements. It also makes possible international output and productivity comparisons by industry, which are also discussed.

The concepts and problems of measuring the factor inputs were the subject of the third session. Somewhat more attention is devoted to real-capital stocks and services than to labor input, in part because the conceptual and statistical problems of capital measurement seem greater. Problems of factor substitutions are considered, and existing capital estimates are subjected to critical review.

Although the main focus of this conference was on conceptual and methodological problems, a number of the papers are devoted to reviews of data or available estimates, and several sets of estimates are presented for the first time in this volume. While it is obvious from perusal of the papers that we have not wholly deprived future researchers of the joy of solving difficult problems in this area, it is also apparent that much progress has been and can be made toward the goal of an integrated set of total and partial productivity measures within the national accounts. Completion of this work will open new vistas for the analysts who are concerned with causes and effects of productivity change.

Preview of Conference Papers

The following preview of the conference papers is intended to highlight the major issues discussed in the papers, to indicate their interrelationship, and to summarize some of the main conclusions. It is certainly not intended as a digest type of substitute for the originals, but merely as a stimulus and a background that will make for fuller understanding of the volume as a whole.

THE CONCEPT AND MEASUREMENT OF PRODUCTIVITY

The opening paper by Irving Siegel is well designed to disabuse the innocents in the field of the notion that there is any general-purpose productivity index, and to warn of the complexities involved in preparing appropriate indexes for specific purposes. He finds that many makers and users of index numbers "tend to overlook the strict demands and implications of *literal* algebra while meeting the easy requirements of *verbal* algebra. Both kinds of algebra must be taken into account, however, in the design of consistent output and input measures, the design of productivity measures that are compatible with index numbers of other associated variables (e.g., wages and prices), and the evaluation of indicators that actually are constructed or used." In particular, he would require that output, input, and productivity estimates have the same coverage, represent an internal average of the component relatives, and that each be derivable from the other two as quotient or product. The national income accounting framework certainly conduces to these objectives.

These requirements necessitate adequate basic data. Siegel is not happy about the progress of productivity measurement since the good old days of the WPA National Research Project, but he is encouraged by the growing tendency of companies to estimate their own productivity changes, which will strengthen the establishment basis of reporting. "Mutually adapted" weighting systems are also necessary. Consistency with related measures would make it possible to express the productivity index as the ratio of input price to output price indexes.

Siegel considers in some detail technical aspects of both the so-called "labor productivity" indexes, and indexes of total, or "multifactor," productivity, and he develops various interesting verbal identities relating to each type of measure. Differing output and input concepts may, of course, enter the productivity formulas. For example, output may be measured gross, net, or in terms of subproducts; labor input in terms of persons engaged, employees, or production workers only, or man-hours worked or paid for; and alternative capital measures

7

are also numerous. Siegel does not view pecuniary weights as necessarily superior to or more "economic" than other types of weights, such as man-hours. "Furthermore, since all indexes are artifices, their construction and use must be reckoned as closer to accounting than to economics."

This is one point at which his discussant, Carl Christ, is forced to disagree; Christ feels "that shifts of production functions are what productivity indexes are really about." He also would seem to disagree with Siegel's proposition that labor productivity indexes should be made as weighted means of relatives by use of man-hour weights for output; rather, Christ thinks "that any improvement in social organization which permits the transfer of resources from a less productive to a more productive industry ought to be regarded in one sense as an increase in productivity." Christ later goes further and suggests that one should try to get independent measures of all the forces that may account for increases in total factor productivity. This would give us greater understanding of the dynamics of economic growth, and perhaps enable us "to push forward our production frontier more rapidly or more cheaply than we now know how to do." As a contribution to this objective, he suggests several kinds of empirical studies of the process by which knowledge concerning technical possibilities is diffused.

Professor George Stigler's paper complements Siegel's in that Stigler is concerned with the *economic* problems in measuring and interpreting productivity change. He points out that while the traditional output-per-man-hour measures are partial and unreliable as measures of output per unit of total input, especially over short periods, they nevertheless will "generally rank the commodity-producing industries correctly with respect to true productivity changes." Turning to the total productivity measures, he develops theoretically the major components of productivity change as measured. He would prefer to confine the indexes to the measurement of technological change by segregating the effects of changing scale, rates of utilization of capacity, and changing inherent quality of inputs.

The component of total productivity change which he considers potentially largest, and the most difficult to separate from technical change as such, is the net effect of external scale economies. Here, Stigler presents the results of some econometric studies, based on fitting a production function to Creamer's estimates for domestic manufacturing, and on an international cross-section analysis. His results lead him to conclude that "economies of scale are potentially of the same order of magnitude as technical progress."

Robert Solow comments that it is hard to measure economies of

8

scale in time series, since the effects of increasing return to scale and of technical advance are mixed together. He questions the meaningfulness of the international cross-section study and demonstrates that "universal constant returns to scale might lead to just such an appearance of increasing returns" as Stigler finds, but for different reasons. Morris Copeland also criticizes Stigler's cross-section analysis, and produces an alternative statistical analysis of the same data which results in the appearance of decreasing returns. Copeland regrets that Stigler did not find it possible to attempt to quantify the other components of productivity change as measured.

Stigler's remarks need not be interpreted as detracting from the value of total productivity measures; they do underscore the caution that users must be aware that the present measures reflect more than pure technical advance. It would undoubtedly be useful for the study of economic growth to know how important the scale factor has been, although the broad productivity measures are still indispensable. One suspects that we may in the end have to rely more on the hunches of a Stigler than on neat econometric solutions to the puzzle of distinguishing the effects of scale economies from those of technical progress

In passing, Stigler mentions the tendency toward diminishing return in extractive industry, but does not consider its potential magnitude as an offset to increasing return. Harold Barnett of Wayne State University and Resources for the Future devotes his paper to this problem. Looking at it first from a theoretical standpoint, he maintains that the premise of a dynamized law of diminishing return—*economic* scarcity of natural resources—must be viewed as a hypothesis and not a fact. He attempts a partial test of the hypothesis by comparing the extractive and nonextractive sectors of the economy with respect to trend in both average prices and output per man-hour.

The productivity comparisons are based on estimates presented in a separate conference paper by Neal Potter and Francis T. Christy, Jr. The price and productivity comparisons either do not support or are adverse to the hypothesis of resource scarcity with respect to agriculture and mineral industries, but do support the hypothesis in the timber industry. Barnett hastens to add that his tentative conclusions would be modified if there had been differential change in the two sectors with respect to other parameters such as technology.

William Vickrey develops other theoretical qualifications to the tests; also the very practical empirical point that output units are quite standard over time in extractive industry, while in many other sectors there has been a gradual net quality improvement which imparts a persistent bias to the relative price and productivity movements.

9

It is also apparent, as Barnett notes, that the productivity comparisons would have been even more convincing if they had taken account of capital and intermediate product inputs as well as the labor inputs. Nonetheless, the Potter-Christy paper adds considerably to our knowledge of the extractive sector. It is also useful, as pointed up by the comments of Vivian Spencer, in illustrating the difficulties encountered in estimating output and labor input over a long time span in a major industry segment.

The availability of data for the measurement of output and manhours for all segments of the United States economy is reviewed in a final paper by Leon Greenberg, who directs the program of productivity measurement in the Labor Department. He covers methodological problems of estimation, and also pinpoints weaknesses and gaps in the underlying data. Particularly valuable is the compilation he presents for all industries showing availability of data on output quantities, values, prices, employment, and hours. The paper's discussant, Raymond T. Bowman, comments: "In the years ahead, it should be possible to use the information to strengthen the basic sources of productivity data and fill in the more important gaps." This comment has added significance, coming from the Assistant Director for Statistical Standards of the Bureau of the Budget, under whose aegis the Greenberg survey was instigated.

ESTIMATES OF REAL PRODUCT

The second portion of the conference was devoted to the concepts and measurement of output, with particular emphasis on the estimation of industry real products. The industry approach, as noted earlier, makes possible estimates of productivity by industry which are consistent with national productivity measures.

It was appropriate that the session was opened with a paper by V. R. Berlinguette and F. H. Leacy of the Dominion Bureau of Statistics, since Canada has probably gone further with implementing the industry product approach than has the United States. The authors point out that the Dominion Bureau has found the industry real-product (net output) estimates to be useful (a) as a check on the results of deflating the gross national expenditure, (b) for current analysis of the industrial composition of changes in the volume of total real product and productivity, (c) for analysis of price-volume components of value changes, and (d) as a basis for economic projections incorporating component industry detail.

The Canadian industry real-product figures reconcile quite well with the aggregate deflated expenditure estimates on an annual basis, and tolerably well quarterly. An interesting feature of the Berlin-guette-Leacy paper is a comparison of the movement of net and gross output measures for the industries, comprising about one-third of gross domestic product, for which both types of estimates are possible. In general, shifts in product mix are seen to account for most of the discrepant movement between the net and gross measures, although materials savings and greater processing of particular goods may be significant in some cases. The authors also present comparisons of aggregates, using national income versus census value-added weights for the industry components and factor cost versus market price weights. The alternative weighting systems are found to make little difference. Many other technical aspects of deflating national product both by type of expenditure and by industry of origin are discussed.

The paper by Jack Alterman and Eva Jacobs presents exploratory estimates of real product originating in all major industry divisions of the U.S. economy annually since 1947, a description of methodology, and some analysis of the results. This project was undertaken at the request and with cooperation of an Interagency Committee on Production and Productivity Statistics sponsored by the Office of Statistical Standards in the Bureau of the Budget. It is gratifying that the real gross national product derived as the sum of the real product of fourteen industry divisions, for which estimates are presented, is quite close in all years to the real GNP estimates derived by deflating final expenditures by type, as published by the Department of Commerce. Encouraged by the results of this exploratory study, in which its representatives also participated, the National Income Division of the Commerce Department in fiscal year 1960 has begun to devote resources to the estimation of national product by industry grouping, which it is hoped will eventually become part of the official national accounts.

National product estimates by industry not only provide an additional approach to and check on the aggregate but they also permit new and useful lines of analysis, two examples of which are provided by Alterman and Jacobs. The new estimates make possible analysis of the changing industrial structure of production and, when related to associated inputs, the analysis of relative productivity change by industry. Thus, the reader who consults Table 1 of the paper will see that business and personal services show average increases in real product per man-hour well below average, while farming and public utilities have been on the high end of the scale in the postwar period. The estimates also make possible the calculation of the effect on productivity of interindustry manpower shifts. Between 1947 and 1955, only 4 per cent of the over-all increase in real product per man-hour

11

is traced to this cause—a significantly smaller proportion than has been revealed by studies covering longer time spans.

The notes on sources, methods, and techniques provide a relatively solid point of departure in most sectors for further work along these lines. It should be noted that the estimates described by Alterman and Jacobs were based on then-available data. New tabulations from the 1958 censuses, the interindustry chart for that year also being undertaken by the National Income Division, and expansion of the BLS price-collection program will help substantially in preparation of yet more reliable industry product figures.

Prior to the estimates presented by Alterman and Jacobs, only three major sets of industry real-product estimates had been published—those by Kendrick and Jones for the farm sector (which have been continued by the Commerce Department), the net output series for manufacturing developed by the Labor Department, and an earlier set of estimates for various industries prepared by Simon Kuznets. The methodology underlying these series is carefully reviewed by Almarin Phillips. Except for agriculture, Kuznets' industry output estimates were obtained by extrapolating base-period national income by gross output measures. Their validity depends on the generally untested assumption that the ratio of net to gross constant dollar output remains unchanged. This comment applies as well to the industries treated likewise in the estimates presented in the papers just discussed. With respect to the true net output series, Phillips finds them "virtually devoid of serious conceptual error," but points out specific needs for better data. He makes a real contribution to further work by calling attention to and developing one variant of Kuznets' deflation technique that has gone largely unnoticed. By this method, current dollar value added or industry product can be deflated by "a weighted average of the difference between the gross output and the input price indexes." This technique is most useful when industry product estimates are available, but not the necessary data on sales and purchased intermediate products. Phillips tests this method applied to manufacturing value added against the results obtained by BLS using "double deflation."

Since the Phillips paper is, in a sense, a commentary on the Alterman-Jacobs work, Charles Schultze, who was scheduled as a discussant of the latter paper, was free to give the conference a bonus by illustrating applications of the industry real-product series in price-change analysis. He demonstrates that in conjunction with current dollar industry-product estimates (which Schultze built up from the Commerce Department's industry income figures), the consistent real-product series can be used to obtain industry unit value-added indexes that reconcile with economy price indexes. The industry indexes, in turn, can be decomposed into unit labor costs, unit property costs, and unit depreciation and indirect business taxes. The proportionate contributions of changes in each of these types of unit costs to the total unit value-added change can then be computed. This type of decomposition does not reveal causal relations, but it does provide the basis for more revealing analysis than is possible without the detail. The analysis would be even more revealing, however, if the unit labor and capital cost measures were further decomposed into factor price and productivity indexes. In a subsequent discussion, George Tolley attempts to do just this for the agricultural sector.

The OEEC has recently been experimenting with international comparisons of real product by industry. This work is not to be confused with the reports issued in 1954 and 1958 which compared national product by expenditure class for several member countries and the United States.

Milton Gilbert and Wilfred Beckerman, in their discussion of this recent work, devote much of their paper to the theoretical problems involved in international product comparisons—treatment of net income from abroad, the effect of differences in tastes and income distribution among nations, quality differences and unique products, and differences in relative price weights. With respect to tastes, for example, they argue that international differences are less than differences over long time spans in the same country. They support this position by reference to their statistical studies: "It was remarkable how greatly the observed international differences in consumption patterns appeared to be explained by differences in incomes and relative prices." This conclusion was concurred in by their discussant, Tibor Scitovsky.

In general, Gilbert and Beckerman feel that conceptual limitations on intercountry comparisons are no greater than those which apply to intertemporal comparisons, and are not great enough seriously to affect the order of magnitude of the results.

The results of a comparison of real product by major industry division for the United States and United Kingdom in the year 1950, together with employment comparisons, are given in tables. The aggregate industry product estimates are compared with the real-expenditure totals for the same year. The effect of the alternative country weights are somewhat different in the two sets of estimates, and the authors discuss the relative reliability of the statistical underpinnings of each. The implied net output per worker comparisons by industry are very interesting, and one hopes that the corresponding

13

capital coefficients will some day be available to help in the explanation of international productivity differences by industry.

Tibor Scitovsky opens his comments on the Gilbert-Beckerman paper by reference to the "tug of war between the more imaginative statisticians and the more rigorous—or should I say more pedantic—theorists." Although cast in the role of the pedant, Scitovsky declared himself as quite sympathetic to the OEEC attempts at international real-income comparisons. He goes on to discuss further the economic meaning of the comparisons in both their welfare and productivity aspects, and argues that the estimates are more ambiguous in meaning from the productivity viewpoint.

THE MEASUREMENT OF INPUT

The third and final session of the conference was devoted to problems in the concepts and measures of economic input. In planning the program the Committee placed particular emphasis on capital, the estimation of which is peculiarly elusive.

In his introductory paper, Kenneth Boulding points out that definitions of input vary with the context. Whereas, in studies of income distribution and resource allocation, inputs must be defined as equal to output, in productivity studies it is essential that input be defined in such a way that its changes will *not* equal output changes. This leads to the problem of differentiating between significant and nonsignificant inputs. In a later discussion, Zvi Griliches suggests trying to measure *all* input in an attempt fully to explain output change. But in any case, it is apparent that the change in "efficiency" indicated by a productivity index depends on the scope and definitions of the inputs.

Like Stigler, Boulding is interested in identifying productivity change in terms of shifts in production function. He discusses theoretically various types of "factor-saving" shifts, and his discussant, Murray Kemp, pushes the analysis somewhat further. Unfortunately, statistical measures cannot precisely reveal the shifts except under an unholy alliance of assumptions of linear, homogeneous production functions, competitive markets, and constant input proportions.

The first part of Boulding's discussion is based on the assumption that labor and capital inputs can be measured in homogeneous units over time. He then raises questions as to how "labor" use of time may be separated from nonlabor use, and how the intensity of labor may be measured. Dangers in measuring capital-output ratios are noted: "The composition and physical nature of capital changes all the time, and any measure of its aggregate becomes increasingly arbitrary as time goes on." Despite his avowed failure to find solutions, Boulding pleads that "accurate" input measures should not be

14

substituted for "significant" ones, and he concludes by warning against "the danger of our information system controlling the questions instead of the questions the information system."

The problems of measuring labor input were assigned to Edward Denison and his two scheduled discussants, George Tolley and Murray Wernick. Before settling down to the main issue, Denison could not resist the temptation briefly to renew the discussion concerning the proper scope of national product estimates. He argues that "social overhead" outlays must be included in product; their exclusion as advocated by Kuznets would, in effect, "omit from the measurement of output provision for the satisfaction of all needs that change over time because of changes in individuals' external environment." Denison thinks this "destroys the national product as a measure of the total output that actually is available to satisfy wants and needs." The narrower treatment would also produce changes in productivity due solely to external environmental changes, unless the resources devoted to the excluded output were omitted from the input measures, which would involve difficult allocations.

Turning to labor input as such, Denison argues that man-hours worked are a better measure than employment of real cost in terms of disutility. Thus, he considers man-hours to be the appropriate gauge of labor input to combine with other input measures to derive measures of productivity, "or the efficiency with which an economy maximizes output to satisfy its members' wants while minimizing real costs." Denison enters more controversial territory, however, when he claims that employment is a better measure than man-hours of effective labor input in terms of the contribution labor makes to production. He argues that output per man will vary less than output per man-hour with changes in hours at all points above thirty or so per week, and thus employment is a labor input measure "that is crudely adjusted for one form of quality change—the quality of an hour's work that is due to shortening of hours." The effect of a shorter week on hourly production is seen to work through several channels: reduction of worker fatigue and, more important, stimulation of management efficiency and substitution of capital for labor. With regard to the latter, Tolley asks: "Do we want productivity measures to obscure these effects?" Wernick also favors man-hours measures, and makes some cogent criticisms of the estimates of full-time equivalent employment as prepared by the Office of Business Economics.

Denison next considers the adequacy of employment and man-hour data. He points out the "enormous advantage in statistical interdependence between the measures of output and labor input" in the national accounts. Use of the gross national product estimates calculated from the income side in conjunction with persons-engaged series consistent with the labor compensation component maximizes this advantage in short-run comparisons, although over the long run the statistical discrepancy is not important. Based on his long experience in income work at the Commerce Department, Denison guesses the average error in the annual rate of change in real national product per person resulting from errors in the "persons-engaged" series to be roughly 0.2 percentage points for year-to-year comparisons, and to be negligible for periods longer than two or three years. Since data for average hours of work are less reliable and complete than employment data, Denison puts the error in the man-hour series at several times that in the persons-engaged estimates. He doubts whether the error is serious in long-term comparisons of output per man-hour, although it may be for short-term changes. "However, year-to-year variations in productivity change are so great that even rather crude measures may be useful in distinguishing years of large from those of small or negative productivity increase."

Denison prefers to use unweighted man-hours in productivity ratios, rather than weight by average hourly earnings in the various occupations or industries, so that the effects of shifts will show up in the productivity measures. He believes, nevertheless, that "comparison of output per man-hour with output per unit of 'labor input' in Kendrick's sense [weighted man-hours] . . . provides a useful measure of the contribution of industry shifts to past increases of productivity, and hence also a useful tool for projections." Tolley presents some new statistical evidence on this point, based on labor force estimates weighted in terms of fifty-five occupational groups for the period 1910–50. He concludes that "Changing quality of labor inputs associated with occupational mix seems to have been a minor source of U.S. growth from 1910 to date." Wernick urges further investigation of this factor, as well as of changing composition of the work force with reference to sex, industry, and· production as compared with nonproduction workers.

In their paper on concepts of real-capital stocks and services for productivity measurement purposes, Richard and Nancy Ruggles make no attempt to gloss over the inherent difficulties. They are critical of the conventional measures of real capital based on what it would cost in the base year to produce a given year's stock. Such measures attempt to treat capital in terms of standard units, adjusting to exclude changing efficiency of the capital goods but not for the changing efficiency with which they are produced. This attempt runs into difficulties because, for one thing, the designs of products interact with their costs of production. More broadly: "The basic fact is

16

that capital in general has no physical units, and any arbitrary solution will predetermine the answers we get." With changes in quality and new kinds of capital goods, it is not possible to know what they would have cost in an earlier, base period. Further, the Ruggleses see an incongruity in not adjusting capital goods for improved efficiency, but yet adjusting net capital stocks downward for the effects of obsolescence. The usual problem of aggregation is posed by changing relative prices, which in the case of capital items are affected by changes in the relative quantities of cooperating inputs as well as by changing technology and other supply and demand forces.

The alternatives of measuring capital in terms of real input, or of capacity, are discussed, but their limitations from a productivity standpoint preclude much support.

Despite the conceptual problems, the Ruggleses find the studies of the National Bureau of Economic Research in the areas of capital-output ratios to be illuminating. This usefulness they trace to the fact that price deflators for capital and for output do not diverge widely, so the ratios in terms of physical volumes move similarly to those based on current dollars, which the authors consider to have significance.

In addition to their treatment of capital stocks and services, the Ruggleses also seek to clarify the treatment of capital formation in the national accounts. They propose adjustment for efficiency change parallel with that extended to consumer goods, and inclusion of certain types of intangible investment and governmental capital formation.

Evsey Domar's first reaction to the Ruggleses' paper was a feeling of relief for having been spared the job himself! He points to attributes of capital which complicate measurement: longevity, impermanence, technological change, source of future income, and a limited second-hand market. Yet, as he notes, most of these attributes also attach to labor, but they "do not prevent our labor friends from merrily aggregating man-hours among industries and over time."

Milton Gilbert, who also contributes a commentary on the Ruggleses' paper, is much more sanguine than they about the possibilities of constructing meaningful capital measures. He thinks that there are enough capital goods that retain their basic characteristics over long enough periods of time to permit the construction of estimates without much more resort to convention than is necessary in the national product estimates as a whole.

Daniel Creamer's paper is devoted to a review and appraisal of the capital, or "wealth," estimates for the major sectors of the U.S. economy, prepared for the National Bureau of Economic Research in

17

connection with its study of "Trends in Capital Formation and Financing." All possible methods were employed in these estimates: censuses or balance sheet data were used for agriculture, mining, and manufactures; cumulation of annual net expenditures for nonfarm residential construction; and a combination of these methods for the regulated industries. Creamer describes in some detail the sources of basic data, methodology used, and other characteristics of each of the sets of estimates. For all sectors except mining, he finds it possible to test the estimates by comparison with other more or less independent estimates.

He also aggregates the real net fixed capital estimates for the five sectors and compares them with Kuznets' estimates obtained by cumulating net fixed capital formation in constant (1929) dollars for all private, profit-making sectors of the national economy by decade intervals, 1880–1948. The relative movement of the two series over the period as a whole appears reasonable, although large differences in rates of change in certain decades are disturbing.

Raymond Goldsmith concludes from Creamer's materials that "our best hope for the future is the systematic development of the perpetual inventory method of measuring the stock of capital, i.e., the cumulation of price-adjusted and properly depreciated figures for gross capital expenditures, sectorally classified and broken down by main types . . . ." The indispensable gross capital expenditure figures are available, but Goldsmith sees three chief obstacles to their transformation into stock estimates: (1) better capital goods price indexes are needed, (2) considerable effort is needed to develop realistic depreciation rates, and (3) at least one postwar benchmark estimate of capital stock is required. To supply the last need, Goldsmith proposes a census of national wealth. He thinks we are in far better position to take a meaningful census now than we were at the time of the last one in 1922. Addressing himself to this point, Robert W. Burgess notes various unsolved problems of wealth estimation. He suggests that "the Census Bureau can make the greatest feasible contribution toward an ultimate 'census of wealth' by contributing the results now provided by the various censuses and making some relatively modest changes and supplementary studies that will make these results more useful in the field of wealth. After more material of this general type has been accumulated, and more helpful conceptual analyses have been made, the Bureau might be in a position to cooperate effectively in conducting a single, comprehensive census of wealth."

Whether it is possible to measure capital at all precisely, much precise thought has been devoted to the analysis of conditions of factor substitutions. This problem was of concern to the conference if only

18

because relative changes in input quantities and prices create the same index number problem in measuring inputs that beset the estimator of output. More broadly, there is the question of the forces behind factor substitution, and their possible relation to advances in technology and productivity.

Against this background, Eric Schiff first takes up the question whether upward pressure on wage rates, as by labor unions, stimulates research and invention in industry "by making the search for new labor-saving procedures even more imperative than it would otherwise be." On admittedly scanty evidence, he concludes that there is little or no relation. Vernon Ruttan points out that there is even some question whether unions have been able to raise wages generally above equilibrium levels in the first place. Schiff then asks whether wage boosts accelerate the rate at which managements adopt known labor-saving devices. In most nonfarm industry, he argues, "process variation by merely changing 'doses' of individual input elements is precluded by fairly strict technological complementarity constraints." After an interesting review of considerable empirical evidence, he suggests that redesigns of industrial processes are largely independent of changes in labor costs. Ruttan would qualify this viewpoint: "In the longer run, where the production function may resemble something closer to its classical form . . . the possibilities for factor substitution may be considerably greater" than in the short run.

Schiff succeeds in eliciting agreement from Ruttan on his proposition regarding the effect of relative factor price changes: "If capital is substituted for labor in response to rising labor costs rather than to declining costs of capital equipment, then the effect on *total* productivity (output per unit of total input) is negative, despite the rise in *labor* productivity."

The other major section of Schiff's paper has to do with the impact of the corporate income tax on factor substitution. His model leads to the conclusion that increases in corporate income tax rates encourage the substitution of processes that are more labor intensive for ones that require more capital and are more efficient at the lower tax rates. Schiff suggests that the increased tax rates of the 1930's may have been one of the causes of the decline in the capital coefficient during that period.

Ruttan points out that Schiff's conclusion hinges on his assumptions, which are not wholly realistic. He offers several alternative hypotheses to explain the thirty-year decline in the capital coefficient following World War I.

Whatever the impression created by the printed conference record,

19

the discussions at the day and a half of meetings were lively, at times heated, and often humorous. In short, a good time was had by the participants. This was a welcome by-product of the presentation of a set of papers which contribute substantially to our growing understanding of the concepts, measures, and meaning of productivity change.

make-up—to the basic output and input data, the weights, and the formula that it embodies.

Unfortunately, few alternative productivity measures are actually constructible from available materials, and the variety of practicable measures will not be quickly or appreciably extended by government and private endeavors to improve economic statistics. Furthermore, if all conceivable measures could be computed for a single industry or economic sector, they would not give identical results and might even disagree sharply for intervals of significant change in economic structure (e.g., transitions between war and peace and between good times and bad). Accordingly, the quotient of any available or constructible pair of output and input measures cannot be regarded as *the* productivity index without appeal to additional cogent criteria that rule out all rivals. The odds are overwhelming that this quotient is only *a* productivity index, rather than the best—the most pertinent —of the many conceivable specific measures. For the uses to which it is put, it may lack certain desirable properties and even possess some undesirable ones.

The customer, in other words, is not always right; nor is the producer. Neither of them is really at liberty to attach to a productivity quotient any economic or other meaning that he chooses or that an occasion demands. The meaning ascribed to a measure should be congruent with the operational meaning, with the implications of the literal algebra involved. Only those who would live by faith alone could risk accepting an official, general-purpose, or other authoritative measure as universally applicable, as appropriate for any problem situation, without reference to its literal meaning.

Literal Consistency within Productivity Definition

PROPERTIES OF "REASONABLE" INDEXES

NOTE: Some revisions have been made in the text and footnotes of the paper originally presented. John W. Kendrick offered many helpful comments as a member of the Reading Committee.

Let us now turn to the design of index numbers untrammeled by limitations of data, funds, time, and patience. What conditions of literal algebra might reasonably be imposed on measures satisfying the bald verbal definition of productivity as the quotient of output and input? In the first instance, we treat this question as involving no additional verbal identity. That is, the output, input, and productivity indexes are considered to describe a complete and closed system, to comprise the entire statistical apparatus needed for the universe of discourse.

25

Common sense—or, if one prefers, intuition—suggests that the three indexes should preferably (1) be similar in general form, (2) make equally good operational sense, and (3) be invariant to the order of their derivation. More explicitly, it seems reasonable to require (1) homologous structure of the measures of all three variables, (2) equivalence of each measure to an internal average of the corresponding relatives, and (3) derivability of each measure from the other two (as a quotient or product).

If the first requirement is interpreted somewhat generously, many formulas immediately come to mind as qualifying. It is not essential for our purposes to add criteria or to cite circumstances that would eliminate all eligible sets of measures but one. In the remainder of this paper, however, no notice will be given to geometric means of relatives. Attention will be confined to the types of indexes that are commonly approximated—weighted aggregative measures and weighted arithmetic and harmonic means of relatives. All these are ratios with dimensionally comparable numerators and denominators. Occasional reference will be made to combinations of two or more qualifying measures into Fisher-type "ideal" averages.[1]

The three requirements cannot be satisfied exactly with normally available data. The consistent theoretical measures, being mutually determined, are tethered one to the other by specially forged links of literal algebra. The particular concept of output, input, or productivity that enters explicitly into one measure must be retained in the companion measures. An output index, furthermore, may have to incorporate weights other than the usual pecuniary variety (e.g., man-hours). In short, the demands of consistency cannot be met precisely unless the basic data are available in proper kind, detail, and amount.

Of special importance is the requirement of derivability of any measure from the other two. This property may be guaranteed by the design of the index-number systems in such a manner as to achieve a cancellation upon multiplication or division. The condensation of the product or quotient of two indexes to a ratio of only two compatible aggregates implies the conditional equivalence of weighted output

---

[1] The chain index is not explicitly considered. Even though discontinuities in data are conventionally handled by resort to this type of index, the author believes that it should be regarded as a crude alternative to a "free composition" aggregative measure, which is an extension of the ordinary Laspeyres or Paasche measure to cover *all* the products made at some time in the whole span under consideration. Thus, in the free composition index, fictitious weights and zero quantity entries may be required in the numerator or denominator for products not yet made or already obsolete. The conventions of this index, strange though they may seem, are much more sensible than those of the chain index, which never registers a rise from, or a fall to, zero for any product class and implies that nonexistent products show exactly the same changes over time as the products actually included in the measurement. See footnote 10.

26

and input. But this equivalence could not obtain in particular instances unless the mutually adapted weighting systems assure the direct dimensional comparability of output and input aggregates in the first place. In other words, the weights assigned to output and input quantity figures that are initially expressed in characteristic output or input units reduce all these figures to a single common denominator for all periods.

From the statements just made, useful corollaries flow. The cancellation criterion is as essential to thinking about consistent index numbers as the principle of conservation is to physics and the principle of exhaustiveness to accounting. It even provides a rule for the selection of output and input weights when productivity measurement does not embrace all factor inputs.[2] It offers the key to clean deflation, to the design of a suitable matching price index for literally as well as nominally converting a value index into a quantity measure. It permits expression of a productivity index as a ratio of appropriately constructed *price* measures for input and output.[3] The notion of direct comparability of output and input not only underlies cancellation but also permits (1) the expression of net output in any period as a difference between weighted gross output and weighted nonfactor input (e.g., materials and energy) and (2) the interpretation of an aggregative productivity index as a ratio between two expressions for weighted output or between two expressions for weighted input.

LABOR PRODUCTIVITY

In the thirties, the WPA National Research Project pioneered a program of consistent measurement of production, man-hours, and labor productivity in the manufacturing and mining industries.[4] The formulas were developed with reference to the primary aim of the Project—the study of unemployment and re-employment in a changing technological environment.

Consistent formulas were devised by WPA within the framework of

---

[2] See footnote 8 for an example of the application of the cancellation criterion to the case of productivity based on gross output and only one (labor) input.

[3] Let $QP = V = V' = Q'P'$, where Q and P represent quantity and price indexes for output; Q' and P', quantity and price indexes for input; and V, and V' value indexes for output and input. For productivity, we have

$$\Pi = \frac{Q}{Q'} = \frac{V/P}{V'/P'} = \frac{P'}{P}.$$

See footnote 15 for an explicit example.

[4] See H. Magdoff, I. H. Siegel, and M. B. Davis, *Production, Employment, and Productivity in 59 Manufacturing Industries, 1919–36*, WPA National Research Project Report No. S-1 (Philadelphia, 1939), 3 vols.; and V. E. Spencer, *Production, Employment, and Productivity in the Mineral Extractive Industries: 1880–1938*, WPA National Research Project Report No. S-2 (Philadelphia, 1940).

the verbal identity: Man-hours=Output × Unit man-hour requirements. Since unweighted man-hours were accepted for the input measure, two Paasche-Laspeyres sets were obtained for the other two variables. In the output formulas, the quantities were weighted by unit labor requirements; in the formulas for unit labor requirements, the weights were output quantities. The numerators and denominators of all these aggregative formulas were dimensionally equal to man-hours (which could also be interpreted as weighted output, if necessary). The reciprocals of the two indicators of unit man-hour requirements were internal means of productivity relatives.[5]

In practice, the WPA Project could seldom satisfy the strict demands of the literal algebra and accordingly had to resort to various degrees of approximation. In particular, it almost always had to use conventional output measures with unit-value weights for individual industries. But this very compromise could have defeated the WPA program objective: The quotients of such output measures and unweighted man-hours indexes need not be internal means of productivity relatives.[6]

If appropriately detailed data were available for weighting the man-hours expended on individual products,[7] WPA could have achieved

---

[5] One set of indexes satisfying the verbal identity is:

$$\frac{\sum q_i l_i}{\sum q_o l_o} = \frac{\sum q_i l_o}{\sum q_o l_o} \cdot \frac{\sum q_i l_i}{\sum q_i l_o},$$

where the q's and l's refer to output and unit man-hour requirements. The reciprocal of the second index on the right is an aggregative productivity measure, which, of course, may be rewritten as an internal mean of relatives.

[6] See I. H. Siegel, *Concepts and Measurement of Production and Productivity*, U.S. Bureau of Labor Statistics (March 1952), pp. 53–4. In general, an output index that is not designed for consistency with an input index yields a productivity quotient which may be factored into two terms, one being an internal mean of productivity relatives. The second term, however, may be such that the quotient falls outside the range of productivity relatives.

An egregious example of externality (and a troublesome one, too, in view of the increasing political importance of the rate of economic growth) is provided in the long-term productivity measures for our private economy and its agricultural and non-agricultural components. Thus, *Bulletin No. 1249* of the U.S. Department of Labor (published in December 1959, a year after this paper was presented) shows an average annual increase of 2.3 per cent in the real output per man-hour in the private sector during the period 1909–58, but smaller increases for both the agricultural and non-agricultural components—2.1 and 2.0 per cent, respectively. A variant set of measures for the same period shows corresponding rates of 2.4, 2.1 , and 2.1 per cent.

[7] It should be recognized, of course, that the joint or overhead labor expended in, say, a plant or company on a group of products can be allocated only by procedures that are in some degree arbitrary. Value added cannot strictly be measured for individual products either. At least in principle, the subproduct approach (see footnote 10), which distinguishes the results of processing stages or operations instead of treating individual products as wholes, would minimize or avoid the need for arbitrary allocations of man-hours or value added. In other words, joint or overhead operations may be regarded as yielding subproducts meriting separate classification and measurement.

its technical objective by another route. Thus, if the conventional value-weighted output measures are considered satisfactory, it is possible to design weighted companion indexes yielding productivity quotients that must be internal averages of relatives. Corresponding to the Laspeyres-type output measure in this case are two sets of productivity and man-hours indexes rather than one. Similarly, for the output measure of the Paasche variety, two other sets of matching measures are derivable for the other variables (i.e., for man-hours and productivity).[8]

Economic analysts often wish to decompose the percentage change in man-hours between two years into particles reflecting percentage changes in output and in unit labor requirements. Actually, there are three particles rather than two, so the verbal identity is frequently stated incorrectly in the first place. The identity should read:

$$\left. \begin{array}{c} \text{Percentage change} \\ \text{in man-hours} \end{array} \right\} = \left\{ \begin{array}{l} \text{Percentage change in output} + \text{per-} \\ \text{centage change in unit man-hour} \\ \text{requirements} + \text{joint percentage} \\ \text{change in both output and unit} \\ \text{man-hour requirements.} \end{array} \right.$$

The third particle is sometimes ignored; sometimes absorbed into one of the other two particles; sometimes distributed equally between the other two particles (with the result that the time reference of the "weights" differs from the time base for the computation of percentage changes); or sometimes incorrectly attributed to factors other than output and unit man-hour requirements. The joint particle has a distinct meaning in terms of algebra, geometry, or a Taylor expansion, and it should accordingly not be absorbed into either or both of the other particles. When it is not absorbed, it should not be interpreted in terms of variables extraneous to the identity. Furthermore, since

---

[8] To assure cancellation, we make one weighted output term equal to a (differently) weighted input term—say

$$\sum p_o q_o = \sum \left(\frac{p_o q_o}{m_o} . m_o \right).$$

For the verbal identity shown in the text, we then have

$$\frac{\sum \left(\frac{p_o q_o}{m_o} . m_i \right)}{\sum \left(\frac{p_o q_o}{m_o} . m_o \right)} = \frac{\sum p_o q_i}{\sum p_o q_o} . L,$$

if we choose the Laspeyres production index; and L, an index of unit man-hour requirements, is equivalent to a weighted mean of relatives of the form $\left(\frac{m_i}{m_o} \div \frac{q_i}{q_o} \right)$. Three other sets of similar measures may be worked out.

See *Index Numbers of Industrial Production*, United Nations Statistical Office Studies in Methods No. 1 (New York, September 15, 1950), pp. 57–8.

partitioning is more like anatomy than physiology, it seems desirable to avoid causal language—to avoid labeling components as "due to", or showing the effects of, the particular variables involved.

Since output normally increases and unit labor requirements tend to decline over a span of years, the corresponding percentage changes are typically different in sign. In these circumstances, the distribution of the joint particle between the other two may have particularly awkward results. A difference in signs may often be avoided if the basic identity is rewritten so that output equals man-hours times productivity. Productivity, the reciprocal of unit labor requirements, commonly has an upward trend and, over long periods, man-hours too are likely to increase.

Beyond the verbal algebra of partitioning, there is still the matter of literal algebra. Percentage changes should be measured as differences between appropriate indexes and unity. If a Laspeyres (Paasche) index is used for production, the Paasche (Laspeyres) formula is indicated for unit man-hour requirements or productivity.[9]

A few additional points should be made before we turn our attention to productivity measures involving a broader input base:

1. The Fisher "ideal" index could be used to reduce the two sets of WPA measures to one. Similarly, geometric means could be taken of the two sets of formulas built around the Laspeyres value-weighted

---

[9] The partitioning identity may be written as:

$$(M-1) = (Q-1)+(L-1)+(Q-1)(L-1),$$

where M, Q, and L refer to indexes of man-hours, output, and unit man-hour requirements and, of course, $M=QL$. If M is an unweighted index, then, as in footnote 5, Q may represent a Laspeyres index and L a Paasche index. The identity is also satisfied by the Paasche formula for Q and the Laspeyres formula for L.

The particles are more likely to have the same sign if we write $Q=M\Pi$ and

$$(Q-1) = (M-1)+(\Pi-1)+(M-1)(\Pi-1).$$

If M and Q are defined as in the preceding paragraph, then Π is the reciprocal of the measure used for L.

The purely formal character of partitioning and the inappropriateness of the practice of distributing the joint particle may be effectively illustrated by a plausible case of $M=QL$, in which $Q-1=2$ and $L-1=-1/2$, so that $M-1=1/2$ and $(Q-1)(L-1)=-1$. The "effect" of the joint change in Q and L is a decline of 100 per cent in M, which is ridiculous; and if the joint particle is equally distributed between the other two, as is so often done, the change in M "due to" the change in L becomes minus 100 per cent!

On partition formulas including only two variables, see *Concepts and Measurement* . . ., *op. cit.*, pp. 86–90.

On the proper way to introduce extraneous variables into a discussion of partition identities, see a comment by I. H. Siegel in *Proceedings of the Business and Economic Statistics Section, American Statistical Association, 1957,* p. 309.

The position taken in this paper is not only at variance with common practice but is also opposed to the Divisia approach to index-number design and to the rationale more recently offered by Stuvel (*Econometrica*, January 1957 and July 1958).

output index, or of the two sets consistent with the Paasche value-weighted index.

2. Many different output and labor concepts may enter into the formulas intended literally to satisfy the verbal algebra. Thus, the output figures could refer to completed products, net output, or subproducts (which correspond to the arcs of production cycles). The man-hours could relate to hours worked or hours compensated, to wage workers or all employees. The verbal identity may also define a consistent set of generalized aggregative indexes that take account of the entry of new products and the exit of defunct products without chaining.[10]

3. In the interpretation of labor productivity measures, account must be taken of the special difficulties besetting the quantification of output and of the manner in which these difficulties are met. Among the problems frequently encountered are lags in reporting of quantities of new products, the heterogeneity of product classes, quality change, and the noncommodity character of many "services" performed by manufacturing company personnel (e.g., research,

[10] On the subproduct concept, see I. H. Siegel, "The Concept of Productive Activity," *Journal of the American Statistical Association*, June 1944, pp. 218–28. On extended aggregative indexes intended to replace chain indexes, see *Concepts and Measurement . . .*, *op. cit.*, pp. 70–4, and I. H. Siegel, "Aspects of Productivity Measurement and Meaning," in G. Deurinck, ed., *Productivity Measurement, I: Concepts*, Organization for European Economic Cooperation (Paris, August 1955), pp. 50–6.

As already suggested in footnote 7, subproducts are the results of the discrete activities that lead to the end products normally measured. According to the subproduct approach, automobile production is much more than final assembly of the completed product; it should also include the manufacture of components, which in turn may be visualized as a series of discrete steps. Production measures based on subproducts would have many advantages; they would reflect the structure of productive activity more accurately, provide better indicators for industries making heterogeneous end products, and avoid distortions associated with changes in the degree of technical integration.

The following equation illustrates the satisfaction of the verbal identity considered in footnote 5 with free composition indexes:

$$\frac{\sum q_i l_i + \overline{\sum} q_i l_i + \overline{\overline{\sum}} q_i l_i}{\sum q_o l_o + \overline{\sum} q_o l_o + \sum q_o l_o} = \frac{\sum q_i l_o + \overline{\sum} q_i l_o + \overline{\overline{\sum}} q_i l_o}{\sum q_o l_o + \overline{\sum} q_o l_o + \sum q_o l_o} \cdot \frac{\sum q_i l_i + \overline{\sum} q_i l_i + \overline{\overline{\sum}} q_i l_i}{\sum q_i l_o + \overline{\sum} q_i l_o + \sum q_i l_o}.$$

The index on the left refers to man-hours; those on the right, to output (Laspeyres) and unit man-hour requirements (Paasche). In each of the aggregates, a single bar designates the partial sum for products common to both of the compared periods; a double bar, the partial sum for products not made in the base period; and a triple bar, the partial sum for products not available in the comparison period. A strike-through indicates that a particular partial sum equals zero because the output quantities equal zero. The l_o's for the partial sums with the double bars and the l_i's for the partial sums with the triple bars are fictitious; they may be estimated as the lowest unit labor requirements consistent with zero output in the given period. The numerator of the output index and the denominator of the input index are identical, but cancellation marks are not shown as in other footnotes in order to avoid confusion with the strike-throughs.

starting-up of new facilities, office work, and minor construction). Although some of these services represent quasi-investments and the corresponding labor often is included in input, their economic contributions are not recorded as discounted equivalent current product.

4. The true character of an output measure derived by deflation is determined by the concepts, composition, structure, and compatibility of the two indexes employed in this process. If the same value index may be written in several meaningful ways (as in the case of net value of output), each form calls for a different matching price deflator and implies a different production quotient. If an appropriate unit of measurement for a particular type of output (e.g., research) cannot be directly visualized, it certainly cannot be established by deflation of the corresponding value (or man-hours) by a vaguely pertinent price (or unit man-hour requirement) measure. The literal sense of an output measure obtained by deflation must be understood before a subsequently derived productivity index may be interpreted.

5. Manufacturing and other output measures with pecuniary weights are not necessarily superior to, or more "economic" than, measures incorporating labor weights. They are easier to make, and their weights are more comprehensive, but they need not be the most suitable measures for any particular analysis. Furthermore, since all indexes are artifices, their construction and use must be reckoned as closer to accounting than to economics—a point suggested in the introductory section of this paper.

6. The incorporation of labor weights in production measures does not imply acceptance of a labor theory of value, and the construction of labor productivity indexes does not imply that labor is the only productive input. Index computations in terms of labor units or any other units (including money) are a species of accounting divorced from the process of market valuation. Since historical productivity measures refer to average ratios for changing technologies, rather than to marginal ratios for a given technology, they have no imputational significance that is obvious.

7. A productivity index which is not an internal mean of relatives cannot be properly understood until it is rewritten as, say, the product of an internal productivity average and a factor representing everything else.[11]

---

[11] When an output index with unit value weights is divided by the index of unweighted man-hours, the quotient may be factored into a WPA-type productivity index and another term. See footnote 6.

32

8. Despite increases in the amount, and improvements in the scope, of government and private statistics since the 1930's, the task to which the WPA National Research Project addressed itself remains unmanageable. The compilation of detailed establishment information on a product or subproduct basis is essential for the development of literally consistent output and input measures. With the end of the biennial census system in 1939, this prospect, perhaps never brilliant, perceptibly dimmed for manufacturing. At any rate, extant government programs to revitalize productivity measurement contemplate no fundamental or extensive change in the basic information system for manufacturing. Beyond a certain point, ingenuity cannot substitute for limited or nonexistent detailed coordinate data for production and other variables.[11a]

MULTIFACTOR PRODUCTIVITY

It is much easier to write consistent formulas for multifactor productivity than actually to measure nonlabor factor inputs in suitable characteristic units. The process of setting down formulas is simplified by the introduction of a second summation sign, to cover (factor or nonfactor) inputs entering into each gross product. As for assuring that the productivity formulas are internal means of relatives, we again invoke the cancellation rule. Specifically, we employ a concept of net output that is identical in scope with factor input. We also use weights that make output and input dimensionally comparable and that equalize them (i.e., cause cancellation) for one of the two compared times. If the inputs refer, say, to labor and capital, the net output concept should ideally be restricted to the value added by these factors.

The verbal identity, Multifactor input=Net output × Unit factor requirements, leads to at least two kinds of consistent formulas. In one case, the net output measure is really a Paasche or Laspeyres aggregative index of gross quantities with "nettifying" unit-value-added weights. Since the input concept corresponds to net output in scope, valuation at cost permits us to write a Paasche or Laspeyres input index that yields a productivity measure containing only two weighted aggregates. This productivity measure may be rewritten as a weighted mean of relatives, the numerators of which refer to gross

[11a] Man-hour series adjusted for presumed productivity changes account for about half of the 1957 weighted aggregate in the revised FR production index for manufacturing and mining and for about 54 per cent of the aggregate relating only to manufacturing.

See *Industrial Production: 1959 Revision*, Board of Governors of the Federal Reserve System (Washington, July 1960).

output of individual ratios and the denominators of which refer to a narrower concept of factor input.[12]

A second system of aggregative formulas satisfying the above verbal identity is built around the Fabricant-Geary measure of net output. This measure has two aggregates, a minuend and subtrahend, in both numerator and denominator. In the common version, one aggregate refers to weighted gross output, the other to weighted non-factor input (e.g., materials and energy). For exact correspondence with factor input in scope, however, the measure must either be interpreted in terms of subproducts or altered in some other manner to allow for net change in the inventories of goods in various stages of processing. If the measure is interpreted in terms of subproducts, then the value added in each of the compared periods is determined incrementally; intermediate subproducts made and consumed in the same period appear in both minuend and subtrahend and hence cancel. If, instead, the minuends are reserved for finished products and the subtrahends refer either to the corresponding nonfactor input or to all the nonfactor input of the period, adjustment terms have to be added to the formula to assure coextensiveness with the factor-input index.[13]

The Fabricant-Geary output formula has Laspeyres and Paasche variants, both of which are equivalent to aggregative indexes of net output. Using the same weighted factor-input indexes as we did in conjunction with the output measures weighted by value added, we again effect the desired cancellations in deriving productivity expressions. In this case, however, the productivity relatives, rather than simply the weights, are net. That is, the numerator of each productivity relative actually refers to the net output of an individual

[12] The verbal identity becomes, for the Laspeyres input and output variants,

$$\frac{\sum Sw_of_i}{\sum Sw_of_o} = \frac{\sum q_i\left(p_o - \dfrac{SP_oQ_o}{q_o}\right)}{\sum q_o\left(p_o - \dfrac{SP_oQ_o}{q_o}\right)} \cdot L';$$

and L' may be rewritten as a weighted mean of relatives of the form $\dfrac{Sw_of_i}{Sw_of_o} \Big/ \dfrac{q_i}{q_o}$. S signifies a summation corresponding to a gross product, and the w's stand for the remuneration of the factor inputs, the f's. In the expression for gross output with unit-value-added weights, the q's stand for gross outputs, the p's for gross prices; and the Q's and P's refer to nonfactor inputs (e.g., purchased materials and energy).

The approach discussed in this section should well satisfy a measurement need mentioned in Christ's comments: It not only recognizes the difference between gross and net product but also permits the derivation of consistent measures for both of these concepts, factor inputs, other inputs (e.g., materials and energy), and gross and net productivity.

[13] See *Concepts and Measurement . . ., op. cit.*, pp. 61–2.

product. In the earlier case, it will be recalled, the relatives had gross output numerators.[14]

In both systems, productivity change may be viewed *sub specie pretii* as well as *sub specie quantitatis*. Thus, the ratio of Laspeyres (Paasche) net output and factor input measures equals a ratio of Paasche (Laspeyres) price measures. This conversion is based on the identity of values of net output and factor input when the price and quantity subscripts match. It also implies the equivalence of value indexes for net output and factor input and their factorability in turn into compatible quantity and net price indexes.[15]

Whichever net output formula is taken as the starting point, the appropriate Laspeyres and Paasche product price measures are net, not gross. This important fact is typically overlooked in the deflation of national product, of the nongovernment component, and of the value added in industries for which output is not measured directly.

For students interested in the anatomy of multifactor productivity increase over time, a close study of the expressions already discussed will prove rewarding. Economists, for example, may obtain new insights by viewing productivity advance as *the asymmetrical change of prices for the same resources defined as net output and as factor input.* Equality obtains when these resources are valued as output and as input in prices of the same period, but the productivity aggregates that are left after cancellation show that the equality no longer holds when

---

[14] The verbal identity for the Laspeyres situation is

$$\frac{\sum Sw_o f_i}{\sum Sw_o f_o} = \frac{\sum p_o q - \sum SP_o Q_i}{\sum p_o q_o - \sum SP_o Q_o} \cdot L'';$$

and L'' may be written as a weighted mean of relatives of the form

$$\frac{Sw_o f_i}{Sw_o f_o} \div \frac{\left(q_i - \dfrac{SP_o Q_i}{p_o} \right)}{\left(q_o - \dfrac{SP_o Q_o}{p_o} \right)}.$$

[15] The Laspeyres productivity index derived in footnote 12 (i.e., l/L') is equivalent to the quotient of two Paasche price measures:

$$\Pi' = \frac{\sum Sw_i f_i}{\sum Sw_o f_i} \div \frac{\sum q_i \left(p_i - \dfrac{SP_i Q_i}{q_i} \right)}{\sum q_i \left(p_o - \dfrac{SP_o Q_o}{q_o} \right)}.$$

The productivity index derived in footnote 14 (i.e., l/L'') is equivalent to:

$$\Pi'' = \frac{\sum Sw_i f_i}{\sum Sw_o f_i} \bigg/ \frac{\sum p_i q_i - \sum SP_i Q_i}{\sum p_o q_i - \sum SP_o Q_i}.$$

In both of these cases, we have simply inserted $\sum Sw_i f_i = \sum q_i \left(p_i - \dfrac{SP_i Q_i}{q_i} \right) = \sum p_{it} q - \sum SP_i Q_i$, which states the equivalence of weighted factor input and weighted net output in period i. See *Concepts and Measurement . . ., op. cit.*, pp. 74–5.

the prices refer to some other period. Furthermore, the price indexes show that a productivity rise implies the fall of the net-output price with respect to the factor-input price of the same resources.[16]

The theory underlying static production functions and marginal productivity determination must be distinguished from, although it has some relation to, the basic idea stressed here that input and output time series are measures of the "same" resources from different viewpoints. A production function, which is not expected to remain a literally valid description of technological relationships over any length of time, mathematically connects small changes in input and output as though they were cause and effect. For the limited period to which the function applies, it may be thought to have a live economic meaning, an imputational significance. But no similar claim is justifiable for indexes that report historical changes in average output per unit of composite factor input—changes reflecting, among other things, the transition from one static production function to another.[17]

Acknowledgment should be made of some of the challenges presented by multifactor productivity measurement in addition to that of designing consistent indexes. One basic problem is the expression of factors other than labor, such as capital (which changes in quality over time) and enterprise in significant quantitative units. Another problem is the proper representation of certain kinds of output, such as the current production equivalent of current research input, in indexes conventionally restricted to commodity measurement. Finally, we should note the difficulty of completely enumerating the factors relevant to output, including factors that are not compensated. Thus,

[16] This paragraph carries a message concerning efforts, mentioned by Christ, to identify completely the sources of observed changes in the output. It suggests that, even if all factors could be taken into account and properly weighted, a productivity "gap" or residual would still arise in time comparisons.

A constant composite productivity index of unity, however, may be obtained by design, and without an exhaustive accounting of inputs. Thus, the measure of every recognized factor input could be "adjusted" for the most significant "quality" change of all—the very productivity change indicated for that factor. Such adjustments, which compensate for the omission of various inputs as well as for changes in the character of the acknowledged inputs, could lead to constant productivity series for labor, capital, and so forth, and for the multifactor composite too.

[17] Reference is made, here as elsewhere in this paper, to the static production function because it is usually assumed in discussions of marginal productivity and the theory of income distribution. The text could be suitably modified, of course, to reflect the increasing interest in empirical dynamic production functions, from which time series are derivable for marginal as well as average productivity. Comments made earlier on efforts to determine the contributions of recognized variables to changes in an aggregate also apply to attempts to isolate the roles of labor, capital, and so-called "technological change" (or "organization," in Aukrust's terminology) in explaining the difference between two values of a dynamic production function.

36

government services might be overlooked; and, in the case of agriculture, better-than-normal amounts of rain and sunshine should be reckoned as technical inputs even if normal amounts are taken for granted as part of the environment of production.

Literal Consistency beyond Productivity Definition

So far, we have discussed the design of consistent index-number systems for only those situations in which productivity, output, and input have the stage to themselves. But economists, statisticians, government officials, business and labor leaders, news commentators, editorial writers, and assorted speechmakers are often concerned with problems in which one or more of these variables must share attention with others of coordinate importance. In such instances, the verbal identities may be much more complex than the kind already considered, and the aggregates may involve three or more variables, rather than two as in the familiar Laspeyres and Paasche formulas.

The problem of achieving consistency beyond the productivity definition arises, for example, when wages and employment are discussed in conjunction with productivity. For such situations, it seems reasonable to require homologous, aggregative measures satisfying one of these two verbal identities:

Payrolls = Unit labor cost × Man-hour productivity × Man-hours

   = Average hourly earnings × Unit man-hour requirements × Output.

In either case, many sets of consistent aggregative formulas may be written. A particular formula for any variable may occur in more than one set, in different combinations with others. If the geometric mean is applied to all possible sets, generalized ideal indexes are obtained. These indexes have such desirable properties as meeting the time-reversal and (generalized) factor-reversal tests in addition to remaining internal means of relatives.[18]

The number of sets of formulas satisfying the above verbal identities may be reduced by the introduction of additional subsidiary requirements. Thus, we may stipulate that indexes of productivity and man-hours entering into the first of these identities should meet the

---

[18] All aggregates entering into the first identity would have the form $\Sigma\, c \Pi m$ while differing in their time subscripts. All the aggregates entering into the second identity would have the form $\Sigma\, elq$. Here, c stands for unit labor cost and e for average hourly earnings. Note that $\sum c_o \Pi_o m_o = \Sigma\, e_o l_o q_o$ and $\Sigma\, c_i \Pi_i m_i = \Sigma\, e_i l_i q_i$. See *Concepts and Measurement . . ., op. cit.*, 84–5; and I. H. Siegel, "The Generalized 'Ideal' Index-Number Formula," *Journal of the American Statistical Association*, December 1945, pp. 520–3.

cancellation criterion upon multiplication—in other words, that the resulting index of output should be a ratio of two aggregates and an unequivocal internal mean of output relatives. Or we may invoke the cancellation criterion for the man-hours index formed as the product of measures of unit man-hour requirements and output in the second identity. The introduction of these supplementary cancellation conditions in effect simplifies the original verbal identities to

Payrolls = Unit labor cost × Output

= Average hourly earnings × Man-hours;

and these statements are satisfied by only two sets of simplified measures for the indicated variables.[19]

Another verbal identity involving payrolls should be mentioned because it is especially appropriate to the discussion of the productivity-wage-price connection:

$$\text{Payrolls} = \frac{\text{Average hourly earnings}}{\text{Output per man-hour}} \times \frac{\text{Value of output}}{\text{Price}}.$$

Since a number of the variables are of coordinate importance, it is reasonable to require that the measures be conceptually compatible, have a certain structural similarity, and reduce to internal means of relatives. So crude are existing quantitative tools compared to the ones required that clamor for more detailed and more complete basic statistics would surely seem as appropriate as the babel of diagnosis and prescription heard throughout the land.

It is a curious fact that at least two distinct aggregative formula systems may be designed to satisfy the last payroll identity; and, within each system, many sets of compatible measures may be written down.[20] Again, if subsidiary cancellation conditions are introduced, fewer aggregative measures are eligible, the number of sets of consistent measures is reduced, and the identity is telescoped. Thus, we may wish to stipulate that the first quotient on the right-hand side of the identity be a guaranteed internal mean of unit-labor-cost relatives, and that the second quotient be an internal mean of output quantity relatives.

One other point should be mentioned before this section is concluded. Indexes for the same variable are not necessarily equal if they arise in connection with different verbal identities. Similarly, an index

[19] The eligible aggregates in footnote 16 are limited to those that may, by virtue of the compatibility of time subscripts, be rewritten as $\Sigma\, c\Pi m = \Sigma\, cq$ and $\Sigma\, elq = \Sigma\, em$.

[20] According to one system, all of the aggregates would have the form $\sum elr$ while differing in time subscripts. According to the other, all aggregates would have the form $\sum pelq$. Here, r is the ratio of value of output to wages for each product. Note that $e_i l_i r_i = p_i$; and that various partial products of $pelq$ (which itself is dimensionally exceptionable!) also have pertinent meanings (e.g., pq = value of output).

of unit man-hour requirements satisfying one identity need not be the reciprocal of an index of man-hour productivity entering into another identity. Thus, the productivity measures derived for the first payroll identity cited above are not the same as those implied by the last payroll identity. Furthermore, only two of the four productivity measures literally satisfying the first payroll identity are exactly equal to the reciprocals of two of the four measures of unit man-hour requirements satisfying the second payroll identity.[21]

Conclusion

MORE HONORED IN THE BREACH

As we look about, we find little current awareness of, or interest in, the basic ideas that inform this paper.[22] One reason, of course, is the paucity of data. Another is the enshrinement of various indexes alleged to be suitable for general purposes. Still another is optimism, the belief that only in one's own specialty can the difference between tweedledum and tweedledee ever really matter. Without pretending to exhaust this fascinating topic, we must also mention the reluctance of sophisticated employees and consultants to footnote their findings with skull and crossbones, to risk undermining with candor the complacency of their "practical" employers and clients.

Everywhere we see the distinction between literal and verbal algebra blurred. "Any old" index with a suitable name is frequently used as though the details of its construction are of no moment and the purpose to which it is put is irrelevant. The mismatching of concepts, like deflation of the value of net product by gross rather than net price, is routine. The libelous anachronistic label of "nonproduction" employees is pinned on research workers and other personnel engaged in quasi-investment activities; and the failure to reckon their discounted product in current output is hardly taken into account in discussions of such phenomena as productivity "slowdown" or profit "squeeze". A price-deflated index of output value is commonly said to

---

[21] This sentence corrects too sweeping a statement made in *Concepts and Measurement . . ., op. cit.*, p. 85.

The equivalent indexes of the first and second payroll identities are:

$$\frac{\sum c_o \Pi_i m_i}{\sum c_o \Pi_o m_i} = \frac{\sum e_o l_o q_i}{\sum e_o l_i q_i}$$

and

$$\frac{\sum c_i \Pi_i m_o}{\sum c_i \Pi_o m_o} = \frac{\sum e_i l_o q_o}{\sum e_i l_i q_o}.$$

[22] It is pleasant to record, however, that works like R. Stone's *Quantity and Price Indexes in National Accounts*, Organization for European Economic Cooperation (Paris, November 1956), still appear occasionally and, of course, that conferences such as the present one are held too.

represent output in constant dollars of the base period even though the story told by the literal algebra is different and more complex. Chain production and price indexes are usually interpreted as though they were of the ordinary Paasche or Laspeyres variety. The changes shown by the leading index of manufacturing production are chronicled as though they convey message without noise, as though the huge gaps filled with data synthesized by verbal algebra were actually filled by the real thing. Changes indicated by, say, a man-hours (or production) index, are often broken arbitrarily into two parts, one said to be "due to" a change in production (or man-hours) and the other "due to" a change in productivity. Analysts of the productivity-wage-price relationship typically overlook the incompatibility of the concepts, scope, and weighting systems of the aggregate measures that they actually use. Users of available productivity indexes often do not seem to know or care whether these measures are internal averages of productivity relatives or reflect something more. In short, on the contemporary scene, we find too little vigilance exercised to distinguish a properly weighted index from a loaded one.

A LITTLE ONWARD

The history of productivity measurement, especially the recent record, does not encourage hope for rapid or cumulative improvement of practice. Perhaps, leadership in developing and utilizing data more nearly in accord with theoretical requirements will pass to the younger industrial nations, which have a clear need to raise productivity and are less encumbered by statistical custom. In our own country, the renewed vigorous advance of productivity measurement must not be expected to result from intermittent flurries of government support induced by labor-management controversy, fears of inflation, or failures of measures to accord with expectations and beliefs. Instead, fundamental progress will probably come about, if at all, as companies, remaining preoccupied with cost control and profit-making and having adopted electronic data processing systems, gradually introduce private programs of productivity measurement and generally strengthen the establishment basis of statistical reporting.[23]

No powerful lobby may be expected to arise in support of more and better productivity statistics, but movement toward these twin objectives could be encouraged by the development and display of a more critical attitude by makers and users of productivity and related

---

[23] For other remarks by the author on the same subject, see *Concepts and Measurement . . ., op. cit.*, pp. 99–103; and "Next Tasks in the Measurement of Production and Productivity," *Estadistica*, September–December 1955, pp. 390–2.

measures. In particular, it seems desirable to keep a constant eye on the divergence between practical and theoretically preferred indexes. More attention should accordingly be given to methods of investigating this divergence and of estimating the numerical consequences of compromise. These methods employ elementary, vector, and matrix algebra. They make effective use of the Pearsonian, rank, and von Bortkiewicz correlation coefficients; the generalized Lagrange identity; and correct partition formulas, the terms of which correspond to those of Taylor expansions.[24] Finally, it is hoped this paper has demonstrated the value of multiplicative identities as frameworks for consistent formula design and for the appraisal of available data and of current practice in measuring.[25]

COMMENT

CARL F. CHRIST, University of Chicago

Siegel's paper deals mainly with the choice of index-number formulas to be used in measuring input, output, and productivity. While we were both at Johns Hopkins University I learned a good deal from him on this subject. I have very little to add to what he has said in his paper, except to second most of it firmly. I agree with the main points that he makes, which I take the liberty of selecting as follows:

1. Each index should be a ratio of two aggregates or, in other words, a weighted arithmetic or harmonic mean of corresponding relatives.

2. The data for the three indexes for any economy or sector should have the same coverage. That is, they should apply to the same economy or the same sector, and if (as is almost always the case) they are based on a sample of the goods and services in the economy or sector, they should all be based on the same sample.

3. The indexes should be consistently designed, so that the productivity index is the ratio of the output index to the input index, i.e., so that any one of the three can be obtained directly from the other two.

4. The three foregoing requirements can be satisfied by more than one formula (e.g., Laspeyres and Paasche), and numerical results obtained will be different for the different acceptable formulas.

[24] See *Concepts and Measurement* . . . *op. cit.*, Chapter 3 and pp. 90–2, and various articles by the author in *Journal of the American Statistical Association* on index-number differences (September 1941, December 1941, June 1943).

[25] For comments by the author on two productivity publications appearing after this paper was presented, see reviews in *Journal of Business*, January 1960, pp. 63–4, and *Personnel and Guidance Journal*, May 1960, pp. 764–5.

5. The choice of the formula which satisfies conditions 1 to 3, as well as the choice of the procedures to be used in collecting data for the formula, should depend on the purpose for which the indexes are wanted.

6. In many, if not most cases, the data that have already been collected by somebody else are not those that one would want for constructing the indexes. In such a case it is necessary either to collect the desired data or to fashion some kind of approximation of the readily available data.

I can object to only two points that Siegel makes. First, he suggests that the classical theory of index numbers is sufficient for our purpose and that the so-called economic theory of index numbers, dealing with indifference curves and production functions, is of no help at all in designing productivity indexes. Of course he is right if he means that there are terrible problems involved in trying to aggregate indifference curves and production possibility curves, and that without quite severe simplifying assumptions we cannot easily interpret the results of such aggregation. Nevertheless, I feel that shifts of production functions are what productivity indexes are really about, and that in trying to measure productivity we will be ahead if we remember that production functions are in the theoretical background of what we are doing.

My second disagreement with Siegel is probably not a disagreement in substance at all. He says that an increase of efficiency in an economy which is the result merely of transfer of resources from less productive to more productive industries, with no change of productivity within any industry, should not be called an increase in productivity. This statement is made in connection with his plea that every productivity index should be a weighted mean of productivity relativities, which I referred to as item 1 above. I believe, as George Stigler said in his paper for this conference, that social organization is a kind of factor of production, and that any improvement in social organization which permits the transfer of resources from a less productive to a more productive industry ought to be regarded in one sense as an increase in productivity. I would agree with Siegel that this kind of increase in productivity ought to be clearly separated from the kind of increase which occurs within individual industries.

Siegel's brief discussion of partioning and eight "additional points" on labor productivity (see Section II) is particularly noteworthy. Some of these touch on many of the important issues of productivity measurement.

The paper contains a large number of references to Siegel's "Concepts and Measurement of Production and Productivity," a 108-page mimeographed document of the Bureau of Labor Statistics dated March 1952. This document, I am very sorry to say, is not readily available, but those who take Siegel's message to heart will find a great deal more detail there.[1]

I should now like to return to a discussion of three broader comments on productivity measurement.

First, I believe that the distribution of knowledge concerning technological possibilities is important. It is worth distinguishing two kinds of lags in the use of new knowledge. First, there are lags because capital equipment embodies the knowledge available when the equipment was designed, and capital equipment lasts quite a long time, so that at any moment there is a large amount of capital in use which is inferior to currently designed capital equipment based on better knowledge. Second, there is a lag in the use of new knowledge by people who are currently investing in new capital, because some designers of capital equipment have not yet learned about recent advances that would cause them to improve their designs.

These remarks suggest that three kinds of empirical study might be useful. First, a time series study of the productivity, when new, of plants constructed in successive years in a single industry, in order to discover the rate of progress of knowledge about how to build plants. An example of a study of this type is that by Anne Grosse (Carter) entitled "The Technological Structure of the Cotton Textile Industry," in Leontief's volume, *Studies in the Structure of the American Economy*. Second, a cross-section study of the productivity, when new, of a number of plants constructed in the same year in a single industry, in order to discover the dispersion of knowledge about how to build a plant at any point of time. Third, a time-series study of the productivity of each of several given plants, beginning when they were new and extending over their lifetime, to determine the extent to which the original design of a plant "freezes in" the knowledge available when the plant was designed, and to what extent new discoveries can be used to improve the productivity of existing plants. (I was glad to be told by Professor Leontief, in a comment from the floor following these remarks, that he believes he will be able to obtain data to perform some studies of these three types.)

The second of my three broader comments on productivity measurement deals with the relationship between materials and fuels on the one hand, and indexes of output, input, and productivity on

[1] Siegel advises that arrangements were made for another run (the third) in the summer of 1960.

the other. Except for input-output analysis of the Leontief type, most studies of production functions explicitly mention as input only things like labor and capital, ignoring materials and fuels. It seems to me that this is a theoretical oversight, or at best a failure to make explicit the assumptions used. Surely the better approach is to begin with a production function that explicitly makes gross output depend on labor, capital, and materials inputs. Net output or value added is then gross output minus materials input.

When dealing with a closed economy as a whole, of course, the distinction between gross and net output is not quantitatively important because a closed economy has no materials input except for things like minerals, fish, air, water, and sunshine, and hence nearly all of the value of gross output is value added. However, for any economy with substantial imports or for any sector of an economy the distinction becomes important.

It is not hard to show that if material input is a stable function of gross output, and if the production function just mentioned is stable, then gross output can be expressed as a stable function of labor and capital input alone, or alternatively, net output can be expressed as a function of labor and capital input alone. However, there is a big "if" involved, because materials input need not be a stable function of gross output. Indeed, if the price of materials changes relative to the price of labor and capital, then one can expect a substitution between materials on the one hand and labor and capital on the other. Thus, for example, the ratio of gross output to labor and capital input can rise in response to a reduction in the relative price of materials, without any change in any production function. It can also happen, of course, that the fall in the relative price of materials can be the result of a technological improvement somewhere in the economy, either a material-saving improvement in the material-using industry or an increase in productivity in the material-producing industry; or it can be the result of a reduction in the demand for the material on the part of some other user.

These considerations suggest that it is important to use productivity indexes in which attention is given to material input.

The last of my three general comments concerns the objectives of productivity research. Many authors of papers for this conference have said, I think rightly, that the kind of productivity measure we want depends on the question we want to answer. Let me try to sketch a framework within which I think we might agree on what kinds of things we are trying to measure. I think we have a twofold objective in productivity research. One objective is to make it possible to push forward our production frontier more rapidly or more cheaply than we now know how to do. This is a practical sort of objective. The other objective, I would say, is to understand both past and future increases in the money value of gross output, looked at from the supply side. This is a seeking-after-truth-for-its-own-sake sort of objective, though, of course, if we attain it we will be better able to attain the practical objective too.

Concerning the attempt to understand increases of money value of gross output, we as a profession have already proceeded as follows.

1. We have devised measurements of price change, and when their effect is taken account of, we are left with a change in *real* gross output.

2. We have subtracted real materials inputs to obtain a measure of real *net* output or real *value added*.

3. We have tried to measure inputs in the form of labor and capital, and we have divided the real value added measured by this real labor-and-capital input measure. The result is the now familiar *index of output over input*, i.e., real net output divided by real labor-and-capital input, of the type put forth by Abramovitz, Kendrick, Schultz, and others.

At first it seemed enough to compute such an index, to note that it appears to increase at about 1 per cent per year, and to attribute this growth to increases in technological knowledge. This is no longer sufficient. It is now necessary to try to get independent measurements of things that we believe are components of the index of real net output divided by real labor-and-capital input and see whether they account for observed rate of growth of that index. In other words, we should try to force to zero the residual or unexplained part of the increase in the money value of gross output. The following possibilities have been suggested (I continue to number them in series with the preceding steps):

4. Changes in the quality of the labor force.

5. Changes in the quality of the stock of capital, or in the ratio of the quantity of services produced by capital to the stock of capital.

6. Increasing returns to scale.

7. The fruits of investment in the search for new knowledge about production possibilities. Here I imagine a conventional production function, in which output depends on inputs of labor, capital, and materials, and also on a parameter describing the current state of technology. Also I envision a second production function, whose output consists of improvement in the technology that enters into the

45

conventional production function, and whose input consists of resources devoted to research activities.

I believe that if we can succeed in getting the residual down to zero, we will have a much better understanding of economic growth than we have now. There will then be plenty of time to discuss what factors to include in the definition of productivity and what factors to call by some other name, such as improvements in the quality of inputs, increasing returns to scale, and the like.

Economic Problems
in Measuring Changes in Productivity

GEORGE J. STIGLER
UNIVERSITY OF CHICAGO

Labor Productivity as an Index of Productivity

PRODUCTIVITY measurement occupies an unusual and possibly unique place in the history of quantitative economic research.

Most important measurable concepts have a long history of theoretical discussion before the actual measurements begin on a large scale. The national income concept was discussed from the time of the mercantilists, the concept of a price level or the purchasing power of money has a similarly ancient theoretical tradition, and one could say much the same of the terms of trade, taxable capacity, the incidence of taxes, etc. Once the task of measurement became important, new theoretical difficulties were always uncovered, but the measurers had some initial guidance.

A second set of economic measurements appeared without much assistance from earlier theoretical tradition. The studies of the distribution of income by size are an example of this work, and so too is the derivation of Engel (income-expenditure) curves. In these cases the quantitative worker had to formulate his own concepts and do his own theorizing until his results began to attract the attention of the theorists, who then came to aid and thwart him with their refinements.

But only productivity measures of important economic magnitudes arose in the face of a theoretical tradition which denied them any relevance to economic structure or policy. A productivity measure, until recently, was a measure of the average product of some class of productive services. When they began to be calculated on a large scale it was already a basic proposition of economics that one should never look at average products, only at marginal products.

The equality of marginal products in all uses is a necessary condition for efficient use of a resource, and hence for maximum output. The marginal productivities are basic elements of the demands for productive factors. The dependence of marginal products on the quantities of and proportions among productive factors is the essence of the theory of production. These are illustrative statements of the fundamental role of marginal products in economic analysis. So far as I know, not a single theoretical statement of any importance can be made about the average products of factors.[1]

Yet certainly the product, and possibly even the productivity, of calculators of productivity indexes continued to increase. Does this mean that a set of statistically unsound quasi-random numbers were being supplied to careless users, or that the economic theorists were purists who did not recognize the great usefulness of approximate data? The answer is not easy.

An approximate answer depends upon the closeness of the approximation and the question which is being asked. For a lame ant the statement that the height of a house and of the Eiffel Tower are equal is a satisfactory approximation; a pilot might need a closer approximation. The uses of productivity data, however, are infinitely varied, and it does not seem possible to present any objective criterion of the minimum goodness of approximation that is generally required.

We may say a trifle more about the accuracy of a labor productivity measure as an estimate of a capital-and-labor productivity measure. Labor is quantitatively the largest input (in marginal units of measure, i.e., as a share of income) so large changes in labor productivity over time are likely to reflect at least roughly the movements of a properly defined measure of productivity. But in general the labor productivity measure will exceed it by more, the more capital has grown relative to labor.[2] Labor productivity will therefore be a better measure of total productivity, the more nearly proportional the increases of labor and other resources over time, and the smaller the relative weight of nonlabor resources in total input.

The extent to which capital and labor change together over time proves to be fairly close in the manufacturing sector. Using Kendrick's

---

[1] What propositions there are about average products—such as that average product should be maximized to maximize output if only one factor is scarce—are polar cases.

[2] Let $P = A(t)f(C,L)$, where P is output, C is capital, L is labor, and $A(t)$ is the index of productivity. If technical progress is independent of the proportions between the factors, as this production function assumes, and there are constant returns to scale, one may derive the equation,

$$\frac{d\left(\frac{P}{L}\right)/dt}{P/L} - \frac{A'(t)}{A(t)} = \frac{w_c d\left(\frac{C}{L}\right)/dt}{C/L},$$

where w_c is the share of capital return in the total product, i.e., $w_c = \frac{\partial P}{\partial C} \cdot \frac{C}{P}$. [See R. M. Solow, "Technical Change and the Aggregate Production Function," *Review of Economics and Statistics*, XXXIX (1957), 312 ff.] It follows that the relative change in output per worker will be in excess of the true index of productivity if capital increases relative to labor, and the two estimates will approach equality as w_c approaches zero, for given relative changes in the factors.

48

data, we may calculate the coefficients of correlation between inputs of man-hours and capital:

All manufacturing, 1869–1953, $r = .984$ ($n = 10$)
Two-digit manufacturing industries
    1929–53 change for each industry, $r = .860$ ($n = 20$)
    1948–53 change for each industry, $r = .728$ ($n = 20$)
    1952–53 change for each industry, $r = .257$ ($n = 20$)[a]
    1949–50 change for each industry, $r = .610$ ($n = 22$)[a]
    1950–51 change for each industry, $r = .868$ ($n = 22$)[a]
    1951–52 change for each industry, $r = .574$ ($n = 22$)[a]

[a] Based upon my data.

Our interest is primarily in the interindustry correlations, which indicate that the industrial pattern of labor input changes is fairly closely correlated with the corresponding pattern of capital input changes over considerable periods, but that the correlation is smaller and more unstable the shorter the period of comparison. The correlation for annual changes is at times so small as to make the labor productivity index highly unreliable as an index of capital productivity.

Even if the movements of man-hours and capital are very different, a labor productivity index will provide a tolerable estimate of total productivity if the weight assigned to capital is small. In manufacturing this proves to be the case: in Kendrick's two-digit manufacturing industries the weight of capital to that of labor is 1 to 3.23, on average, with a range, however, from 1 to 11 (apparel) to 1 to .75 (products of petroleum and coal).[3] The remark seems only partly relevant to these figures,[4] but it should be emphasized that the common but erroneous practice of excluding working capital from capital leads to exaggerated relative weight for labor inputs.

A labor productivity index seems generally to rank the commodity-producing industries correctly with respect to true productivity changes. It does not follow that the actual numerical changes in productivity are reliable. In fact they are biased, and substantially so. Only when changes in labor and other inputs are proportional will the labor index be unbiased.[5] In all manufacturing, the regression of

[3] The apparel ratio is undoubtedly too low because of the omission of rented capital.
[4] Kendrick's weights are based upon the total remuneration to capital and labor, although his index of the quantity of capital is restricted to durable capital plus inventories. I do not know how good an index of total capital this combination is.
[5] Using the notation of footnote 2, if w_c is stable the excess of labor productivity over true productivity changes between periods 0 and 1 will be

$$w_c \log \left(\frac{C_1}{L_1} \middle/ \frac{C_0}{L_0} \right).$$

If $C = a + bL$, the sign of expression is positive if $aL_0 > aL_1$, which holds if $a < 0$, $L_0 < L_1$.

capital on man-hours for the period 1869 to 1953 was

$$C = -34.8 + 1.232L,$$

where C is capital and L is man-hours. Labor increases were accompanied by larger relative capital increases, so labor productivity measures overstated true productivity changes. On the other hand, in the interindustry comparison of inputs for 1929–53,

$$C = 25.9 + .832L,$$

so here the labor productivity index understated the differences among industries in the true productivity changes. In the annual changes, a is negative in two years and positive in the other two, so the direction of bias was unstable.

Are the labor productivity measures valuable approximate answers to an important question, or are they misleading pieces of arithmetic? In comparisons of productivity changes over long periods, and comparisons among industries with widely differing rates of productivity increase, the rankings of productivity increases by labor productivity increases are tolerably reliable. Even this tentative conclusion, which I interpret to be adverse to most short-run uses of labor productivity measures, assumes the accuracy of the total productivity measures, and it is to this, the main problem of this paper, that I now turn.

General Considerations

A pure measure of economic progress measures the increase in the output of given resources, or the decrease in the inputs for a given product.[6] The shifting mixtures of inputs which are responses to changes in their relative prices do not constitute advances in productivity, which come only from changes in the "state of the arts."

The state of the arts is the heritage of technical and economic knowledge which is possessed (by whom we consider later) at a given time. Its relevant content is summarized by the list of technologies which are not inferior in the sense that no technology in this list uses more of some inputs (and no less of others) than any other technology.

This set of noninferior technologies is displayed graphically by an isoquant—a curve showing the minimum combinations of inputs necessary to produce a given quantity of a given product. (Inferior technologies lie above the curve.) In Chart 1 we draw a curve displaying all combinations of (say) capital (C) and labor (L) which in the existing state of the arts will produce a specified amount of a given product. This is our isoquant; under the normal assumptions of

[6] The two are equivalent only if the production function is linear and homogeneous; this problem is discussed later.

diminishing returns to each productive factor (and, in the multifactor case, general complementarity of inputs), this curve is convex to the origin.[7] The entire quadrant above the curve represents less efficient methods of production, in the sense that the given product is there made with more of one input and no less of the other than would be required by available alternative techniques.

Suppose now that we observe a new process of production, Q_2 or Q_3, at a subsequent time; how can we tell whether it is more or less efficient than that indicated by P_1? In formal theory we postulate a known production function, and we would unhesitatingly say that Q_3 is an inferior technique—knowledge has retrogressed—and Q_2 a superior technique. Lacking this knowledge of the production function, we can say only that points in the rectangle whose northeast

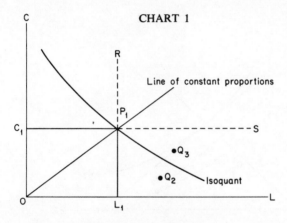

CHART 1

corner is at $P_1(OL_1P_1C_1)$ represent techniques superior to P_1, and those in the infinite rectangle whose southwest corner is at $P_1(RP_1S)$ represent techniques which are inferior to P_1. Even this weak conclusion depends upon the assumption that the qualities of the inputs have remained constant: if they have deteriorated, the rectangles are no longer well-defined.

So far, of course, we have not used one part of our observational information: the relative prices of inputs in periods 1 and 2. Under

---

[7] Let the production function be $P=f(C,L)$. Then the slope of an isoquant is given by $dP=0$, or

$$\frac{dC}{dL} = -\frac{f_l}{f_c}.$$

Then

$$\frac{d^2C}{dL^2} = -\frac{f_c^2 f_{ll}+f_l^2 f_{cc}-2f_c f_l f_{cl}}{f_c^3}.$$

Since $f_{ll}<0$ and $f_{cc}<0$, the second derivative is necessarily positive if f_{cl} (or a sum of such terms in the general case) is positive.

51

competition (we look at monopoly later), the entrepreneur who mini-
mizes costs in each period operates where marginal products are
proportional to factor prices, or, in terms of Chart 2, where a factor
price line is tangent to the relevant isoquant. Any process falling
below the price line (π_1) was unattainable in period 1 or it would have
been adopted because it would lower costs. In our illustrative example, we may say that relative to P_1, Q_2 is certainly a superior technique
and Q_3 possibly a superior or inferior one. The process Q_2 represents
an improvement of approximately a/OP_1, for the inputs would have
fallen (in period 1 prices) in the proportion, a/OP_1.

These approximations may be rather poor if price relatives in the
second period were substantially different. There may exist another
process ($Q_2^!$) which would have been even cheaper at period 1 relative

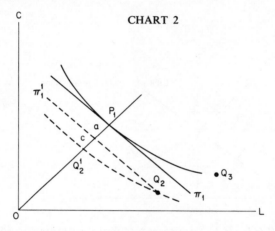

CHART 2

prices, so that the increase in efficiency is actually $(a+c)/P_1$. Whether
this is true, or contrariwise the approximation exaggerates the gain
in efficiency (and $Q_2^!$ lies above $\pi_1^!$), depends upon the shape of the
new isoquant relative to the earlier isoquant.[8] The two isoquants
can even intersect if once-known techniques are forgotten, or the
qualities of some inputs deteriorate. Advances in technology do not
have to lead to constant displacements of the isoquants; only one input may be economized by a given advance.[9]

[8] There are obvious parallels between our ratios and consumer index numbers, but
the analogy is far from complete. The cost of living indexes rest upon the assumption of
constant tastes, and lose their meaning if tastes change. In productivity analyses, on the
contrary, the essence of the problem is the measurement of the change in the state of
the arts, the analogue of tastes.

[9] Only if the isoquants bear a very special relationship to one another will the gain in
efficiency measured on a ray from the origin through P_1 equal that measured on a ray
through Q_2. If the production function has a very simple form, such as $Q_2(C,L)=$

52

Of course a change in the relative prices of inputs will also lead to a change in inputs, even if the state of the arts does not change. Thus, in Chart 3 the maximum profit position is at Q_1 if the price line is π_1, and at Q_2 if the price line is π_2. If combination Q_1 is valued at π_2 prices, a relative rise in efficiency from period 1 to period 2 of a/OQ_2 is indicated; and if Q_2 is valued at π_1 prices, a relative fall in efficiency from period 1 to period 2 of b/OQ_1 is indicated. In fact if these relationships failed to hold, a change in technology would be demonstrated. A price line with the average of the slopes of π_1 and π_2 will not necessarily pass through both Q_1 and Q_2, so changes in relative prices will, with the usual index number formulas, lead to some change in

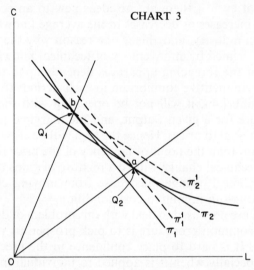

CHART 3

reported efficiency, although none has taken place. The ambiguity could be eliminated only if one knew the production function.

If the total output of the commodity changes when the new technique is adopted, as is usually the case, along which isoquant should we measure productivity changes? If the production function is linear and homogeneous, no choice is necessary: then to produce m times as much as P_1, we originally needed mL_1 and mC_1 and the family of all possible isoquants has the same slope at all points along the line of fixed proportions, OP_1[10]. Nothing but a scale factor is involved, and we can assert that real inputs fell in the proportion of the

$kP_1(C,L)$, with each production function homogeneous of degree one, the measurements along the two rays will be equal.

[10] For $dC/dL = -f_l/f_c$, and if f is homogeneous of degree 1, its derivatives are homogeneous of degree zero, i.e., changing inputs by a multiple m leaves each marginal product unchanged.

fall in inputs necessary to produce P_1. If the production function does not have this simplifying property, we must recognize a new element, which (under competition) is the presence of external economies. We discuss this problem in the final section.

Let us recur to the question of what a given state of the arts means. In formal theory it is usually taken to be the sum total of existing knowledge, no matter how much of this knowledge any one entrepreneur possesses at a given time, because in long-run equilibrium in a stationary economy, everybody eventually learns everything relevant. In the changing economy this will hardly do; what is relevant is the frequency distribution of knowledge among entrepreneurs. So we must recognize that even if there are no ideas new to an economy, there can be large increases or decreases in the average knowledge of entrepreneurs in an industry, and this is one reason why the state of the arts cannot be defined by an inventory of technical knowledge.

The relevance of the foregoing apparatus depends upon the existence of long-run competitive equilibrium in each period. If a given firm is not in equilibrium, it will not be operating with the lowest possible expenditure for a given output, and the marginal products will not be proportional to prices. Hence the firm will be elsewhere on a short-run isoquant than the point of tangency of the price line, and the measure of a technical change will be a mixture of gains or losses from any such technical change plus those from moving closer or farther from the long-run minimum cost condition.

Two procedures are now used to deal with this problem of disequilibrium. The more common procedure is to pick prosperous years for one's calculations. It is hard to place confidence in the precision of this procedure, especially when it is applied to individual industries which may be in a state of depression while business is generally good.[11] Over long periods the estimates should not be seriously biased, but this is a further reason for distrusting short-run estimates.

The other procedure is, in effect, to scale down the nominal amount of inputs which are not fully used—presumably capital, as a rule.[12] If the technical proportions between the inputs are rigid, this procedure is clearly (half) correct: the effective input of the surplus factor varies proportionally with the nonsurplus factor.[13] But even then the

[11] For example, in Kendrick's terminal year (1953) for two-digit manufacturing industries, apparel products were earning only 2.6 per cent on assets (3.1 per cent in 1947 prices) after taxes, a lower rate than in any preceding year since 1938.

[12] One of the first to do this, in an oblique way, was J. M. Clark, "Inductive Evidence on Marginal Productivity" (*American Economic Review*, 1928), reprinted in *Preface to Social Economics* (New York, 1936).

[13] Of course, any one input then yields a correct estimate of changes in "technical" efficiency.

procedure is half wrong: it measures technical possibilities, not the efficiency of an economic organization. If entrepreneurs generally keep too much of one input around, whether for reason of esthetics or stupidity or nepotism, this is a source of inefficiency to be treated on a full parity with "technical" inefficiency.[14] When the proportions between inputs are variable, the adjustment is also incorrect in estimating the efficiency of available technical methods. Greater capital per laborer increases the marginal productivity of labor, and only a portion of the capital is, in an esoteric sense, excessive.[15]

The Presence of Monopoly

Prices equal marginal costs under competition, and they do not under monopoly. Hence decisions of entrepreneurs are guided by quantities which are (in principle) reported and observable under competition, but are guided by quantities which are not observable or reported under monopoly. What difference does this make in our ability to interpret the evidence on economic progress? We consider first the effects of monopsony in the factor market, and then monopoly in the selling markets. They affect, alternatively, the measures of input and output.

The monopsonist is guided in his combination of productive services by their marginal costs. His condition for maximum profits is:

$$\frac{\text{Marginal product of } C}{\text{Marginal cost of } C} = \frac{\text{Marginal product of } L}{\text{Marginal cost of } L}.$$

In terms of our isoquants, the line of equal outlay (π_1 of Chart 2) becomes a curve, which is usually concave to the origin.[16] In Chart 4,

[14] Of course, to the extent that the unemployment of capital is due to factors outside the control or reasonable anticipation of the entrepreneur, the procedure aims at a meaningful question: How efficient are the entrepreneurs within the area where their own decisions are determining? But I doubt that one can give a useful answer, since this area of self-determination is ambiguous analytically as well as empirically.

[15] The issues involved seem to be identical with those encountered in the determination of "excess capacity."

[16] Total cost is $C = cp_c + lp_l$, and the slope of the equal outlay curve is given by

$$\frac{dC}{dl} = 0 = c\frac{dp_c}{dc}\frac{dc}{dl} + p_c\frac{dc}{dl} + p_l + l\frac{dp_l}{dl}$$

or

$$\frac{dc}{dl} = -\frac{p_l + l\dfrac{dp_l}{dl}}{p_c + c\dfrac{dp_c}{dc}} = -\frac{(MC_l)}{(MC_c)}.$$

$$\frac{d^2c}{dl^2} = -\frac{MC_c\left(l\dfrac{d^2p_l}{dl^2} + 2\dfrac{dp_l}{dl}\right) - MC_l\left(c\dfrac{d^2p_c}{dc^2}\dfrac{dc}{dl} + 2\dfrac{dp_c}{dc}\dfrac{dc}{dl}\right)}{MC_c^2}.$$

This expression is negative if the first and second derivatives of the supply functions of the factors are positive or zero.

55

the monopsonist operates at Q_m, where the equal output and equal outlay curves are tangent.

Let us assume that the monopsonist has control over the wage rate he pays, but not over the price of capital. Then the marginal cost of labor will exceed its price (on the reasonable assumption that the supply curve of labor is positively sloping), and the slope of the constant outlay curve will be steeper, at the indicated inputs of labor (OL_m) and capital (OC_m) inputs, than the corresponding price ratio.[17]

CHART 4

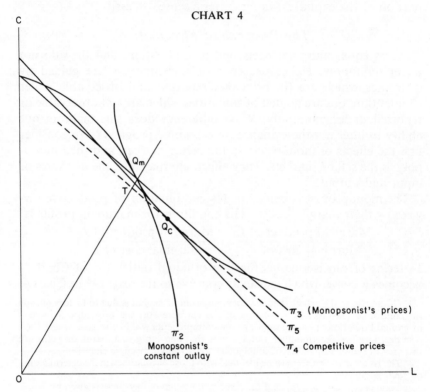

That is, the prices paid by the monopsonist generate a price line (π_3) which is flatter than the isoquant at its point of tangency (Qm) with the constant outlay curve (π_2).

[17] Let P^0 be the specific price of capital services of which C_m units are purchased, and P_l^0 the price of labor when L_m units are purchased. Then the slope of the monopsonist's constant outlay curve will be

$$-\frac{P_l^0 + L_m\left(\dfrac{dp_l}{dl}\right)l = L_m}{P_c^0}$$

and the slope of the corresponding price line is $-P_l^0/P_c^0$, which is algebraically larger, for the second term in the numerator of the previous expression is also positive.

56

If the monopsonist is replaced by a large number of firms so that competition is established in the labor market, the individual competitor will face the factor price line π_4.[18] The price of labor will be higher relative to that of capital because more labor will be used; more labor will be used because the marginal cost of labor to a competitive buyer does not exceed its price. The price line π_4 is accordingly steeper than π_3. It is tangent to the isoquant at Q_c. The competitive inputs, valued at the monopsonist's prices (π_5 parallel to π_3), indicate that the removal of monopsony increased efficiency in the proportion TQ_m/OQ_m.

This calculated increase in productivity as a result of eliminating monopsony is essentially misleading. It is similar to, although not

CHART 5

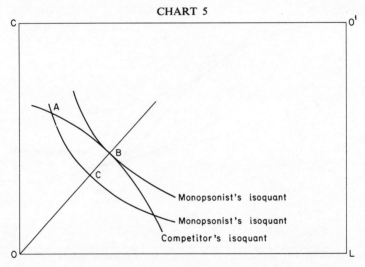

really identical with, the apparent changes in productivity that arise in the competitive case when relative input prices change. Yet it is true that monopsony leads to an inefficient allocation of resources among industries, so its elimination should lead to an increase in the productivity of the economic system. The conventional argument to this end may be illustrated with the familiar "box" diagram in Chart 5. The sides of the box measure the total quantities of capital and labor, the output isoquants of the monopsonized sector are drawn with respect to 0, and those of the competitive sector with respect to 0'. The original situation of the monopsonist and the competitive sector is at A. If the monopsony is eliminated, the new

---

[18] With n competitors, and no economies or diseconomies of scale, the isoquant of the competitor will be the same as that of the monopsonist except that corresponding points on the input scales will be $1/n$ times as large.

position *B* is reached, with the monopsonist's output the larger by *BC/OC*. (The actual equilibrium position will lie on a contract ourve of which *B* is one point; a knowledge of demand conditions is necessary to determine it.)

The increase in efficiency is not due to any change in the state of the arts, as this phrase is customarily used. But if we include in the arts the economic organization of the economy, as we certainly should, there has been an advance when monopsony is eliminated.

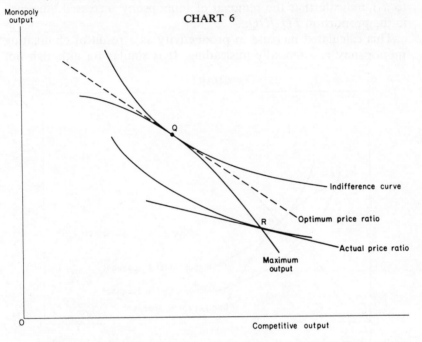

CHART 6

The increase in efficiency cannot be attributed to any one industry, however.

Monopoly power in selling markets is much more important. The value of the marginal product of a factor will be higher in the monopolistic than in the competitive industries, so the elimination of monopoly would allow a redistribution of resources such that real income of the community could be larger. How does the presence of monopoly affect the estimates of economic progress?

Consider a situation in which all resources are fully employed in either the monopolistic or competitive sectors of the economy. There will be a production possibility curve which displays the maximum outputs of the two sectors, given in Chart 6. Subject to difficulties much discussed in welfare economies, there will be a collective consumer indifference curve and an output given by Q.[19] With monopoly the outputs will be at R. The quantities of the resources are the same in both situations and the relative prices of the various resources may also be the same,[20] so efficiency varies between the two situations in proportion to the measure of output.

The monopoly combination R falls on a lower indifference curve than Q, so efficiency rises if monopoly is eliminated. This result is certain to be revealed if the conditions of our diagram are met, for R falls on a lower price line than Q at either monopolistic or competitive prices. But if monopolistic and competitive sectors have constant costs, the production possibility curve coincides with the optimum price line and R falls on this line; in this event removal of monopoly does not lead to an increase of output measured in competitive prices.

The most interesting point raised by the presence of various forms of monopoly is the aggregation problem their effects pose. When these inefficient forms of market organization diminish in scope or quantitative importance, no one industry deserves credit for the resulting increase in productivity. Even if the productivity of each industry is correctly measured, the sum of their advances is not necessarily equal to the social advance in productivity. This can be restated as the proposition that general economic structure is also an input. Unless it is explicitly introduced—and I happily leave this task to the input specialists—there will be unexplained increases or decreases in productivity in the economic system. This is similar to but distinguishable from the effects of external economies (to which I now turn), because this component of the efficiency of an economic structure is independent of its size.

The Economies of Scale

We have so far assumed that the activity we are measuring is subject to constant returns to scale, so an increase of K per cent in every input will lead to a K per cent increase of output—in the absence of economic progress. This assumption, which is explicit or implicit in all productivity calculations, is not obviously correct, and yet its abandonment could have radical influence on these calculations. If a K per cent increase of each input leads to an M ($>K$) per cent increase of output even with a given state of the arts, the conventional calculations overstate the rate of progress, and conversely if $M < K$.

Let us approach this problem through a concrete example. The

[19] We can avoid the difficulties in the concept of community indifference curves by assuming that consumption is independent of the distribution of income.

[20] They will be the same if the monopolistic and competitive sectors use various resources in the same proportions.

real quantities of labor, capital, and value added in American manufacturing industries are given in Table 1. We may fit to these data the so-called Cobb-Douglas production function,

$$P = aC^\alpha L^\beta,$$

where P is product, C is capital, L is labor, and a is a scale constant.

TABLE 1

Employment, Capital, and Value Added in Manufacturing Industries, 1900-48
(1929 prices)

Year	Capital (millions of dollars)	Laborers Employed (thousands)	Value Added (millions of dollars)
1900	17,452	5,063	9,275
1909	31,734	7,226	13,674
1919	46,094	9,665	18,042
1929	63,022	10,502	30,591 (ca.)
1937	55,319	10,619	30,581
1948	82,427	15,322	49,801

SOURCE: Daniel Creamer, *Capital and Output Trends in Manufacturing, 1880–1948*, p. 18.

When Douglas fitted such a function, the sum of the exponents $\alpha + \beta$ was approximately unity, so there were approximately constant returns to scale.[21] This result depended partly upon the period he covered (1899–1922), partly on the deficiencies in his data. When we use Creamer's data (in Table 1), we obtain the equation,

$$P = .19C^{.46}L^{.90},$$

and the sum of the exponents is 1.36.

Before we turn to the discussion of this result, let us simplify it by expressing all inputs in terms of capital, and thus put aside the question of changes in the proportions of inputs. This simplification can be made, at least approximately, by expressing labor in terms of capital by use of the rate of substitution between labor and capital in 1919.[22] The production function of manufacturing for the period

---

[21] In *The Theory of Wages* (New York, 1934), β was set equal to $(1 - \alpha)$; in "Are There Laws of Production?" *American Economic Review*, March 1948, the sum of the coefficients was 1.04 with the same data.

[22] With the production function in the text,

$$\frac{\partial P/\partial C}{\partial P/\partial L} = \frac{.46aL^{.90}C^{-.54}}{.90aL^{-.10}C^{.46}} = \frac{46L}{90C},$$

and substituting the values of capital and labor for 1919,

$$\frac{\partial P/\partial C}{\partial P/\partial L} = \frac{1}{9.33},$$

if we multiply the labor inputs by 9.33, the total "capital" (input) was \$64.7 billions in 1900, \$225.4 billions in 1948.

can then be written,

$$P = bC^{1.36}.$$

The equation summarizes the basic finding that the increase in "capital" (inputs) from 1900 to 1948 of 248.4 per cent led to an increase in output of 435.5 per cent. The conventional measures of progress say that the increase was $(535.5/348.4-1)$ $100=53.7$ per cent, or 1.08 per cent per year on average.[23]

This estimation of the rate of progress obviously rests upon the assumption that in the absence of progress the production function would have been $P=bC$. But suppose that there were increasing returns to scale, so in the absence of progress the production function would have been $P=bC^{1.1}$. Then if capital increased from 1 to 3.384 the product would have risen from $P_{1,900}$ to $(3.48)^{1.1} \times P_{1,900}$, or to 3.947 times the initial output, and the measure of progress over the period would be $(535.5/394.7-1)100=35.7$ per cent. If the function in the absence of progress had been $P=bC^{1.2}$, progress would have been only 19.7 per cent over the period. With constant returns to scale, the estimate was 53.7 per cent, so these alternative production functions reduce the estimate of progress by almost one-third and three-fifths respectively. Any considerable economies of scale would have a large effect upon our estimates of technical progress.

A larger economy should be more efficient than a small economy: this has been the standard view of economists since the one important disadvantage of the large economy, diminishing returns to natural resources, has proved to be unimportant. The large economy can practise specialization in innumerable ways not open to the small (closed) economy. The labor force can specialize in more sharply defined functions; we can have economists who specialize in national income estimation, tax avoidance techniques, measurement of productivity, or writing textbooks. The business sector can have enterprises specializing in collecting oil prices, in repairing old machinery, in printing calendars, in advertising industrial equipment. The transport system can be large enough to allow innumerable specialized forms of transport, such as pipelines, particular types of chemical containers, and the like.

The argument, familiar since Adam Smith's time, surely is valid. The question is: how important are the economies of scale of the economy (or industrial subsets of the economy)? We cannot use time

[23] The output per unit of input is

$$\frac{P}{C} = bC^{.36}$$

and if $C=ke^{rt}$, i.e., if input grows at the rate of r per cent, "efficiency" grows at the (percentage) rate of $.36r$.

61

series on the inputs and outputs to answer this question because we have no independent measure of economic progress.

It might appear more promising to fit a cross-sectional production function to numerous industries, and estimate the extent of increasing returns from this function. Such an estimate would be too low; it would at best measure the extent of economies of size of individual industries and therefore ignore economies which are due to the growth of the entire economy, which are shared by all industries. Thus the gains from specialization in large industries would be measured, those from improved transport and banking systems would be excluded.

Such a function has of course been calculated several times; the function for American manufacturing in 1909, for example, was found to be

$$P = .90L^{.74}C^{.32}.\ [24]$$

This function displays increasing returns ($.74+.32=1.06$). But a function derived in this way is essentially meaningless; under competition the return per unit of labor or capital (product measured in value terms) will be the same in large and small industries. At best, therefore, the cross-sectional functions measure only monopoly returns or short-run disequilibria. To use this approach would require a measure of output that did not wash out the superior efficiency of large scale.

The method would be more attractive if the interindustry comparisons were international, for then the measure of the effects of scale would not be obscured by the forces of competition (unless mobility of resources between the nations were high), and the measure would not exclude the economies of scale of the entire economy which are shared by all industries. Unfortunately, there are apparently no countries that have approximately the same state of the arts as the United States and also possess satisfactory data on inputs and output.[25] A rough comparison of the United States with Great Britain will have to serve as an example.

We may compare the physical outputs of corresponding industries in the United States and Great Britain in 1947 and 1948, using Frankel's data.[26] Let us assume that the production function (not technique) of an industry is the same in both countries, so if the function for Great Britain is

$$P_e = aL^aC^\beta,$$

[24] M. Bronfenbrenner and P. H. Douglas, "Cross-Section Studies in the Cobb-Douglas Function," *Journal of Political Economy*, December 1939.

[25] The Canadian economy, which meets these conditions, is so closely related to our economy that it reaps a large part of our gains of specialization.

[26] Marvin Frankel, *British and American Manufacturing Productivity*, University of Illinois Bulletin (Urbana, 1957).

that of the United States is $P_a = b(\lambda_l L)^\alpha (\lambda_c C)^\beta = k\lambda_l^\alpha \lambda_c^\beta P_e$, where λ_l and λ_c are the ratios of labor and capital of the American industry to the corresponding quantities for the British industry. We may fit a function,

$$\frac{P_a}{P_e} = k\lambda_l^\alpha \lambda_c^\beta,$$

and calculate $(\alpha+\beta)$. The function, estimated from twenty-three industries,[27] is

$$\frac{P_a}{P_e} = 1.45\lambda_i^{.827}\lambda_c^{.444} \quad (R^2 = .806),$$

so $(\alpha+\beta)=1.27$.[28] This equation displays extremely powerful economies of scale: applied to the 48-year period covered by Creamer's data, it would reduce the effects of technical progress to an 8.5 per cent increase in output, or to one-sixth of the amount yielded by a constant-returns-to-scale assumption.[29]

This estimate of the economies of scale is no doubt biased upward. The ratio of American to British inputs is very probably understated. This is especially likely for capital, where we follow Frankel in using fuel consumption as an index of capital. The American data suggest that this index does not vary in close proportion with capital.[30] Even the labor figures, which are simple counts of employees, may have the same bias because our labor force has benefited from much more educational investment.

The conclusion to be drawn, aside from the inevitable one that more work should be done, is that economies of scale are potentially of the same order of magnitude as technical progress. I consider the problem of establishing the approximate magnitude of these economies a major one, not merely of productivity calculations, which are not especially important, but of the theory of economic growth.

[27] One can obtain P_a/P_e and calculate λ_l from Table 10 of Frankel; from Table 5 one can obtain λ_l/λ_l and hence λ_c.

[28] The standard error of α is .19; that of β, .17. The algebraic values of the residuals are not correlated with the absolute size of the American industry, but there is a moderate positive correlation of the absolute values of the residuals with absolute size of industry.

[29] J. B. Heath has recently made a similar comparison of Great Britain and Canada in "British-Canadian Industrial Productivity," *Economic Journal*, December 1957. The chief difference is the use of horsepower as a measure of nonlabor inputs. For fourteen industries he obtains the equation

$$P = 1.55\lambda_i^{.73}\lambda_c^{.31} \quad (R^2 = .9705),$$

where the variables represent the ratio of Canadian to British quantities. The main objection to this comparison is given in footnote 25.

[30] The 1954 capitals (in 1947 prices) may be correlated with fuel purchases for the twenty-two two-digit American manufacturing industries; the Pearsonian coefficient is only .536.

COMMENT

ROBERT M. SOLOW, Massachusetts Institute of Technology

I had almost come to the end of Stigler's paper, nodding agreement as he laid it on the line for the statisticians, when I suddenly realized that I hadn't thought of anything to say. And in our profession to be struck dumb is considerably more damaging to a reputation than simply making mistakes. But fortunately for me, two pages before the end I found an important point on which Stigler and I disagree. It bears on what we both think to be one of the essential and neglected aspects of the problem—the question of increasing returns to scale.

The natural places to try to catch the effects of increasing (or decreasing) returns to scale are aggregate time series like Stigler's Table 1, or their microeconomic analogues. But then we run into a familiar kind of identification problem. Over long periods of time, capital, labor, and output grow. The effects of increasing scale and of technical change are mixed. The data provide no sure and simple way of segregating those increases in output per unit of input which would have occurred through the mere passage of time and increase of knowledge, even if inputs were constant, from those increases which would in fact have been available earlier if only the system had been larger. It is true that over shorter periods one can find decreases in employment and even in capital inputs so that any increases in output should be attributable to some kind of improvement in technique or efficiency (compare 1929 and 1937 in Table 1). But no one likes to hang an argument on these depression observations, on the ground that the equilibrium relationships we seek are likely to be disturbed in such times of rapid, short-run adjustment.

I leave aside all the additional difficulties, such as the inputs we don't measure at all (entrepreneurship is the standard example), the inputs whose measures are systematically biased by quality changes, and shifts between market and nonmarket activity.

One turns next to the possibility of some sort of cross-section measure which will hold time, and therefore the state of the arts, constant. Stigler considers for a moment the standard sort of Cobb-Douglas cross-section study applied to a single economy and finds it "essentially meaningless." I consider this much too generous an evaluation. He goes on to suggest that the cross-section production function makes more sense if it is used to compare two similar but quite separate economies, for then competition need not require factor returns to be equal in the two countries even if the state of the arts is identical in identical industries. This idea is followed up in an ingenious way and leads to estimates of the Cobb-Douglas elasticities which add up to 1.27, a strong case of increasing returns to scale.

This is where I have to find fault. I don't think this device really dodges the nonsense in the cross-section approach. The results suffer from much the same difficulty of interpretation and may in fact mean something quite different from what they appear to say. I think I can show that under plausible (though not necessarily true) assumptions, universal constant returns to scale might lead to just such an appearance of increasing returns.

The difficulty goes back to the ordinary cross-section technique of Douglas and his followers. Suppose there *is* competition everywhere, and suppose every industry operates under constant returns to scale. Suppose you plot output per man-hour against capital per man-hour, one point for each industry, which is essentially what the cross-section technique does. Then what you get is not meaningless, but it is simply not a production function. The points should lie on or near a straight line whose vertical intercept should be the real wage and whose slope should be the real return on capital. This line will be the envelope of the production functions of the several industries. You can fit a log-log function to it if you're in the mood, but you're wasting your time. This theoretical point is surely well known. There are some remarkable recent results by Tibor Barna which show that nature imitates art, and what is theoretically expected actually shows up in the data.

Now let us turn to the international comparison. In a notation as close to Stigler's as I can conveniently make it, let Q_i^e and Q_i^a be the outputs of the ith industry in England and America. Then if each industry has a Cobb-Douglas production function, the same in both countries, we can write

$$Q_i^e = L_i^{\alpha_i} C_i^{\beta_i}$$
$$Q_i^a = b(\lambda_i L_i)^{\alpha_i}(\mu_i C_i)^{\beta_i}$$

where L_i and C_i are the labor and capital inputs into the ith industry in England and λ_i and μ_i are the ratios of American labor and capital inputs to English in the ith industry. It would, of course, be a gross coincidence if every industry's technology were describable in this constant elasticity form. I suspect the Cobb-Douglas function has been grossly overdone (and I have done my share of overdoing). But at least I am allowing each industry its own elasticity. I am sure Stigler is under no illusions about the meaning to be attached to the single interindustry α and β in his cross-section function.

Suppose there is approximate competition everywhere. If there are strong increasing returns to scale it is hard to make sense out of an

65

assumption of competition—unless the economies of scale are all purely external, which is in itself not an attractive assumption and could in any case pose very difficult analytical peculiarities. But my argument does not depend too much on the assumption of competitive product markets, so I make the assumption for convenience. Then we have the marginal productivity equations:

$$w^e = p^e_i \frac{Q^e_i}{L_i} a_i \qquad w^a = p^a_i \frac{Q^a_i a_i}{\lambda_i L_i}$$

$$r^e = p^e_i \frac{Q^e_i}{C_i} \beta_i \qquad r^a = p^a_i \frac{Q^a_i \beta_i}{\mu_i C_i},$$

where w^e, r^e, w^a, r^a are the wage rate and rental of capital services in England and America and p^e_i and p^a_i are the prices of the ith commodity in the two countries. From these equations it is easily deduced that

$$\frac{p^a_i Q^a_i}{p^e_i Q^e_i} = \frac{w^a}{w^e} \lambda_i \quad \text{and} \quad \frac{p^a_i Q^a_i}{p^e_i Q^e_i} = \frac{r^a}{r^e} \mu_i.$$

Finally we can conclude that

1. $$\frac{w^a}{w_e} \lambda_i = \frac{r^a}{r^e} \mu_i \quad \text{or} \quad \frac{\mu_i}{\lambda_i} = \frac{w^a r^e}{w^e r^a};$$

2. $$\frac{p^a_i Q^a_i}{p^e_i Q^e_i} = \sqrt{\frac{w^a r^a}{w^e r^e}} \ \sqrt{\lambda_i \mu_i}.$$

The first of these states, remarkably enough, that the ratio μ_i/λ_i (the ratio of capital per worker in the ith industry in America to capital per worker in the same industry in England) is independent of i; that is, it is the same for all industries. A glance at the first column of Frankel's Table 5 indicates at once that the data do not behave in this way. I suggest that among the reasons they do not are the following:

1. English and American industries do not always have the same production function.

2. The degree of monopoly may differ from industry to industry and country to country.

3. Fuel input may be a poor measure of capital services; dentistry may be more capital intensive than marshmallow-toasting.

4. In many industries the production function may be quite different from the Cobb-Douglas, and this result depends on the constant elasticity form.

66

5. Different industries may vary in the average skill level of their work forces and therefore it is a mistake to measure labor input by employment and another mistake to imagine each industry as paying the same wage rate even under competitive conditions.

The second conclusion above states that if ratios of values of output for each industry are plotted against λ_i and μ_i, the points should fall along a Cobb-Douglas surface of degree one, in fact with equal exponents. But these are monetary values whereas I understand Frankel's figures are attempts at physical output measurement. If value ratios behave in this special way, how might output ratios Q_i^a/Q_i^e be expected to behave? That depends on the observed relation between the price ratio p_i^a/p_i^e on one hand and λ_i and μ_i on the other. If industries with relatively high values of λ_i and μ_i are associated with relatively low values of p_i^a/p_i^e, i.e., if America tends to specialize in commodities for which it has a price advantage; then for high values of λ_i and μ_i, Q_i^a/Q_i^e will tend to be rather higher than the value ratio, and for low values of λ_i and μ_i, Q_i^a/Q_i^e will tend to be rather lower than the value ratio. Thus both the Law of Demand and the Principle of Comparative Advantage seem to suggest that a regression of the output ratio for various industries against λ_i and μ_i will be biased in the direction of increasing returns even if each underlying production function exhibits constant returns to scale.

I am afraid I may have left two misleading impressions, which I would like to correct.

First, I do not believe that the Frankel data or similar figures will bear the refined interpretation I have put on them. I have pointed out one way in which they fail to behave as they theoretically should and I have suggested a number of reasons (all of which I believe to be empirically true) why they may be deficient for this kind of theorizing. This is no reflection at all on Frankel, who never intended the figures for this purpose. What I have been trying to show is that Stigler's attempt to use a purified cross-section production function approach to the measurement of economies of scale escapes some but not all of the pitfalls. The results must be handled cautiously.

Second, I am not trying to debunk increasing returns to scale. As an economic theorist I would gladly pay tithes to a Society for the Preservation of Constant Returns to Scale, and consider the money well spent. But analytical convenience aside, the way of the world is surely quite different. I agree completely with Stigler about the potential magnitude of scale effects, and about their probable actual importance. The problem of measuring economies of scale and distinguishing their effects from those of technical progress is an econometric puzzle worthy of anybody's talents.

REPLY: George J. Stigler.

Because of Frankel's kindness in supplying the value data underlying his study, it is possible to evade one of Solow's criticisms. One may compare relative prices with relative outputs, and thus disregard the multiplicity of inputs (which is an unwelcome complication in this context). The resulting equation is

$$\log \left(\frac{\text{price in U.S.}}{\text{price in G.B.}}\right) = 2.005 - .263 \log \left(\frac{P_a}{P_e}\right),$$
$$(.075)$$

with $n=24$. The equation implies a production function of degree $1/(1-.263)=1.34$, which is substantially identical with that in the text.

Solow's main criticism, that the demand conditions can produce a spurious finding of increasing returns even when constant returns prevail, is of course disquieting. International specialization is probably not a large source of bias; the commodities are primarily domestic in Frankel's sample. The effects of domestic demands, however, do not seem capable of easy summary. I would welcome a showing of some bias because the present estimates of increasing returns are embarrassingly large.

POSTSCRIPT: Robert M. Solow.

Controversy over the source and nature of increasing returns to scale goes back a long way in the literature of economics. Not many of Clapham's "empty boxes" have been filled. To the extent that there are unexploited economies of scale internal to individual firms, data pertaining to individual firms should be studied. Stigler has suggested to me that it is also worth studying economies of scale of various degrees of externality, and I think he is right. In particular he has suggested one of the classical cases, in which economies of scale are external to each firm in the industry, but internal to the industry as a whole.

In this case, my equation (1) when written for each firm in the ith industry would show constant returns to scale ($\alpha_i + \beta_i = 1$), but the multiplying constants a and b would be increasing functions of the output of the industry, i.e., of the sum of firms' outputs. This implies that the aggregate production function for the industry would exhibit increasing returns to scale. This in turn suggests that equations like (2), if they had to be written for the industry, would overexhaust the product.

On these assumptions I think the proper way to proceed is slightly different. Since the economies of scale are external to the firm, it is still permissible to suppose that each firm takes the prices of factors and the output of the industry as parameters. Then for each firm (supposed equal in size, for simplicity) the usual value-of-marginal-product conditions will hold. In addition, if equilibrium is to exist for the industry, the price of the product must equal the unit cost of production. It can then be shown that equations (2) undergo, for the industry, only a slight modification. They become:

$$\frac{w^e}{1-\gamma_i^e} = \frac{p_i^e Q_i^e a_i}{L_i} \qquad \frac{w^a}{1-\gamma_i^a} = \frac{p_i^a Q_i^a a_i}{\lambda_i L_i}$$

$$\frac{r^e}{1-\gamma_i^e} = \frac{p_i^e Q_i^e \beta_i}{C_i} \qquad \frac{r^a}{1-\gamma_i^a} = \frac{p_i^a Q_i^a \beta_i}{\mu_i C_i}$$

where γ_i^e and γ_i^a are respectively the elasticities of a and b with regard to the industry output.

Then the first of my two numbered conclusions holds exactly as it stands and the second is modified only by the appearance on the right-hand side of the additional multiplicative factor $(1-\gamma_i^e)/(1-\gamma_i^a)$. If anything, this reinforces the conclusion, since one would expect λ_i and μ_i to be large in those industries for which γ_i^a is large relative to γ_i^e.

Morris A. Copeland, Cornell University

This Conference was started some twenty-odd years ago to afford workers in the field of national income and social accounting, both the producers of the figures and the users, an opportunity to meet and discuss problems of common interest. As time has gone on the scope of topics considered at Conference sessions has gradually expanded. It currently includes about everything that comes under the head of empirical aggregative economic inquiries.

This expansion of Conference interest is a natural and, I think, a desirable one. The statistical measurements with which aggregative economics concerns itself consist of estimates of social accounting magnitudes like GNP and national wealth, as well as other closely related quantities. All things considered the Conference may well take its major objective to be fostering and facilitating statistical investigations of a macroeconomic nature.

It is probably inevitable that the process of expansion of the scope of Conference interest should have gone even farther. Macro-economic inquiries are not all statistical. There is another kind that I venture to call a priori model analysis because of the tenuous connection between the neoclassical economic models it investigates and the real world. On a number of occasions, participants in Conference sessions have engaged in a priori model analysis. Such analysis was

69

particularly in evidence in the 1958 sessions, and it is this fact that prompts the following comments.

I do not mean to suggest that such analysis should be excluded from Conference proceedings in future. Exclusion would be contrary to the spirit of intellectual freedom. I urge that such analysis be clearly recognized for what it is, and be clearly labeled, because the distinction between a priori analysis and empirical research seems to have been particularly blurred in the 1958 Conference proceedings.

It would require lengthy comment to do an adequate job of grade labeling. In the interests of brevity, I have decided to discuss a single example. The example I have chosen is the second, third, and fourth sections of Stigler's paper. I have made this choice with three considerations in mind. First, among those who have devoted themselves extensively to neoclassical model analysis Stigler stands out as an especially careful thinker. Second, he has made, over a period of years, a particular effort to find some connection between his models and the world of fact. And third, his theoretical pronouncements are often couched in arrogant language that seems to imply there is no competent economist who disagrees with him.

In his first section, Stigler discusses the use of labor productivity measures as substitutes for capital-and-labor productivity measures. He deals with this topic in the spirit of empirical science, and his findings are significant.

The remaining sections of his paper are concerned with the following hypothesis: Ratios of aggregate physical volume of output to physical volume of input are crude in the technical statistical sense. An upward trend in such a crude ratio can be resolved into four main parts: (1) changes in input price relationships; (2) increases in the competitive nature of the economy (or decreases in its monopolistic nature); (3) economies of scale resulting from mere increases in the size of the economy; and (4) "pure" economic progress resulting from a change in the "state of the arts."

Much of his discussion runs in terms of models for which the equations are specified only in broad terms, such as the signs of the first and second derivatives of functions and restrictions that confine the analysis to real values of the variables. Such a priori model-analysis is not specific in the sense that each equation is given a specific analytical form with parameters that can be determined as least squares fits.

Of course Stigler gives us equations of this very specific form, too, and parameters that have been determined as best fits. If this hypothesis is valid and significant, it seems reasonable to insist that

NOTE: These comments were not written until after the Conference sessions.

it lend itself to exploration in terms of specific equations of the best-fit kind and that such equations provide empirical support for thinking that each of the four components has, for some period of years, a value materially different from zero. The question I am particularly concerned to consider is, Does he present statistical evidence that his input-price-change component, his monopoly-vs.-competition component, and his economies-of-scale component do in fact assume values materially different from zero?

In the second section Stigler finds that "changes in relative [input] prices will, with the usual index-number formulas, lead to some change in reported efficiency, although none has taken place." If one grants that a firm can be counted on to behave as if it operated with a production function of the type implied in his Chart 3, this conclusion is logically inescapable. But Stigler might have postulated behavior in accordance with a production function in which capital and labor are perfect complements. On this assumption no change in relative input prices would lead to any change in efficiency. Therefore, the extent of the influence of changes in relative input prices on reported efficiency depends on the nature of the production functions to which business behavior in fact conforms. The more closely they approximate perfect complementarity, the more nearly negligible the influence. But Stigler makes no attempt to show that the influence is material.

In an imperfectly complementary case the influence of a change in relative input prices on reported efficiency could be either plus or minus. Conceivably then, even assuming far from perfect complementarity, the influence on an aggregate measure of efficiency for, say, all manufacturing industries might be negligible because, with changing techniques, the pluses offset the minuses. The second does not consider this possibility.

Stigler refers to input prices as "one part of our observational information." This seems to imply that satisfactory measures for both prices are available. I dare say the difficulties in providing an aggregate statistical measure of the cost of labor are not too serious, but I wish Stigler would give us his solution of the problem of providing a statistical measure of the cost of capital.

Next as to his monopoly-vs.-competition component of an increase in an output-input ratio. In theory at least, this component might be either positive or negative. Hence the exploration of his hypothesis seems to call for some measure of the extent to which there is movement toward more monopoly or toward more competition. Stigler finds that elimination of monopoly or monopsony always improves economic efficiency. As applied to his Charts 5 and 6 this proposition

will doubtless command general agreement. As applied to the real world, however, where competition between selling enterprises includes quality of goods, terms of sale, and sales effort and where employer competition mixes wages and working conditions, this proposition is certainly somewhat controversial, yet there is nothing in Stigler's third section that relates to this influence in the real world. The argument proceeds exclusively in terms of a priori models with competition always conceived as "perfect competition."

Stigler may be right in thinking recent increases in aggregate U.S. output-input ratios reflect in part changes in the degree of monopoly or of competition in the economy, but he presents no empirical support, nor does he offer us any measure of this type of change. No doubt he is painfully aware of the difficulties of providing such a statistical measure. At any rate, he does not even attempt to say whether the change in recent years has been toward or away from a more competitive form of organization.

The third section of his paper is purely deductive from start to finish. And it seems fair to conclude that the part of his hypothesis with which it is concerned does not readily lend itself to empirical investigation in terms of the statistical data currently available.

Stigler's third component of increases in crude output-input ratios is the influence of "economies of scale." His hypothesis here is that a production function may be such that an increase of x per cent in each input may, "in the absence of progress," result in an increase of more than x per cent in output. In examining this possibility in connection with time-series data a need is observed to find some way to distinguish between (1) the increase in an output-input ratio that would have occurred with an increase in scale but no change in the production function (i.e., "in the absence of progress") and (2) the part of the actual increase in an output-input ratio that is attributable to "progress" (i.e., to a change in the production function.)[1] Likewise in an intercountry comparison which shows higher output-input ratios for Country A than for Country B there is need to find some way to say how much, if any, of this showing is due to differences in scale and how much is due to differences in production functions.

When Stigler concludes that "economies of scale are potentially of the same order of magnitude as technical progress," he presumably has in mind mainly what I would call aggregative economies of scale. It could be argued that his U.S.-British comparison in large part reflects economies of scale at the plant or enterprise level, and that

---

[1] Stigler refers to his equation, $P=bC^{1.36}$ (which does not make such a distinction), as a "production function." This use of the term is confusing. It might better be called a "state-of-the-arts function."

American businessmen have generally developed plants and business organizations of optimum size while their British cousins have not. But the hypothesis that differences in the state of the arts have resulted in differences in approximation to optimum size is more likely to appeal to those who do not have a pro-American bias. At all events, economies of scale at the industry level can hardly have contributed significantly to the finding of an $(\alpha+\beta)$ of 1.27. Such so-called external economies imply an input with a supply schedule that descends to the right. And practically the only situation that can yield this kind of schedule under anything remotely resembling perfect competition is one in which the input is itself a product made with an input that has a decreasing supply price. External economies that result from the larger size of the American economy seem a more plausible possibility than the one Stigler has in mind.[2]

Stigler attaches more weight to his intercountry comparison than to his Cobb-Douglas fit to Creamer's data.[3] But there is need in both cases to distinguish between differences in an output-input ratio that involve no change in production function and differences that are due to such a change. We do have a technique of sorts for making such a distinction in a time-series analysis, but no comparable technique for an intercountry comparison.

The technique I refer to requires us to assume that output is a particular analytical function of inputs and time. If for the moment we avoid being specific analytically, we must assume $P=f(C, L, t)$. Presumably we will expect $\partial P/\partial t$ to be >0, for we will take time as an indicator of the state of the arts. In other words, we will expect technological progress. Having fitted a function of this kind to data such as Creamer's, we can then hold time constant and with it the state of the arts, and investigate the way output changes with changes in inputs. Also we can hold the inputs constant and investigate the way output varies with time and the state of the arts.

There is an obvious objection to this procedure. The line is drawn according to the specific analytical form assumed for $P=f(C, L, t)$. However, if I propose for Creamer's data an analytical form that gives no suggestion of aggregate economies of scale, and if Stigler wishes to raise this objection, it would seem incumbent on him to offer an alternative form of $P=f(C, L, t)$ that gives at least as good a fit and does exhibit economies of scale.

A comment here on his U.S.-British comparison: He assumes that

[2] "The large economy can practice specialization in innumerable ways not open to the small (closed) economy."

[3] In fact he goes so far as to say, incorrectly I think, that "We cannot use time series on inputs and outputs to answer this question"—viz., "How important are the economies of scale of the economy . . . ?"

73

the output-input "function (not technique) of an industry is the same in both countries."[4] Since this function includes only C and L as independent variables, with no separate independent variable as an indicator of the more progressive state of the arts in the United States, his anlysis does not distinguish the influence of external economies from that of differences in the state of the arts, and does not indicate whether there are increasing or decreasing returns with scale. His comparison is, therefore, completely irrelevant to the conclusion that he seems to have drawn from it. This leaves the final section without pertinent statistical support.

The hypothesis I propose to fit to Creamer's data is extremely simple. I will take $\partial P/\partial C = 0$, so long as there is any excess capacity in the economy. This means my hypothesis exhausts no more degrees of freedom than Stigler's did when he found that $\log P = \log (.19) + .46 \log C + .90 \log L$. My hypothesis is that output is an increasing function of time (as an indicator of the state of the arts) and of the economy's capacity factor (i.e., the percentage of capacity at which the economy is operating). I will take as an indicator of the capacity factor a deviation-from-trend computation for labor input. Specifically, I assume that $\log P = m \varDelta \log L + ht + k$, where $\varDelta \log L$ is the deviation from its linear trend of $\log L$. With t measured in years and $1900 = 0$, I find the following best fit:

$$\log P = .396\varDelta \log L + .0148t + .9875.$$

This equation gives an appreciably better fit than does Stigler's.[5] And since .396 is markedly less than 1, it clearly suggests decreasing rather than increasing returns with scale.[6]

No doubt Stigler will regard the capacity factor as reflecting short-run disequilibria. My hypothesis certainly emphasizes short-run adjustments, but I protest his normative language. It is principally short-run adjustments that we have learned how to explore statistically. The idea of a functional relation between output and inputs that represents the long-run adjustments for various price situations and for a given state of the arts does not readily lend itself to statistical exploration. If Stigler has a way of exploring such a relation I wish he would tell us about it.

RAYMOND L. RICHMAN, University of Pittsburgh

In his section on "Labor Productivity as an Index of Productivity," Stigler complains that index makers began constructing indexes of

---

[4] Here again, the confusing term "production function." See footnote 1.

[5] The standard error of my predicted $\log P$'s is .081. The standard error of his predicted $\log P$'s is .141.

[6] It may be convenient to think of my formula in the following form:

$$P = \text{a constant} \times L^m \times C^0 \times f(t).$$

labor productivity when "it was already a basic proposition of economics that one should never look at *average* products, only at *marginal* products." Later he adds, "So far as I know, not a single theoretical statement of any importance can be made about the average product of labor."

These statements are completely misleading. All of the industry, sector, and national productivity measures are measures of long-run changes in productivity. Average product is of more theoretical importance in the long-run case than is marginal product.

First, in the long run under competitive conditions, price tends to minimum average cost. Average cost is composed of the prices of the factors of production divided by their average products.

Second, businessmen have long been pricing on the basis of their average costs. Wages and prices are set over long periods. In labor negotiations businessmen have been concerned with the effect of a wage increase on their average costs. This is not the place to discuss average cost pricing, but it is surely time that economists paid more attention to how the economic system works, although it is not irrelevant how it should work. Further, under some assumptions about the shape of the production function, they might achieve about the same results as they would if they were using marginal costs, e.g., where one assumes a production function (average product) "kinked" at the point of designed capacity.

Third, the production function implies certain precise relations between marginal productivity, average productivity, and total production. From what is happening to average product, what is happening to marginal product can be deduced. As a practical matter, no entrepreneur would ever know his production function by trying to determine marginal product without going through the intermediate stage of learning average product. Cost accountants would still be looking for clues if most economists, including Stigler, had not, perhaps by oversight since it has "no theoretical importance," included drawings of average product when they drew marginal product curves, and if the cost accountants did not know that profits were the difference between average costs and price, not marginal costs and price.

Perhaps most important, the exception which Stigler relegates to a footnote as a "polar case" is of fundamental importance in distributing income among the factors of production, and is pregnant with political and ideological significance. As he phrased it, "What propositions there are about average products—such as that average product should be maximized to maximize output if only one factor is scarce—are polar cases." To translate it to the problem of capital

75

and labor inputs, as the proportion of capital inputs to labor increases, *ceteris paribus*, wages increase and interest decreases until the marginal product of capital is zero, where average product of labor and total product are maximized. A major economic goal is to maximize the average product of labor. The long-run change in the average product of labor is indeed an important measure of economic progress.

Stigler next discusses the accuracy of an index of labor productivity as an estimate of changes in total productivity, that is, capital-and-labor productivity. He draws the obvious conclusion that labor productivity is a better measure of total productivity the more nearly proportional the changes in the various inputs and the larger the labor input is to total inputs. In the individual firm, the capital inputs come largely from outside the firm. (Similarly, changes in the degree of subcontracting, of integration, of power, and other inputs represent changes in inputs from outside the firm.) Under the conditions applying to the individual firm, labor productivity is a good index of total productivity only under the conditions specified by Stigler. However, in the case of a closed economy where all inputs come from within the economy, an increase in capital is not an input independent of labor input. The condition that labor be a large input relative to total input is always satisfied, because most of the capital input is itself a labor input. To represent capital as an independent input is to understate the gain of the economy by double-counting some of the labor input.

ROBERT EISNER, Northwestern University

I shall address myself only to the section of Stigler's paper in which he indicates that certain empirical data collected by Marvin Frankel suggest increasing returns to scale. While I shall call into question the weight to be attached to this suggestion, my concern is not the substantive issue, about which I offer no judgment. Rather, I should like to take Stigler's estimates as a point of departure for an exposure of some pitfalls in presuming to estimate parameters of an economic relation when that relation is not adequately specified.

Utilizing a cross section of twenty-three industries with data as to output and labor and capital inputs in the United States and the United Kingdom, Stigler derives estimates of parameters of a Cobb-Douglas-type production function which indicate that a plus b, the sum of the labor and capital coefficients, equals 1.27. More precisely, where P_a is output in an industry in America and P_e the corresponding output in England, and λ_L and λ_C are the ratios of American to English inputs in the industry for labor and capital respectively,

76

Stigler finds that

$$P_a/P_e = 1.45\lambda_L^{.827}\lambda_C^{.444}.$$

But now suppose each industry has resources or factors specific to its output and different countries are differently endowed. We may classify these other resources as "land," "know-how," or entre-preneurship and label them R_{ij}, where i refers to the ith industry and j goes from 1 to n. Then, if the production function, or functions, are of the Cobb-Douglas type, they may really be given by

$$Q_i = aL_i^\alpha C_i^\beta \left(\prod_{j=1}^{n} R_{ij}^{\gamma_j} \right) + u_i,$$

where u_i is the usual stochastic term and the other variables are as Stigler has defined them.

But if these other factors or resources contributing to production do exist and this is the form of the function, it must follow that $\gamma_j \geqslant 0$ for all j and hence that the partial derivatives of output (Q) with respect to each factor as well as all cross partial derivatives must be positive. Thus industries relatively well-endowed with other resources (R_j) would have higher marginal product curves for labor (L) and capital (C). Because of imperfect mobility the remuneration of labor and capital would tend to be higher in industries relatively well-endowed with other factors, and the ratio of labor and capital to these other factors would tend to be relatively low. This is all that is necessary to establish that industries well-endowed with other factors relative to the same industries in another country would attract relatively more labor and capital and have a relatively higher ratio of output to the sum of labor and capital inputs. (This last is analogous to Stigler's demonstration that a relatively higher capital input would raise the average product of labor.)[1] It follows, under these circumstances, that there would be an upward bias to the estimates of the sum of the labor and capital coefficients ($\alpha + \beta$) and to the estimate of the degree of the Stigler-Frankel production function. Until the amount of this bias can be calculated, the evidence that Stigler presents for increasing returns cannot therefore be accepted as valid.

[1] Page 48 and footnote 2.

The Measurement of Change
in Natural Resource Economic Scarcity

HAROLD J. BARNETT
WAYNE STATE UNIVERSITY AND RESOURCES FOR THE FUTURE, INC.

Introduction

NOTE: Part of this paper draws upon a larger collaborative study undertaken by Professor Chandler Morse and myself for Resources for the Future, Inc., and to be published in book form by this organization. I wish also to acknowledge helpful suggestions from other colleagues.

MANY economists and the general public believe that natural resources (hereafter resources) are scarce and becoming more so, and that this has economic significance. The belief is that resource scarcity inflicts diminishing returns, in some sense; and that these impair economic welfare and growth. The notions seem to be simple and straightforward. Indeed such views are usually expressed as factual statements requiring no proofs.

I am sure that the concepts are not simple and straightforward, and I do not know whether they are true. At the conceptual level, I find much ambiguity and some confusion as to the forms which natural resource scarcity take, and the nature of the diminishing returns which scarcity inflicts. Sorting out the concepts as best I have been able, I have uncovered a multiplicity of theoretical propositions. It appears to me, further, that these propositions are not factual ones, but hypotheses. I have learned, also, that, because of the implicit or explicit assumption that "facts" need no empirical proof, they have had none in the literature. And, finally, I have discovered that, because of the ambiguities and complexities in the simple view of natural resource scarcity and effect, empirical testing is rendered difficult, as much from uncertainty as to what should be tested as from how to test it.

PUBLIC OPINION

I first briefly discuss non-economist public opinion, in order to show that the scarcity doctrine is socially important. The literature is quite voluminous and it is weighted strongly in the belief that the natural resource scarcity problem is significant and urgent. Some of the expressions are of alarm, while others of them are merely of serious concern.

Samuel Ordway, prominent contemporary conservationist, believes that, within foreseeable time, increasing consumption of resources can produce scarcities serious enough to destroy our present culture.[1] The American Association of School Administrators, a department of the National Education Association, states that unless we in the United States use natural resources more prudently, we shall soon be on the road to lower living standards and national decline.[2] William Vogt believes that unless world populations are reduced, there will be drastic lowering of living standards, and that there is not time for reliance upon voluntary population adjustments.[3]

Recent years have seen a spurt of similar literature from outstanding physical scientists. Among others, Harrison Brown, Sir Charles Galton Darwin, Dr. Allen Gregg, Dr. A. J. Carlson, and Robert C. Cook have stated that natural resource scarcity is inconsistent with contemporary growth rates of living levels and population numbers. For example, geneticist Cook writes, "The world's growing population will force the use of marginal lands, which in general are extremely expensive to exploit. More and more human energy will have to be devoted to the basic problem of producing food, and the standard of living, instead of going up, will remain at the subsistence level in the areas where it now stands at that, while the wealthier areas will find their standards of living declining. Already the pressures of population in most parts of the world have compelled an unwise exploitation of the good lands."[4]

At the level of high government policy, the natural resources platforms of both political parties in this country, as well as a long list of state and federal statutes, are concerned with natural resource scarcity and its adverse economic effects. Governmental concern is not confined to peacetime domestic welfare alone. The State Department warns Foreign Service officers that the industrial and military power of the United States is due in part to its mineral resources; and "that unfortunately mineral resources are exhaustible, from which it follows that the faster a nation grows in industrial strength and military potency—a growth made possible largely through increased mineral output—the faster it liquidates the very basis of its power." Admiral Rickover, in response to a recent question as to

[1] Samuel H. Ordway, *Resources and the American Dream* (New York, 1953), Foreword.
[2] *Conservation Education in American Schools*, 29th Yearbook, American Association of School Administrators, department of the National Education Association, p. 11.
[3] William Vogt, *Road to Survival* (New York, 1948), p. 265.
[4] Robert C. Cook, *Human Fertility, The Modern Dilemma* (London, 1951), p. 296.

whether he was concerned about using up our natural resources and our natural sources of power, answered, "Yes, I am. We are using our energy sources at a very great rate, not only fuels but also minerals . . . If we keep on using minerals . . . and fuels . . . at the rate we do, there is no question that within a generation or two there will be a shortage. It is my firm conviction that that nation which controls energy sources will become the dominant nation in the world."[5]

These public views of natural resource scarcity and diminishing returns do not derive from examination of U.S. economic history. Diminishing returns in the simple meaning of declining output per unit labor input has not occurred. Rather, the record is of increasing returns averaging about 1 ½ to 2 per cent per year compounded, since 1870 at least. Perhaps the general public believes that diminishing returns from the natural resource scarcity phenomenon apply to the extractive sector alone, but the tables of output per unit labor input in extraction, presented in this volume by my colleagues, Potter and Christy, also show a trend of increasing average returns of 1 ½ to 2 per cent per year. And if output is measured in a net manner, this would produce similar results. Still another commonsense type of measure might go this way: the extractive sector is hypothesized to experience diminishing returns and increasing costs; and, therefore, the size of the nation's bill for extractive goods will increase relative to GNP, and the fraction of the nation's labor force required for the extractive sector will rise. But the facts do not bear out such theorizing. In modern U.S. economic history, the percentage of the U.S. labor force engaged in extraction declines steadily from about 56 per cent in 1880 to about 14 per cent in 1955.

I think lay opinions on natural resource scarcity and diminishing returns therefrom derive substantially from the teachings and writings of professional economists.[6] "The ideas of economists and political philosophers, both when they are right and when they are wrong, are more powerful than is commonly understood."[7]

[5] United States Government, Department of State, Division of Foreign Reporting Services, November 1945. Economic Manual (*A Guide for Reporting Officers in the Foreign Service of the United States of America*), Dept. of State publication 2556, Chapter 10. Admiral Rickover in an interview on "See It Now" TV program manuscript, November 18, 1956, Columbia Broadcasting System, New York. Cf. H. J. Barnett, "The Changing Relation of Natural Resources to National Security," *Economic Geography*, July 1958 (also available as a reprint from Resources for the Future, Inc., Washington, D.C.).

[6] Concerning origins of the scarcity doctrine see H. J. Barnett, "Malthusianism and Conservation." Available as a preprint from Resources for the Future, Inc., Washington, D.C.

[7] J. M. Keynes, *The General Theory of Employment* (London, 1936), p. 383.

ECONOMISTS

It is easier to come to grips with economists' views on natural resource scarcity and its effects than with lay opinions. There are ambiguity and confusion here also but they stem from neglect, brevity of statement, omission, or error, rather than from basic incapacity of the discipline or its practitioners to form the propositions adequately.

Economists seem to present two propositions concerning natural resource scarcity and effect. First is a classical static model in which natural resource scarcity is assumed to be present and to inflict diminishing marginal returns to labor and capital. This concept is then mentally dynamized, and the scarcity force is viewed as occurring among other forces which work in the contrary direction. The hypothesis does not, therefore, require that the historical course of returns be diminishing, since favorable forces can more than offset the adverse natural resource influence. But in such conceptions natural resource scarcity is present and does, *ceteris paribus*, inflict diminishing marginal returns to labor and capital. Thus, for example, Schultz refers to land, the nonreproducible factor, always acting as a drag on economic growth because of the element of diminishing returns.[8] But he sets this in a discussion of favorable influences to returns, such as improvement of the quality of people as productive agents and improvement of the level of productive arts. Bach presents a similar formulation, and other similar presentations occur in Mill and Marshall.

The second form of the scarcity doctrine starts with the proposition just described and embodies it in a prognostication and policy judgment. It suggests that the natural resource scarcity force has a tendency to become stronger with the passage of time, and that in the contest between natural resource scarcity on the one hand, and favorable dynamic influence on the other, the former threatens to become dominant or at least relatively more important. For example, Spengler recently expressed the opinion that "our demands on the resources which cannot be augmented by technological progress will soon result in large-scale scarcities and the prohibitive prices and costs which accompany scarcities."[9] Villard has written on related lines, and Ise, Pigou, and Mitchell expressed concern over resource depletion in such a way that I infer that they project increasingly adverse influence from natural resource scarcity.

[8] *The Economic Test in Latin America* (Ithaca: August 1956), pp. 19–20. Also Theodore W. Schultz, "Latin-American Economic Policy Lessons," *American Economic Review*, XLVI 2 (May 1956), p. 431.

[9] Joseph J. Spengler, "Population Threatens Prosperity," *Harvard Business Review*, (January–February 1956), p. 88.

My interest here is to test empirically the first of the above economic doctrines of natural resource scarcity and impulse to diminishing returns. Clearly, the appropriate way to make a start at improved understanding of the effects of this scarcity, and operational testing of the doctrine, is to formulate explicitly the static models which underlie the doctrines. In this attempt my first task is to distinguish the several different natural resource scarcity conceptions, define the diminishing returns which flow therefrom for a simplified, essentially static situation, and relate these to economic welfare and growth.[10] I then puzzle over how to test these empirically in a dynamic economy. Finally, I suggest a device for measuring natural resource scarcity and its economic effects in a dynamic economy, and in a preliminary and tentative way apply it to U.S. history since 1870.

Simple Static Scarcity Models

Let there be a static, linear, and homogeneous social production function of the type

$$O = f(R, L, C),$$

where O=units of output, R=units of natural resources, L=units of labor, and C=units of capital. Each of the three inputs and the output is a homogeneous, physical variable. Labor and capital are assumed available in constant-proportion doses. The function is assumed to be what Allen has termed a "more general normal type," specifically

$$O = \sqrt{2H(L+C)R - A(L+C)^2 - B(R)^2},$$

where A, B, and H are positive constants such that H^2 is greater than AB.[11]

The expansion path for *resource plenitude* (=no scarcity), and no institutional basis for limiting resource use or charging for use, is OG in Chart 1 (in this chart $H=2$; $A=B=1$).

We can now immediately define the first case of natural resource scarcity—*Malthusian-type scarcity*—by specifying that total resource availability is r_1. In this case, the expansion path is OEH. Given sociotechnical conditions, we find that:

1. *Natural resource scarcity* is defined as a small limit of R availability relative to $L+C$, small being further defined as an amount less than r_1/a_1.

[10] For elaboration on these models, see C. Morse and H. J. Barnett, "A Theoretical Analysis of Natural Scarcity and Economic Growth" (published in 1960 in an SSRC-RFF Conference volume, by The Johns Hopkins Press, Baltimore).

[11] R. G. D. Allen, *Mathematical Analysis For Economists* (London, 1947), pp. 288, 322.

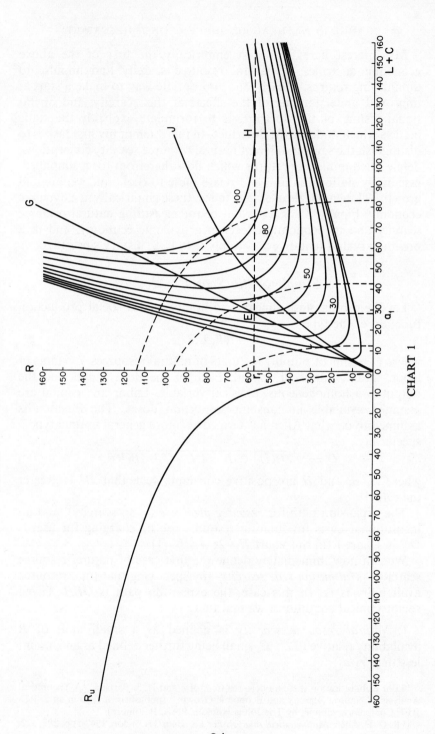

CHART 1

84

2. *Diminishing returns from natural resource scarcity* is defined as the decline, which occurs from E onward, in marginal productivity of $L+C$, due to the small limits of R availability.

3. *Impairment of economic welfare* from natural resource scarcity is defined as the decline in output per capita, when this begins to occur at E.

4. If we stipulate that economic growth is increase in total output, then *impairment of economic growth* from natural resource scarcity is limitation of output at a level not exceeding 100. Let there be a conventional or physical "subsistence" level per unit $L+C$ equal to kO, where k is greater than $100 \div L+C$, and let $L+C$ always increase to the limit of subsistence. Then impairment of economic growth from natural resource scarcity is the stabilization of output at some point on the path EH short of H. The exact point depends on the value of k. Such cessation of growth contrasts with endless increase in output along OEG, in the resource plenitude case.

In the second case of natural resource scarcity—*Ricardian scarcity* —there is no limit on total resources available, but their economic qualities decline steadily as a function of volume employed. This relaxes the earlier assumption of constant quality. To represent this case, the original social production function is modified as follows:

$$O = f_1(R, L, C) - f_2(R_u).$$

R_u represents resources of steadily declining economic quality, but is equal to R in quantitative physical units (e.g., acres). If we assume the social production function is the same one, except for the retardation term, there is a special case in which we may use the same isoquant diagram, and handle the absorption of labor and capital required to upgrade R_u to R economic quality on a bent axis. The original equation,

$$O = \sqrt{2H(L+C)R - A(L+C)^2 - B(R)^2},$$

becomes in this case

$$O = \sqrt{2H[(L+C) - e^{R_u m}]R_u - A[(L+C) - e^{R_u m}]^2 - B(R_u)^2},$$

where m is any positive constant (in Chart 1, $m = .03912$). The new expansion path, derived by employing natural resources to the point where marginal productivity of $(L+C)$ is maximized (which is the point where marginal productivity of resources equals zero), is OJ. We find that:

1. *Natural resource scarcity* is the decline in quality of resources, irrespective of unlimited total quantity.

85

2. *Diminishing returns from natural resource scarcity* is the immediate and steady decline in marginal productivity of $(L+C)$, due to steady quality decline of incremental resources.

3. *Impairment of economic welfare* from natural resource scarcity is the decline in output per capita, along *OJ*.

4. Again stipulating that economic growth is increase in total output, that there is a "subsistence" level per unit $L+C$ of kO, and that $L+C$ increases to this limit, then *impairment of economic growth* from natural resource scarcity is stabilization of output someplace along *OJ*, where $O/(L+C)=k$, rather than endless increase along *OG*.

The scarcity effect is now characterized for the case of small limits of total resource availability relative to population and sociotechnical conditions, and for qualitative decline in resources as a function of scale of employment of such resources.

The third case of scarcity, a depletion conception, cannot be shown in the chart without relaxing the assumption of a static model, since resource extinction is a function of time, among other things. But Chart 1 can help us visualize the economic effects of depletion. We must try to imagine successive Chart 1's in time. Then depletion eats away the resource axis from the bottom. If resource availability is that of the first case, the expansion path, *OG*, remains unchanged because there are always more constant quality resources than are needed, and there is neither scarcity nor effect. If resource availability is that of the Malthusian case, then the horizontal portion of the expansion path, *EH*, falls to successively lower levels, corresponding to the successive depletions of resources. If resource availability is that of the Ricardian case, *OJ*, then it is the bent axis which is depleted (gnawed away from the bottom—best resource first), and a flatter and lower expansion path results. It must be emphasized that the depletion case does not exert an economic scarcity impulse or produce a scarcity effect if grafted on to our resource plenitude situation. It is only if a Malthusian or Ricardian scarcity exists, or can be brought into being by depletion, that depletion then becomes economically operative. Then:

1. *Natural resource scarcity* is the extinction of resources where the quantity availability was already limited and small; or the extinction of high quality resources, where quality was already declining; or both.

2. *Diminishing returns from resource scarcity* and *impairment of economic welfare* are as given in the first two cases, but with aggravated severity.

86

3. *Impairment of economic growth* is eventual decline in total output, a contrast with the other scarcity cases in which growth merely ceased.

I do not develop here various other cases which are combinations of Malthusian, Ricardian, and depletion scarcities. For example, there could be a large but limited volume of high quality resources, and then endless quantities of declining quality ones. Resource qualities could exist in quantity plateaus, and the decline of quality as a function of quantity be in discrete, rather than continuous, steps. Depletion affects Malthusian and Ricardian scarcities differently. Quality depletion is possible, in addition to quantity depletion, and so forth. I also do not attend to another interesting set of scarcity propositions. It is possible to conceive of the variety of natural resources as a system of interdependent variables in "ecological balance." Then scarcity of quantity limits or of qualities can be conceived from the fact that man's resource needs, although small relative to total resources, have a different composition from the natural ecological balance, and scarcity is experienced from quantity or quality limits of a single resource. Further, aggregate natural resource availability can experience manifold reduction from depletion of individual key resources.

Relaxation of Conditions

If all of the assumed conditions are present, then it is easy to detect scarcity effects in the ways described above. What happens if we relax conditions?

Assume, for example, that the static social production function is characterized by increasing returns to scale. Then the appearance of diminishing marginal returns to labor and capital due to (say) Ricardian scarcity can be indefinitely delayed, depending on the strengths of the opposing forces. But the scarcity force would still be operative, and effects would still be experienced. Thus, let us assume we could compute an expansion path of output as a function of labor plus capital for the conditions of increasing returns to scale and resource plenitude and, holding other things constant, compare this with the actual (say) Ricardian scarcity case. We would find the latter to be lower, even though perhaps accelerating. The scarcity effect is represented by the difference between the two paths.

Let us admit, now, great improvement in manufacturing technology. Then again it would be true that with (say) Ricardian resource availability, an expansion path might show output as a function of labor and capital to be accelerating. But nevertheless this path would

87

fall below the comparable expansion path under conditions of resource plenitude. There would thus be scarcity effect which, in theory, is measured by the difference between the paths.

In general, the same continues to be true no matter what other conditions are relaxed, no matter how dynamic the economy, so long as (say) Ricardian scarcity is to be a continuous, dynamic force.

This poses our next questions.

WHAT DOES RESOURCE SCARCITY MEAN? IS IT FACT OR HYPOTHESIS?

Cosmologists hold different views on whether the universe is limited. For our purposes here, however, let us take it as fact that the natural resources available to man are physically limited. From this, however, it does not follow that Malthusian *economic* scarcity of natural resources must exist. Economic scarcity, as distinguished from physical, requires the additional assumption that the limits of resource availability be small relative to demands placed on them. The size of demands, in turn, depends upon the size of population and capital stock and the sociotechnical parameters. But if the presence or absence or Malthusian economic scarcity depends upon these economic determinants of demand, then it is a relative matter which cannot be deduced from the fact that the physical environment has bounds. Adam and Eve lived in a resource-limited, but not a resource-scarce, world. I conclude, then, that Malthusian economic scarcity of natural resources must be viewed as a hypothesis, and not accepted as fact.

Ricardian economic scarcity as defined, requires as one assumption —taken here as a fact—that the world's natural resources be viewed as heterogeneous in physical properties. However, it also requires that society be able to array the physically varying natural resources in a declining order of *economic* qualities, and that the order remain invariant through time; that it use them in this order; and that the decline in economic quality not be permanently interrupted by access to indefinitely great expanses of unused resources of unchanging marginal economic quality. To elaborate:

1. Ordering according to economic quality clearly requires relating known and stable physical properties of resources to equally known and stable sociotechnical parameters in such a way as to arrive at a *unique and permanent economic ordering.* Yet historically, for example, copper and tin came into use early, iron later, and the light metals last. Consider, similarly, the order of use of energy commodities.[12] If we view both knowledge (ignorance) and production

[12] See, for example, H. J. Barnett, *Energy Uses and Supplies* (Washington, 1950) Charts A and E and Table 18.

parameter stability (instability) with hindsight, it would seem that success in translating physical properties into economic qualities should not be viewed as fact, but hypothesis.

2. Even if translation of physical properties into economic qualities were always successful, does society necessarily use resources in this order? For a number of reasons, the answer would seem to be, "not always." Impediments are international trade barriers, government reservation of resources, distances from population centers, recognized by Ricardo as an influence distinct from intrinsic physical properties, and institutional obstacles (such as the hunting preserves of former European nobility), etc. On the other hand, there is powerful economic motivation to use resources in order of physical properties, where economic quality can be determined to be a function of physical properties.

3. Assume now use in declining order of economic quality. Is the decline necessarily an economic continuum? It is relatively so for certain things, particularly if these are defined narrowly, like northeastern cherry wood or high-grade manganese in Virginia. But it is not for others, such as sea water magnesium, taconite, aluminium clays, low-grade manganese ores, lateritic nickel, uranium in granite, solar energy, and so forth.

All three propositions are hypotheses rather than facts.

Finally, is depletion of natural resources an economic fact? In a sense it is, although, because of physical laws of conservation of matter-energy, it is not an ultimate physical fact. But the notion of depletion as an economic scarcity force must be subjoined to Malthusian or Ricardian economic scarcity, which I have just argued should be viewed not as facts but as hypotheses. And, so, even if we accept depletion as an economic fact, depletion as an economic scarcity force which produces some kind of economic scarcity effect must be viewed as a hypothesis.

The question to answer empirically is not the size of the scarcity effect. It is, rather, whether or not there has been scarcity force in the first instance.

SUMMARY AND TENTATIVE CONCLUSIONS

Our scarcity models are invalid as descriptions of reality. Since the logic is correct, though briefly stated, the invalidity of the models must be found in one or more of the premises or assumptions. Thus the notion of a social production function characterized by a static law of variable proportions, as manifest in the general shape of the output isoquants in Chart 1, could be at fault. The assumption that such function is characterized by constant returns, in addition, is today being sharply challenged. The assumption of invariant socio-technical parameters is erroneous.[13] Finally—and this is what concerns me here—it is possible that resources are not economically scarce, after all.

The diminishing returns scarcity effects in the models derive from *all* the assumed conditions, not just from resource scarcity. The failure of historical evidence to show diminishing returns does not disprove such economic scarcity. Scarcity could be present while returns were increasing if, for example, improved sociotechnical parameters increased output more rapidly than resource scarcity retarded it, the social production function were characterized by increasing returns to scale, or capital were increasing at a rate sufficient to more than offset such scarcity.

In liberating the embarrassing question of whether natural resource economic scarcity exists, how empirically to prove that it does or does not, and how to measure it, we must somehow disentangle the single condition of resource economic availability from its milieu of widespread parametric change, possibly increasing returns to social scale, and other forces.

NATURAL RESOURCE SCARCITY IN INCREASING RETURNS ECONOMIES

For progressing (dynamic increasing returns) economies our problem is to devise a method for data observation in which other things are held constant, in order to learn from examination of returns whether resource availability in an economic sense, as defined in the models above, is economically poorer in period t_n than in t_o. Elsewhere I have considered, and found possibly useful, but not very promising, the prospect of learning this for the economy as a whole from examination of physical stocks or inventories of resources. The one way I deal with the question here is as follows.

I first assume an identifiable extractive sector (E) to which natural resources are a significant productive input. There is an identifiable N sector, the remainder of the economy, to which natural resources are not a significant productive input. I characterize agriculture, mining, forestry, and fishing as extractive, and all other economic activity as nonextractive. The trend of labor productivity performance in the two sectors would, *ceteris paribus*, tend to be the same, in a mobile economy such as that of the United States. But natural resource economic scarcity if present would produce a tendency toward

---

[13] The growth of what Earl Stevenson has felicitously termed "molecular engineering" is particularly responsible. For insight into the magnitude and significance of the chemical industry advances, see H. J. Barnett and F. T. Moore, "Long Range Growth of Chemical Industries," *Chemical and Engineering News* (April 1958), pp. 78–84, 142.

diminishing returns to labor in E but not in N, and this tendency would operate with greater effect in E than in $N+E$.

I now assume that all other dynamic, scale, and institutional forces in the economy are neutral. This means, for example, that changes in capital-output ratios and changes in purchased materials-output ratios impinge with equal force in both E and N, and that the effects of demand changes upon the E and N sectors are neutral too. The result is that except for resource scarcity, *changes* in gross productivity of labor between t_o and t_n would be identical, that is:

$$\left(\frac{E_L}{(N+E)_L}\right)_{t_n} - \left(\frac{E_L}{(N+E)_L}\right)_{t_o} = \Delta = \text{zero,}$$

where E_L stands for labor input per unit E output, and so forth. But if resource economic scarcity develops or increases between t_o and t_n in the E sector, then the improvement in gross labor productivity in the economy as a whole $(N+E)$ will be greater than in the E sector. This will force increases in the ratios $E_L/(E+N)_L$ as time progresses, and make the successive Δ's positive figures.

I now go further and assume that there is such mobility of factors—labor, capital, and purchased materials—between E and N that their rates of remuneration per unit input are either equal, or if not equal, maintain a constant ratio through time. I also assume that prices of products are competitively set at the sum of labor, capital, and purchased material costs. These tentative assumptions together with the productivity hypothesis above produce the result that extractive goods prices will rise relative to all $(N+E)$ prices through time, if natural resource economic scarcity occurs and increases through time.

Tentatively, therefore, I expect that natural-resource economic scarcity if present will produce (1) an increasing trend of labor input per unit of output in extractive sectors relative to the whole economy, and (2) an increasing trend of unit prices of extractive goods relative to all goods.

This will be true, given the assumptions, for any of the economic scarcity forms defined in the Malthusian, Ricardian, and depletion models, above. All the models yield adverse real cost effects in any sector (E) in which resource scarcity exerts a diminishing returns force relative to any sector (N) which may be taken as a stand-in for economic activity not subject to this influence. My task will be to measure the trends of relative productivity and relative price, assuming that they are indicators of relative real cost changes.

The results must be viewed as only *tentative* indicators of the presence or absence of scarcity. This is because of the strenuous assumptions that other parametric change would be identical as between

91

the two sectors; that demand changes have neutral effects; that scale changes would not affect the sectors differently, except with respect to natural resource availability; that ratios of capital/output and purchased materials/output in E to those in $(N+E)$ did not change significantly between t_o and t_n; etc.[14]

Development of resource scarcity in the progressing economy can only be detected if other influences on cost are held equal. The above proposal holds other things equal in a somewhat unorthodox way. The proposal does *not* hold other things constant in the conventional way, which would compare the ratios of t_o and t_n by utilizing the production function of period t_o. The device of focussing on change in ratios of E productivity and price to N productivity and price, in effect, holds change other than resource availability between t_o and t_n to be equal, or in the proportions of t_o in the two sectors. Consequently changes in resource availability include not only possible recourse to lower qualities, depletion, and other adverse resource circumstances, but also possible favorable ones, as, for instance, discovery of new resources and new ways to use old ones. Our interest is resource availability in the dynamic economy. To hold other things constant between t_o and t_n in the conditions of t_o would test the rationality of the t_o economy, not the differential resource economic availability in t_o as compared with t_n.

Quantitative Test

In this quantitative test, unless otherwise stated, I use data from the paper prepared by my colleagues, Potter and Christy, in this volume, and from the manuscript, *U.S. Natural Resource Statistics, 1870–1956 —Measures of Price, Output, Foreign Trade, Consumption, and Productivity*, of their study for Resources for the Future, Inc. I refrain from repeated cautions concerning index-number problems, alternative-weight indexes, and possible errors in early data. I am fully aware that these warnings apply with even greater force than usual to

[14] Jaroslav Vanek has suggested that I should not feel so uncomfortable about my heroic assumption of "neutrality," as between the E and N sectors, of all influences other than resource availability. He observes my approach is essentially to view natural resource scarcity as having economic meaning only in a dynamic, general equilibrium setting, which includes resource endowments, technology, tastes, etc. Then movements of relative prices (and, possibly with some reservations, relative labor productivities) are value indexes reflecting relative scarcities of products from the two sectors, a significant and operational economic conception. In this conception, conditions (1) and (2), above, become definitions in themselves. If the problem is viewed in this way, he points out, the assumption of neutrality, as between E and N, of influences other than resource endowment is not needed. Vanek is right. Putting the question this way tends to limit further inquiry into the *reasons* for the relative price and productivity movements, however; and this is why I have chosen the present, more complex formulation.

extremely long-term, highly aggregated data, taken from an uncompleted study. My presentation here is a preliminary effort to test the scarcity hypothesis. Thus when I do not seek explanation of the movements of aggregates in individual commodity series, this does not imply lack of interest or intent. My test is confined to the 1954 weighted extractive indexes; the Potter-Christy index constructions based on 1929 and 1902 weights, as well as the comparisons with other weight indexes, were still being computed at the time this paper was prepared. In all respects, therefore, the present test should be viewed as trial run, the major purposes of which are reconnaissance and exploration.

RELATIVE PRICES OF EXTRACTIVE GOODS

Between 1870 and 1956, there was approximately a 10 per cent increase in unit prices of extractive goods (agriculture, minerals, timber, fish) relative to the BLS wholesale price index. This is tentative evidence in support of the resource scarcity hypothesis. But the relative price change is small in several respects. It is small relative to the length of period, the size of short-term fluctuations, the possible deficiencies in validity of the data, and my impression of variability among group prices indexes from causes other than resource scarcity.

During the eighty-six year period, for example, there were almost twenty short-term, plus or minus movements in relative extractive prices of equal or greater magnitude. These short-term changes reflect primarily cyclical, weather, and war influences, unrelated to the long-run scarcity hypothesis. By indicating that if either terminal date is shifted, the size of relative price change could change substantially, they weaken our ability to test the scarcity hypothesis and are adverse to it. A long-term change no greater than numerous short-term ones raises doubt about the social significance of the hypothesized phenomenon.

In addition to concern over terminal dates, there are two other reasons for breaking the long span into subperiods. One is that pre-1900 data are poorer than later data. The other is that the scarcity hypothesis in general contemplates that resource availability becomes increasingly adverse as a nation grows; this is particularly relevant for our long period. See, for example, Boulding's paper in this volume, where he states,

> "... in the United States ... at least since about 1890 the 'land' factor has certainly expanded much less than the labor and capital factors. The assumption of equal proportional increases of factors is not perhaps wholly inapplicable before 1890, but this is a rare type of episode in

human history: for the most part labor and capital expand against a much less expansible land and resources barrier."[15]

We therefore reconstruct the relative extractive price data in sub-periods:

	Percentage change from *beginning date*
1870–1900	−13
1900–29	+31
1929–56	−2
1900–56	+25
1870–1956	+12

The 1900–56 relative price change helps the hypothesis; and the noncontinuance or reversal of the 1900–29 increase during the 1929–56 period hurts it.

Finally, the course of 1954 weighted relative extractive prices 1870 to 1956 is presented in Chart 2. As I interpret these data I find an absence of long-term trend until World War I, a higher level, but again without trend in the 1920's, sharp declines during the depression 1930's, sharp increases during World War II, and a steady, gradual decline since the war. The only long-term movement that looks at first as if it might support the scarcity hypothesis is a steady, gradual up-drift from 1905 to 1945. But 1945 is clearly an undesirable final terminus for observing long-term "normal" movements.

We now turn to the major components of the extractive index where it is valuable to look at the components separately. Signs of scarcity or plenty will be clearer in them than in the alloyed, heterogeneous extractive total.

In 1870, almost 90 per cent of the total value of extractive output was agricultural. Since that time, the importance of agriculture in the extractive total has declined steadily and substantially, but today, agriculture still acounts for approximately 60 per cent. The figures are virtually the same if value added is used instead of total value of output. Agriculture, therefore, dominates the extractive index.

Over the 1870–1956 period, relative agriculture price also increased about 10 per cent, composed of no change, 1870–1900; a 30 per cent increase, 1900–29; and a 13 per cent decrease, 1929–56. All of agriculture's major relative price movements, from our long-term viewpoint, are so similar to those of the extractive total that it is not

[15] I think it was the Census Bureau which, on the basis of an arbitrary population density benchmark, originated the statement that the frontier disappeared about 1890. Actually, more original land entries took place in the 1900–10 decade, due to the Homestead Acts, than in any other decade in history; and the entries for 1910–20 were almost as large.

CHART 2

Extractive Product Prices (1954 weights) Relative to BLS Wholesale Price Index
(1947–49 = 100)

All extractive

Agriculture

Minerals

Timber

Ratio scale

1870   '80   '90   1900   '10   '20   '30   '40   '50   '56

Source: Appendix Table.

worthwhile to comment in detail here. Repeating the conclusions for all extraction, there is a relative price increase which could be the effect of scarcity, but it is very small, and its time sequence is disturbing to the hypothesis.

The next most important extractive industry is minerals—about 5 per cent of value of output in 1870 and 30 per cent in 1954. The value added percentages are similar. The change of relative mineral prices, 1870–1956, is dull for our scarcity hypothesis—a 5 to 10 per cent decline.

The picture becomes more interesting if we ignore the first thirty years when minerals output was economically insignificant and data are poor. We find that relative mineral prices increased by about 50 per cent between 1900 and the present. This is more promising for the scarcity hypothesis, particularly for the Ricardian and depletion forms of it.

The long-term mineral series shown in Chart 2 may be character- ized as having two subperiods. There is a level course which runs from before 1900 to the first World War; and there is another level trend, about half-again higher, following that War to the present. The absence of more steady rise is strongly disconcerting for the scarcity hypothesis. The abrupt rise would appear, initially at any rate, as likely to reflect differential parametric change—industrial organiza- tion and market structure changes, for example—as diminished economic availability of resources. I therefore judge that, while inter- esting, the case is less promising than it at first appeared, and reach the conclusion that further investigation is needed.

The final component I consider is timber products—about 6 per cent of extractive output in 1870, and 8 to 9 per cent in 1909 and 1954. This category is interesting enough to show the data at approximately ten-year intervals, for the timber products total, and for its two major components, lumber and pulpwood. The data appear in Table 1.

TABLE 1

Timber Product Prices (1954 Weights) Relative to
BLS Wholesale Price Index
(1947–49 = 100)

	All	Lumber	Pulpwood
1870	27	22	
1879	30	24	
1889	35	28	
1899	40	32	94[a]
1909	43	38	76
1919	44	42	60
1929	53	50	65
1939	63	62	67
1949	99	99	98
1955	109	109[b]	102

[a] 1900.
[b] 1953.

Source: Potter and Christy, *op. cit.*

Relative prices of all timber products quadrupled over the eighty- five year span. And, moreover, they increased steadily. There is an increase in every interval of roughly a decade shown in the table. This is very promising evidence in support of the scarcity hypothesis. There is further support in the fact that present output levels are no greater than at the turn of the century (peak output was reached a bit later, in 1907), while present relative prices are almost treble those of 1900. It is interesting that lumbering, which was of major influence in inciting the original conservation movement, yields the only striking preliminary evidence of scarcity effect. If the price evidence is evidence of resource scarcity, then Gifford Pinchot was correct in his forecast of price increases, although not in his forecast of disastrous general economic consequences:

"For example, it is certain that the rate of consumption of timber will increase enormously in the future, as it has in the past, so long as supplies remain to draw upon. Exact knowledge of many other factors is needed before closely accurate results can be obtained. The figures cited are, however, sufficiently reliable to make it certain that the United States has already crossed the verge of a timber famine so severe that its blighting effects will be felt in every household in the land. The rise in the price of lumber which marked the opening of the present century is the beginning of a vastly greater and more rapid rise which is to come. We must necessarily begin to suffer from the scarcity of timber long before our supplies are completely exhausted.

"It is well to remember that there is no foreign source from which we can draw cheap and abundant supplies of timber to meet a demand per capita so large as to be without parallel in the world, and that the suffering which will result from the progressive failure of our timber has been but faintly foreshadowed by temporary scarcities of coal.

"What will happen when the forests fail? In the first place, the business of lumbering will disappear. It is now the fourth greatest industry in the United States. All forms of building industries will suffer with it, and the occupants of houses, offices, and stores must pay the added cost. Mining will become vastly more expensive; and with the rise in the cost of mining there must follow a corresponding rise in the price of coal, iron, and other minerals. The railways, which have as yet failed entirely to develop a satisfactory substitute for the wooden tie (and must, in the opinion of their best engineers, continue to fail), will be profoundly affected, and the cost of transportation will suffer a corresponding increase. Water power for lighting, manufacturing, and transportation, and the movement of freight and passengers by inland water-ways, will be affected still more directly than the steam rail-ways. The cultivation of the soil, with or without irrigation, will be hampered by the increased cost of agricultural tools, fencing, and the wood needed for other purposes about the farm."[16]

The separate lumber and pulpwood columns present interesting additional information. Until World War II, the relative price rise in the total series was entirely due to the lumber component. Woodpulp relative prices were approximately level from 1903 to 1939, except for some violent fluctuations, which canceled out, associated with World War I. And they have been without trend since 1940, as well, but at a level 50 per cent above the former one.

RELATIVE LABOR PRODUCTIVITY

The Potter-Christy paper for this volume makes its major contribution in the measurement of productivity movements. This permits brevity here as to whether movements of labor productivity in extractive industry, relative to labor productivity in the whole economy, indicate resource economic scarcity:

1. Labor productivity in the extractive sector has, since 1880, increased faster than real GNP per unit of labor input. The trend of relative labor productivity was level until the beginning of World War II. Since then, it has increased by half. Both pieces of evidence are, tentatively, adverse to the resource-scarcity hypothesis.

2. The relative labor productivity series of agriculture tells the same story.

3. Labor productivity in mining relative to labor productivity in the economy as a whole has trended upward since 1880. The rate of improvement in the relative series has increased significantly since the close of World War I. The relative series (1947–49=100) show a 20–25 per cent improvement, in the first half of the seventy-five year period, and a 70–80 per cent improvement in the second half. This evidence is, tentatively, in severe opposition to the scarcity hypothesis.

4. The labor productivity record in timber, relative to that in the economy as a whole, tentatively strongly supports the scarcity hypothesis. Except for an interruption in the 1900 data, the time series show steady decline in timber's labor productivity, relative to that in the economy as a whole, during the entire period. Relative labor productivity in timber has fallen by 70 to 80 per cent. That is, labor input per unit of timber output relative to labor input per unit of real

[16] Gifford Pinchot, *The Fight for Conservation* (New York, 1910), pp. 15–17.

GNP quadrupled from 1880 to 1950. This is also the positive scarcity indication which the relative price series gave us.

SUMMARY

I summarize the quantitative exploration with relation to the scarcity hypothesis as follows:

	Relative Price Indicator	Relative Labor Productivity Indicator
All extraction	Does not support hypothesis	Adverse to hypothesis
Agriculture	Does not support hypothesis	Adverse to hypothesis
Minerals	Supports hypothesis ambiguously	Adverse to hypothesis
Timber	Supports hypothesis	Supports hypothesis

Differential Parametric Change

Adverse conditions of natural resource availability will be reflected in adverse trends of prices and productivities in the E sector relative to those in the N sector or the whole economy $(N+E)$ because the adverse force is *differentially* operative in the E sector. But I must warn again how strenuous the assumptions are which have to be made in order for the relative trends to be interpreted as definitive indicators of increasing or decreasing natural resource scarcity. Any other influences differential between the two sectors will also be reflected in these trends.

I shall not attempt to incorporate consideration of differential parametric changes in my quantitative tests. Rather I provide an incomplete catalogue of economic influences which operate on my "scarcity indicators," but which I neutralized with a blithe *ceteris paribus*. The check list will serve as warning on how distant the analysis here is from firm conclusions.[17]

FOREIGN TRADE

We have to decide whether we are testing the scarcity hypothesis for a self-sufficient United States or for the United States as part of the world economy. If the former, then the tests have to be redesigned in order to eliminate the influences of net imports of foreign supplies on extractive goods prices and labor productivity. If the latter, then there is no need to consider the sources of the supply. I dissent from the current view that the switch from net exports to net imports of minerals, which occurred in the twenties and thirties, by itself supports the hypothesis of domestic minerals scarcity. This is like saying that teenagers mow lawns because adults are incapable of doing so.

[17] See, however, Vanek's comment in footnote 14.

DIFFERENTIAL CHANGES IN FACTOR REMUNERATION RATES

The hypothesis involves movements in real cost per unit of extractive goods relative to all goods. If wage, interest, profit, and other rates change differentially in extraction as compared to nonextraction, these affect the relative price scarcity indicator and have to be taken into account. Differential changes in labor rates and degrees of market control seem particularly important. The relative productivity scarcity indicator is not directly affected.

GOVERNMENT INTERVENTIONS

If government behavior changes between t_o and t_n and this differentially affects the extractive *vs.* the nonextractive sector, then relative prices and relative productivities or both will be affected. The range of actions which have to be considered before we can properly interpret the scarcity indicators include farm price support and minerals price incentive statutes, differential tax preferences and more direct subsidies, production limitations, such as acreage and oil quota controls, and public investment in resource improvement.

PURCHASED INPUTS—CAPITAL AND MATERIALS

The productivity measures involve total output relative to labor input. If the ratio of purchased inputs (capital and materials) relative to labor changed differentially between the extractive and nonextractive sectors, relative productivity would have to be adjusted before it could be interpreted as a scarcity indicator. The relative price scarcity indicator, on the other hand, covers all inputs (costs) and is not subject to this defect. Differential movement of purchased inputs could be the reason the relative minerals productivity ratio improves so markedly following World War I, while relative prices increase significantly.

TRANSPORTATION AND LOCATIONS OF PEOPLE AND ECONOMIC ACTIVITY

The influence of transportation changes and economic location changes on scarcity indicators, and on the entire scarcity conception, is very great. Conceptual work is needed on these influences in a dynamic setting before we can even talk about taking them into account in scarcity indicator analysis. Ricardo's fundamental law of diminishing returns was based on the dual factors of cost of transportation and land quality decline, and Mason has shown that over a long period, transportation innovation was more important an influence in

TABLE 2

Extractive Product Prices (1954 Weights) Relative to BLS Wholesale Price Index
(1947–49 = 100)

	All Extractive	Agriculture	Minerals	Timber	Fish
1870	78	69	119	27	37
1871	80	65	137	28	33
1872	75	62	126	28	38
1873	66	62	86	29	35
1874	65	67	67	29	40
1875	67	69	71	28	50
1876	73	66	102	28	38
1877	75	68	98	28	48
1878	60	60	67	28	40
1879	63	65	61	30	39
1880	66	69	66	29	38
1881	72	76	68	32	41
1882	74	81	64	32	60
1883	69	74	64	32	67
1884	69	74	60	34	69
1885	68	68	66	35	62
1886	63	66	59	36	63
1887	65	71	57	36	65
1888	70	72	62	35	80
1889	64	67	64	35	78
1890	66	68	65	36	38
1891	69	72	63	36	83
1892	68	74	59	37	35
1893	69	78	54	36	72
1894	68	74	61	40	68
1895	69	69	72	38	66
1896	66	66	72	40	43
1897	66	69	62	38	63
1898	67	70	64	39	95
1899	68	68	75	40	83
1900	68	68	73	40	82
1901	72	75	70	39	81
1902	70	76	67	38	65
1903	70	72	74	38	44
1904	72	72	72	39	41
1905	69	72	69	41	61
1906	70	72	74	44	32
1907	73	73	76	44	52
1908	76	78	76	44	54
1909	77	82	70	43	55
1910	76	83	64	41	52
1911	78	83	69	44	62
1912	78	80	73	43	58
1913	82	84	84	44	29
1914	81	84	78	43	29

101

(TABLE 2 concluded)

	All Extractive	Agriculture	Minerals	Timber	Fish
1915	80	82	82	40	29
1916	83	79	103	42	25
1917	86	86	96	39	52
1918	88	89	96	37	46
1919	85	89	84	44	41
1920	83	78	105	62	44
1921	79	73	108	52	50
1922	84	76	110	55	49
1923	84	80	102	60	41
1924	86	83	103	54	49
1925	88	86	104	52	52
1926	88	83	112	54	37
1927	85	84	97	53	52
1928	86	87	92	50	67
1929	89	89	96	53	66
1930	86	82	98	54	71
1931	72	68	88	53	76
1932	69	57	101	49	64
1933	68	61	93	58	63
1934	76	68	99	61	57
1935	79	77	91	54	56
1936	82	80	96	57	55
1937	82	80	96	63	57
1938	78	70	103	60	45
1939	76	70	99	63	78
1940	78	72	98	70	92
1941	85	81	96	74	90
1942	90	92	89	70	101
1943	100	106	88	71	111
1944	102	108	89	76	105
1945	105	110	89	75	105
1946	103	111	87	76	104
1947	102	106	90	98	88
1948	102	102	103	103	108
1949	97	93	107	99	103
1950	96	92	103	108	78
1951	98	97	96	106	97
1952	97	95	99	106	96
1953	92	86	106	106	85
1954	90	83	107	104	84
1955	(89)	(80)	(108)	(109)	
1956	(87)	(77)	(110)	(109)	

Source: N. Potter and F. T. Christy, Jr., *U.S. Natural Resource Statistics, 1870–1956*. To be published by Resources for the Future, Inc., Washington, D.C. Data are preliminary, pending completion and review of the manuscript. The authors state that the fish data, particularly, are subject to radical revision.

reducing delivered energy cost than innovation in the energy sector proper.[18]

DIFFERENTIAL TECHNOLOGICAL CHANGE

If for any reason technological change is not uniform as between extractive and nonextractive sectors, then both the relative price and relative productivity scarcity indicators will be affected, and this will obscure the influence of resource availability. Tomato and tobacco cultivation, for example, are less susceptible to efficiency improvement than most manufacturing processes. I am impressed by the phenomenon of technological change induced by economic pressure. Schumpeter would, as a third view, have expected technological change to be differential as among industries on the grounds of differential susceptibility to market control.

URBAN LAND

I have not yet been able to figure out whether urban land scarcity should be within or outside the scarcity hypothesis I am testing. It is now outside.

OTHER DIFFERENTIAL SOCIAL AND INSTITUTIONAL CHANGES

This caption is inserted to warn that I have given only an incomplete list of influences, other than resource scarcity, which could be responsible for differential parametric change in the two sectors and which thereby would influence my relative price and relative productivity ratios.

COMMENT

WILLIAM VICKREY, Columbia University

In a world of perfect competition and no uncertainty about the future, scarcity of nonrenewable, appropriable resources must be considered a relative matter, not an absolute one. In a world of perfect foresight, the price at which a well-defined body of ore would change hands would advance through time at a rate corresponding to the ordinary money rate of interest, otherwise investment in the purchase of such an asset would be attractive or unattractive relative to other investments. The rate of advance in price would be the same whether the mineral in question were rare or plentiful relative to current and anticipated needs. It is therefore likely to be misleading to take price

---

[18] Edward S. Mason, *Productive Uses of Nuclear Energy*, Report on Energy Requirements and Economic Growth, National Planning Association, Washington, D.C., pp. 20, 21.

trends as a measure of "diminishing returns" traceable to the limited total stock of nonrenewable natural resources. Indeed, in a world of certainty, it is difficult to define the economic criteria for distinguishing one nonrenewable mineral as being "scarcer" than another, in any way that reflects the imminence of exhaustion. One resource may be cheaper than another, assuming some common value unit to have been selected, but that is all.

To be sure, sometimes relative cheapness may be so extreme as to create a difference almost in kind rather than in degree. If Adam had offered to sell Seth a coal mine which he had discovered, but which was of a nature not to be economically exploitable before the twentieth century, the discounting of the modern price for 6,000 years, even at minimal rates of interest, would yield a price far below the smallest coin available.

If prices of nonrenewable resources *in situ* deviate from this normal interest-rate-determined trend, it must be as a result of changing expectations. One possibility would be changing expectations regarding interest rates, which would affect all mineral properties alike: inauguration of a cheap money policy might then be falsely interpreted as an increasing scarcity of natural resources. Other possibilities are changes in expectations about demand through the development of new uses, or of substitutes, or of better methods of processing; or about supply, almost entirely through further exploration of the extent of deposits and possibly the development of new means of exploiting hitherto unworkable deposits. Prices trends of resources are thus not a measure of absolute scarcity, or even of scarcity at a given time relative to current rates of use, but are rather an indication of the extent to which the evolution of prospects for interest rates, demand, and supply deviate from previously held expectations, an entirely different matter.

In practice, comparable prices or price indexes for resources covering extended periods of time are not readily available, and instead prices of the products derived from the natural resources after more or less processing are used. In this price the depletion factor, representing the contribution of the scarcity element to the total cost, will rarely contribute more than 30 per cent. In the "Malthusian" case of a resource limited in total stock but of uniform quality and accessibility, putting i for the rate of interest and d for the share of depletion in total cost, one could expect that under conditions of constant technology the price would increase at the rate of id per year regardless of the rate at which the fixed stock is being exhausted.

The "Ricardian" case of a total stock of variable accessibility and

104

quality is not so different from this as might at first appear. Suppose a simple case of a resource existing in two grades: grade A requiring processing costs of $2 per unit of marketable product, and grade B requiring processing costs of $4 per unit. Suppose that the exhaustion of grade A occurs at time t_a, and that at that time the general scarcity of the resource is such as to induce a price of $5 for the finished product, thus yielding $3 per unit in royalties to the owner of the last unit of A processed, and $1 in royalties to the owner of the first unit of B processed after time t_a. Before t_a, the product price must have been increasing at a rate of $i \cdot \$3$ per year, assuming constant technology, if the holders of the grade A deposits were to get a normal return on their investment. After t_a the requisite rate of price increase is only $i \cdot \$1$ per unit, since it is now the B grade that is controlling. Before t_a it is unprofitable to process grade B: owners of this grade can get a better net discounted return by waiting to process it until some time after t_a. Similarly owners of grade A would only stand to lose if they waited until after t_a to process their deposits in the hope of a better return.

The intertemporal equilibrium situation is then correctly stated as one in which deposits are exploited in order of increasing processing costs. But if we assume perfect foresight on the part of the owners of the raw resources, the trend of the price of the finished product will not indicate the degree of Ricardian scarcity. Increasing scarcity as measured by the degree to which the poorer deposits are used will be reflected in two ways: by a *decline* in the *rate of increase* of the price of the finished product, and by a *decline* in the share of the total cost represented by depletion charges. For nonrenewable resources in a context of constant technology and perfect foresight, it is accordingly difficult to see any direct relation between long-term trends of the price of the finished product and the degree of Ricardian scarcity. A better indicator would be the rate of deceleration of the price increase, or perhaps the decline in the ratio of depletion charges to total costs.

Transfer of these conclusions from a hypothetical world of perfect foresight, constant technology, and competitive markets to a real world of changing expectations, advancing technology, and imperfect competition of course requires major qualifications. Nevertheless, it would seem that for the nonrenewable sector, observations of price trends of marketable products is more nearly indicative of technological advance and changes in expectations about demand, supply, and interest rates, than they are of absolute levels of ultimate resource availability as viewed at a given point of time.

One specific source of bias in any comparison of price trends between extractive and other industries may be worth pointing out. Products priced as the proximate output of the mining industry are, generally speaking, standardized items retaining their essential characteristics over long periods of time, whereas the outputs of the economy as a whole, or of the manufacturing sector in particular, are so much more subject to innovation and quality improvement through time that it is difficult to evaluate them for the purposes of constructing productivity, price, or quantity indexes. If we say that the price of copper has exhibited such and such a trend, or even that mining products generally have risen or fallen in output or price by such and such a percentage, we know fairly well what we mean. If we say that automobiles or refrigerators have increased in price or in physical output by a specified percentage, we are much less sure of what we mean. On the whole it seems likely that technological improvements reflected in a changed quality of output are less important in mining than elsewhere, and that there is here a possible source of persistent bias that would cause an overstatement of the relative productivity advance in the mining sector.

There remains to be examined the question of whether there are circumstances which would justify treating a nonrenewable resource that is expected to be in limited supply some time in the future as a free good, in its raw state, in the present, aside from the obvious possibility that the value to be imputed by reason of long-term discounting may be so small as to be negligible, as in the case of Adam's coal mine. We may take the maximization of the value of the heritage as the social objective to be passed on to future generations, given the maintenance of a specified current consumption level. Under a perfectly competitive regime uncomplicated by economies of scale or imperfect foresight, all resources that would ever have a price would always have a positive price, and the production pattern so defined would be one that would maximize the social heritage under the given constraint as to current consumption. If, however, there are economies of scale in the extractive process, or if there are external economies tied up with the utilization of the nonrenewable resource, a situation may occur where the social heritage would be maximized by making the resource available at no charge for depletion, even though in private hands it would be held at a positive value. Unfortunately it is not at all easy to determine whether or where such situations in fact exist.

The analysis of the renewable sector of course differs in that the possibilities for intertemporal transfer are more limited. Soil depletion and the cutting of virgin timber may be important factors in a newly developed area, but for long-settled areas these factors become

106

relatively insignificant. Here there is opportunity for diminishing returns due to scarcity of natural resources to be reflected in price trends, and with appropriate care it may be proper to draw conclusions on relative scarcity or the tendency to diminishing returns from an examination of the price trends.

Employment and Output
in the Natural Resource Industries, 1870–1955

NEAL POTTER AND FRANCIS T. CHRISTY, JR.

RESOURCES FOR THE FUTURE, INC.

INPUT and output in the resource industries are of interest from several points of view. Malthusians with an analytical turn of mind might look for falling productivity in this area of the economy as a measure of overpopulation and a forecast of calamity. Much popular opinion attaches this kind of significance to resources problems. Economists regard the resource area as one of inelastic demands or necessities. They note that it is subject to violent fluctuations as a result of business cycles, and there is a view that these industries are basic. Legislators look at resources as a measure of the nation's self-sufficiency, power, and prosperity. It is partly for this reason that these industries furnish a springboard for numerous subsidy schemes.

This paper does not address these policy problems. It represents, rather, part of an attempt to measure trends in labor input and output in the extractive sector of the economy, over the eighty-five year period from 1870 to 1955. Thus it ranges from the days of free land and virtually untapped minerals to the present era. It is part of a larger study[1] in which the authors have gathered data providing economic measures of the extractive sector of the economy: its prices, outputs, imports and exports, domestic consumption and employment.

In this enterprise we have of course been dependent on a multiplicity of sources. Very few studies or sources of data cover so long a time span. This has forced us to splice series which are frequently independent and unconnected. We have checked for consistency of movements in the different series, where overlap presented this possibility. We have found a gratifying number of cases of apparent consistency, nearly as many as in the supposedly continuous series.

Output

Tables 1 and 2 show our estimates of output in the extractive sector of the economy and its principal subsectors, with indexes of manufacturing output and GNP as scales for comparison.

[1] *U.S. Natural Resource Statistics, 1870–1955: Measures of Price, Output, Foreign Trade, Consumption, Employment, and Productivity*, a forthcoming study to be published by Resources for the Future, Inc. We wish to acknowledge many helpful suggestions and criticisms from our colleagues, particularly Harold J. Barnett, who has given general supervision to the study during its two and a half years of preparation.

109

TABLE 1

Output of Resource Industries (billions of dollars, in 1954 prices)

	Agriculture	Timber	Mining	Fish, Fuel-wood, and Waterpower	All Extractive	GNP
1869		.84				
1870	5.8		.33		7.6	19
1871	5.9		.41		7.8	19
1872	6.2		.46		8.1	24
1873	6.2		.52		8.3	24
1874	6.2		.49		8.3	24
1875	6.8		.48		8.8	24
1876	7.1		.51		9.3	26
1877	8.0		.59		10.2	28
1878	8.3		.58		10.6	29
1879	8.6	1.19	.68		11.0	32
1880	9.1		.71	.60	11.6	36
1881	8.1		.81	.58	10.8	37
1882	9.4		.95	.58	12.4	39
1883	9.2		1.01	.57	12.2	39
1884	9.9		1.04	.56	13.0	41
1885	9.8		1.01	.56	12.8	41
1886	9.8		1.08	.54	13.0	44
1887	9.6		1.21	.53	13.1	45
1888	10.3		1.36	.54	13.9	44
1889	10.8	1.78	1.35	.55	14.5	46
1890	10.3		1.49	.55	14.1	50
1891	11.5		1.59	.54	15.5	52
1892	10.1		1.67	.54	14.2	57
1893	10.2		1.64	.52	14.4	54
1894	10.5		1.57	.51	14.7	53
1895	11.4		1.77	.51	15.8	53
1896	12.2		1.80	.50	16.7	59
1897	13.1		1.86	.49	17.6	63
1898	13.8		1.99	.49	18.6	65
1899	13.7	2.32	2.25	.48	18.8	71
1900	13.8	2.78	2.40	.48	19.5	72
1901	13.4	2.84	2.58	.48	19.3	81
1902	14.0	2.86	2.64	.49	20.0	82
1903	13.9	2.86	3.10	.48	20.3	86
1904	14.6	2.86	3.11	.47	21.0	85
1905	14.6	2.87	3.54	.46	21.5	91
1906	15.5	3.02	3.65	.47	22.6	101
1907	14.4	3.06	4.18	.47	22.1	103
1908	15.0	2.80	3.78	.47	22.0	95
1909	14.8	2.98	4.20	.48	22.5	104
1910	15.5	2.98	4.54	.48	23.5	107
1911	15.0	2.84	4.49	.48	22.8	110
1912	16.8	2.97	4.78	.49	25.0	116

(TABLE 1 concluded)

Output of Resource Industries (billions of dollars, in 1954 prices)

	Agriculture	Timber	Mining	Fish, Fuelwood, and Waterpower	All Extractive	GNP
1913	15.2	2.94	5.11	.49	23.7	117
1914	16.8	2.73	4.74	.50	24.8	112
1915	17.3	2.57	5.0	.51	25.4	111
1916	15.7	2.72	5.7	.51	24.6	120
1917	16.5	2.51	6.1	.52	25.6	120
1918	16.8	2.30	6.2	.52	25.8	133
1919	16.8	2.43	5.3	.52	25.1	133
1920	17.8	2.46	6.1	.52	26.9	126
1921	15.7	2.09	4.9	.51	23.2	115
1922	17.3	2.38	5.2	.50	25.4	133
1923	17.5	2.65	7.1	.51	27.8	149
1924	17.3	2.56	6.6	.52	27.0	149
1925	17.8	2.61	6.9	.54	27.8	162
1926	18.5	2.53	7.4	.55	29.0	171
1927	18.3	2.44	7.5	.58	28.8	170
1928	19.0	2.42	7.4	.61	29.4	172
1929	18.8	2.56	8.1	.65	30.1	182
1930	18.3	1.95	7.1	.62	28.0	165
1931	20.1	1.45	5.9	.56	28.0	153
1932	19.3	1.07	4.8	.55	25.7	130
1933	17.8	1.24	5.3	.59	24.9	127
1934	15.2	1.35	5.7	.67	22.9	138
1935	18.3	1.61	6.1	.72	26.7	153
1936	16.5	1.87	7.2	.73	26.3	173
1937	20.8	1.95	8.0	.72	31.5	183
1938	20.1	1.72	6.8	.72	29.3	175
1939	20.3	1.94	7.6	.74	30.6	189
1940	21.1	2.06	8.4	.74	32.3	206
1941	21.8	2.32	9.2	.79	34.1	238
1942	24.4	2.34	9.8	.79	37.3	267
1943	23.9	2.22	10.0	.86	37.0	297
1944	24.6	2.17	10.5	.89	38.2	318
1945	24.4	1.91	10.2	.91	37.4	314
1946	24.9	2.22	10.0	.88	38.0	282
1947	24.1	2.32	11.2	.88	38.5	282
1948	26.4	2.40	11.7	.92	41.4	293
1949	25.7	2.12	10.2	.97	39.0	293
1950	25.4	2.46	11.3	1.01	40.2	318
1951	26.2	2.51	12.5	.99	42.2	342
1952	27.2	2.51	12.3	1.00	43.0	353
1953	27.4	2.51	12.5	1.01	43.4	369
1954	27.4	2.50	12.1	.99	43.0	363
1955	28.4	2.72	13·1	1·06	45·2	393

Source: See Table 2.

111

TABLE 2
Output Indexes, 1947–49 = 100

	Agriculture	Timber	Mining	All Extractive	Manufac-turing	GNP in 1954 prices
1870	23	(37)	3.0	19	3.8	6.6
1871	23		3.7	20	4.1	6.6
1872	24		4.1	21	5.0	8.3
1873	25		4.7	21	4.9	8.3
1874	24		4.5	21	4.8	8.3
1875	27		4.4	22	4.6	8.3
1876	28		4.6	24	4.6	9.0
1877	32		5.4	26	5.2	9.7
1878	32		5.3	27	5.5	10.0
1879	34	52	6.2	28	5.9	11.1
1880	36		6.5	29	7.4	12.4
1881	32		7.4	27	7.5	12.8
1882	37		8.6	31	8.5	13.5
1883	36		9.2	31	8.4	13.5
1884	39		9.4	33	8.4	14.2
1885	38		9.1	32	8.1	14.2
1886	39		9.8	33	9.7	15.2
1887	38		11.0	33	10.0	15.6
1888	40		12.3	35	10.2	15.2
1889	42	78	12.3	37	11.4	15.9
1890	41		13.5	36	12.1	17.3
1891	45		14.4	39	13.3	18.0
1892	40		15.1	36	13.3	19.7
1893	40		14.8	36	11.8	18.7
1894	41		14.2	37	11.6	18.3
1895	45		16.1	40	14.1	18.3
1896	48		16.4	42	12.9	20.4
1897	52		16.9	44	14.5	21.8
1898	54		18.0	47	15.7	22.5
1899	54	102	20.4	48	16.0	24.5
1900	54	122	21.7	49	16.3	25
1901	53	125	23.4	49	18.4	28
1902	55	125	23.9	51	20.6	28
1903	55	126	28.1	51	21.1	30
1904	58	125	28.2	53	19.8	29
1905	58	126	32.1	54	23.7	31
1906	61	132	33.1	57	25.4	35
1907	57	134	37.9	56	25.7	36
1908	59	123	34.2	56	21.3	33
1909	58	131	38.1	57	25.2	36
1910	61	130	41.1	59	26.8	37
1911	59	125	40.7	58	25.7	38
1912	66	130	43.3	63	29.6	40
1913	60	129	46.3	60	31.6	40
1914	66	120	42.9	63	29.7	39

(TABLE 2 concluded)
Output Indexes, 1947–49 = 100

	Agriculture	Timber	Mining	All Extractive	Manufac-turing	GNP in 1954 prices
1915	68	113	46	64	35	38
1916	62	119	52	62	41	41
1917	65	110	55	65	41	42
1918	66	101	56	65	41	46
1919	66	106	48	63	38	46
1920	70	108	55	68	39	44
1921	62	92	44	59	30	40
1922	68	104	47	64	39	46
1923	69	116	65	70	45	52
1924	68	112	60	68	43	51
1925	70	114	62	70	48	56
1926	73	111	67	73	50	59
1927	72	107	68	73	50	59
1928	75	106	67	74	52	59
1929	74	112	73	76	58	63
1930	72	86	64	71	48	57
1931	79	64	54	71	39	53
1932	76	47	44	65	30	45
1933	70	55	48	63	36	44
1934	60	59	51	58	39	48
1935	72	71	55	67	46	53
1936	65	82	65	66	55	60
1937	82	86	73	80	60	63
1938	79	76	62	74	46	60
1939	80	85	69	77	57	65
1940	83	90	76	82	66	71
1941	86	102	83	86	88	82
1942	96	103	89	94	110	92
1943	94	98	91	93	133	103
1944	97	95	95	97	130	110
1945	96	84	92	94	110	109
1946	98	97	90	96	90	98
1947	95	102	102	97	100	98
1948	104	105	106	105	103	101
1949	101	93	92	99	97	101
1950	100	108	103	102	113	110
1951	103	110	113	107	121	118
1952	107	110	111	109	125	122
1953	108	110	114	110	136	128
1954	108	110	109	109	127	125
1955	112	119	119	114	140	136

Sources: The general nature of our sources for the extractive output data are given in the text. For detailed sources, see the authors' forthcoming study, *U.S. Natural Resource Statistics, 1870–1955.*

The manufacturing output index was prepared by linking Warren Person's index *Forecasting Business Cycles* to Solomon Fabricant's index *Output of Manufacturing Industries, 1899–1937*, and this to the Federal Reserve Board Index. Overlap periods were, of course, compared. The dates of linkage chosen were 1899–1909 and 1919–29.

The Gross National Product estimates are those of the Department of Commerce for 1909–55. To this were linked tentative estimates prepared by the authors, with the aid of preliminary estimates made available by Simon Kuznets and John W. Kendrick, to whom we make grateful acknowledgement. They should not be charged with any errors which appear, however, as we have made a number of changes.

Most noteworthy is the relative decline in the extractive industries (except for mining) since the 1870's. While real GNP expanded nearly sixteen times from 1870 to 1955, the extractive industries expanded five and a half times. In terms of output in 1954 prices, this means that the extractive industries dropped from producing about one-third of GNP to only 12 per cent. As can be seen from Chart 1 and the indexes in Table 2, the greatest decline is in forestry, with fishing, etc., next in order of decline (though the data here are quite thin), and agriculture a strong third. Output in mining, on the other hand, rose as a percentage of GNP.

These data reflect the familiar fact that manufacturing, trade, and service activities have increased more than real GNP, while consumer nondurable goods have increased less. Food and fiber output have risen approximately in proportion to population, and these cover the bulk of farming and fishing. Farm output has risen to four and a half times its level of the early 1870's, while population has risen to four times its level in that period. Timber output appears to have risen to only about three times its 1870 level.

Additional insight may be gained by observing the timing of the movements (see Chart 1). Agricultural output has risen very nearly in step with population all the way. Timber output, however, rose a good deal more rapidly than population until 1900, apparently as fast as GNP. Since 1900 there have been no important short-term increases in timber output, while there have been some important declines; there may be a down trend. The decline of timber relative to real GNP and the other extractive industries has thus been severe, from 4 per cent of the GNP down to less than 1 per cent (in 1954 prices).

The growth of mining output up to 1900 was even more rapid than output of timber, manufacturing, or real GNP. In 1954 prices, mining output was only 1.5 per cent of GNP in 1870, but it had grown to 3.5 per cent by 1900. Mining continued to grow more rapidly than GNP until World War I. It held its peak in the 1920's, and has since shown a moderate decline relative to GNP. The present mining/real GNP relationship is the same as in 1900.

The all-extractive output index is constructed by combining the

114

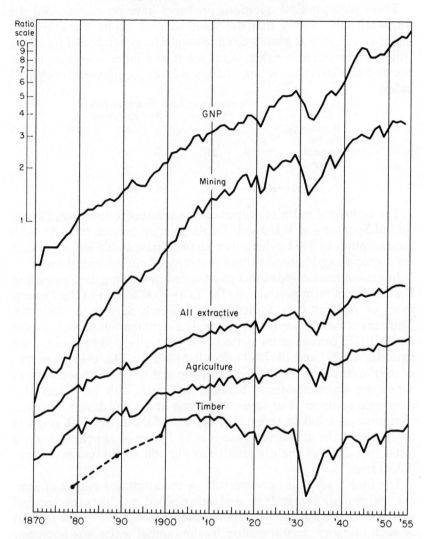

CHART 1
Output: Extractive Industries and GNP

Ratio
scale

10
9
8
7
6
5

4

3

2

1

GNP

Mining

All extractive

Agriculture

Timber

1870   '80   '90   1900   '10   '20   '30   '40   '50 '55

indexes of output in the separate sectors, with weights proportioned
to values of output in 1954. How suitable for the economic concept of
extraction are these weights? Is agriculture overweighted because the
commodities it produces are more nearly finished than iron ore or
crude oil? Or is agriculture underweighted because we have used
value of output rather than employment as our weighting factor? Are
sawlogs or finished lumber more comparable to threshed wheat and
shipped milk? Does monopolistic pricing in one field overweigh that
field relative to the others?

115

These philosophical questions probably have no answer, but the following table shows that the value weights we have chosen give about three times as great a relative weight to minerals and timber as would employment weights. As a result, the index shows a greater rise for all-extractive output than would an employment-weighted index.

Percentage of Total Weight in 1954

	By Value	By Employment
Agriculture	64	86
Timber	6	2
Minerals	28	10
Other	2	2
All Extractive	100	100

The combined index of output of all resources follows very closely that of Spencer and Wardwell[2] for the overlap period, 1900–52, with the exception of 1934, where they seem to have made less allowance for a drop in agricultural output than any of our sources show.

In agriculture the index was constructed by splicing the Strauss and Bean index of farm production[3] for 1870–1909 to that of the Department of Agriculture's Agricultural Research Service for 1910–55. This means that the weighting system is a combination of current year and 1910–13 prices for the period 1870–1909; 1935–39 prices for the period 1910–39; and 1947–49 prices for 1940–55. The 1910–37 period of overlap between the Strauss and Bean and the ARS indexes shows very close correspondence between the two, with no discernible difference in trend. The series of Barger and Landsberg,[4] however, computed as a linked series with the use of the Edgeworth formula (weighted by the average of base-year and given-year prices) shows a trend that declines slightly relative to our spliced Strauss and Bean-ARS series.

The timber series is our own sum of the estimated output of lumber, pulpwood, veneer logs, and other wood products (except fuel wood), each multiplied by an approximate average 1954 price for logs of each category. Extrapolation by the lumber series was necessary

[2] Vivian Eberle Spencer and Charles A. R. Wardwell, *Raw Materials in the United States Economy, 1900–1952* (Bureau of the Census, 1954: processed), p. 72.

[3] Frederick Strauss and Louis H. Bean, *Gross Farm Income and Indices of Farm Production and Prices in the United States, 1869–1937*, Table 60. We have used the index computed according to Irving Fisher's "ideal" index, which is the index favored by the authors; it uses a geometric mean of indexes computed with base period weights and with current year weights—that is, it is a geometric mean of a Laspeyres Index and a Paasche Index.

[4] Harold Barger and Hans H. Landsberg, *American Agriculture, 1899–1939: A Study of Output, Employment, and Productivity*, National Bureau of Economic Research, 1942, Table 5.

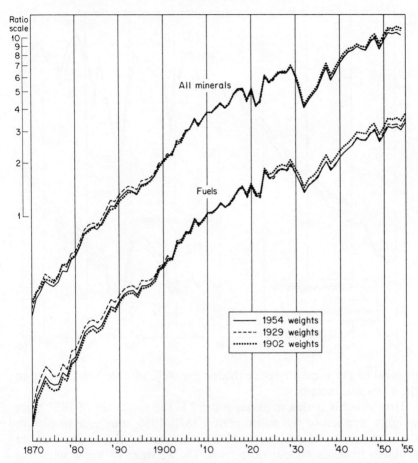

to extend the Forest Service series for miscellaneous wood products to years before 1899. This is a considerable deficiency, as these products are estimated at about 25 per cent of all timber output in 1899, and may have varied considerably relative to lumber over the thirty-year period. Pulpwood and veneer logs must also be handled by extrapolation before 1899. This appears to be a minor matter, as large uses of pulp and plywood did not appear until later.

The minerals index is a weighted sum of the physical output of all the significant minerals produced, accounting for about 97 per cent of all employment in mining as given in the 1954 Census of Mineral Industries. (The principal omissions are the uranium group, unimportant before World War II, and some minor nonmetals.) The weights are as near as we could come to the 1954 value of each

117

CHART 3
Output Indexes with Alternative Weights: Metals and Nonfuel Nonmetals

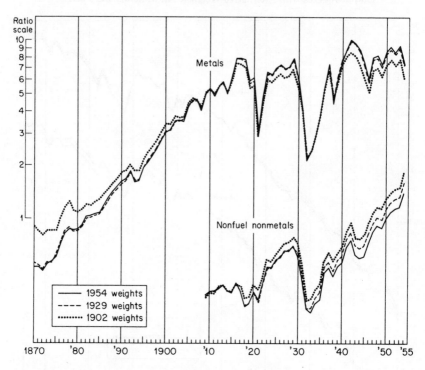

mineral at the mine or concentrator (or well, pit, etc.), according to the Census concepts.

How reliable is this minerals index? Is the single set of 1954 price weights, applied to the entire period 1870–1955, adequate to picture the movements of real output? The answer to this index-number problem depends on our objectives. Do we want to know what the rate of growth was in terms of present-day values, or in terms of the values of some "normal" period like 1926, 1935–39, or 1947–49?

The problem may be a minor one relative to our general conclusions, mainly because there is so much similarity of growth in output among the minerals. We have computed indexes for all minerals and the major sectors with 1902, 1929, and 1954 price-weights;[5] the results are shown in Charts 2 and 3.

The all-minerals indexes nearly coincide over the whole eighty-five-year period. The maximum difference is between the 1902-weighted

[5] These years were chosen because there is a Mineral Census for each of them. In fuels, the data were taken from the Minerals Yearbook, as Census did not cover oil and gas in 1929; the differences were very small in years where both Bureaus had coverage. For natural gas in 1902, an estimate of value at wells had to be made, as *Mineral Resources* gave only value at point of consumption.

118

index and the 1954-weighted index; the difference (see Chart 2) is that of a 4.3 per cent (with 1902 weights) and a 4.4 per cent annual increase. The fuels indexes are separated slightly more, with a maximum difference of 4.8 per cent annual growth (1902 weights) *versus* 4.5 per cent. For metals, the 1929-weighted index is almost identical in movement to that with 1954 weights (Chart 3); with 1902 weights, however, the index rises less rapidly. [6]

In the nonmetals, data are too skimpy prior to 1902 to warrant comparisons of this sort. For the 1902–54 period, however, we note (Chart 3) that the 1929- and 1954-weighted indexes are closely parallel. The 1902-weighted index rises faster, with a 4.6 per cent annual rate of growth for the fifty-two-year period, as against 3.6 per cent per year for the 1954-weighted index.

When we compare the present minerals index (with 1954 weights) with indexes computed by others (Y. S. Leong, Bureau of Mines, Barger and Schurr, Federal Reserve Board, Paley Commission), we find differences which are generally small (less than 5 per cent) over the whole span of years in which the indexes overlap. There is, however, a tendency for our series to run higher than the others for the period 1899–1921. Individual pairs of years may show differences considerably larger than 5 per cent.

Employment

Indexes of labor input or employment are presented in Tables 3 and 4 and in Chart 4. It is apparent that the extractive industries have declined as employers relative to the national total. In the early 1870's they used about 55 per cent of all labor; in the early 1950's they used only about 15 per cent. The greatest relative decline was in agriculture, which also was and is the largest sector of the extractive industries. The absolute increase in agricultural employment over the eighty-five years was less than 10 per cent, while the national total of employment rose over 300 per cent, mining employment about 500 per cent, and timber perhaps 400 per cent.

Agriculture has declined relative to the national total almost continuously since 1870. An absolute decline in agricultural employment started after World War I and has continued practically without interruption, accelerating after 1945. Mining increased its share of

[6] This is chiefly because gold (whose output actually *decreased* over the period) is assigned a relatively heavier weight by 1902 prices, while iron and copper (the large growing items) are assigned relatively lighter weights. It will be noted from Chart 3, however, that a large part of the difference is in the period 1870–90. If we start with 1890, we find only a moderate divergence: with 1902 weights, the rise is 1.9 per cent per year; with 1954 weights, it is 2.4 per cent per year.

CHART 4
Employment: Extractive Industries and Total U.S.

Ratio scale

Total U.S.

All extractive

Agriculture

Mining

Timber

1870 '80 '90 1900 '10 '20 '30 '40 '50 '55

the national total of employment from 1870 to 1920, then started an absolute as well as relative decline which almost parallels that of agriculture. Logging employment rose relative to the national total until 1920 and has declined a little absolutely (and a great deal relatively) since that time. The result of these changes is that agricultural employment declined from 95 per cent of the extractive total to eighty-five per cent, while mining rose from less than 3 per cent to over 10 per cent.

In preparing these indexes, we sought measures of employment which would properly represent the trends of real labor inputs required to produce the output of each industry. This ideal is, of

120

TABLE 3
Employment in Resource Industries (millions)

	Agriculture	Timber	Mining	Fishing	All Extractive	Manufac- turing	Total U.S.
1869						2.1	
1870	6.3	.03	.19	.04	6.6		12.6
1879						2.9	
1880	8.4	.05	.30	.05	8.8		17.0
1889			.56			4.0	
1890	9.8	.10		.08	10.5		23.1
1900	10.5	.12		.09	11.5	5.4	28.4
1901						5.7	29.7
1902			.81			6.2	30.9
1903						6.4	31.6
1904						6.1	31.5
1905						6.6	32.8
1906						7.1	34.2
1907						7.2	34.8
1908						6.5	33.9
1909			1.07			7.5	35.9
1910	11.1	.15		.09	12.4	7.7	36.5
1911	11.1					7.7	37.0
1912	11.1					8.2	38.2
1913	11.1					8.6	39.4
1914	11.1					8.1	38.7
1915	11.1					8.1	38.6
1916	11.2					9.5	41.2
1917	11.1					9.7	42.3
1918	11.0					10.0	45.5
1919	10.8		1.15		12.3	10.5	44.4
1920	11.0	.19	1.18	.07	12.4	10.5	43.6
1921	11.0		1.15		12.4	8.1	41.2
1922	10.9		1.21	.07	12.4	9.0	42.9
1923	10.8		1.28	.07	12.3	10.2	45.4
1924	10.7		1.18	.08	12.1	9.5	44.8
1925	10.7		1.15	.08	12.1	9.8	45.7
1926	10.6		1.16	.09	12.0	10.0	47.0
1927	10.4		1.16	.10	11.8	9.8	47.0
1928	10.4		1.06	.10	11.7	9.8	47.3
1929	10.4		1.03	.10	11.7	10.5	47.7
1930	10.3	.15	.98	.10	11.6	9.4	45.7
1931	10.3		.87	.10	11.4	8.0	42.6
1932	10.2		.75	.09	11.1	6.8	39.1

(TABLE 3 concluded)

Employment in Resource Industries (millions)

	Agriculture	Timber	Mining	Fishing	All Extractive	Manufac-turing	Total U.S.
1933	10.1		.76	.10	11.1	7.3	39.4
1934	9.9		.86	.10	11.0	8.3	42.5
1935	10.1		.89	.10	11.2	8.9	44.1
1936	10.0		.94	.10	11.2	9.7	47.1
1937	9.8		.99	.10	11.1	10.6	48.4
1938	9.7		.92	.10	10.8	9.3	46.7
1939	9.6		.91	.10	10.8	10.1	48.2
1940	9.5	.16	.95	.10	10.8	10.8	50.2
1941	9.1		.99	.09	10.3	13.0	54.2
1942	9.2		.97	.09	10.5	15.1	59.7
1943	9.1		.89	.09	10.2	17.4	65.4
1944	9.0		.86	.10	10.1	17.1	66.6
1945	8.6		.84	.12	9.7	15.3	64.7
1946	8.3		.89	.14	9.5	14.5	58.9
1947	8.3		.94	.14	9.5	15.3	59.1
1948	8.0		.98	.14	9.3	15.3	59.8
1949	8.0		.96	.14	9.3	14.2	58.7
1950	7.5	.17	.94	.13	8.8	15.0	60.0
1951	7.1		.93	.12	8.3	16.1	64.0
1952	6.8		.90	.12	8.0	16.3	65.2
1953	6.6		.87	.12	7.7	17.2	66.0
1954	6.5		.79	.12	7.6	16.0	64.3
1955	6.7		.80	.12	7.8	16.6	66.1

Source: See Table 4.

TABLE 4

Indexes of Employment in Resource Industries

(1947–49 = 100)

	Agriculture	Timber	Mining	Fishing	All Extractive	Manufac-turing	Total U.S.
1870	78	18	20	29	70	15[a]	21
1879						19	
1880	104	29	31	36	94		29
1889			58			27	
1890	121	59		58	112	28	39
1900	129	71		66	123	36	48
1901						38	50
1902			84			42	52
1903						43	53
1904						42	53

122

(TABLE 4 continued)

Indexes of Employment in Resource Industries

(1947–49 = 100)

	Agriculture	Timber	Mining	Fishing	All Extractive	Manufac-turing	Total U.S.
1905						45	55
1906						48	58
1907						48	59
1908						44	57
1909			111			50	61
1910	137	88		66	132	52	62
1911	137					52	63
1912	137					55	65
1913	137					58	67
1914	137					54	65
1915	138					54	65
1916	138					64	70
1917	137					65	71
1918	136					67	77
1919	134		120		131	71	75
1920	136	112	123	51	132	71	74
1921	136		120		132	54	70
1922	135		126	49	132	60	72
1923	133		133	52	131	68	77
1924	132		123	56	129	64	76
1925	132		120	61	129	66	77
1926	131		121	68	128	67	79
1927	128		121	75	126	66	79
1928	128		110	72	125	66	80
1929	129		107	73	125	71	81
1930	128	88	102	71	124	63	77
1931	127		91	71	122	54	72
1932	126		78	67	118	46	66
1933	125		79	69	118	49	67
1934	122		90	72	117	56	72
1935	125		93	74	120	60	74
1936	124		98	74	120	65	80
1937	121		103	74	118	71	82
1938	120		96	75	115	62	79
1939	119		95	76	115	68	81
1940	118	94	99	72	115	72	85
1941	112		103	68	110	87	92
1942	114		101	63	112	101	101
1943	112		93	68	109	116	110
1944	111		90	71	108	115	113
1945	106		88	86	103	102	109
1946	103		93	103	101	97	99

123

(TABLE 4 concluded)

Indexes of Employment in Resource Industries

(1947–49 = 100)

	Agriculture	Timber	Mining	Fishing	All Extractive	Manufac-turing	Total U.S.
1947	102		98	101	101	102	100
1948	98		102	101	99	103	101
1949	99		100	98	99	95	99
1950	93	100	98	95	94	100	101
1951	87		97	91	89	108	108
1952	84		94	87	85	109	110
1953	81		91	89	82	116	111
1954	80		82	88	81	108	109
1955	83		83	88	83	111	112

[a] Calculated by interpolation.

Sources, Tables 3 and 4:

Agriculture: 1929–55, *Economic Report of the President, 1957,* p. 140 (sources, Department of Labor and Census' *Monthly Report on the Labor Force*); 1910–28, U.S. Department of Agriculture, Agricultural Marketing Service, *Farm Labor* bulletin, January 10, 1956, p. 9, linked to above series; 1870–1900, Daniel Carson, "Industrial Composition of Manpower," in *Studies in Income and Wealth,* Vol. XI, p. 47, based on Census of Population (Occupations), linked to above series.

Timber: The data cover logging only, as sawmills are engaged in manufacturing. Figures based on Census (Occupations).

Mining: These data are a summation of series we have gathered and spliced from a number of sources, principally Bureau of Mines, the *Census of Mineral Industries,* Bureau of Labor Statistics, Barger and Schurr's *The Mining Industries,* Department of Commerce National Income Division, and the WPA National Research Project. The concepts used are not always consistent with each other (see text). We have sought to get consistent indicators of the movement (rather than the level) of labor input required to produce fuels or ores ready for use or refining. We have tried to avoid inclusion of manufacturing operations but attempted to include all operations required to extract and prepare a commodity of uniform quality—metal ores ready for smelting, coal separated from slate, etc.

Fishing: Data from U.S. Fish and Wildlife Service, *Fishery Statistics of the U.S.,* linked to Census Occupation data for years prior to the 1920's. Since the ratio between the Census data and the Fish and Wildlife data is not very stable in the period of overlap (1930, 1940, 1950), the resulting series is only a rough approximation.

Manufacturing: A series prepared for us by Stanley Lebergott. He used Bureau of Labor Statistics *Employment and Payrolls* reports, extrapolated with adjusted Census of Population (Occupations) figures, and interpolated by unpublished estimates of Edwin Frickey.

Total U.S. Employment: 1929-55, Department of Commerce *National Income* figures, adjusted to use our figures on farm employment, since Commerce omits family labor; 1900–28, Sum of our agricultural employment, plus a series on nonfarm employees prepared for us by Stanley Lebergott, plus a series on nonfarm proprietors prepared by Alba Edwards for the 1940 *Census of Population,* plus a series on government prepared by John W. Kendrick, linked to above series; 1870–90, Daniel Carson's "Manpower" series, prepared from Census of Population (Occupations) data (in *Studies in Income and Wealth,* Vol. XI), linked to above series.

course, nowhere attainable over the whole eighty-five-year period, and we have used a variety of substitutes. In choosing substitutes, we put long-term consistency for each series above consistency of concept as between series (e.g., between agriculture and mining, or among mining industries).

WEIGHTING

The employment data are not "weighted," as we have followed the usual practice of simply adding all persons engaged in each industry. However, perhaps employment data should be weighted, as there are certainly qualitative differences among workers, between different classes of workers, and between industries. Much farm labor, for instance, is unskilled, casual, and juvenile, while mining and timber use large proportions of skilled adult males. If allowances for quality were made, the decline in extractive employment might be less than is shown in our figures, for farming would have a smaller relative weight, and its quality may be increasing relatively as well as absolutely.

CONSISTENCY

In data over a long period and as between industries, consistency is, of course, not attainable in any complete sense, as we have been forced to utilize different sources for different industries and different time-periods. Different agencies collect data by different questions and methods, and classify them differently. In mining, for example, the Bureau of Mines has collected data on workers subject to accident hazards, without regard to their wage or salary status, type of work, etc. The Census has collected data on "production and development workers" (called "wage earners" in earlier years), plus "other employees" and "proprietors." Since about 1913 the Bureau of Mines has separated men working in mills, smelters, and concentrators from those mining ores. Census makes this separation only for man-hours and only for 1939 and 1954. The Bureau of Mines averages employment for active periods, i.e., when the mine was open and operating. Census gets average employment over an entire twelve months, including periods of zero employment. Mines frequently includes Alaska, Hawaii, Puerto Rico, Canal Zone, etc., under "United States"; Census does not. The Department of Agriculture defines farm employment as working one hour or more per week on a farm. The Census Monthly Report on the Labor Force counts only those working a majority of their time on a farm.

Wherever we have been forced to use apparently inconsistent data in this way, we have attempted to appraise the different series and the

125

reasons for divergencies. We have also checked as long an overlap period as possible and made the link on an average basis, or at the point where there was nil or trivial difference.

DEFICIENCIES OF DATA

In agriculture and timber there are acute data problems which we would like to mention. Farmers are poor record-keepers, in any case. The problems of keeping adequate and meaningful records of labor input on the farm are enormous even when serious attention is given to them. Much of the labor is seasonal, migratory, or has irregular hours. Most important, a large portion is family labor, and it is often difficult to tell when people are merely living on a farm and when they are working on it. The efficiency of the labor varies over a very wide range, due to variations in skill, strength, energy, and intelligence. The problem is so serious that the Department of Commerce National Income Division excludes any allowance for family labor in its "persons engaged" figures.[7]

This problem, together with the insuperable problem of allocating labor input among the various crops and livestock products, leads the Department of Agriculture to discard its employment data when it comes to estimating productivity on the farm. The Agricultural Research Service estimates output-per-man-hour-equivalent ratios, which means they estimate the standard adult male labor it would have taken to produce the year's output, rather than the actual hours it did take.

Finally, farming presents the problem of the labor devoted to supplying services, food, etc., to the household, rather than to the market. This is still an important problem in the measurement of labor input required for agricultural output. In 1870 it was a much larger problem, for most farm households then supplied not only much of their food but also their own fuel and frequently housing, clothing, and refrigeration as well. We do not have data on the amount of labor that went into supporting these services, but we can be sure that the effect of our being unable to exclude it introduces a bias into our employment series. This overstates the decline in labor input to produce farm products and consequently the decline in labor cost per unit of such output.[8]

The timber employment data are perhaps even more subject to

[7] *National Income*, 1954 edition, Table 28, footnote 1.
[8] It is true that the farm output series include some products consumed on the farm as well as those sold; but numerous minor products and all services are excluded, and the excluded outputs must surely have declined, causing the above-mentioned bias.

126

error than those for agriculture. The difficulties are great; the labor used to "extract" the resource—that is, labor used to fell trees, and to bring logs and pulpwood to the mill—is customarily associated closely with manufacturing operations, principally sawmills. The sawmills generally use considerably more labor than is employed in logging operations, so that a small error in segregating workers hired by sawmill companies might produce an error of as much as 100 per cent in the estimates of logging labor. Moreover, lumber mills themselves have been handled in several ways in the different censuses. The basic sawing of the logs is closely associated with operations of trimming, planing, and further manufacture, and different questionnaires and classifications seem to have produced erratic results, as indicated for example by Fabricant's employment-to-output ratios in *Employment in Manufacturing* (p. 311). Thus there is no line of demarcation which is altogether satisfactory.

In the case of pulpwood, we have a material coming largely from unorganized small operators and farmers, so data on the cost of gathering this type of timber is rare or nonexistent.

EMPLOYMENT VS. MAN-HOURS

A note should be given on our reasons for presenting employment data but not man-hour data, commonly used as a measure of labor input. Estimates of man-hours usually require not only estimates of employment but also a series of hard-to-get estimates of hours per week or per year for each type of labor. Much of this data is of too low a degree of accuracy to provide any improvement in the measure of trend in labor input over that provided by our employment series.

In agriculture, in particular, there are extant the most widely divergent views or estimates of the average length of the workweek. The Twentieth Century Fund has estimated that the farm workweek rises as we go backward in time to something like sixty hours in 1910, while the Agricultural Research Service gives figures in connection with its productivity estimates which imply that the week on the farm has remained constant at a little under forty hours on the average. There is also considerable doubt whether man-hours on the whole are a better measure of labor input than is employment. There has been very great progress in the past eighty-five years in reducing the amount of idleness in a day's work and in increasing the time lost in commuting. Reductions in weekly hours have often been accompanied by a tightening-up of working procedures so as to get as much output from an eight-hour day as from a ten-hour day. (See Denison's paper in this conference.)

127

Labor Cost

In Table 5 and in Charts 5–12, we present the input-output or unit labor cost data. It is apparent that employment per unit of output (hereafter "labor cost" for short) in resource industries has fallen about as rapidly as in manufacturing and slightly more rapidly than in production of GNP. In view of the difficulties with the data, one should hesitate to say there has been a discernibly greater rate of increase in productivity in the resource industries than in the rest of the economy over the eighty-five-year period. It can certainly be said there has been no important lag.

We now look at the trends of labor cost in the subsectors and individual commodities of the resource industries.

TABLE 5
Indexes of Employment per Unit of Output
(1947–49 = 100)

	Agriculture	Timber	Mining	All Extractive	Manufac- turing	GNP
1870	341	48	598	370	384	320
1879					329	
1880	291	58	446	320		230
1889			435		236	
1890	298	85		310	233	226
1900	238	63		250	222	192
1902			326		202	184
1909			271		200	169
19??	225	73		220	193	167
1911	232				202	164
1912	207				185	161
1913	228				183	165
1914	207				182	169
1915	203				155	170
1916	222				153	168
1917	211				158	172
1918	205				165	167
1919	203		233		186	163
1920	194	112	210	194	181	169
1921	219		257	225	182	175
1922	199		255	206	154	158
1923	193		197	186	151	149
1924	194		195	189	148	147

128

(TABLE 5 concluded)

Indexes of Employment per Unit of Output
(1947–49 = 100)

	Agriculture	Timber	Mining	All Extractive	Manufac- turing	GNP
1925	188		183	184	134	138
1926	180		172	175	134	134
1927	178		171	173	132	135
1928	172		158	168	126	134
1929	174		142	164	122	128
1930	178	111	155	175	131	135
1931	161		164	172	138	136
1932	165		175	182	152	147
1933	178		164	188	135	151
1934	204		173	203	143	150
1935	173		166	177	130	141
1936	190		148	180	118	133
1937	148		140	149	118	129
1938	152		153	152	135	130
1939	148		135	149	118	125
1940	142	114	127	141	109	119
1941	131		122	127	99	112
1942	119		111	119	92	109
1943	120		100	116	88	107
1944	114		93	111	88	102
1945	110		94	109	93	101
1946	105		101	105	108	102
1947	107		96	104	102	103
1948	95		96	95	100	100
1949	98		107	100	98	98
1950	93	100	95	92	89	92
1951	84		85	83	89	91
1952	79		84	78	88	90
1953	75		80	75	85	87
1954	74		75	75	84	86
1955	74		70	73	80	82

129

CHART 5. Employment per Unit of Output: GNP and Major Extractive Sectors
(labor cost)

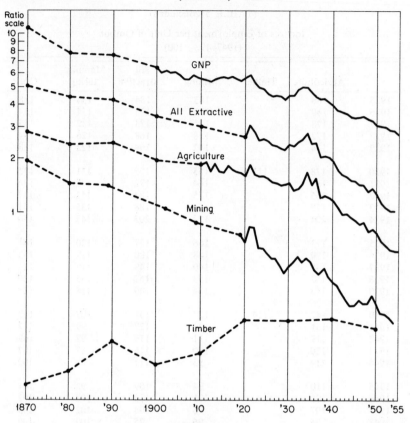

CHART 6. Agriculture and Sectors: Labor Cost

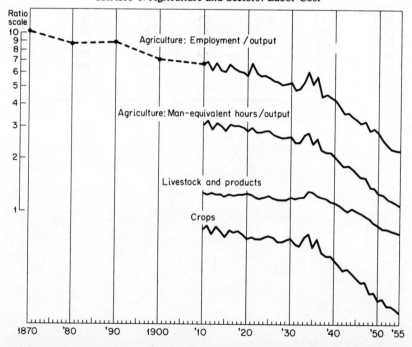

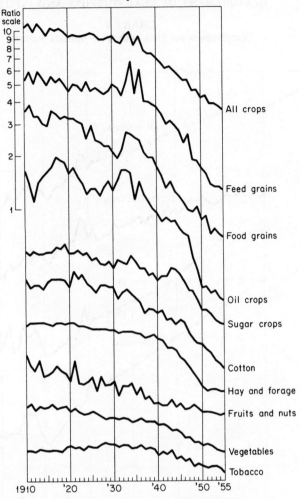

CHART 7. Crops: Labor Cost

Ratio
scale

All crops

Feed grains

Food grains

Oil crops

Sugar crops

Cotton

Hay and forage

Fruits and nuts

Vegetables

Tobacco

1910   '20   '30   '40   '50 '55

CHART 8. Livestock and Products: Labor Cost (1947–49 = 100)

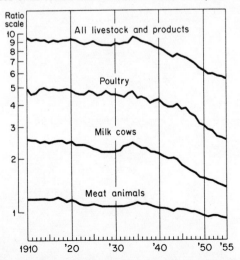

Ratio
scale

All livestock and products

Poultry

Milk cows

Meat animals

1910   '20   '30   '40   '50 '55

CHART 9
Employment per Unit of Output: Mineral Sectors

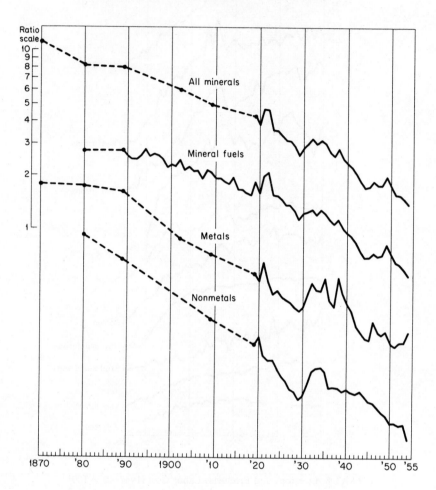

CHART 10
Mineral Fuels and Components: Labor Cost (1947–49 = 100)

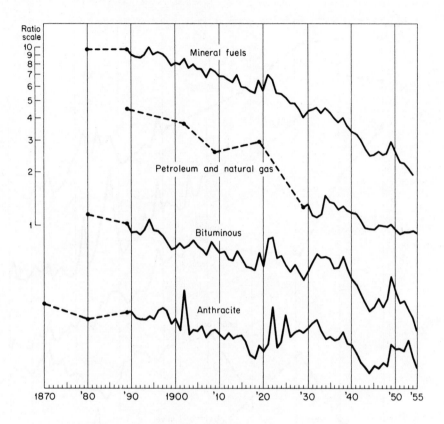

CHART 11
Metals and Major Components: Labor Cost

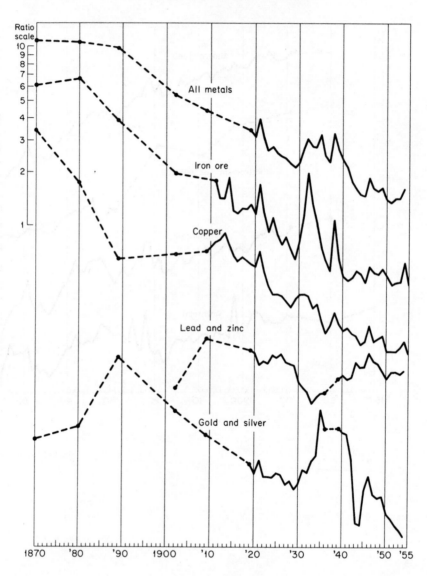

CHART 12
Nonmetals: Labor Cost

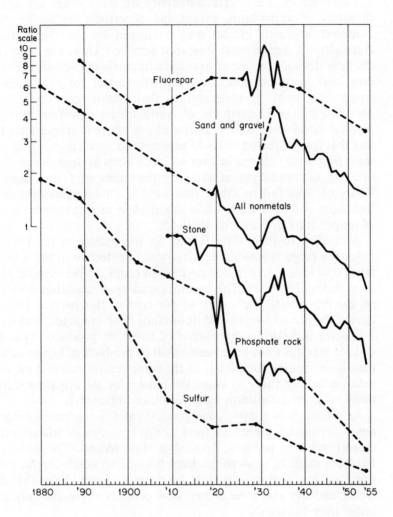

AGRICULTURE

There are no data on productivity or labor costs for any sub-divisions of agriculture, except the constructs begun by WPA's National Research Project and continued by the Department of Agriculture's Agricultural Research Service.[9] These are estimates of the time it would require an average adult male to produce the various crop and livestock products, with allowances for the techniques, equipment, weather, geographical distribution of plantings, etc., observed by the Department of Agriculture's reporters. While this method raises some doubts in our minds, there is reassurance in the fact that for the period 1910–55 this method yields approximately the same percentage change in over-all labor costs as does our method of dividing our employment data by the index of farm output (see Chart 6). The fall in labor cost for the "man-equivalent hours" technique is 65 per cent, while our decline in employment per unit of output is 67 per cent for 1910–55.

According to these data (Chart 6), the decline in the labor cost index for crops is almost identical with the decline in the total farm labor cost index: 66 per cent decline for crops, 65 per cent for the all-farm index (1910–55). The livestock-and-products labor cost index, on the other hand, falls only 41 per cent in this period. There was during the period a relative shift of labor from crops to livestock, and a relative increase in the output of livestock products. One might deduce that this must have been a shift to products of higher value per man-hour, but the complexity of the computation makes it impossible without further study to know the reason for the apparent inconsistency between the allfarm index and its components.

As indicated in Chart 7, the greatest rates in decline in labor cost among crops have been in food grains (principally wheat) with oil crops (soybeans, peanuts, flaxseed) a close second. The slowest gain has been made in tobacco, perhaps because so much careful cultivation, picking, and curing must be done by hand. Vegetable crops, fruits, and hay also have shown slow productivity gains only a little faster than tobacco's.

Among livestock and products (Chart 8), meat animals have been the slowest to gain (only 21 per cent decrease in labor cost since 1910), while dairies show a 46 per cent decline in labor cost.

MINING

Here we can give a more complete analysis, as we have not

[9] U.S. Work Projects Administration, *Changing Technology and Employment in Agriculture*, published by the Bureau of Agricultural Economics, 1941; USDA, Agricultural Research Service, *Changes in Farm Production and Efficiency*, published annually in June.

depended upon unknown methods and unpublished worksheets of others. Our indexes are simple quotients of employment and output, weighted by average unit values in the case of the group indexes for output, as noted above.

Since about 1902, the unit labor cost of fuels has declined at the same rate as all minerals (Chart 9). This reflects in part the close parallels among the three mineral sectors, and the fact that fuels constituted about two-thirds of the total value of output in 1870 and about three-quarters in 1954. However, the principal constituent was anthracite in the earlier period and is now petroleum, whose value is as great as that of all other minerals put together. As can be seen in Chart 10, the fuels whose employment/output ratios have fallen fastest have been oil and gas (employment for these two fuels cannot be separated). Yet the decline of the all-fuels index is as great as that for oil and gas, because of the considerable shift of the distribution of employment from the coals to oil and gas, where output per man has generally been about three times that in coal (valued in 1954, 1929, or 1902 prices). In recent years this effect has been somewhat augmented by the shift from anthracite to bituminous coal. In the earlier years, however, this movement had an adverse effect on the all-fuels productivity index, as output per man in anthracite was then generally higher than in bituminous coal (both valued in constant 1954, 1929, or 1902 prices).

The unit labor cost of metals declines at the same rate as that of all minerals since 1902, but more rapidly than the other minerals from 1870 to 1902, when output expanded most rapidly. All the major metals—iron, copper, and gold and silver—show this same rate of decline in unit labor input, about 3 per cent per year (Chart 11). Gold and silver appear to have had a sharp increase in labor cost between 1870 and 1889, but thereafter they fall more or less in line with iron and copper. Of the minor metals, lead, zinc, and mercury show almost horizontal trends in labor cost, while bauxite (a very minor employer) shows an irregular and sharp decline, and manganese shows a moderate decline. (These last two are not charted.)

The nonfuel nonmetals labor cost index shows a downtrend similar to that of all minerals for the period since 1919, but a considerably less sharp dropoff in the earlier period. We offer this conclusion with some trepidation, however. The data are quite thin, and dependent on backward extrapolative estimates with respect to stone, which is a highly heterogeneous group of commodities, with a range of labor costs from about an eighth of a man-year to ten man-years per 1,000 tons (1954 Census data).

In phosphate rock, where the best data on employment and output

137

in the nonmetal field appears, we observe a fall in labor costs that is more rapid than that for the other nonmetals (Chart 12). Sulfur has shown a much more moderate decline in labor costs, after the big drop in costs that came with the introduction of the Frasch process in the first decade of the century. Fluorspar shows a slow rate of decline throughout the period.

Sand and gravel show a steep rate of decline since 1933, when regular statistics from the Bureau of Mines became available. The Census data (not shown here) indicate a significant rise in labor cost over the decade 1929–39. This is a surprising result, for which we have not yet found an explanation.[10]

Stone output dominated the nonmetals picture until the 1920's, so there is little difference between the trend in labor cost of stone and of all nonmetals until 1919. After that year, however, in the period in which we have better data, the labor cost of stone has declined more rapidly than that for all nonmetals.

In timber, the trends are the opposite of those in agriculture and mining. Labor cost increases absolutely, as well as quite steeply relative to the other sectors. It may be that falling quality and decreasing accessibility of timber has more than offset the advantages of the improved machinery for making roads, hauling, cutting, etc., but a review of the employment estimates indicates that these interesting results may be due to defects in our data.

It will be clear from the foregoing review of labor input and output data in the resources field that much remains to be desired, especially in the earlier period, when the Director of the 1870 Census (Francis Walker) commented:

"... The Statistics of Mining and Fishing Industry in the United States, with the present modes of collection, are so distressingly inadequate to the known facts of the case, that their admission to The Tables of Manufacturing Industry amounts to a positive disparagement of the latter. The Statistics of Manufactures have their own faults, as is elsewhere frankly acknowledged, under the present census system of the United States; but they are incomparably more complete and accurate than any Statistics of Mining or Fishing Industry to be obtained by existing machinery."[11]

Yet the attempt to picture the development of the Nation from the period of primeval forests, unbroken sod, and unexplored mines to

---

[10] A correction for the number of man-shifts per year in 1929 and 1939 (worked out on a rough basis from a table in the 1929 Census, classifying plants by ranges of days open per year) gives a more moderate rise than the simple employment data.

[11] *Ninth Census of the U.S.*, Vol. 3, "Statistics of the Wealth and Industry," p. 383.

the present inevitably involves the use of such data, at least on the first attempt. We have tried to remove the errors and inconsistencies which were apparent in the summary data from various sources. Our next hope is that those with more detailed knowledge in the specialized fields can offer corrections which will enable us to make these indexes a more adequate representation of the "known facts of the case."

COMMENT

VIVIAN EBERLE SPENCER, Bureau of the Census

The production series covering the years 1870 to 1955, presented by Potter and Christy, are closely related to the President's Materials Policy Commission Census series, which begin with 1900. Their paper throws light on the effect of changes in the weighting systems, adds figures for years before 1900, and provides some groupings of raw materials slightly different from those used in the PMPC-Census reports. New measures of employment for the raw materials industries are also presented for the period 1870 through 1954 and on an annual basis from 1919 through 1954. Productivity measures have been calculated by dividing the employment series by the production series. Since the implications of the types of trends shown are discussed in other papers, my remarks are confined primarily to the statistics as related to other available measures. However, in attempting to appraise the validity of these new measures, I have been somewhat hampered by lack of full detail on actual sources and methods used.[1]

Let us consider in order the three Potter-Christy measures: (1) the "output of resource industries" series as related to the PMPC-Census measures of raw materials production from 1900 to the present; (2) the employment measures as related to various concepts of employment; and (3) the productivity measures as derived from the employment and production series.

Production Series

The Potter-Christy production series, like those of the PMPC-Census, give raw materials figures in terms of constant dollar aggregates, separately for agriculture, mining, and two other groups of raw materials. The third Potter-Christy series is called timber and seems to differ in concept from the PMPC-Census series for forest products principally by the exclusion of fuel wood in the former. The fourth Potter-Christy series is called fish, fuel wood, and water

[1] These were available to me, in part only, from an unpublished manuscript.

power, and the fourth PMPC-Census series fishery and wildlife products.

A series for "hydro energy" for the period 1900–50 was presented in the PMPC report, but it was not included as a component of the all-raw materials aggregates because of some obvious questions of significance. For example, it would seem equally appropriate to include in the raw materials aggregates a measure for use of water for purposes other than energy, and such use is implicitly included in the GNP figures as a component of the statistics for services and governments. Wildlife production was not covered by Potter and Christy. Nevertheless, whatever the differences in these fringe series, both sources agree that they amount to only about 2 per cent of the all-raw materials or all-extractive totals.

Indexes of the Potter-Christy and original PMPC-Census series on a 1947–49 base follow each other, in general, very closely. This is particularly true of indexes of the minerals series, which differ in all years before 1953 by 3 points or less. Both series were based on 97 per cent or more coverage of mineral products, uranium ore being the principal commodity completely omitted in both. The Potter-Christy series also excludes stone and clay produced and used in the same establishment in manufacturing cement and structural clay products. Note that near identity of the indexes is achieved even though the Potter-Christy series uses 1954 weights, while the Census series used 1935–39 weights.

The agriculture series from the two sources, expressed as indexes, diverge only slightly more. Both consist primarily of Department of Agriculture aggregates, but different Agriculture Department series were selected for the later years. Potter and Christy used an agriculture production series developed especially for measuring productivity, whereas the PMPC-Census used the Bureau of Agricultural Economics series, "Production for Sale and for Farm Home Consumption."[2] In the early years the movement of the two indexes is very similar, since both were based on the Strauss and Bean index of farm production for 1909 and previous years.

An index of the Potter-Christy timber series agrees fairly closely with an index of the PMPC-Census series including fuel wood. But when fuel wood is removed from Census figures, it exceeds the latter index in the early period by 50 to 70 per cent. The significant difference between the trends shown by the two series of more comparable coverage seems to be due primarily to the relatively lower weight given by Potter and Christy to pulpwood and "minor products" as

[2] The new series for "Supply and Utilization of Farm Commodities" was not completed in time to be included in the 1900–52 Census report.

compared with the weight given to lumber. It is also influenced by their use of a somewhat different series for "minor products" and their apparent exclusion of figures for naval stores.

The fish, fuel wood, and water power series, expressed as an index, bears little comparability in the aggregate to related PMPC-Census series because of the different weights assigned to fuel wood. Potter-Christy measures fuel wood in terms of the value of coal which would be required to provide its heat equivalent.

Since indexes of the major series for minerals and agriculture agree closely, indexes of the Census "all-raw materials" series and the Potter-Christy "all-extractive" figures also agree closely. When expressed as indexes with 1947–49 as a base, they differ by 4 points or less in all but one year, by 3 points or less in all but three years, and by 2 points or less in all but eight years.

One of the interesting contributions made is the comparison of segments of the minerals index using different weight bases, presented in Charts 2 and 3. In view of the wide fluctuations over the years in some minerals prices, it is surprising not to find more significant differences when 1902, 1929, and 1954 prices are used as weights. The nearly identical indexes based on the Potter-Christy and PMPC-Census series provide another example of the small effect of changing weight base, since 1954 weights were used by Potter and Christy and 1935–39 weights by the Census.

Employment Measures

The paper lists fairly completely the major problems in developing employment figures for the raw materials area.[3] It is highly desirable to have a measure of labor input for the production of raw materials, including figures on an annual basis insofar as possible. My evaluation of the figures in the Potter-Christy report was hampered by lack of a uniform and clearly stated objective in developing the employment measures. Instead, the authors indicate that the employment series represent an attempt to reveal trends in real labor inputs, but that this ideal is nowhere attainable, and that a variety of substitutes were used. For example, after listing various possibilities, an objective for the employment measure for minerals is not set as either the Census concept of average number of employees during the entire year or as the Bureau of Mines concept of average number of employees on active days—two employment measures that may differ

[3] It was because of such problems that the Census report did not go further than reproduction of broad classifications for number of gainful workers in the raw materials area for the period 1820–1940, with roughly comparable OBE figures for persons engaged full-time for the years 1929, 1940, and 1950.

141

greatly. In the 1954 Census, when both figures were obtained for the coal industries, the average number of employees on active days exceeded the average for twelve months in the anthracite industry by about 29 per cent, and in the bituminous coal industry by 14 per cent.[4] Nor is it made clear by the authors whether the employment figures represent only production and related workers or include all other employees. No statement is made about the inclusion or exclusion of working proprietors. The figures given in the report for the mining series seem to agree fairly closely with those I obtain by use of the Census data for average number of employees for twelve months, including both production and related workers and all other employees, after these are adjusted for omission of certain industries or parts of industries in censuses before 1954, shown below in millions.

Year	Potter-Christy Employment	Adjusted Census Employment
1870	0.19	0.16
1880	0.30	0.31
1889	0.56	0.54
1909	1.07	1.04
1919	1.15	1.10
1939	0.91	0.86
1954	0.79	0.81

These figures differ at most by 5 per cent. The 1954 figure used by Potter and Christy agrees exactly with the total employment in the mineral industries as shown in Table 2 of the General Summary in the 1954 Census of Mineral Industries volumes. This figure does not include the approximately 20,000 employees engaged in mining operations at manufacturing establishments. Such mining employment is included in Table 1 of the 1954 Census General Summary referred to above which furnishes a basis for the adjusted Census employment shown. (This mining employment at manufacturing establishments is required to produce certain mineral products and the production of such products is included in the PMPC-Census production series.) However, the identity of the Potter-Christy employment for 1954 and the Census employment excluding mining at manufacturing operations is, in part, an accident, since the Potter-Christy figures represent the sum of employment from various sources rather than a series adjusted to the 1954 census. In fact, while it excludes employment at quarries operated in conjunction with cement plants it includes employment at quarries associated with

[4] These different definitions, of course, would affect the cyclical trend more than the long time trend, if the same definition is used consistently from year to year.

lime kilns. Again, it includes employment at quarries operated in conjunction with dimension stone dressing plants (which are classified in manufacturing) but excludes employment at the dressing plants.

The Potter-Christy discussion of the problems of measuring employment for the timber series clearly points up the difficulty of measuring logging employment without including employees at associated sawmills. The basic difficulty is the fact that, for a significant portion of this industry, the same employees work in logging and sawmill operations of individual establishments. While it might be more feasible to segregate man-hours for logging and sawmill activities, no adequate series of this type are currently available.

The difficulties in measuring agricultural employment are also well-stated, but again the paper does not make objectives entirely clear. The authors indicate carefully the problems of measuring production and employment and state that the exclusion of some of the production for farm home use introduces a downward bias in the labor cost per unit output series. The evidence presented, however, is not enough to indicate clearly the direction of bias in the over-all measure of agriculture productivity.

The importance of part-time work when using an employment measure rather than a man-hour one, which is emphasized in connection with the agriculture series, should not be disregarded in mining. For example, the 1939 Census of Mineral Industries, which obtained separate data for full-time and part-time workers in the crude petroleum and natural gas industries, showed 19 per cent of all such wage earners as part-time workers.

Productivity Measures

For the productivity measures, I will not discuss the relative significance of using a particular type of index number or of using price rather than employment weights. I would like to emphasize, however, the extreme importance of covering the same areas in a production and an employment series if they are to be used for measuring labor productivity. In the current paper I find too little emphasis on this point. It is hard to measure the bias introduced into these series by lack of availability of comparable output and employment measures for some of the areas covered.

Such comparability was attempted for minerals by excluding stone and clay used in cement and structural clay products plants. However, no adjustment was made to exclude value added by dimension stone dressing at plants operated in conjunction with quarries, even though employment at the dressing plants was excluded. We have been able to check fairly closely the indicated rate of decline in employment

143

per unit output by dividing the PMPC-Census production series (or, for years before 1900, the Potter-Christy output measure) by the adjusted Census employment shown above. On a 1954 index base the comparative figures are given below.

Year	Potter-Christy Index	PMPC-Census Index
1870	797	714
1880	595	650
1889	580	602
1909	361	413
1919	310	340
1939	180	178
1954	100	100

The Potter-Christy report includes some discussion of the advantages and disadvantages of using man-hours rather than employment in a productivity measure. For the minerals area, more reliable annual man-hour figures may be available for the last three or four decades than annual employment figures measured under the Census concept, because of the relatively high quality of the man-hour figures in the Bureau of Mines accident reports. In any case, the 1939 and 1954 minerals censuses provide a benchmark check on the effect of measuring labor cost in man-hours. The employment per unit output index given above as 178 for 1939 would have been changed to 153 if man-hours had been used, because of an increase in average hours worked per man-year, from 1,664 in 1939 to 1,933 in 1954.

This effect of changing hours per man-year appears to be the principal explanation of the behavior of the 1929 and 1939 Census sand and gravel figures referred to in the Potter-Christy paper. The Census figures actually show about the same ratio of wages and salaries to value of shipments for the sand and gravel industries for 1929 and 1939. However, the number of employees per unit output for 1939 is about 25 per cent higher than for 1929, and similar ratios occur for each of the major sand and gravel producing states. An analysis of the information in the 1929 Census report shows that over 92 per cent of all sand and gravel establishments were working six full days or more a week in 1929, and that about 36 per cent of them worked over 300 days. In 1939, however, a considerably less-full year appears to have been worked.

The Potter-Christy productivity measure for timber, which shows increasing employment per unit output, is not substantiated by related Census statistics. The authors include a discussion of the

144

weaknesses of the employment figures, based as they are on occupation statistics from the decennial censuses. A rough estimate of 1939 employment in logging operations on the basis of the 1939 Census of Manufactures gives a figure not far from the 0.16 million employees indicated by Potter and Christy. However, our rough computations of the changes in logging productivity indicated by 1919, 1929, 1939, and 1954 Censuses of Manufactures figures, show productivity increasing significantly rather than declining. The upward trend shown in the Potter-Christy labor cost per unit output series is probably the result of dividing employment by an index of production which is not sufficiently comparable to it in coverage. Moreover, the employment coverage may be significantly different from census to census. One may question, for example, whether labor used in the production of fuel wood is actually excluded from the Potter-Christy employment series to the same extent for all years. For recent years, persons devoting part time to the production of fuel wood may frequently be classified in agriculture by census takers; but for early census years, when much more fuel wood was used, a large number of persons cutting fuel wood for sale may have reported themselves as engaged in such an activity as wood chopper. On the other hand, by-product fuel wood employment would be included for all years, but in later years, such wood constitutes a larger proportion of all wood used for fuel.

In closing, it should be noted that the reliability of a productivity index computed as the quotient of two indexes of this type is, in general, less than that of the component indexes. For example, if the production and employment indexes are of equal reliability, the computed "labor cost" index will be roughly one-half as reliable as the component indexes.

Data Available for the Measurement of Output per Man-Hour

LEON GREENBERG

BUREAU OF LABOR STATISTICS, DEPARTMENT OF LABOR

Introduction

NOTE: This paper was prepared with the assistance of Robert T. Adams, Eva Jacobs, and Jerome A. Mark of the Division of Productivity and Technological Developments of the Bureau of Labor Statistics.

IN VIEW of the importance of productivity statistics in many areas of investigation, questions have been raised as to the adequacy of the available measures and the needed improvements in basic data. Pertinent analyses such as the report of the Joint Economic Committee of the President,[1] the more recent report of the National Accounts Review Committee,[2] and numerous internal memoranda of various agencies have been concerned more with the general improvement of basic statistical sources than with the specific area of productivity measurement. Therefore, the Interagency Productivity Committee of the Bureau of the Budget concluded that a more intensive examination of productivity data was required. This report is an outgrowth of that decision.

Part I of this report defines the major types of productivity measures, discusses the general problems attendant on their construction, as well as the kinds of data required, and summarizes the available data by sectors. Part II presents a comprehensive compilation of the data available by industries. From these tabulations it is hoped that specific gaps may be readily ascertained. The tabulations are not exhaustive since the study was limited to regularly published, readily available sources. Sampling techniques and sampling errors have not been evaluated. Also, since my primary purpose is to indicate weaknesses in the available data, the positive value of the existing series is not discussed.

---

[1] *Statistical Gaps,* Report of the Joint Committee on the Economic Report, 1948; *Employment and Unemployment Statistics,* Hearings before the Joint Committee on the Economic Report, 1955; *Economic Statistics,* Hearings before the Joint Committee on the Economic Report, 1954.

[2] *The National Accounts of the United States,* Hearings before the Subcommittee on Economic Statistics, October 29–30, 1957.

147

Productivity: Concepts and Data Requirements

A productivity measure is the ratio between output and input both specifically and comparably defined. The ratio can be expressed in terms of selected inputs or all inputs combined. However, the measures which have been most generally used are those which relate output to man-hours, sometimes known as labor productivity.

Measures of aggregate output per man-hour fall into three general categories. First, there are the physical productivity measures which show changes in the labor time required to produce a fixed composite of goods and services. These measure changes in technical efficiency alone. Second, there are the gross productivity measures which take into account shifts in the relative importance of component sectors with different levels of output per man-hour, as well as changes in output per man-hour within sectors. Third, there are the net output per man-hour measures which reflect, in addition to changes in physical productivity and shifts between sectors, changes in material requirements per unit of output. Since they reflect the effect of changes in resource allocation, the gross and net measures may record changes even when there is no movement in the productivity of component sectors. Each of the categories specified requires different kinds of data.

Data for the measurement of physical productivity should include the physical quantities of the various goods produced and the unit man-hours required in their production. However, only rarely is such information available for all commodities in an industry on a continuous basis. Where unit man-hours are not available, physical quantities are combined using weights which are assumed to be proportional to this variable. In order of preference, substitute weights which would be used are unit labor cost, unit value added, and unit value. In practice, these weights have been used in the reverse order at the commodity level. In combining industries, man-hour weights are used.

Gross productivity measures generally are derived by deflating production values by appropriate price indexes. The latter should be sufficiently detailed to relate to the value of output in question. Deflated value series are sometimes used as approximations of physical productivity measures.

Net output productivity measures, the third category, are based upon aggregates of dollar value added. These measures require the same data as the gross output measures and also information on materials and services consumed, with appropriate deflators.

148

Output

AGGREGATE MEASURES

Because of expedients adopted to fill gaps in the data, none of the current output series can be defined as purely physical, gross, or net measures.

Annual production indexes have been developed by the Bureau of Labor Statistics for manufacturing and by the Federal Reserve Board for manufacturing and mining (with different weighting systems), using quantity data wherever possible. Both series, with variations, include industries where output change is estimated from materials consumed and deflated shipments. The FRB also uses man-hours (adjusted for estimated productivity change). The BLS estimates that the industries for which data other than physical quantities were used represent almost 30 per cent of the production workers in the industries included in 1947. The FRB estimates that 38 per cent of the value added of its annual indexes represents data other than quantities produced and shipped.

There is no single series based entirely on the concept of gross output using deflated values of production. However, deflated value measures are important because they can be computed on an industry basis for a larger proportion of the total economy than can either of the other two output measures. They are used mainly as substitutes for parts of the other two types of series.

The closest approximation to a net output measure for the entire private economy is the estimate of constant dollars GNP prepared by the National Income Division of the Department of Commerce. This estimate includes the market value of all final goods and services. Since intermediate products are excluded, the duplication inherent in an aggregation of industry gross output is eliminated. The method of approach consists of estimating the deflated value of final product consumption. However, departures in certain sectors are necessary because current expenditures data or appropriate deflators are lacking.[3] For example, the current value of personal consumption expenditures for some service industries is estimated from wage payments deflated by a price index or, more generally, by an index of wage rates. The resulting real value essentially reflects the movement of employment and does not take into account possible changes in productivity. On aggregation, therefore, the total real GNP includes values which are inappropriate for measuring output per man-hour.

---

[3] George Jaszi, "The Statistical Foundations of the Gross National Product," *Review of Economics and Statistics*, May 1956. See also *National Economic Accounts of the U.S.*, Joint Economic Committee, Cong. of the U.S., 1957.

Since the GNP estimates are derived from the product side without explicit recognition of the industry of origin, they do not permit analysis of the relative trends in component sectors. For this purpose, estimates of net output per sector are needed. Most such estimates represent industry gross output measures combined with net output weights because net output data are not available. However, for agriculture and manufacturing it has been possible to derive deflated net output as a residual after deducting deflated materials consumed from deflated shipments.[4] The net output index of manufacturing is not conceptually identical to GNP originating in manufacturing but is an approximation. The deviations are the direct result of data deficiencies.

BASIC DATA, BY SECTORS

It is difficult to summarize the deficiencies of the output data because they are attributable to such varied factors as lack of homogeneity of product or service, lack of over-all control totals, a diversity of sources, and conceptual problems of output definition. Nevertheless, it appears that the quantity and quality of the data available depends upon the level of detail which is presented separately. Most aggregations are built up from data collected from smaller units. For example, a sector physical production index cannot be constructed without first creating indexes for the component industries for which data are available, and making imputations where necessary. However, the presentation is not always in the required detail because data are nonexistent, sample estimates of smaller aggregates are considered unreliable, or funds are not available for publication. Of course, when the analysis is broadened to include the total economy, weaknesses which may be of great concern in the analysis of smaller aggregates tend to cancel out.

A review of the industry coverage of different kinds of output data by major sectors follows. A discussion of the quality of the data available is deferred until Part II.

Agriculture. Information on the quantity and value of production is available for major crop and livestock activities for total United States, by geographic regions, and by states. Thus, measures of gross output on almost any conceivable basis are possible. Information is similarly available for gross farm income and expenditures and net farm income. Price indexes are available for deflating both gross income and expenditures and, therefore, for deriving net output. The estimates of gross and net income, like the production estimates, are

[4] Jack Alterman and Eva Jacobs, "Estimates of Real Product in the United States by Industrial Sector, 1947–55," and Almarin Phillips, "A Review of Three Estimates of Industry Output," this volume.

generally derived from survey samples and tied to the agricultural census every five years. There are, however, areas for which sample data are not available, and here only broad approximations are possible.

Mining. Coverage here is substantially complete. Data are available in four-digit industry detail from the quinquennial Cenus of Minerals Industries on the quantity and value of ore produced, value of shipments, minerals received for preparation, supplies, fuel and electrical energy, and value added.

For intercensal years, data are available from the Regular Commodity Canvasses and the Accident Analysis Canvasses of the Bureau of Mines. Data from the former source include the quantity and value of production and/or shipments on a commodity basis (wherever made). These data are generally published in the *Minerals Yearbook*, although for major minerals they are available monthly or quarterly. The statistics are compiled from complete canvasses, and are, therefore, less than benchmark only in that they may be tested against Census data periodically. A reconciliation between Census and *Minerals Yearbook* data is difficult because of the large amount of mining occurring in other sectors of the economy—up to 25 per cent in the case of total nonmetallic minerals except fuels, and for specific industries, a much higher percentage. The 1954 Census includes partial data on mining operations in nonmining industries.

The Accident Analysis Canvass results in quantity data on a modified four-digit industry basis for all mining except petroleum and natural gas. This series covers only crude ore produced, but is comparable to the employment and man-hour series published by the Bureau of Mines. This material is not now published, but it is readily available.

Manufacturing. Table 1 is a frequency distribution showing the extent to which quantity data are available in the Census of Manufactures.

TABLE 1

Percentage of Total Output Covered by Quantity Data, Manufacturing Industries

Coverage	Number of Industries	Percentage of Employment
Total	446	100.0
Per cent		
75–100	171	46.9
50–74	59	14.2
25–49	36	7.5
0–24[a]	180	33.4

[a] Includes zero coverage of 155 industries, 29.6 per cent of employment.

Source: Value of shipments for which quantity data are available divided by the total value of shipments, both on a wherever-made basis, as reported in the *1954 Census of Manufactures*.

For industries responsible for 60 per cent of total manufacturing employment, half the value of total output is covered by quantity data. For industries representing almost 30 per cent of total employment, no quantity data are available.

Except where there are problems of disclosure or extensive duplication in the figures, value data from the *1954 Census of Manufactures* are available for all industries. Although shipments are reported in some cases and production in others, either may be derived by adjusting for the net change in inventories.

The 1954 Census also presents data on total materials consumed, for all industries. For some industries a commodity breakdown is also included, while for others, commodity data are available only if the industry consumes an important material. Table 2 presents ratios

TABLE 2

Percentage of Total Materials Consumed Covered by Commodity Data, Manufacturing Industries

Coverage	Number of Industries	Percentage of Employment
Total	446	100.0
Per cent		
75–100	43	18
50–74	64	17
25–49	87	17
0–24a	250	48

a Includes zero coverage of 206 industries, 39 per cent of employment.

Source: Value of individual products consumed for which quantity or value data are available, divided by the total value of materials consumed, as reported in the *1954 Census of Manufacturers*.

which indicate the portion of total materials consumed in an industry, for which some commodity detail is available. For industries representing 34 per cent of manufacturing employment, no materials distribution is available from the primary sources.

TABLE 3

Number of Manufacturing Industries Covered by Less than Benchmark Quantity Data

Time Period	Number of Industries	Percentage of Employment	Value Added
Monthly	83	42	41
Quarterly	9	4	4
Annually	65	32	31

Annual data on the value of industry shipments and inventories are available from the Annual Survey of Manufactures on a basis comparable to the Census. Only insignificant amounts of value data are available for lesser periods. Table 3 indicates the availability of less than benchmark quantity data. The figures are not additive since

152

data are available several ways for certain industries. However, some coverage is available for about 100 four-digit industries representing about 59 per cent of both value added and employment. Such data as are available for less than annual periods have a limited value. The coverage is uncertain and it is from widely different sources and for nonuniform time periods.

Noncommodity Sectors. The industries here can be grouped according to the types of data available. First, there are the industries which are included in the *1954 Census of Business*, namely, wholesale and retail trade and service. The Censuses of Business provide benchmarks for sales or receipts of these industries, which constituted more than one-quarter of total private employment in 1954. For interim periods, sample survey data are collected by the Census Bureau for trade but not for services. The Internal Revenue Service has recently begun publishing current estimates of annual gross receipts for trade and services derived from a sample of income tax returns.[5]

The second group of industries are those for which data are collected by regulatory agencies. These include the utilities, transportation, banking and insurance, and accounting which together accounted for about 13 per cent of total private employment in 1954. Annual and less than annual data in this area are fairly plentiful. However, problems arise in adapting these data to production index use when the regulated segment of an industry is not representative of the whole. Some of the information collected is neither tabulated nor published because of lack of resources or because it is not usable for the agency's purposes. Such data might help to fill gaps in the statistical measures.

The remaining industries, covering about 15 per cent of total private employment, include real estate, contract construction, and services not covered by the Census. In general, data for this group are nonexistent, irregular, or otherwise seriously deficient. The publication of IRS gross receipts data has provided a better basis for estimating the annual output value of some of these industries but the problem of securing adequate deflators and less-than-annual data remains.

Price Indexes

In order to deflate gross or net value series, appropriate price indexes are needed. Several price series are compiled by the government but none are collected specifically for deriving real production indexes. As a result, problems of classification, reconciliation,

[5] *Business Indicators*, Internal Revenue Service, April 1958.

weights, etc., arise when the existing price data are adapted to this purpose.

Some limitations common to most price indexes are not readily overcome. For example, it is generally impossible to express in commodity specifications all of the changing qualitative aspects of the goods priced. To the extent that price indexes fail to allow for improvements in quality they are overstated and, if used for deflation, they result in an understatement of the real output value. When quality deterioration occurs, the opposite tendencies prevail.

WHOLESALE PRICE INDEX

The index most frequently used for deflating value of shipments data is the BLS Wholesale Price Index. While this series is perhaps the best single source of deflators, it has several limitations for use in deriving production indexes.

Since it is not feasible to collect prices for every grade, size, style, or even every kind of commodity, the WPI contains a large degree of imputation, both within and between product classes. An analysis of the extent of imputation is extremely difficult, because the definition of the term is not always consistent. For example, the extent of imputation could be taken to refer only to those commodity classes for which no single product is priced. It could also be considered to refer to all products which are not directly priced regardless of commodity classification. The BLS employs the first definition. Ratios thus computed are shown in Part II.[6]

The proportion of imputations for a commodity group or industry is not by itself an indication of the accuracy of a given index, since the imputed values may be valid. However, imputed weights should reflect the price determining factors for individual commodities and these may be difficult to appraise. For example, is the price of copper base alloy pipes and tubes moved by the price of yellow brass sheets or by that of copper water tubing? Not enough analysis has been done to permit an over-all evaluation in this area.

There are also important groups of commodities for which no data are collected because it is too difficult to price or even define a typical item. The problem commodities are generally "custom built," and include special industry machinery, elaborate machine tools, airplanes, locomotives, and ships. Under the present WPI system, the price index for the whole machinery and motive power group is imputed to these products—an unsatisfactory expedient for any but the most aggregative kind of analysis. An alternative has been to determine indexes for these products by pricing inputs, a method

6 See Tables 6 and 8.

which faces conceptual obstacles and misses the effect of productivity changes in assembling. Frequently too, there are insufficient data on some of the components, such as material input quantities and profit margins.

The WPI embodies quoted, rather than actual prices, and the two may differ. In times of material shortages, premiums may raise actual prices above the published levels with the result that the index is understated. When supplies are plentiful, the index may be over-stated because of the prevalence of discounts. When either of these conditions is widespread and the differentials are measurable, some correction is generally applied. However, since there is usually a lag between the development and recognition of price differentials, they continue to have an effect on short-run changes in deflated output.

Research with an interesting potential for evaluating the WPI was undertaken in connection with the BLS-Census-FRB benchmark production indexes for 1947–54. Unit values from Census data were computed for all commodities for which quantity data were available for 1947 and 1954. The unit value index of those commodities which are priced for the WPI was compared with the WPI for the same commodities. This analysis was not completed because of limitations of research resources, but there were indications that product mix shifts rather than reporting errors in the Census data or lack of representativeness in the BLS sample were responsible for many of the discrepancies noted.

INDUSTRY PRICE INDEXES

During 1953, to meet the needs of the appraisal phase of the 1947 input-output project, the BLS began arranging the WPI commodity indexes into industry price indexes. The procedure involved coding each WPI commodity with its corresponding Census commodity classification and assigning its weight to the producing industries. A tabulation was prepared which showed for each industry the component commodities and indexes, their respective weights, the proportion of total shipments covered by direct pricing, and the combined index. In addition to achieving a useful set of industry indexes, this procedure brought out clearly those industries for which no commodity was directly priced. It also made explicit all the imputations in the WPI weighting system so that it could be readily determined which price movement was being imputed to which commodity.

These industry indexes are limited in that only the primary products of each industry are included. Also, weights are available only for the Census year, so that the indexes are base year weighted. When

155

an index of value is deflated by a base weighted price index, the resultant production index is currently weighted, although an aggregate index would be base-weighted in terms of the component industry production indexes. A conceptually desirable base year weighted production index, therefore, cannot be derived with these data. Further investigation is required before the significance of the resulting biases, if any, can be evaluated.

Table 4 shows the coverage available as a result of the 1947 interindustry price tabulations. The industry series are now being

TABLE 4

Percentage of Total Shipments Covered by Direct Pricing, Manufacturing Industries, 1947

Price Coverage Ratios	Number of Industries	Percentage of Value Added
Total	446	100
Per cent		
75–100	110	29
50–74	72	19
25–49	57	17
0–24[a]	207	35

[a] Includes zero coverage of 187 industries, 29 per cent of value added.

Source: BLS wholesale price indexes by industry.

continued through 1956. The extended indexes will incorporate the weights of the 1954 Census. While the over-all coverage will not be significantly altered (no substantial improvement is expected in those areas where pricing is most difficult), large differences could occur in individual industries because of changes in classification between the 1947 and 1954 Censuses.

CONSUMER PRICE INDEX

In the noncommodity producing area, the Consumer Price Index is the major source of price data. It is officially described as measuring "the average change in retail prices of goods, rents and services customarily purchased by city wage-earner and clerical-worker families." These prices may not be representative of all purchases but there has been no over-all study of whether the price movements of goods and services purchased by higher income groups or persons living in rural areas show significant differences.

In deflating the value of commodities in personal consumption expenditures, the CPI is frequently combined with the Department of Agriculture series on prices paid by farmers, to achieve a broader representation of economic groups. The latter series is not conceptually consistent with the CPI since it does not deal with commodities with standard specifications but with products of the kind and

156

quality most commonly purchased. These are not necessarily the same through time. How much of the difference between the two series is attributable to technical differences and how much to the distinction between economic groups is not known.

The criticism of "quoted prices" levied against the WPI is in some respects also applicable here. Changes in buying habits and shifts to discount houses or other low mark-up retail outlets are not immediately reflected in the index. Over the short-run this may lead to an upward bias.

UNCOVERED AREAS

For those industries whose output is almost entirely purchased by business, such as advertising, legal, engineering, and accounting services, no price data are available. For those industries whose output is shared by business and households, such as telephone, telegraph, gas and electric, and laundry services, where a CPI is available it has been used to represent the price movement of the entire output of the industry.

Employment and Hours

TOTAL NONFARM

Employment. Primary data are available from the Current Population Surveys of the Census Bureau (CPS) and the employment surveys of the Bureau of Labor Statistics. CPS data are published in the Monthly and Annual *Report of the Labor Force* (MRLF and ARLF) and the BLS data in *Employment and Earnings,* which is also published monthly.

The BLS employment series are available at a level roughly corresponding to the three-digit Standard Industrial Classification code. However, some three-digit groups are omitted from the detail and it is, therefore, not possible to derive complete productivity data on this basis. Four-digit data are available only where the four-digit industry comprises the entire three-digit classification (e.g., SIC Industry 291, which consists entirely of SIC Industry 2911—Petroleum Refining).

The Census Bureau and the BLS attempt to measure different universes of total employment. Their concepts differ and they employ different sampling techniques and estimating procedures, resulting in considerable variation in findings for comparable sectors.

The CPS estimates are based upon personal interviews of a household sample selected in accordance with a probability design while BLS statistics are derived largely from a modified cut-off sample which includes all firms with a specified level of employment. The cut-off point is set separately for each industry and the criteria for its determination are that the sample should "represent a substantial proportion of total employment in an industry" as well as "provide an appropriate standard of accuracy." In a few industries, special sample designs and procedures are used.

Essentially, the Current Population Surveys count persons while the BLS surveys count jobs. Thus, in the ARLF estimates, a worker is counted only once—in the industry of his major employment. In the BLS figures, a worker is counted more than once if he held more than one job covered by the sample. Some analysts have estimated that the number of persons holding two or more nonagricultural jobs might at times range between 750,000 and 1,000,000 persons. However, a more recent study suggests that these figures are understated.[7] Since the importance of multiple job holdings varies during the year, the difference between the CPS and BLS monthly estimates will fluctuate seasonally.

The ARLF estimates are based upon a labor force concept and include all persons aged fourteen or more, including paid industry employees, proprietors, unpaid family workers, and household domestics. The BLS estimates refer only to paid industry employees. The ARLF estimates include "persons with a job but not at work" because of "vacations, illness, industrial disputes, bad weather" or other voluntary reasons. The BLS estimates include only those absent workers who are paid for their time off.

A complete reconciliation between the two series has never been effected. The small discrepancy which remains after taking account of all known differences could come from errors in the population and benchmark estimates against which the respective sample estimates are checked, or from errors in enumeration or reporting.

Another source of employment data is the Commerce Department. The National Income Division of the Office of Business Economics publishes three employment series: (1) "Average Number of Full- and Part-time Employees," (2) "Number of Full-time Equivalent Employees" (two half-time employees equaling one full-time employee), and (3) "Number of Persons Engaged in Production." These estimates are conceptually consistent with the national income and GNP estimates. They are based almost entirely on secondary sources, usually Unemployment Insurance data. Estimates of proprietors, which along with wage and salary employees represent "persons engaged in production," are derived during Census years from the Industrial and Population Census and for intercensal years, from an

---

[7] *Employment and Unemployment Statistics*, Hearings before the Joint Committee on the Economic Report, November 7–8, 1955, p. 28.

estimated factor based on business population data developed by the National Income Division.

For selected years, the Census of Manufactures provides estimates of total employment for all four-digit manufacturing industries except where the information might be identified with a specific establishment. Between censuses, the Annual Survey of Manufactures provides a continuous and consistent source of data. These Census Bureau estimates are almost identical in character to those of the BLS. Nevertheless, significant differences have appeared in the manufacturing series of both agencies, especially at the three-digit industry level. The reasons, while under frequent study, have not been determined. The compensating nature of the differences between individual industries is more indicative of the effect of random factors than of a bias in either method of estimating.

The administrative reports of the Bureau of Employment Security and the Social Security Board, are still other sources of data. While these figures are not used directly for constructing employment estimates, they are an important element in the estimating systems of both the BLS and the Census of Manufactures.

Table 5 provides a recapitulation of these various sources of data and their characteristics.

Hours. The surveys of the BLS and the Census Bureau also provide data on average weekly hours. The BLS series theoretically covers all hours paid for regardless of work stoppages, absenteeism, vacations, sick leave, and overtime. Although the data are obtained from the employment sample previously described, all respondents do not report man-hours and the effective coverage is somewhat less.

The CPS estimates include only the hours of persons actually at work during the survey week. Conceptually, this is the greatest difference between this series and the BLS but it may be obscured by statistical discrepancies. The CPS hours are obtained from the same sample as the employment figures but since they are limited to time spent on the job, coverage is more restricted. The Census and Annual Survey of Manufactures provides data on man-hours for production workers in all four-digit manufacturing industries. This series covers all hours paid for (including overtime) providing the employee is at the plant. Except for work stoppages, this concept approximates that of the CPS.

Since the BLS collects only the hours of production and nonsupervisory employees, any estimate of total hours for an industry must assume that the workweek of other employees fluctuates directly with that of the included workers, or else that it is constantly maintained. Since the CPS average hours reflect only employees actually at

159

work, the employment base must be adjusted to exclude persons with a job but not at work.

Total man-hours for the economy cannot be directly derived by combining the hours and employment estimates. Estimates of average weekly hours are not published for certain industries in the noncommodity producing area. For manufacturing, average weekly hours are

TABLE 5

Sources of Nonfarm Employment Data and Their Characteristics

Item	BLS	Annual Survey and Census of Manufactures	CPS	U.I.	BOASI
Concept	Jobs	Jobs	Persons	Jobs	Jobs
Reporting unit	Establishment	Establishment	Household	Firm	Firm[a]
Coverage	All paid persons	All paid persons	Persons over 14, including unpaid	All paid persons	All paid persons
Type of survey	Mail survey	Mail survey	Personal interview	Administrative report	Administrative report
Reporting period	Monthly	Annually[b]	Monthly	Quarterly	First Quarter
Type of sample	Modified cut off	Probability sample	Probability sample	All firms	All firms
Survey period	Pay period ending nearest 15th of month	Week ending 15th of Mar., May, Aug., Nov.[c]	Week including 12th of month	Week ending nearest 15th of every month	Week ending nearest the 15th of March
Level of aggregation	SIC 3-digit	SIC 4-digit	[d]	3-digit[e] SSB	3-digit[e] SSB

[a] Except manufacturing, which is generally on an establishment basis.

[b] The Annual Surveys cover non-Census years. Censuses of Manufactures have occurred in selected years 1947, 1954, 1958, etc.

[c] Except seasonal industries, which include period ending nearest the fifteenth of each month.

[d] Not available.

[e] Approximation.

available for about 191 four-digit industries which account for 68 per cent of total manufacturing employment but the employment estimates are generally available only on a three-digit level.

Farm. Securing a satisfactory measure of labor input for the farm sector is uniquely difficult. The farm house is both the living quarters and the place of employment of the farm family. Over two-thirds of the farm work force consists of proprietors and unpaid family workers

160

who alternate between farm and household chores. Records are not generally available to furnish a basis for separation. Therefore, the time spent on farm work by the major portion of the work force can not be determined by conventional methods, and the available measures of employment and man-hours reflect considerable subjective judgment. In some cases, consistency with the definition of employment in other sectors becomes an important criterion for allocation of work time.

Employment. Data are available from the Census Population Survey and the Agricultural Research Service of the Department of Agriculture. Employment data from the latter source are published monthly under the title *Farm Labor*.

The CPS estimate of farm employment has the same characteristics as the nonfarm estimate included in its reports on the labor force, i.e., it is based on personal interviews with a probability sample of farm households, and the survey week includes the twelfth of the month. The ARS estimate is based on a mail survey of a non-cross-section sample of 20,000–25,000 farmers. The survey week is the last complete calendar week in the month.

Both series cover farm operators and hired workers who spend at least one hour of the survey week on farm work. Unpaid family workers are included only if they spend at least fifteen hours on farm work. This cut-off point may result in the exclusion of substantial amounts of labor from the estimates. A survey covering the month of August 1951 revealed 1.5 million workers in this category, one-half of whom worked fourteen hours a week.[8]

The ARS estimates include all employed children; the CPS excludes those under fourteen years of age. The ARS counts jobs, while the CPS counts persons. These differences in concept and coverage, along with statistical differences, cause variations in the level and short-run behavior of the two series.

Hours. Average weekly hours from the CPS reports are the only data available. Although the basis for the estimate is identical to that for the CPS estimates of hours for other sectors, the peculiar problems of measuring employment render an estimate of total man-hours (derived as the product of average employment times average hours) less satisfactory here than elsewhere.

The number of children not counted by the CPS may number nearly one million during certain seasons. If the workday were eight hours, eight million hours could thus be lost from the estimate in a single day. Multiple job holders also present greater difficulties in the

---

[8] "Farm Employment," unpublished memorandum, Bureau of the Census, 1951.

farm sector than the nonfarm sector largely because of their relatively greater number. The number of persons holding jobs on farms, but who work most of their hours in other industries, fluctuates between one-half and one million persons at different times of the year. The farm hours of these workers are classified in the nonfarm sector while the hours farm workers spend in secondary employment are credited to the farm sector. Data are not available for a statistical determination of the net effect of multiple job holding on total farm man-hours.

In order to develop estimates of total man-hours in the farm sector, the USDA has derived a "man-hour requirements" series. It is derived from benchmark estimates of the number of hours of direct labor required by an average adult male worker to cultivate an acre or produce a unit of livestock or livestock products. The benchmark estimates are from farm management studies, and are made for crop and livestock activities by separate areas within states. Total direct man-hours required are derived as the product of average requirements times the number of acres of crop or units of livestock. The hours of indirect labor are separately estimated and added. The estimates are summarized for states, regions, and the total economy. For nonbenchmark years, the estimates are derived from changes in acreage or livestock units modified to take into account changes in yield and changes in methods of production. The series is thus independent of employment estimates. It is essentially an adaptation of the standard labor unit procedure of cost accounting, although less precise.

It has been said that the taking account of the impact of technological change and yield between benchmark years builds into the series a predetermined productivity estimate. This is not true for benchmark years, and to the extent that the series is adjusted to benchmark levels the influence of such "circularity" is minimized over the long run.

Comparability between Output and Man-Hours

With few exceptions the estimates of output and man-hours are obtained from different sources. Consequently, in order to derive meaningful productivity measures, it is important to evaluate the extent to which these separate measures are consistent with each other, bearing in mind that the problem of comparability lessens as the level of comparison broadens.

When output and employment are to be related, the classification basis for reporting the two sets of data should be the same. Despite tremendous strides toward attainment of a uniform system of classification codes, not all data sources use the system, and the assignment

162

of establishments to industries is made at different points in time, with different purposes in mind. Variations in classification may account for a large part of the observed differences between Census and BLS employment data. Similar variations occur between output and employment data.

One of the basic problems in reconciling industry output and man-hour data is the "wherever made" versus the "establishment" form of classification. Output data in manufacturing generally include total shipments or production of products primary to a particular industry wherever they happen to be made, while input data include hours employed in the production of both primary and secondary products in establishments classified within a particular industry. The following diagram indicates the nature of the problem.

	Given Industry	Other Industries
Primary Products	A	C
Secondary Products	B	

Physical output data are generally available on the basis of AC while man-hours always relate to AB.

Because of this situation, changes in the total output of products primary to an industry are not necessarily associated with changes in the labor input of that industry. Classifying employment and man-hours on a basis comparable to output is usually impractical. It might be possible to adjust output data to man-hours data but this would require an extensive retabulation of Census data which might create other problems. Fortunately, a high percentage of most commodities is generally produced within the primary industry, while secondary production in an industry is usually a very small proportion of total output.[9]

Where the deflated value of industry shipments is used as the industry measure of output, there is another problem. Although the value data are on an establishment basis, the price indexes refer to primary products wherever made.

Another difficulty sometimes arises because output data are reported on a company basis while input data are reported on an establishment basis. Since company activities may cover more than one industry or major sector, the two measures may not correspond.

Employees in central offices and auxiliaries who service all the

[9] This is discussed further in Part II, where the appropriate product specialization ratios are provided.

163

establishments of a firm, such as personnel administrators, purchasing agents, warehousing and storage employees, repair and maintenance men, and research and development employees, present another problem since the establishments which they service are not necessarily classified in the same industry. Treatment of these employees varies according to the source of employment data. The Census of Manufactures includes data on the total number of central office employees, but makes no attempt to distribute them to particular industries. The BLS includes such employees in the industry which constitutes the major portion of the company's activities. In either case, the employment and output aggregates are inconsistent.

Problems of comparability also arise from the treatment of expenditures for scientific research and development, which represent a steadily rising percentage of total economic activity. The results of such outlays are inherently uncertain and usually intangible. When a patent does result, industry may capitalize the associated research expenditure and amortize it over the life of this asset. When research is unsuccessful, it is charged against current account. As a result, the value of research output is excluded from most output measures. On the other hand, the hours of research and development employees are included in the man-hour aggregates embodied in over-all productivity estimates. One solution would be to remove the hours of research employees from the estimates of total man-hours. However, this procedure would involve collecting more refined information, since the hours of research employees are not presently identifiable. Another solution would be to capitalize total private expenditure for research and development and include it as part of gross private domestic investment.

A similar problem occurs in industries in which establishments customarily perform their own construction work. The output measures of these industries do not include the value of this construction but the hours of the force account construction employees are included in man-hours. From the data currently collected it is not possible to separate the force account hours. While all industries are affected by this inconsistency to some degree, it is particularly troublesome in industries such as railroads and utilities where the amount of such construction is significant.

The production of purely military products in an industry which normally produces civilian goods, may create another problem. The usual tabulations of production data do not include military items, while the time applied to their production are included in man-hour statistics. Adjustments are made to avoid a downward bias in productivity estimates when military production is rising. This applies only to physical productivity indexes because value data generally include the value of military production.

Recommendations

Certain recommendations concerning steps that may be taken to improve the collection of data follow from the preceding review. With regard to output data, it is suggested that censuses be taken at regular and predictable intervals. Not only does this source provide benchmarks for many statistical series, but in many cases it provides the only information available. The benchmarks, in turn, provide the basis for evaluating methods of extrapolation. Surveys of nonmanufacturing sectors for intercensal years should be of such quality, in terms of sampling procedure, that they could be related to the censuses to form reliable continuing series. A third suggestion is that the Annual Survey of Manufactures be tested empirically in a census year by tabulating data for the Survey sample separately within the Census universe.

For benchmark years, additional physical quantity data should be collected in the Census of Manufactures, where feasible. Quantity data collected on an annual basis should conform to Census quantity data both in coverage and classification. Key monthly quantity data should be collected for more industries. It would be helpful if the value of purchased services were tabulated from data presently available on income tax returns, and if additional data on materials consumed were collected in the Census of Manufactures to provide the basis for improving net output measures. The final recommendation concerning output data is that the cost of goods sold be collected for both wholesale and retail trade. If such direct reporting is not considered feasible, margins can be derived from income tax returns. If the latter alternative is to be adopted, a regular sampling procedure must be instituted. Margin data would also be useful in adjusting producer prices to purchaser prices.

On the subject of price data, it is suggested that the sources of consumer price information be expanded to include coverage of additional segments of the population, more consumer items, and additional retail outlets. Industry indexes might profitably be computed from the Wholesale Price Index and, with respect to the latter, prices might be collected at the wholesale level to supplement prices currently obtained from manufacturers. Prices might also be collected for categories not now covered by the WPI, including business services and special types of purchases such as those made by government.

Coming to employment and man-hours data, it is suggested that estimates be provided, at least at the two-digit level, for employment in the services sector and for average hours in the transportation, finance, communications, and services sectors. Hours worked consistent with published hours paid need to be collected (a program designed to accomplish this objective is already underway). Hours of nonproduction workers should be collected; also the hours of force account employees in those industries where they represent a significant proportion of total employment, e.g., telephone and electric and gas utilities. Further, it would be helpful if occasional surveys were made of farm labor to determine hours worked on farms by persons under fourteen years of age and those whose major employment is in the nonfarm sector.

Implementing these suggestions would involve methodological problems and further work would have to be done to solve the measurement problems in certain industries where, because of lack of homogeneity and the custom-made nature of the products, quantity and price data cannot be obtained directly. In such instances it would be necessary to study alternative methods of measurement, for example the possibility of deriving quantity figures by the use of weight, area, or materials consumption information, and obtaining prices on the basis of hypothetical or standardized products. Appraisal of these and other possibilities might be assisted by plant level studies. Recommendations resulting from such a study would be a guide to all users of these data.

Industry Data

This section summarizes for each industry the sources and extent of the data available for deriving production and productivity indexes. Included is information on output quantities and values, and employment and man-hours. Price data, usable with value data to yield gross output measures, are noted, along with materials consumed data which constitute a vital element in the construction of net output measures. The information was prepared in the finest industry levels practical, generally in terms of the Standard Industrial Classification (SIC). Measures of the relative importance of each industry are provided to aid students in assessing the significance of data gaps. A distinction is made between benchmark and nonbenchmark periods. Data for the former is, by definition, derived from a Census covering the general subject matter of an industry. Data for other than benchmark periods comes from sample surveys or extrapolations.

The commodity producing sectors—agriculture, mining, and

166

manufacturing, and the noncommodity producing sectors are analyzed separately. The information for manufacturing, mining, and services is presented in tabular form. The information for the remaining sectors is given narrative form because the variety of sources, the difficulty of ascertaining coverage ratios, and/or the alternative ways of defining and measuring output, made tabulation impractical.

Commodity Producing Sectors

MANUFACTURING

Table 6 provides information on the data available for years when a complete census of manufactures was taken and interim periods. Only a sample page of the table is reproduced here. It is believed that the complete table, with all the four-digit industry detail would not be of interest to the general reader. However, anyone who is interested in the specific industries may obtain copies of the complete table upon request to the author.

The availability of quantity data is expressed in terms coverage of ratios which relate the value of primary products wherever made, for which quantity data are available, to the like value total. Ideally, the ratios should relate the value of primary and secondary products for which there is quantity data to the total value of industry shipments. However, since quantity data are available only on the basis of primary products wherever made, this was the determining factor.

Production indexes based on quantity data by implication impute the movement of an industry's primary products to its secondary products, and assume that the movement of primary products wherever made is the same as that of primary products actually made within the industry. As an indication of the significance of these imputations, data are provided for each industry showing the importance of primary products in relation to total shipments (specialization ratio), and the importance of primary products made "at home" in relation to primary products, wherever made.

Coverage is virtually complete in the case of output value, so only the form of the data available is shown. Coverage ratios are used, however, to indicate the extent to which imputation is employed in developing a price index of an industry's primary products. When examined in conjunction with the industry specialization ratio, some indication of the validity of the price index as a deflator can be obtained.

While the data for manufacturing are generally plentiful, there remain areas that could be improved. A summary of industries

167

TABLE 6

Productivity Data for Manufacturing Industries

INDUSTRY CODE			RELATIVE IMPORTANCE		QUANTITY DATA					
					Benchmark Periods				Nonbenchmark Periods	
					Per cent of Coverage		Primary Products			
2-Digit	3-Digit	4-Digit	2-Digit	3-4-Digit	1947–1954	1954 Only	Per cent Industry Specialization	Per cent Industry Coverage	Form of Data and Frequency of Publication	Approximate Coverage
(1)	(2)	(3)	(4)	(5)	(6)	(7)	(8)	(9)	(10)	(11)
20			8.7	100.0	84					
	201			14.4	98				P,M	
		2011		10.4	99		98	87		
		2013		2.5	96		83	28		
		2015		1.5	97		96	97		
	202			16.8	92					86.1
		2021		1.0	100.0		74	77	P,M	
		2022		.7	96		83	74	P,M	
		2023		1.3	44	99	82	68		
		2024		2.5	93		93	70		
		2025		.4	88		90	56		
		2026		.7 ⎫	95		82	94		
		2027		10.3 ⎭			82	94		
	203			9.7	23				P,A	96.0
		2031		.5	20	100	96	94		
		2032		.1	88		97	91		
		2033		6.2			90	94	P,A	
		2034		.4			95	97	P,A	
		2035		1.1	86		80	75	P,A	
		2036		.3	79		94	95		
		2037		1.1			88	84	P,A	
	204			9.1	89					
		2041		2.4	85		94	84	C,M	
		2042		4.4	95		95	90		
		2043		1.3	97		77	80		
		2044		.3	98		99	100		
		2045		.8			71	45		
	205			14.8	96					
		2051		11.7	96		98	99		
		2052		3.0	100		97	93		

TABLE 6 (concluded)

VALUE DATA	MATERIALS CONSUMED	PRICE INDEXES		EMPLOYMENT			MAN-HOURS
		Source	*Per cent Direct Pricing*	*Relative Importance*		*Source*	*Source*
Form Available	Per cent of Commodity Coverage			2-Digit	3–4-Digit		
(12)	(13)	(14)	(15)	(16)	(17)	(18)	(19)
	71			10.5	100.0	C,L,S	C,L
	90				18.9	C,L,S	C,L
S	92	WPI	91		13.4	C	C
S	80	,,	85		2.7	C	C
S	86	,,	72		2.8	C	C
	79				17.2	C,L,S	C,L
S	78	,,	99		1.3	C	C
S	88	,,	99		.8	C	C
S	73	,,	97		.8	C	C,L
S	60	,,	96		2.2	C	C,L
S	76	,,	67		.4	C	C
S	} 81				.9	C	C
S					10.8	C	C
	34				12.0	C,L,S	C,L
P	58	,,	100		.9	C	C,L
P	76	,,	100		.1	C	C
P	35	,,	71		7.3	C	C
P		,,	81		.4	C	C
P	10	,,	26		1.3	C	C
P	34				.7		
P	54	,,	57		1.3	C	C
	76				6.6	C,L,S	C,L
S	88	,,	87		1.8	C	C,L
S	70	,,	2		3.6	C	C,L
S	47	,,	71		.7	C	C
S	92	,,	82		.2	C	C
S	46	,,	28		.3	C	C
	58				17.7	C,L,S	C,L
S	59	,,	41		15.0	C	C,L
S	54	,,	97		2.7	C	C,L

Notes to Table 6 on the following page.

169

Cols. 1–3: Based on the *1954 Census of Manufactures*. This code is a variant of the SIC system. Most of the differences between the two represent combinations at the four-digit level (see the *1954 Census of Manufactures*, Vol. II, Pts. 1 and 2, for details).

Col. 4: The ratio of national income originating in each two-digit industry to total national income originating in manufacturing, as computed from Table 13 in the *Survey of Current Business*, July 1957.

Col. 5: The ratio of value added of each four-digit industry to the value added of the corresponding two-digit industry, computed from data in the *1954 Census of Manufactures*. Since national income data are not available below the two-digit level, these ratios are used as an approximation thereto.

Col. 6: The 1954 value of primary products, wherever made, for which quantity data are available on a comparable basis in 1947 and 1954, divided by the 1954 value of shipments for all primary products wherever made. The two-digit and three-digit totals are weighted by value added.

Col. 7: The value of primary products, wherever made, for which quantity data are available in 1954, divided by the 1954 value of shipments for all primary products, wherever made. This ratio indicates the amount of quantity data available in 1954 for those industries for which the benchmark ratio is less than 50 per cent.

Col. 8: Ratio of an industry's shipments of its primary products to its shipments of all products.

Col. 9: Ratio of an industry's shipments of its primary products to the value of shipments of these products, wherever made.

Col. 10: Legend indicates form of data available and frequency of availability: production (P), consumption (C), shipments (S), annually (A), quarterly (Q), monthly (M). Data are from *Facts for Industry* and other sources, a complete list of which is available separately.

Col. 11: Ratio of the value of products for which quantity data were currently available to the total value of industry shipments as of 1947.

Col. 12: Legend indicates that the data are available in the form of production (P) or shipments (S), the latter requiring adjustment for inventory change to obtain production.

Col. 13: The proportion of the total value of materials consumed by each industry for which some commodity distribution data are available. Computed from data in Table 7, *1954 Census of Manufactures*, Vol. II, Industry Statistics. The base of the ratio does not include fuels which are available for most industries. Contract services are also omitted.

Col. 14: WPI is the Wholesale Price Index, CPI, the Consumer Price Index.

Col. 15: Ratio of the value of each industry's primary products, wherever made, which are directly priced, to total in 1947. Asterisk indicates lack of comparability between the 1947 and 1954 industry classifications.

Col. 16: Ratio of total employment in an industry to total employment in manufacturing.

Col. 17: Ratio of employment in each four-digit industry to employment in the corresponding two-digit industry.

Col. 18: Legend indicates that data are available from one or more of the following sources: Census Bureau, *Census of Manufactures* (C), Bureau of Labor Statistics, *Employment and Earnings* (L), Bureau of Employment Security, *Employment and Wages* (S).

Col. 19: Legend indicates that data are available from the Census Bureau (C) and/or the Bureau of Labor Statistics (L), in the same publications, as above.

---

lacking or weak in benchmark data is presented in Table 7. In order to describe the extent of lack of data briefly and quantitatively, the material was summarized on a two- and three-digit basis and an arbitrary standard of 50 per cent or less was adopted to indicate poor coverage.

TABLE 7

Summary of Gaps in Data for Manufacturing Industries

		THREE-DIGIT INDUSTRIES WITH DATA COVERING LESS THAN 50 PER CENT OF THE INDUSTRY								
		Kind of Data								
		Quantity[a]			Price[b]			Materials Consumed[c]		
INDUSTRY	SIC CODE	Number of Industries	3-Digit Code	Per Cent of 2-Digit Value Added	Number of Industries	3-Digit Code	Per Cent of 2-Digit Shipments	Number of Industries	3-Digit Code	Per Cent of 2-Digit Materials Consumed
Total Manufacturing		72			84			102		
Nondurables		24			35			49		
Food	20	1	203	$\frac{10}{10}$	3	202 204 207	$\frac{32}{17}$ 12 4	4	203 207 208 209	$\frac{29}{8}$ 3 6 12
Tobacco	21	3	212 213 214	$\frac{31}{17}$ 8 7	1	214	$\frac{33}{}$	4	211[d] 212[d] 213[d] 214[d]	$\frac{100}{44}$ 8 4 45

[a] Coverage is defined as the value of "Q" items divided by value of "Q+N" items as established by the Census-FRB Benchmark Project.

[b] Coverage is defined as the value of shipments of "directly priced" items divided by total wherever made shipments.

[c] Coverage is defined as the value of materials identifiable by commodity divided by total materials, parts, containers, and supplies of the industry.

[d] Totals may not add because of rounding.

TABLE 7 (continued)

THREE-DIGIT INDUSTRIES WITH DATA COVERING LESS THAN 50 PER CENT OF THE INDUSTRY

INDUSTRY	SIC CODE	Quantity[a]			Price[b]			Materials Consumed[c]		
		Number of Industries	3-Digit Code	Per Cent of 2-Digit Value Added	Number of Industries	3-Digit Code	Per Cent of 2-Digit Shipments	Number of Industries	3-Digit Code	Per Cent of 2-Digit Materials Consumed
Textiles	22	1	227	8 / 8	3	224, 226[d], 228	12 / 2, 9, 1	6	221[d], 222[d], 223[d], 226[d], 228, 229	75 / 12, 13, 34, 1, 7, 7
Apparel	23	2	237[d], 239	14 / 2, 12	3	236, 238, 239	25 / 6, 5, 14	9	231[d], 232[d], 233[d], 234[d], 235[d], 236[d], 237[d], 238[d], 239[d]	100 / 9, 21, 28, 10, 1, 6, 3, 5, 18
Paper and pulp	26	—		—	5	261, 264, 265[d], 267, 269	94 / 51, 6, 2, 21, 15	—		—

TABLE 7 (continued)

THREE-DIGIT INDUSTRIES WITH DATA COVERING LESS THAN 50 PER CENT OF THE INDUSTRY

		Kind of Data								
		Quantity[a]			Price[b]			Materials Consumed[c]		
INDUSTRY	SIC CODE	Number of Industries	3-Digit Code	Per Cent of 2-Digit Value Added	Number of Industries	3-Digit Code	Per Cent of 2-Digit Shipments	Number of Industries	3-Digit Code	Per Cent of 2-Digit Materials Consumed
Printing and publishing	27	7		53	9		100	3		8
			273d	9		271d	32		274	2
			274d	2		272d	15		278	3
			275d	22		273d	9		279d	2
			276d	9		274d	2			
			277d	2		275d	23			
			278d	3		276d	10			
			279d	6		277d	2			
						278d	3			
						279d	5			
Chemicals	28	5		78	4		57	8		93
			281d	15		281	13		281	8
			282	34		282	33		282	31
			283d	14		286	1		283	7
			287d	3		289	11		284	8
			289	12					285d	11
									286	1
									288d	18
									289	9

[a] Coverage is defined as the value of "Q" items divided by value of "Q+N" items as established by the Census-FRB Benchmark Project.

[b] Coverage is defined as the value of shipments of "directly priced" items divided by total wherever made shipments.

[c] Coverage is defined as the value of materials identifiable by commodity divided by total materials, parts, containers, and supplies of the industry.

[d] Totals may not add because of rounding.

TABLE 7 (continued)

THREE-DIGIT INDUSTRIES WITH DATA COVERING LESS THAN 50 PER CENT OF THE INDUSTRY

		Kind of Data								
		Quantity[a]			Price[b]			Materials Consumed[c]		
INDUSTRY	SIC CODE	Number of Industries	3-Digit Code	Per Cent of 2-Digit Value Added	Number of Industries	3-Digit Code	Per Cent of 2-Digit Shipments	Number of Industries	3-Digit Code	Per Cent of 2-Digit Materials Consumed
Petroleum and coal products	29	1	299	4 4	2	295 299[d]	6 4 2	2	295	4 3 1
Rubber	30	—		—	1	309	45 45	4	301 302 303 } 309 }	100 55 3 41
Leather	31	3	312[d] 314 319	64 2 60 2	3	316 317 319[d]	14	8	311[d] 312[d] 313[d] 314[d] 315[d] 316[d] 317[d] 319[d]	100 23 2 9 52 1 5 7 1

[a] Coverage is defined as the value of "Q" items divided by the value of "Q+N" items as established by the Census-FRB Benchmark Project.

[b] Coverage is defined as the value of shipments of "directly priced" items divided by total wherever made shipments.

TABLE 7 (continued)

THREE-DIGIT INDUSTRIES WITH DATA COVERING LESS THAN 50 PER CENT OF THE INDUSTRY

		Kind of Data								
		Quantity[a]			Price[b]			Materials Consumed[c]		
INDUSTRY	SIC CODE	Number of Industries	3-Digit Code	Per Cent of 2-Digit Value Added	Number of Industries	3-Digit Code	Per Cent of 2-Digit Shipments	Number of Industries	3-Digit Code	Per Cent of 2-Digit Materials Consumed
Durables		48								
Lumber	24	4	241[d] 243 244 249	50 12 22 7 9	3	241[d] 244[d] 249[d]	26 11 7 9	—		—
Furniture	25	5	252[d] 253[d] 254[d] 256 259[d]	32 8 6 12 6 1	5	251 253[d] 254[d] 256[d] 259[d]	94 —	5	252 253 254 256 259	28 5 5 9 8 1
Stone clay and glass	32	5	322 323 326 328[d] 329	50 18 5 7 3 17	3	322 326 328[d] 329	45 17 6 3 19	9	321 322 323 324[d] 325[d] 326[d] 327[d] 328[d] 329	100 5 16 9 8 5 5 26 3 24

c Coverage is defined as the value of materials identifiable by commodity divided by total materials, parts, containers, and supplies of the industry.

d Totals may not add because of rounding.

TABLE 7 (continued)

THREE-DIGIT INDUSTRIES WITH DATA COVERING LESS THAN 50 PER CENT OF THE INDUSTRY

INDUSTRY	SIC CODE	Quantity[a]			Price[b]			Materials Consumed[c]		
		Number of Industries	3-Digit Code	Per Cent of 2-Digit Value Added	Number of Industries	3-Digit Code	Per Cent of 2-Digit Shipments	Number of Industries	3-Digit Code	Per Cent of 2-Digit Materials Consumed
Primary metals	33	2	333, 339	19 / 7, 13	1	336[d]	4 / 4	1	339	12 / 12
Fab. metal products	34	5	342, 344, 346[d], 347[d], 349	77 / 14, 29, 16, 4, 14	5	342, 344, 347, 348, 349	65 / 12, 30, 4, 5, 13	3	342, 343, 347	25 / 10, 11, 5
Machinery (except electric)	35	8	351, 353, 354, 355, 356, 357, 358, 359	92	8	351, 352, 354, 355[d], 356, 357, 358, 359	92 / 6, 11, 16, 9, 15, 5, 16, 14	9	351, 352, 353, 354, 355, 356, 357, 358, 359	100 / 7, 14, 8, 11, 8, 15, 4, 21, 12

TABLE 7 (continued)

THREE-DIGIT INDUSTRIES WITH DATA COVERING LESS THAN 50 PER CENT OF THE INDUSTRY

INDUSTRY	SIC CODE	Quantity[a]			Price[b]			Materials Consumed[c]		
		Number of Industries	3-Digit Code	Per Cent of 2-Digit Value Added	Number of Industries	3-Digit Code	Per Cent of 2-Digit Shipments	Number of Industries	3-Digit Code	Per Cent of 2-Digit Materials Consumed
Electrical machinery	36	4		87	5		95	6		96
			361	38		361	34		361	30
			363d	2		362	6		362	6
			366	43		363	2		364	4
			369	4		364d	5		365d	2
						365	2		366	48
						366	45		367	6
Transportation equipment	37	3		51	5		40	6		100
			372d	45		372d	33		371	71
			373d	6		373d	3		372	24
			379d	1		374	3		373	2
						375d	0		374	2
						379d	0		375	—
									379d	—

a Coverage is defined as the value of "Q" items divided by the value of "Q+N" items as established by the Census-FRB Benchmark Project.

b Coverage is defined as the value of shipments of "directly priced" items divided by total wherever made shipments.

c Coverage is defined as the value of materials identifiable by commodity divided by total materials, parts, containers, and supplies of the industry.

d Totals may not add because of rounding.

TABLE 7 (concluded)

THREE-DIGIT INDUSTRIES WITH DATA COVERING LESS THAN 50 PER CENT OF THE INDUSTRY

INDUSTRY	SIC CODE	Quantity[a]			Price[b]			Materials Consumed[c]		
		Number of Industries	3-Digit Code	Per Cent of 2-Digit Value Added	Number of Industries	3-Digit Code	Per Cent of 2-Digit Shipments	Number of Industries	3-Digit Code	Per Cent of 2-Digit Materials Consumed
Inst. and related	38	4		59	6		86	7		100
			381[d]	17		381[d]	17		381	18
			382[d]	26		382[d]	24		382	21
			383[d]	4		383[d]	3		383[d]	2
			384[d]	13		385[d]	5		384[d]	17
						386[d]	26		385[d]	4
						387	11		386	25
									387	14
Misc. Mfg.	39	8		61	8		93	8		74
			391[d]	7		391	11		391	11
			393	2		393	3		393[d]	3
			394	11		394	18		394[d]	18
			395	4		396	11		395[d]	6
			396	7		397[d]	24		396	10
			397[d]	13		398	12		398	13
			398	7		399	14		399[d]	13
			399[d]	9						

[a] Coverage is defined as the value of "Q" items divided by value of "Q+N" items as established by the Census-FRB Benchmark Project.

[b] Coverage is defined as the value of shipments of "directly priced" items divided by total wherever made shipments.

[c] Coverage is defined as the value of materials identifiable by commodity divided by total materials, parts, containers, and supplies of the industry.

[d] Totals may not add because of rounding.

For periods other than benchmark data on value of production, shipments, inventories, materials consumed, employment, and man-hours are available from the Annual Survey of Manufactures for the same industries as in the Census of Manufactures. Where the standard error of a survey estimate is considered too large or the estimates otherwise fail to meet a general consistency review, the data are not published. Such cases are limited in number and vary from year to year. Moreover, the data are generally made available upon request.

The availability and coverage of the Wholesale Price Index is the same on a monthly basis as on an annual basis. The same is true of the BLS employment and man-hour estimates.

The situation is different with regard to quantity data. Of the 446 Census four-digit industries, quantity data are available for only 151. Table 6, columns 10 and 11, indicates the characteristics and frequency of nonbenchmark data.

AGRICULTURE

Only the crop and livestock output of farms is included here. Agricultural services and forestry are included in other sectors.

Output. The quinquennial Census of Agriculture provides the benchmark data for constructing gross output measures. The data available include acreage, yield, and production of crops, and the inventory number of livestock.

For intercensal years, quantity and value data are available from a variety of sources within the Department of Agriculture. *Agriculture Handbook No. 118*, published during 1956, lists seventy-six separate statistical reports, each dealing with some phase of farm commodity activity.[10] The data are based upon sample estimates which are checked against a number of other sources such as State Farm Censuses. The estimates range from semi-monthly to annual, depending on the importance of the commodity. They are generally available for states, areas, and for the United States.

The net output of farms is defined as the sum of cash receipts from farm marketings, the value of home consumption, the rental value of farm dwellings, and government payments, less the value of purchased intermediate products consumed. Data for these estimates are available in the *Farm Income Situation* published monthly and summarized annually by the Agricultural Research Service of the Department of Agriculture. Coverage is complete. The ARS estimates have been rearranged to accord with national accounting definitions by the

[10] Major Statistical Series of the U.S. Department of Agriculture, Vol. 8, 1956, pp. 10–11.

OBE to obtain farm national product and income, now published regularly.

Prices. Two indexes of farm prices are published monthly by the Department of Agriculture in the Agricultural Marketing Service report, *Agricultural Prices.* These are the "Index of Prices Received by Farmers" and the "Index of Prices Paid by Farmers." The former is linked from two base weighted indexes of "average" prices received by farmers and measured at the first point of sale out of the farmer's hand. It covers fifty-two farm commodities which account for more than 90 per cent of total farm output.

The Index of Prices Paid by Farmers (the "parity index") measures the average change in the prices of a representative selection of commodities and services generally bought by farmers, along with interest, taxes, and wage rates. The basic information is collected primarily by direct mail from dealers who service farm communities. For some larger items, such as automobiles, the personal interview method is used. Three hundred forty-four commodities were included in the revised index of 1953. In general, these commodities account for at least one-half of the total expenditure for a major commodity group, such as food and tobacco. Data are not available to determine coverage as a per cent of total expenditure for all commodities.

Employment and Hours. The labor input data of farms is described in detail in the first part of this report.

MINING

Table 8 sets forth data available on mining. Since benchmark data from the *1954 Census of Mineral Industries* are available on value of output, materials consumed, and employment and man-hours for virtually all industry classifications, only the availability of quantity data is noted under this heading.

TABLE 8
Productivity Data for Mining Industries

2-Digit (1)	3-Digit (2)	4-Digit (3)	2-Digit (4)	3-4-Digit (5)	Quantity Benchmark[a] (6)	Quantity and Value Non-benchmark (7)	(8)	BES[d] (9)	BLS (10)	BM (11)
		Industry Code		Relative Importance		Output	Price Indexes Coverage[b]	Employment and Man-hours (Nonbenchmark)[c]		
10			15.0	100.0						
	101	1011		40.5	P,S	X	100.0	X	X	X
	102	1021		31.1	P	X		X	X	X
	103			10.0				X	X	X
		1032		.3	P	X				
		1033		.7	P	X				
		1034		9.0	P					
	104			3.3		X		X		
		1042		2.0	P[e]	X				
		1043		.3	P,S	X				X
		1044		1.0	P	X				
	105	1051		1.2	P	X	(100.0)	X		
	106			10.0				X		
		1062		1.7	P	X				X
		1064		3.8	P	X				X
		1063⎫ 1069⎭		4.5		X				X
	108	1081		2.5						
	109			1.4				X		
		1092		.3	P	X				
		1093		1.0		X				
		1094								X
		1099		.1		X				
11			3.3	100.0				X		
	111			100.0					X	X
		1111		84.9	P	X	100.0			
		1112		14.8						
		1113		.3						
12			23.5	100.0						
	121			100.0			100.0	X	X	X
		1211		98.4	P	X		X		
		1212		.7	P	X		X		
		1213		.9						
13			44.5	100.0				X		
	131			79.9			100.0	X	X	X
		1312		74.8	S	X		X		
		1313		5.1	P	X				
		1314			P,S	X				
13										
		1315			P,S	X				
	133			14.6				X		
		1331		8.1						
		1332		.1						
		1339		6.3						
14			13.7	100.0				X	X	
	141			1.3		X		X		

(TABLE 8 concluded)

Industry Code			Relative Importance		Output		Price Indexes Coverage[b]	Employment and Man-Hours (Nonbenchmark)[c]		
2-Digit (1)	3-Digit (2)	4-Digit (3)	2-Digit (4)	3-4-Digit (5)	Quantity Benchmark[a] (6)	Quantity and Value Non-benchmark (7)	(8)	BES[d] (9)	BLS (10)	BM (11)
		1412		.2	S	X				
		1413		.4	S	X				
		1415		.2	S	X				
		1417		.4	S	X				
		1416} 1419}		.1	S	X				
	142			28.5			50.6	X		g
		1422		20.1	S	X		X		
		1423		1.9	S	X				
		1424		.4	S	X				
		1425		.3	S	X				
		1426		2.9	S	X				
		1427		1.9	S	X				
		1429		.9	S					
	144			30.2						
		1441		30.2	S	X	66.4	X		
	145			6.6		X		X		
		1452		1.4	*S	X				
		1453		1.5	*S	X				
		1454		.4	*S	X				
		1455		2.1	*S	X				
		1456		.3	*S	X				
		1457		.1	*S	X				
		1459		.8	*S					
	146			.4	P					
		1462			P	X				
		1469		.4	P	X				
	147			28.8						
		1472		1.2	*S	X				X
		1473		1.3	*S	X				X
		1474		.8	*S	X				X
		1475		7.0	*S	X	100.0			X
		1476		5.3	*S	X	(100.0)			X
		1477		2.5	*S	X	100.0			X
		1479		10.5						
14	148			.4						
		1481		.4						
	149			3.8				X		
		1492			P	X		X		
		1493		.5	P	X				
		1494		.3	P	X				
		1495		.4	P	X				
		1496		.2	P	X				X
		1497		.2		X				
		1498		.8	P	X				
		1499		1.4						

Notes to Table 8 on following page.

a Benchmark (Census of Minerals Industries) data on the value of shipments are available for all three-digit industries and all four-digit industries except 1094. Such data generally represent the gross value of primary and secondary minerals physically transferred, contract work done, and the value of products purchased and resold without further processing. Some duplication is present but where it is significant, a net shipments figure is published.

Benchmark data on value added are similarly available except for industries 1094, 1314, and 1315. Value added here represents the sum of the value of shipments and capital expenditures less the sum of intermediate products consumed and purchased machinery. This definition differs from that used in manufacturing in that it includes the difference between capital expenditures and purchased machinery.

Benchmark data are similarly available on supplies (including the cost of products purchased wholly for resale), fuel, and energy, except for industries 146 and 1462.

b Coverage ratios apply to both benchmark and nonbenchmark periods.

c Benchmark data on production and development employees, all other employees, and working and total proprietors are available for all three- and four-digit industries with the exception that "other employees" are not available for industry 1462. Man-hours of production and development employees who were at the establishment are available for all three- and four-digit industries.

d Employment data only.

e Production defined as the quantity of placer materials washed.

f Gold and silver, other than placer gold, combined.

g No separation of "dimension" stone or "crushed and broken" stone.

Cols. 1–3: Based on the SIC system.

Col. 4: Ratio of national income originating in each two-digit industry to total national income originating in mining, as computed from Table 13 in *Survey of Current Business*, July 1957.

Col. 5: Ratio of value added of each four-digit industry to the value added of the corresponding two-digit industry. Data are derived from the *1954 Census of Mineral Industries*.

Col. 6: Legend indicates whether the data are in units of production (P) or shipments (S). When preceded by an asterisk, "S" refers to net shipments. Source is the *1954 Census of Mineral Industries*.

Col. 7: Derived from the regular Commodity Canvasses of the Bureau of Mines and published in the *Minerals Yearbook*. Data are on a wherever-made basis. Production data are also obtained by the Bureau of Mines from the Accident Analysis Canvasses. These data are not published but are generally available upon request.

Col. 8: Portion of the value of each industry's primary products, wherever made, which are directly priced. Parentheses indicate that the data represent the average value of output from the *Minerals Yearbook*. Otherwise, the source is the BLS Wholesale Price Index.

Col. 9: Bureau of Employment Security data published quarterly in *Employment and Wages*. Included are the total number of wage-earners employed by firms subject to unemployment insurance payments.

Col. 10: BLS data published monthly in *Employment and Earnings*. For a full description, see Part I, section on nonfarm employment.

Col. 11: Bureau of Mines data derived from the Accident Analysis Canvasses and published periodically in Information Circulars and in Mineral Industry Surveys. Employment refers to workers engaged in production, development, maintenance and repair work, supervisory and technical personnel, and office workers.

183

Noncommodity Sectors

SERVICES

Table 9 provides information about the sources and extent of the data available for the construction of productivity measures in this area. The entire table is not published but is available upon request. The major gaps in this area consist of current value data for households and nonprofit institutions, cost of materials and purchased services for all sectors, price indexes for certain consumer services, price indexes for business services, and employment and man-hours in at least two-digit detail.

TABLE 9

Productivity Data for the Services Sector

Industry Code			Relative Importance		Output (Receipts)		Price Index	Employment			Man-hours
2-Digit (1)	3-Digit (2)	4-Digit (3)	2-Digit (4)	3-4-Digit (5)	Census (Bench-mark) (6)	IRS (Annual) (7)	CPI (8)	Census (9)	BLS (10)	BES (11)	(12)
70			6.8			X			X		
	701			(90.3)				X		X	
		7011		87.7	X			X			a
		7012		2.6	X			X			
	702	702(1)								X	
	703			(9.7)				X		X	
		7031		8.6	X			X			
		7032		1.1	X			X			
	704									X	
		7041									
		7042									
72			13.9			X					b
	721			(39.0)		Xc	X	X	X	X	a
		7211		28.5	X			X			
		7212		.9	X			X			
		7213		5.4	X			X			
		7214		.6	X			X			
		7291		.9	X			X			
	722			27.7		Xc	X	X	X	X	a
		7221		27.0	X			X			
		7222		.7	X			X			
	723			(3.4)	X	X		X		X	
		7231									
		7232									
	724			(18.4)		X		X		X	
		7241		7.1	X		X	X			
		7242		10.8	X		X	X			
		7243		.6	X			X			
	725	725(1)		1.7	X		X	X		X	
	726			4.7	X	X		X		X	
		7262									
		7263									

Notes to Table 9 on the following page.

ᵃ BLS publishes estimates for the entire services and miscellaneous group and a few component industries.

ᵇ Unpublished estimates of average weekly hours worked from the Current Population Survey may be obtained from the Census.

ᶜ 721 and 722 combined.

Cols. 1–3: Based on the 1945 SIC. This classification does not always coincide with the system used in the sources but differences have been reconciled wherever possible.

Col. 4: The ratio of national income originating in each two-digit industry to the total national income of the services sector, as given in Table 13, *Survey of Current Business*, July 1955.

Col. 5: Ratio of employment (full workweek) in those three- and four-digit industries for which such data are available in the *Census of Business* to employment in the corresponding two-digit industry. Employment in noncensus industries is not available on a four-digit basis. Value added figures are not available below the two-digit level.

Col. 6: *1954 Census of Business.*

Col. 7: Gross receipts of proprietorships, partnerships, and corporations are available in the Internal Revenue Service publication, *Business Indicators, 1956–57.* These data are to be published annually on a fiscal year basis. Since the classification system is not specified, there may be inconsistencies in the content of the groups which are not recognizable from the industry names. Less than annual output data are not available.

Col. 8: An entry here indicates that some form of this service is represented by an industry in the BLS, Consumer Price Index. These item indexes are calculated quarterly only. There are no indexes for the business services component.

Col. 9: *1954 Census of Business.*

Col. 10: BLS in *Employment and Earnings* provides an estimate of employment for the total services and miscellaneous sector plus four component industries which account for about 10 per cent of employment in the sector. The BLS sector also includes a few industries not part of the SIC sector.

Col. 11: BES, *Employment and Wages*, quarterly.

CONSTRUCTION

(SIC 15–17, relative importance 6 per cent of total private national income).

OUTPUT. Defined as the value of work put in place. There is no quantity measure that adequately covers all of the components of the industry. Available are data on new construction, including the value of major additions and alterations, and force account construction (BLS and the Business and Defense Services Administration jointly—monthly); also, estimates including the value of maintenance and repairs (BDSA—annually). These estimates are based on mixed sources of varying degrees of adequacy. Particularly important is the lack of a reliable basis for estimating the value of alterations and repairs to structures. It is estimated that at least 20 per cent of the total value of new construction as now computed is based largely on judgment. When particular adjustments are made, such as the allocation of work completed to certain time periods, or the inclusion of an allowance for undercoverage and underestimation in the source data, this ratio is even higher. Both agencies responsible for the current estimates have made numerous suggestions for improvement.

PRICE INDEX. None. The constant dollar value of output series published by the BDSA is derived through the use of a cost index. This index is inappropriate as a price deflator and statistically unreliable in several respects.

EMPLOYMENT. Contract construction with some three-digit breakdown (BLS—monthly). Contract construction by three-digit groups (BES). These estimates are not consistent with the output estimates in that the former includes only contract construction while the latter includes contract and force account construction. Also, unlike the constant dollar output series, the employment figures include maintenance and repairs.

MAN-HOURS. Contract construction, average weekly hours of non-supervisory employees (BLS).

MATERIALS CONSUMED. There is no over-all estimate but scattered data are available for a few segments of the industry.

TRANSPORTATION

Railroads—SIC 40, relative importance 45 per cent (here and in the following cases, the reference is to the proportion of sector income originating in a given industry).

OUTPUT. Ton miles and passenger miles for Class I, II, and III roads (ICC—monthly). These items account for about 94 per cent of total revenue. Also available, total revenue of Class I, II, and III roads with breakdown by type of revenue (ICC—monthly). Note: ICC data published in *Transport Statistics, Part I*, unless otherwise specified.

PRICE INDEXES. Annual freight carload traffic rate index based on 1 per cent way-bill sample (ICC Statement R1-1). Such carload traffic accounts for 97 per cent of freight revenue. Also available, railroad passenger fares, coach (CPI—quarterly).

EMPLOYMENT. All employees, by class of work—executive, professional and clerical, maintenance and transportation (ICC—monthly).

MAN-HOURS. Class I roads—total time paid for, service hours including stand-by and held-over time (ICC).

MATERIALS CONSUMED. Quantity and value of fuel and power, Class I carriers (ICC—monthly). Value is about 20 per cent of operating expense less wages and depreciation. Total of other materials may be approximated from total expenses as shown by subtracting wages, taxes, etc.

186

TRANSPORTATION

(Local railways and buslines—SIC 41, relative importance 10 per cent.)

OUTPUT. Total and revenue passengers carried by type of transit (passenger miles not available). Also, operating revenue by type of transit and passenger revenue. The American Transit Association (ATA) provides monthly and annual data based on reports from companies representing 80–90 per cent of the industry.

PRICE INDEXES. Streetcar and bus fares (CPI—quarterly). Fares, average cash rate (ATA—monthly).

EMPLOYMENT. Group as a whole (BLS); three-digit groups (BES); by type of transit (ATA).

MAN-HOURS. Average weekly hours for the industry as a whole (BLS).

MATERIALS CONSUMED. Breakdown of operating materials constituting 50 per cent of total expenditures for materials, including maintenance items.

TRANSPORTATION

(Trucking and warehousing—SIC 42, relative importance 27 per cent; trucking, local and long distance— SIC 421.)

OUTPUT. Local ton miles not available. Total intercity ton miles (ICC-annual estimate based on sample data from the Bureau of Public Roads). This estimate includes ton miles of private trucks which are not in this industry. Intercity ton miles are reported annually to the ICC by carriers whose revenue accounts for about 70 per cent of the total intercity revenue of regulated carriers. Tons of freight carried by Class I intercity carriers (ICC—quarterly). Total revenue and revenue of unregulated carriers (largely local and exempt) not available. Unregulated carriers were estimated to account for 40 per cent of total industry revenue in 1947 (see Interindustry report). Only the revenue of Class I regulated carriers is compiled, although all Classes report quarterly. Class I revenue is estimated to be 80 per cent of the total of Classes I, II, and III.

PRICE INDEX. None.

EMPLOYMENT. Including warehousing (BLS); Class I carriers only, although all file (ICC); by three-digit industry group (BES— quarterly).

MAN-HOURS. BLS—not available. ICC—some reported but not compiled.

187

MATERIALS CONSUMED. Motor oil and fuel, tires and tubes for regulated carriers.

TRANSPORTATION

(Trucking and warehousing, warehousing and storage—
SIC 422–429.)

OUTPUT. By three-digit industry (BES); as part of the combined estimate for trucking and warehousing (BLS). There are no satisfactory data, either annual or less than annual, for industries which include farm product storage, refrigerated warehousing, footlockers, household goods warehousing, and special and general warehousing. While scattered data on quantities of commodities stored are published, such figures do not take into account the storage period and thus do not completely reflect the output of the industry.

TRANSPORTATION

(Highway transportation n.e.c.—SIC 43.)

OUTPUT. Intercity bus passenger miles (ICC). Estimate is based on passenger miles reported by Class I carriers plus additional data gathered from the Bureau of Public Roads and special studies. Carriers reporting miles constitute about 60 per cent of total industry based on operating revenue.

Bus miles and passengers carried by long haul and short haul carriers are reported in McGraw-Hill's publication *Bus Transportation* but use of these would not take account of change in length of trip within these categories. Data on school bus operation are compiled by the Department of Health, Education, and Welfare.

Operating revenues for long and short haul bus operators (McGraw-Hill, *Bus Transportation*). Operating revenue of Class I carriers (ICC Statement Q-750—quarterly). Revenue of Class II and III carriers reported but not published.

PRICE INDEX. None.

EMPLOYMENT. Buslines, except local only (BLS—monthly); buslines, except local (*Bus Transportation*—annually); Class I carriers only, though others report (ICC); by three-digit industry for the total sector (BES—quarterly).

MAN-HOURS. Class I, total hours paid, by hourly employees (ICC).

MATERIALS CONSUMED. Specified items which can be deflated constitute about 30 per cent of operating expenses less compensation and depreciation. These are available for Class I Intercity buses only (ICC—annually).

188

TRANSPORTATION

(Water transportation—SIC 44, relative importance 6
per cent; ocean-borne foreign transportation—SIC 441.)

OUTPUT. Tons of exports and imports, dry cargo and tanker, carried by United States operated (U.S. and foreign flag) vessels (OBE, on the basis of Census data—quarterly). These data do not take account of changes in length of haul, or commodity shifts within the dry cargo category. Additional data, including detailed commodity statistics by trade area and flag of vessel (Census Bureau—monthly, and the Department of the Army, Corps of Engineers). Ton miles are not available.

Number of passengers arriving at and departing from the United States, by flag of vessel and travel area (Department of Justice, Immigration and Naturalization—on a fiscal year basis). Passenger miles, not available.

There are no reported total revenue data for the industry as a whole. Carriers belonging to conference groups file financial reports with the Maritime Commission. It has been estimated that these carriers carried 70 per cent of the total revenue freight in 1947. However, the sample appears to be biased in favor of freight carriers.

Ocean freight revenue of United States carriers (U.S. and foreign flag ships: OBE—quarterly). These estimates are made on the basis of a questionnaire (Form BE-30) sent to United States operators. Response varies for the different types of operators but is estimated at between 50 and 60 per cent of the total. Also available, passenger revenue (OBE—quarterly, on the basis of passenger data described above). Average fares and shipboard expenditures are obtained from questionnaires given to arriving and departing passengers.

PRICE INDEX. Certain freight rates, so-called conference rates, and others, must be filed with the Maritime Administration. While a coverage ratio cannot be computed, the MA feels that the filed rates cover a substantial portion of the freight carried by United States carriers.

EMPLOYMENT. As part of "Other transportation and services" (BLS—monthly); for this industry (BES).

MAN-HOURS. None.

MATERIALS CONSUMED. None.

TRANSPORTATION

(Water transportation other than ocean: coastwise—
SIC 442; Great Lakes—SIC 443; inland waterways—
SIC 444.)

OUTPUT. Tons of freight by commodity and area (Dept. of the

189

Army, Corps of Engineers, *Waterborne Commerce of the U.S.*— annually). Tons of freight reported quarterly to the ICC by Class A, B, and C carriers constitute only 12 per cent of the total, since bulk carriers and private carriers are not subject to regulation. Number of passengers carried reported quarterly to the ICC by carriers accounting for about 85 per cent of passenger revenue. Passenger miles are available only for domestic waterways, published in ICC statement No. 580. Total revenue, not available.

PRICE INDEX. Revenue per ton by commodity and area of trade may be computed from ICC data but these data are not representative of exempt bulk carriers of commodities such as coal, iron ore, petroleum products, and wheat.

EMPLOYMENT. As part of estimate for "other transportation and services" (BLS); by three-digit group (BES); large regulated carriers only (ICC).

MAN-HOURS. None.

MATERIALS CONSUMED. Consumption of fuel by Class A and B carriers (ICC). More detailed expense items are reported but not compiled.

TRANSPORTATION

(Air Transportation, common carrier—SIC 451, relative importance 5 per cent. This industry consists of carriers subject to Civil Aeronautics Board regulation.)

OUTPUT. Passenger miles, ton miles of freight, express and mail for domestic and international operations (CAB, *Air Carrier Traffic Statistics*—monthly and annual reports). Also, revenues by type of carrier and class of revenue (*Air Carrier Financial Statistics*— quarterly reports).

PRICE INDEX. None.

EMPLOYMENT. Air transportation, common carrier (BLS); air transportation (BES).

MAN-HOURS. None.

MATERIALS CONSUMED. Fuel reported to the CAB.

COMMUNICATIONS AND PUBLIC UTILITIES

(Telecommunications—SIC 48, relative importance 41 per cent; telephone—SIC 481.)

OUTPUT. Number of local and toll calls (FCC—monthly). This breakdown, if consistent, would permit taking account of shifts in distance of calls. However, with the continuing enlargement of local calling areas, there is no such consistency and the number of calls inadequately reflects the quantitative output of the industry.

190

Revenues by source are reported to FCC. Revenue from calls accounts for about 90 per cent of total operating revenue.

PRICE INDEX. "Residential telephone services" (CPI—quarterly). Includes sales and excise taxes. Price data for business use, long-distance calls, intrastate or interstate, are not available.

EMPLOYMENT. Monthly (BLS and BES); by class of employee (FCC).

HOURS. Average weekly hours (BLS); scheduled weekly hours (FCC).

MATERIALS CONSUMED. None.

COMMUNICATIONS AND PUBLIC UTILITIES

(Telecommunications; telegraph communication—SIC 482.)

Virtually the entire industry is subject to FCC regulation and required to file annual reports. In addition, the large carriers, representing most of the revenue of the industry, file monthly reports. Annual summaries for the principal carriers, representing over 90 per cent of total revenues, are published in *Statistics of the Communications Industry in the U.S.*

OUTPUT. Number of messages transmitted by the domestic telegraph industry and words transmitted by transoceanic and marine communication facilities are reported. Number of words is the preferable measure but is not available for the domestic telegraph sector which accounts for 80 per cent of message revenue.

TRANSPORTATION

(Oil pipelines—SIC 46, relative importance 2 per cent.)

OUTPUT. Ton miles of all pipelines (ICC, based on reports to that agency and the Bureau of Mines). Barrel mile data by type of pipeline and type of oil which permit the computation of a weighted index are not available. For the regulated sector, barrel miles are reported to the ICC for trunklines but barrels only are reported for gathering lines. Trunklines are responsible for about 70 per cent of the revenues of the industry. These data include the pipeline departments of oil companies. Insofar as they are operated as separate establishments their inclusion is consistent with the employment data. Also available, data on barrels originated and received by large pipelines (ICC quarterly in Statement Q-600).

Revenues are reported quarterly by establishments regulated by the ICC, which account for 85–90 per cent of total revenue of the industry.

PRICE INDEX. None.

191

EMPLOYMENT. As part of "other transportation" (BLS), regulated pipelines (ICC).

MAN-HOURS. None.

MATERIALS CONSUMED. None.

TRANSPORTATION

(Services incidental to transportation—SIC 47, 428, 438, 446, 452, 458, relative importance 6 per cent.)

These industries consist of miscellaneous services such as forwarding and arrangement of transportation and terminal facilities and services associated with freight, passenger, water transportation, and air transportation.

OUTPUT. No current data are available for this group except for some revenues reported to ICC by a minor part of the total.

EMPLOYMENT. As part of "other transportation and services" (BLS); by three-digit group (BES).

HOURS. None.

Revenues of principal carriers by type of revenue are published. All carriers report.

PRICE INDEX. None.

EMPLOYMENT. Monthly (BLS); for principal carriers by class of employee, except officials and assistants (FCC).

HOURS. Domestic employees, excluding messengers, average weekly hours (BLS). Scheduled weekly hours by class of employee (FCC).

MATERIALS CONSUMED. None.

COMMUNICATIONS AND PUBLIC UTILITIES

(Public utilities—SIC 49, relative importance 53 per cent; electric light and power—SIC 491; gas—SIC 492; electric light and gas utilities combined—SIC 493.)

OUTPUT. Kilowatt hours of electric power sold by class of consumer for Class A and B private utilities (Federal Power Commission —monthly and annually). Additional data for public utilities (FPC and the Edison Electric Institute).

Therms of gas by type of gas and class of consumer for all gas utilities, private and public (American Gas Association, *Gas Facts*). The public portion is estimated to be 4 per cent of the total. Comparable revenues are available from the same sources.

PRICE INDEX. BLS, in connection with the Consumer Price Index publishes a monthly price index for two items of electricity, and price indexes for gas for space heating and for other uses. Wholesale price indexes are available for two classes of electric light and power and one of natural gas.

192

EMPLOYMENT. Total employment in gas and electric utilities (BLS). Employment in the separate activities is not available because many establishments engage in both activities, making it difficult to allocate the employment associated with each. BLS publishes separate estimates for establishments whose output consists solely of gas or electric power, and an estimate for the combination establishments.

An estimate of total gas utility employment, including an estimate for the gas portion of combined establishments (AGA, *Gas Facts*). More intensive analysis of the procedures and classification bases of both series would be required before it could be determined whether an estimate of electric utility employment could be derived by subtraction from the BLS total.

HOURS. Average weekly hours on the same basis as employment (BLS).

MATERIALS CONSUMED. Major items of fuel consumption are summarized for electric power by the FPC and in *Gas Facts* for gas utilities.

COMMUNICATIONS AND PUBLIC UTILITIES

(Public utilities; water supply and sanitary services—
SIC 494, 495, 496, 497.)

OUTPUT. Gross receipts for the group as a whole available beginning 1956–57 (IRS, *Business Indicators*). Less than annual data not available.

PRICE INDEX. Residential water rates (CPI). No price indexes for the remainder.

EMPLOYMENT. For the group as a whole (BLS); for three-digit industries (BES).

HOURS. None.

TRADE

(Wholesale trade—SIC 50–51, relative importance 33
per cent.)

In the *1954 Census of Business*, data are presented for different kinds of wholesale business in accordance with the Standard Industrial Classification. Wholesale trade is treated here as one sector because time limitations preclude a detailed analysis.

Undercoverage within the defined limits of the Census is not significant here.

OUTPUT. Sales by type of operation, kind of business and commodity line (Census). Also available are sales of durables and nondurables (OBE in the *Survey of Current Business*—monthly). The

193

latter estimates represent primarily a blow-up of the estimated monthly sales of merchant wholesalers prepared by the Census Bureau from a sample survey. The Census estimates and standard errors of estimate are published in the monthly *Wholesale Trade Report*. Merchant wholesalers accounted for over 50 per cent of sales and 65 per cent of employment in wholesale trade in 1954. Estimates for other wholesalers are based on less reliable data. Commodity line sales are not collected, which raises problems of deflation since each kind of business may handle a variety of commodities.

Output may also be defined as margin. To determine margins one must have either cost of good sold to deduct from sales, or estimates of operating expense plus profit (the conceptual equivalent). Operating expense is reported for the Census but not profit.

Year end inventories at cost (Census). Monthly inventories (OBE in the *Survey of Current Business*—monthly).

PRICE INDEXES. The WPI is generally a producer's price index and does not reflect the effect of changes in wholesale margins. Commodity gaps in the WPI are indicated under the discussion of manufacturing industries.

EMPLOYMENT. Paid employees and active proprietors of unincorporated businesses, by kind of operation and kind of business (Census). Total wholesale and some three-digit detail but kind of business breakdown not the same as Census (BLS).

MAN-HOURS. Average weekly hours, some three-digit detail (BLS).
MATERIALS CONSUMED. None.

TRADE

(Retail trade—SIC 52–59, relative importance 67 per cent.)

In the *1954 Census of Business*, data are presented by kind of business in accordance with the Standard Industrial Classification. Retail trade is treated here as a unit because of time limitations.

Census of Business data have been historically understated. However, some improvement was made in the 1954 Census as the result of a new system of enumeration designed to obtain data from establishments previously unrecognizable as retail establishments and establishments that were not in operation by the end of the year.

OUTPUT. It is difficult to use Census sales data for deriving an output index by deflation because the value of sales includes sales and excise taxes which have to be removed by an independent estimate. Also commodity line sales are not reported. Classification by kind of business is made on the basis of the major commodity line.

194

Since each kind of business may sell a wide variety of commodities, deflation by a price index restricted to the major commodity line would imply that the price movements of all the commodities sold by that business were the same.

The Monthly Retail Trade Report, published by the Census Bureau, contains estimates of total sales and sales for selected kinds of business, based on sample surveys. It is considered generally adequate for use in intercensal years, but is subject to the same limitations as the Census.

Commonly used indicators of output (such as the volume of goods distributed weighted by constant dollar gross margins) are not completely satisfactory. The output of trade for productivity analyses should reflect the amount of services rendered to customers in the distribution of goods. Weighting by a constant dollar gross margin implies that the quantity of services associated with a particular commodity is constant. The rise in discount houses and self-service establishments suggests a decrease in the amount of service associated with particular groups of commodities, although services in the form of store and location facilities, are steadily increasing.

Since "cost of goods sold" data are not collected for the Census or the survey, it is not possible to compute accurate industry margins.

Inventories were not collected for the 1954 Census. However, monthly inventories are estimated by OBE on the basis of unpublished estimates prepared by the Census Bureau from sample data. The sample has been revised recently to provide a reliable estimate for all retail establishments.

PRICE INDEXES. Many consumer price indexes comparable in name to Census kind of business classifications are available monthly or quarterly from the BLS. These may not be appropriate because of the inconsistency of commodity price indexes for variegated business sales, and the general limitations of CPI prices as described earlier.

Indexes are also available from Department of Agriculture's AMS series on Prices Paid by Farmers but these reflect changes in quality and are not conceptually desirable deflators.

EMPLOYMENT. By kind of store (BLS—monthly); by three-digit group (BES—monthly); paid employees and proprietors (Census).

MAN-HOURS. Average weekly hours of employees; eating and drinking places excluded (BLS—monthly).

MATERIALS CONSUMED. None.

FINANCE, INSURANCE, AND REAL ESTATE

(Banking and other financial institutions; Banking—
SIC 60, relative importance 16 per cent; credit agencies
other than banks—SIC 61, 6 per cent; securities and
commodity brokers, dealers, exchanges—SIC 62,
1 per cent.)

OUTPUT. The problem here is less one of data availability than of defining output to reflect the volume of services performed. There are several indicators which can be used, e.g., number of checks, number of accounts, volume of debits, and the volume of loans and investments. However, no one of these reflects total activity and there are many difficulties involved in developing a suitable weighting system.

In the National Income Accounts and in the BLS interindustry study this sector was considered to consist of financial intermediaries performing an investment function for individuals. Under this definition income from lending activities is received by individuals outside the banking sector and is not part of banking output. For purposes of productivity measurement this concept would not be suitable because output should, among other things, reflect the role of the labor input involved in lending activities.

Once a suitable output indicator is selected it may require deflation and the definition of an appropriate price index presents equally difficult problems.

In general, there is a considerable amount of annual and less than annual data available from agencies such as the Federal Deposit Insurance Corporation, the Federal Reserve Board, and the Securities and Exchange Commission. For personal credit institutions there is no central source of data. For this group and some miscellaneous minor groups, the only over-all data available are from Internal Revenue statistics.

EMPLOYMENT. Separate estimates for groups 60 and 62 (BLS). Note—Group 61 included with real estate.

HOURS. An unpublished estimate of average weekly hours for the whole finance, insurance, and real estate sector is available monthly in the Census Current Population Survey.

FINANCE, INSURANCE, AND REAL ESTATE

[Insurance—SIC 63, relative importance 17 per cent
(including agents and combination offices).]

OUTPUT. Because of the differing nature of their activities, the life insurance sector and the nonlife sector require different measures of output. It is difficult to define the output of the former so as to reflect

196

the volume of services. In the National Income Accounts, claims and premiums are disregarded and output is defined as total expenses. However, since the bulk of insurance operating expenses are wages which in real terms move as labor input does, productivity based on this output measure is by implication constant. Possible alternative measures include the value of insurance in force and the value of premiums collected, both of which are published. But, further clarification of the concepts in this area is necessary before a determination can be made.

In the nonlife sector, investment activity and the resultant income is minor. The services provided may be considered as purely insurance services which are related to premiums and claims. As measured in the input-output study, gross output consisted of total premiums earned. This measure is more closely related to the productive activity of employees. Data concerning premiums and claims by type of insurance are published in *Spectator Yearbook* and *Best's Aggregates and Averages*.

PRICE INDEXES. Automobile and hospitalization insurance (CPI).
EMPLOYMENT. Including agents (BLS); by three-digit groups (BES).
HOURS. Average weekly hours, includes agents (BLS).

FINANCE, INSURANCE, AND REAL ESTATE
(Real estate—SIC 65, relative importance 62 per cent;
real estate operators—SIC 651.)

OUTPUT. Data here, which consist of the value of rents received by real estate owners and lessors, are inadequate. The industry is made up of numerous individuals who do not consider themselves in the real estate business, as well as corporations and individuals who conduct regular real estate operations. The most important source of direct data is income tax returns but gross rents reported to IRS are not tabulated. Even such aggregations would require adjustment for under-coverage resulting from poor recordkeeping or incomplete reporting which, in view of the nature of this industry, is probably significant.

Indirect methods have been used to estimate the missing rents received figures for the nonfarm portion of this sector. The procedure involves resort to a wide variety of sources and the use of fragmentary or obsolete data. Inconsistencies in the data used for extrapolating the number of dwelling units from the Census benchmarks and lack of current average rental values have impeded a satisfactory approximation of the value of nonfarm residential rents. Further complications arise when the value is defined in terms of space rental rather than total rents received or paid. If the output of

197

the industry is taken to include the rental value of owner occupied homes, the limitations of data are intensified.

REAL ESTATE

(Agents, etc., title abstract companies, subdividers, and operation builders—SIC 653–656.)

OUTPUT. No reliable data.

PRICE INDEX. Residential rent (CPI). Nonresidential rent and other sectors not available.

INTERMEDIATE COSTS. Rent-breakdown of costs for individuals is not available. Corporate sector obtained from income tax returns.

EMPLOYMENT. As part of "other finance agencies and real estate" (BLS); by three-digit industry (BES).

MAN-HOURS. None.

The nature of this industry prevents a valid comparison of output and employment (or man-hours) and derivation of a productivity ratio. If output is defined as including an imputation for owner occupied homes, there is no equivalent input factor since there is no way of measuring and reporting the hours spent by owners in managing and maintaining their properties. Even without the imputation, the corresponding labor input is not accounted for. Only a small proportion of rented property is managed and maintained by paid employees whose employment would be reported. The hours spent by owners in managing rented property are not accounted for.

RADIO AND TV BROADCASTING

(SIC 77, relative importance 12 per cent.)

OUTPUT. Revenues of all broadcasters broken down by type of revenue, sale of time and talent (FCC).

PRICE INDEX. None available for the time portion, and price of the talent portion would not be measurable.

EMPLOYMENT AND MAN-HOURS. Employment is reported to the FCC, and is available from the BES.

BLS has no separate estimate for employment or hours.

C O M M E N T

RAYMOND T. BOWMAN, Bureau of the Budget

Leon Greenberg and his colleagues are owed a considerable debt for the painstaking way in which they have catalogued the available data, related it to productivity measurement problems, and highlighted its weaknesses. In the years ahead, it should be possible to use this information to strengthen the basic sources of productivity data and fill in the more important gaps.

There are three guiding principles which must now be evoked more positively in the organization and development of economic data.

1. Data needs must be defined more specifically in terms of clearly recognized analytical purposes.

2. The interrelationships involved in the analysis must be more clearly set forth and the data better integrated for these purposes.

3. Better quality control of data collection processes is needed and more attention must be paid to respondent and interviewer biases. The timing and content of tabulations must better accord with user requirements.

A better understanding of the theoretical and practical aspects of measurement in relation to the uses of the data is also necessary. Only thus can more reliable guides for the improvement of data and the construction of statistical series be secured.

It is important to recognize that productivity measurements cannot in themselves provide all the information economists need to explain wage, price, and output relationships. When made for the economy as a whole, they represent little more than special per capita output series. When such measurements are developed for the several industrial sectors in a manner consistent with the economy's total output, information is added concerning the extent to which the over-all change in unit labor output is associated with shifts in the relative importance of different industries as contrasted with changes intra industry. But even within industries there may be shifts in capital intensity or in scale as well as in technology so that changes in productivity, thus defined, can be variously explained.

When more basic deductions are involved, such as the determination of fundamental relationships between input and output so that functional product shares can be imputed, more difficult problems are encountered. These problems cannot be met by improvements in statistical sources and methodology alone; improvements in theoretical and conceptual formulations are also needed.

PART II

The Estimation of Real Product
in the Economy by Industries

The Estimation of Real Domestic Product by Final Expenditure Categories and by Industry of Origin in Canada

V. R. BERLINGUETTE AND F. H. LEACY
DOMINION BUREAU OF STATISTICS

Introduction

THE PURPOSE of this report is to describe the Canadian experience in developing estimates of real output by the expenditure and the production approaches, that is, the deflation of final products and the measurement of real value added by industry. Although we were guided by the conceptual framework implied by the integration of input-output with the main income and product tables, no attempt was made to present the more sophisticated mathematical treatment of the entire system of prices, quantities, and values in national accounts, as developed by Richard Stone and others.[1] Here we are concerned mainly with the measures of output that constitute the numerators of productivity ratios, and the deflation of the factor inputs which constitute the denominators of these ratios is mentioned only briefly.

Industrial output, deflated final products, and input-output have all been developed in close harmony with the general framework and conventions of the national accounts. Within this framework there are choices of concept and procedure on such subjects as factor costs and market prices, national and domestic product, valuation and deflation problems in nonmarket areas of output, and the classification of industrial components. To some extent these choices are affected by uses to which the results are to be put and section 2 is therefore devoted to a closer examination of uses. Section 3 then examines the general concepts and procedures used in measuring both industrial real output and deflated products, with emphasis on

[1] For a mathematical explanation of the complete system, see Richard Stone, *Quantity and Price Indexes in National Accounts* O.E.E.C. (Paris, 1956). See also, Richard Stone and S. J. Prais, "Systems of Aggregate Index Numbers and Their Compatibility," *Economic Journal*, September 1952 (LXII, 247), p. 565. See also John Kendrick's description of the two output measurements in Volume 22 of this series.

conceptual consistency. Sections 4 and 5 describe the procedures used in each measure in detail, while section 6 brings out some problems that arise as a result of these procedures. The results obtained to date are presented in section 7.

BACKGROUND AND PRESENT STAGE OF DEVELOPMENT

Measurement of physical output in Canada was at first confined, as in most other countries, to the industrial production index. This index, using the formula of value added weights times quantity relatives, was first computed in the early twenties, shortly after the Dominion Bureau of Statistics came into existence. At the same time, the annual Census of Industry was providing current dollar data on value added which lent itself to a "rough estimate" of national income, obtained by adding to the net value of production of the commodity-producing industries an estimate of the production of the service industries. In the late thirties and early war years, these estimates were supplanted by ones emphasizing incomes and expenditures, which continued to be published throughout the war.[2] The postwar emphasis on new and better statistical systems led to the development of a modern set of sector accounts, first published in 1946.[3]

The first set of deflated final product estimates by type of expenditure was prepared in connection with an econometric forecasting model set up as a part of the larger program of studies centering about the official paper on employment policy of 1945.[4] (The latter corresponded in certain respects to the U.S. Full Employment Act of 1946.) The ingredients for a much finer deflation existed in the files of the DBS, and so it developed and officially published the estimates in 1950 as a new feature of the national accounts. Attention at that time was being focused upon quarterly developments, statistically as well as analytically. The deflators were therefore recalculated on a quarterly basis, from 1947 to date, on a 1949 time and weight base. This recalculation was refined still further in detail and superseded existing annual calculations.

Returning now to the industrial production index, a series of revisions designed to improve its coverage and weighting system carried out during the war and early postwar years was followed in 1950 by a complete recalculation (base 1935–39=100), which took into account the formula associated with Geary and Fabricant,

---

[2] S. A. Goldberg, "The Development of National Accounts in Canada," *Canadian Journal of Economics and Political Science*, February 1949.

[3] *National Accounts, Income and Expenditure, 1938–1945*, DBS (Ottawa, 1946).

[4] *Employment and Income, with special reference to the Initial Period of Reconstruction*, presented to Parliament by the Minister of Reconstruction (Ottawa, 1945).

204

namely deflated commodity outputs less deflated commodity inputs by industry.[5] It was published in early 1953 and incorporated a considerable number of manufacturing indexes compiled in terms of value added in constant dollars. The monthly indexes were seasonally adjusted by hand methods at the major group level.[6] It soon became apparent that a more recent base period was required and that the use of unadjusted man-hours for a number of industries was imparting a downward bias. A further revision of the index was then undertaken, involving the recomputation on the new 1949 weight-reference base and the development of up-to-date annual benchmarks. For the current period, adjustment factors for man-hours, based on trends in output per man-hour as indicated by the benchmark series, were also developed. At the same time, dependence on man-hour data was reduced by expanding monthly commodity surveys. The revised monthly series were processed for seasonal adjustment on the U.S. Bureau of the Census electronic computer according to Univac Method II. Unfortunately resources were limited, and all this work took more time than expected.

Much more important for present purposes is the expansion of the index to cover all other industries in the economy.[7] This work has been going on concurrently with the revision of the industrial production index. Its main object is to provide a substantially independent estimate of real domestic product via the industry approach, useful partly as a check on deflated final product, but mainly for the industrial detail which underlies the main income and product tables. At the same time that quarterly income and product tables and quarterly deflated products were being developed and gaining recognition as a useful descriptive device around which to marshal the analysis of current economic conditions, the development of the quarterly estimates of real product by industry were being emphasized to provide the missing industrial link. They have been available internally for the past few years, and they have been used in the current quarterly analyses of the national accounts. More refinement and experience will be required before complete details can be officially published.[8]

[5] Solomon Fabricant, *The Output of Manufacturing Industries, 1899–1937*, National Bureau of Economic Research (New York, 1940), p. 25. R. C. Geary, "The Concept of Net Volume of Output with Special Reference to Irish Data," *Journal of the Royal Statistical Society*, Vol. 107, 1944, pp. 251–9.

[6] *Seasonally Adjusted Economic Indicators, 1947–1955*, D.B.S. (Ottawa, 1957).

[7] The Research Department of the Bank of Canada was the first agency to develop an aggregate series of real output and the results of this work were turned over to the DBS for further development.

[8] A first step toward publication was recently taken with the release of a reference paper, *Revised Index of Industrial Production, 1935–1957*, DBS (Ottawa, 1959).

ADMINISTRATIVE ORGANIZATION

At the DBS work on real output has been largely concentrated in the Research and Development Division, which is also responsible for the national accounts, interindustry flow studies, and a program for the development of productivity measures. This centralization facilitates discussion of the many complex conceptual and procedural problems involved and provides an excellent environment for achieving consistency between the various measures so that they can be integrated within a common framework.

Being primarily engaged in the development and operation of broad statistical aggregates, the Division is in a good position to uncover inconsistencies in reported data and to assess the relative importance of gaps in the DBS statistical collection program. It is thus expected to provide assistance and guidance in the improvement of existing series and in the development of new surveys and the subject matter of statistical collection in general.

Uses

Analyses of results may be of two broad types: "normative analyses" or "results statements" tell what happened; "behavioural analyses" attempt to explain why it happened.[9] Although the governmental publications and official analyses seldom reach beyond the normative type, the statistics themselves are used by outside agencies and individuals in a variety of ways, including testing of hypotheses and occasionally approaching the ultimate end of explaining why such and such an event took place.

The descriptive or normative analyses that make use of the real output measures are outlined below in terms of their appearance in such publications as the quarterly national accounts, the annual report of the Bank of Canada, the annual federal budget, and other publications. While these are generally explanations or descriptions of past events, the budget presents an explicit forecast. We therefore go on to discuss other than normative uses, such as the relation of real output measures to short-term forecasting and to long-term projections in general.

OFFICIAL USES IN CURRENT ANALYSIS (PARTICULARLY THE NATIONAL ACCOUNTS)

There are three main uses of industry real output measures:

1. As an independent check on the results of the deflation of gross national expenditure (GNE). The material has been used in this way

---

[9] Somewhat similar distinctions have been drawn by Ingvar Ohlsson in *On National Accounting*, Konjunkturinstitutet (Stockholm, 1953) and by George Jaszi, Volume 22 of this conference, p. 20.

for some years, as an independent check on the reliability of the year-to-year changes in the physical volume of output as shown by the annual constant dollar gross national product (GNP) series. The GNP series is converted to a gross domestic product (GDP) basis for purposes of the comparison. To date the series have reconciled very closely, and only small differences exist in the annual data. Similar comparisons are made with the results of the quarterly constant dollar GNP. While the series on a quarterly basis have tended to reconcile less precisely, the quarterly real output data have nevertheless proven highly useful as a check on the size and direction of change. Both series are now in course of being seasonally adjusted, and we hope to be able to improve the reconciliation of the quarterly data to a point where two independent measures of real output on a seasonally adjusted basis will be available for publication. While these results are at present only experimental, they have already contributed significantly to our current quarterly national accounts analysis, where it is necessary to make some judgment on the latest quarter-to-quarter change in the volume of output.

2. The material provides highly valuable analytical information on the industrial composition of changes in the volume of total real output. It is used extensively in the national accounts to identify the industrial groups responsible for any strength or weakness in the developing economic situation.

3. Perhaps the deflation of GDP can be developed to the point where meaningful price and volume components can be published on a seasonally adjusted basis. The recent inflationary period has pointed up the need for more precise measures of such components of quarterly movements in the current value GDP. At the present time research is being carried out on the development of Laspeyres-type price indicators to match the various elements of the GDP, and not subject to the quarterly weight shifts which vitiate the implicit price deflators for current price analysis. This new price material, together with the seasonally adjusted real output by industry data and the seasonally adjusted constant dollar data showing the disposition of output by main expenditure categories, will be substantially self-checking, and consistent with the current value series.[10] This inter-related set of price-volume-value data should add powerfully to the tools available for current economic analysis.

Other Official Uses. The annual federal budget and the annual report

[10] Consistent except for adjusting entries, e.g., those due to the use of fixed weight rather than currently weighted price deflators, factor cost versus market price weighting adjustments, and adjustments in specific nonmarket areas of output (all described below).

of the Bank of Canada use the real output measures in a variety of ways to describe the events of the past year and to help in assessing the current economic situation. (Of course, they also include many statistics not described here.) Appended to the budget speech is an "Economic Review" which is usually presented to the House of Commons on the day before the budget, providing the economic background to the budget itself. The following quotation illustrates briefly one particular use of the output estimates: "Assuming normal crops, stable prices, and no untoward external events, I am basing my revenue forecasts on a gross national product of $32 billion, which is about 2 per cent above the level achieved in 1957."[11] The estimates underlying this projection are of course detailed in terms of prices, quantities, and values. From the standpoint of the statistician involved, far down the ladder in the budget-making process, the basic ingredients of prices, quantities, and values must be so designed as to come as close as possible to consistency with one another in leading up to the above value projection. If the product of prices and quantities do not equal the value estimate, then the reconciling differences must be clearly explainable.

SHORT-TERM AND LONG-TERM PROJECTIONS

Econometric models are usually detailed in terms of quantity and price variables, and the interrelationships among these. For example, the production function, which is the final supply relationship, is solely in terms of deflated or real values and man-hours. Similarly, demands are expressed in terms of real quantities, explained by real incomes, price levels, and other causal influences. The equating of global supply with global demand becomes, in effect, a global price level determining equation. It is, in fact, very doubtful if a useful econometric model could be constructed from national accounts' data without first separating these into separate quantity and price components. However, as the prices involved among the separate final expenditure categories vary considerably from one another, additional detailing of the price determining equations would be useful.

The Canadian model referred to earlier treats as exogenous the following variables: investment (based on business men's expectations plus other projections for nonbusiness investment), exports of goods and services, and government expenditures. On the supply side it takes into account the growth of the labor force (man-hours), productivity, and imports. It utilizes a general consumption function. After solution, its results are compared with those of the judgment-type

[11] House of Commons Debates, Vol. 102, No. 27 (Ottawa, 1958), p. 1235.

forecasts made by several specialists. What finally emerges is one projection of the main tables of national income and product.

Long-Term Projections. During the past three years, the statistics of industrial output and deflated final products have been available to a specialized research group engaged in projecting Canadian output at five-year intervals to 1980. The Royal Commission on Canada's Economic Prospects has now published its final report, together with a number of monographs on various special aspects of growth. Chief of these, from the view of using real output measures, is the volume by William Hood and Anthony Scott, *Output, Labour and Capital in the Canadian Economy.*[12] It contains a detailed examination of the concepts and procedures used in setting up industrial real-product and deflated final-product estimates, discusses their suitability for this usage, and presents the record, according to their own worksheets and particular classification scheme, from 1926 to 1955. This record is then used for the 1980 projection. The document contains also some tentative estimates of the real capital stock which were a necessary part of the projection.

USES OF REAL OUTPUT FOR PRODUCTIVITY ANALYSIS

Both output measures described below can be used at the aggregative level in the numerator of a global productivity ratio to derive a measure of total economic productivity. One of the main precautions is that estimates of real product originating in government departments and some minor items of household product embody a constant productivity assumption. This assumption appears also in fixed capital deflators, wherever there are no end prices and factor or material input costs are used to represent them. A proper concept for use in a global productivity measure should be the business sector gross domestic product, divided by corresponding man-hours.[13] This measure incorporates the effects of changing product mix at all levels of aggregation.

Another measurement is that of economic productivity by industries, in which gross domestic product at factor cost originating in each industry is divided by man-hours. If the industry mix is held constant, at the finest or four-digit level, we come as close as possible to a technical productivity concept, which cannot be further refined since our calculations do not generally extend down to plant studies and data on man-hours for individual commodities are not obtainable.

---

[12] Royal Commission on Canada's Economic Prospects (Ottawa, 1958).

[13] Kendrick, Vol. 22, *op. cit.*, p. 414. Kendrick also favors relating real product at factor cost to the corresponding total real factor cost (including capital as well as labor inputs) to get a measure of "total factor productivity."

Shortcomings for productivity uses are discussed further in sections 4 and 6.

Common Objectives, Concepts, and General Procedures

At the present time we are trying to develop an aggregate measure of total product in real terms. We are not concerned with the problem of constructing real balancing accounts for the entire national accounting system,[14] but are concentrating our resources on expressing, in constant dollars, the consolidated production account, GDP =personal expenditure+government expenditure+business final expenditure+exports−imports. Deflation of the factor incomes and capital consumption allowances that ultimately comprise the left side of the equation is not, at present, considered feasible owing to the ambiguity involved in the choice of deflators. No one yet knows a good way of expressing such components as profits in terms of physical volume. (Indeed, if unique deflators could be determined, an adjustment to the left side for changes in productivity would be required to balance the account in real terms.)[15]

Although the factor shares are not themselves easily deflated, their total for each industry in the form of real value added can be obtained by subtracting deflated inputs from deflated outputs. In this form all commodity and service transactions can be expressed as quantities and as values. In effect, the two approaches are designed to measure the GDP by summing commodities and services in two different ways. The production approach measures commodities and services at each stage of the production process and removes double counting and foreign-produced items as each industry boundary is crossed. The expenditure approach arrives at the same aggregate by measuring commodities and services as they finally emerge, less a lump sum amount for foreign-produced items. This fundamental proposition of equality of the two approaches depends upon having a common definition of output, consistent data, a complete and mutually exclusive classification system, and a specified method of routing (that is tracing commodities and services through the productive and distributive processes until they emerge as final products). The following example is intended for illustrative purposes only.

Suppose that raw sugar is imported, then refined in a factory where

---

[14] *A System of Price and Quantity Indexes for National Accounts*, Statistical Office of the United Nations (New York, 1958).

[15] The following comment by Kendrick clarifies the position on productivity: "The advantage of deflating both national income and product is that the difference is an efficiency measure. It is not necessary to deflate profits which is one component of capital compensation; rather, base period capital compensation can be extrapolated by an index of real capital stock and services."

factor costs such as wages, rent, interest, and profits are incurred, plus depreciation. The refined sugar emerges in packaged form, is transported to a retail outlet, and sold to the consumer. The process is recorded for two periods of time, period 0 (the base year) and period 1 (the current year), for each of which there exist prices and quantities pertinent to the successive stages of importation, factory shipments, inventory holdings, transportation, and retail selling. To simplify the example, let us assume no indirect taxes, no intermediate inputs into factory production other than raw sugar, no intermediate inputs into transportation, no intermediate inputs into retail selling other than the cost of the sugar and the transportation charges, and no inventory holdings other than refined sugar at the factory valued at average selling prices.

Production Approach

	Period 0	Period 1
Refined Sugar Shipments	100 lbs. @ .20¢	150 lbs. @ .30¢
Imports of Raw Sugar	130 lbs. @ .10¢	150 lbs. @ .12¢
Change in Inventory of Refined Sugar	+10 lbs. @ .20¢	−15 lbs. @ .30¢
Transportation of Refined Sugar	100 lbs. @ .01¢	150 lbs. @ .02¢
Retail Selling	100 lbs. @ .25¢	150 lbs. @ .40¢

In the production approach, value added in constant dollars is computed at each stage of production, transportation, and selling, by subtracting from the gross value or revenue in constant dollars (prices of period 0) the cost of materials and services in constant dollars. Since quantities and prices are available at each stage, the constant-dollar aggregate can be obtained either by multiplying the quantities by base-year prices or by dividing the current values by indexes of prices. In the example, the manufacturer of refined sugar was able to extract proportionately more refined sugar from the imported material in period 1 than in period 0 because of more efficient machinery. Results of the computation, in constant (period 0) prices are:

	Period 0	Period 1
1. Factory Shipments	20.00	30.00
2. Add Inventory Change	2.00	−3.00
3. Less Materials Used	−13.00	−15.00
4. Value Added at Factory	9.00	12.00
Index (period 0=100)	100.0	133.3
5. Value Added in Transportation	1.00	1.50
Index (Period 0=100)	100.0	150.0
6. Retail Sales	25.00	37.50
7. Less Cost of Sugar	20.00	30.00
8. Less Transportation	1.00	1.50
9. Value Added in Retail Selling	4.00	6.00
Index (Period 0=100)	100.0	150.0
10. Total Value Added (4+5+9)	14.00	19.50
Total Index (Period 0=100)	100.0	139.3

211

The total index of 139.3 in period 1 could also be obtained by summing the component indexes on the basis of the value added weights in period 0. If data on raw sugar used at the factory were not available in period 1, it would not be possible to reflect the saving in materials consumed in the factory index; based on gross production, the factory index would be 122.7 instead of 133.3, and the total index 132.5 instead of 139.3. An assumption that gross output moved parallel to net output in this case would be erroneous.

Expenditure Approach[16]

	Period 0	Period 1
1. Consumer Expenditures on Refined Sugar	25.00	60.00
2. Retail Price Index of Refined Sugar	100.0	160.0
3. Consumer Expenditure in Constant Dollars $(1 \div 2)$	25.00	37.50
4. Add Value Change in Inventory (VPC)	2.00	−4.50
5. Price Index of Refined Sugar at Factory	100.0	150.0
6. Inventory Change in Constant Dollars $(4 \div 5)$	2.00	−3.00
7. Value of Imports of Raw Sugar	13.00	18.00
8. Import Price Index	100.0	120.0
9. Imports in Constant Dollars $(7 \div 8)$	13.00	15.00
Total $(3+6-9)$	14.00	19.50
Total Index (Period $0=100$)	100.0	139.3

Deflation by price indexes is most usual in the expenditure approach, direct quantity measurement most usual in the production approach, because quantitative data are more easily obtainable at the initial stages of production while price series are usually more numerous and detailed at the final stages. There is no reason, however, why either method cannot be used, since, assuming no statistical or other inconsistencies, they provide exactly equivalent answers. Weighting is not illustrated here since only one commodity is involved at each stage. However, if bundles of commodities were being handled, the quantities should be base-weighted where the quantity method is used and the prices currently weighted where the deflation method is used, since the important result is the quantity comparison from period to period. The main point is that the sum (retaining signs) of successive constant-dollar inputs and outputs is equal to constant dollar final product.[17]

GROSS PRODUCT AND NET PRODUCT

The inclusion of capital consumption allowances makes the concept of production "gross." When they are subtracted the product is said to be "net" since it is measured after the deduction of output necessary to replace capital used up during a given period by wear,

---

[16] In practice, data may not be available at this level of detail.
[17] See Richard Stone, *Quantity and Price Indexes in National Accounts*, OEEC, *op. cit.*, p. 34.

tear, obsolescence, and so forth. For some general purposes the gross meausre is the more significant since it incorporates all the resources used in the process of production.[18] Moreover, there are statistical difficulties involved in the measurement of real capital consumption allowances and the estimates are presently restricted to the "gross" concept.

DOMESTIC PRODUCT AND NATIONAL PRODUCT

It has long been recognized that to measure the contribution of various industries to total production one must distinguish between domestic product and national product, and that an industrial approach requires a measure of output produced within the geographic boundaries of a country (GDP), a national approach a measure of product accruing to its residents (GNP). Although the present official Canadian estimate of real expenditure is in terms of national product, estimates of output by industry are now being developed on the basis of domestic product.

Among the factor costs inextricably mixed with industry value added are interest and dividends accruing to nationals of other countries. On the other hand, interest and dividends received by domestic industries from other countries are not a part of value added. Thus GDP is the concept at which to aim for a reconciliation based on the identity "GDP plus net factor incomes received from nonresidents (mostly interest and dividends) equals GNP."[19]

GDP has the advantage of being measurable by three largely independent approaches—income, expenditure, and industry value added (as pointed out above, the national concept does not flow naturally from the third approach), and makes a better framework than GNP for income and expenditure accounts, real output by industry, and input-output and productivity studies.

In order to reconcile GNE with gross domestic expenditure (GDE), the entries for total receipts and outpayments of interest and

[18] But Kendrick prefers the net measure for productivity work, thinking of capital consumption as a kind of intermediate product input (Volume 22, p. 414).

[19] The recent United Nations document, *A System of Price and Quantity Indexes for National Accounts, op. cit.* prepared for the tenth session of the Statistical Commission, points out that an additional adjustment is required if the accounts are to balance in real terms as they do in current dollars. The document suggests that the real measure of GNP should incorporate an item to represent the gains or losses from the terms of trade. The real external account would then be balanced by the identity "exports+trading gains=imports+surplus." This real trading gain cannot be defined uniquely and a conservative value should be chosen for it. GNP in real terms would then be equal to the real value of GDP plus net factor incomes received from nonresidents plus the trading gain. Canadian practice takes no account of trading gains in the estimates of real GNE, but the ingredients are available to users who wish to make the extra calculation.

213

dividends are deleted from the national estimates.[20] This incidentally relieves us of the ambiguity involved in attempting to deflate these financial items.[21]

MARKET PRICES AND FACTOR COSTS

When considering the contributions to GDP of different industries, output should be valued at factor cost rather than at market prices. Value added at factor cost is the difference between the selling value of an industry's products excluding indirect taxes on these products[22] and the cost of materials and services used in production, including taxes on these inputs. The difference represents the industry's relative contribution to total output and is a measure of resource allocation particularly relevant for productivity studies.

The statistics which form the basis of the production calculations are principally founded on the factor cost definition. The valuation of output in the annual Canadian census of industry, from which benchmark output data for the mining and manufacturing industries are obtained, excludes sales and other excise taxes. Thus practically as well as theoretically, it appeared preferable to base the measures of production by industry and the weighting system on GDP at factor cost. Another consideration was the advantage of making the industry weights invariant to any changes in indirect taxes particularly since the system is changed only periodically.

On the other hand, the real expenditure approach is associated conceptually with GNP at market prices. Furthermore, the statistical data are given as market values and market prices and therefore the most practical procedure is to leave indirect taxes embodied in both the values of the final products and their price deflators. Once this has been done, however, the resulting quantity series can be recombined, using base period factor cost weights. Although present analytical uses of the deflated final products, concerned as they are with final demand analysis, are better served by the market price procedure, future developments should allow for factor cost weighting as well.[23]

[20] The domestic or geographic concept is extended to include the foreign operations of domestically registered air and water carriers and the activities of legations and armed forces situated in foreign countries. Conversely, the domestic operations of foreign-based air and water carriers, together with the activities in Canada of foreign legations and armed forces, are excluded. The main point here is to ensure that the treatment of these activities adopted in the production approach is consistent with the measure of deflated expenditure.

[21] The domestic product concept is described fully in the United Nations' document F.2, *A System of National Accounts and Supporting Tables* (ST/STAT/SER.F/No. 2).

[22] Taxes such as those on property cannot be allocated to individual products and therefore are not deducted.

[23] See also *National Income Statistics, Sources and Methods*, Central Statistical Office, 'London, H.M.S.O., 1956,' p. 40.

For reconciliation purposes, the production measures at factor cost were inflated to a market price basis, rather than the expenditure estimates at market prices deflated to factor costs. Accordingly, a complete set of market price industry weights was developed to re-weight the production indicators. These weights correspond to the detail available in the 1949 factor cost structure used for the production series and were developed from data used in the construction of the interindustry flow table;[24] control totals for this table were obtained from the national accounts. Indirect taxes and subsidies were allocated to the proper industry factor-cost valuations, an admittedly difficult procedure sometimes. However, in the process of constructing the input-output table, very detailed commodity flow studies were made. Where a commodity was produced by more than one industry group, the flows were kept, as far as possible, separate. Thus taxes were allocated to commodities and to the industries producing them. The results, in general, were judged sufficiently reliable to be used for the present purpose. Subsidies were defined as amounts contributed by governments towards current costs of production and indirect taxes as all taxes which are deductible as expenses from gross revenues of business. Accordingly, the subsidies and taxes were allocated on the basis of the industries receiving the subsidies or paying the taxes.

These market price weights were applied to our experimental industry production indexes and the results are compared in Table 1 with those based on the regular factor cost system. The indexes are shown at various levels of aggregation on the base of 1949=100 for the years 1949–56.

Although the two sets of indexes are similar at the composite level,

TABLE 1

The Effect of Factor Cost and Market Price Weights on Production Indexes

	GDP		Total Manufacturing		Nondurable Manufacturing	
	Factor Cost	Market Prices	Factor Cost	Market Prices	Factor Cost	Market Prices
Weights (%)	100.000	100.000	27.160	29.689	14.644	17.197
1949	100.0	100.0	100.0	100.0	100.0	100.0
1950	106.2	106.1	106.2	106.3	106.0	105.5
1951	113.7	113.1	115.0	113.9	110.8	109.1
1952	120.1	119.6	118.5	118.4	113.2	113.2
1953	124.1	124.1	126.4	127.0	120.2	120.8
1954	122.4	122.6	122.9	123.8	121.2	121.9
1955	134.4	134.6	134.7	135.9	130.4	131.0
1956	145.5	145.5	145.1	146.1	138.1	139.1

[24] *The Inter-industry Flow of Goods and Services, Canada, 1949*, DBS Reference Paper No. 72 (Ottawa, 1956).

215

TABLE 1 (concluded)

	Foods and Beverages		Durable Manufacturing		Electrical Apparatus and Supplies	
	Factor Cost	Market Prices	Factor Cost	Market Prices	Factor Cost	Market Prices
Weights (%)	3.789	4.729	12.516	12.492	1.409	1.497
1949	100.0	100.0	100.0	100.0	100.0	100.0
1950	103.8	103.7	106.5	107.5	112.5	113.4
1951	106.8	106.6	119.9	120.6	120.7	121.3
1952	113.5	114.3	124.8	125.5	124.5	127.7
1953	117.4	119.4	133.6	135.6	150.9	159.2
1954	120.6	121.5	124.8	126.3	151.7	161.7
1955	126.8	128.0	139.7	142.6	176.2	191.6
1956	133.1	135.0	153.3	155.8	191.3	202.5

differences appear at lower levels of aggregation. The effects of a major strike in 1951 in the tobacco products industry (subject to heavy excise taxes and duties) on the two series are clearly distinguishable in the first three groupings. In the manufacturing division, the market price series show a tendency to increase at a slightly greater rate than the factor cost series because most of the industries subject to the heaviest indirect taxes (such as distilleries, tobacco products, petroleum refineries, motor vehicle manufacturers, radio, television, and appliance manufacturers) show larger increases in physical output in recent years than the average of all manufacturing industries. This divergence is particularly noticeable for radio and television manufacturers, whose physical output rose by 443 per cent between 1949 and its peak in 1955, compared with a gain of 35 per cent for total manufacturing over the same period. The marked effect of this rapid advance in one component on the production index for the electrical apparatus and supplies industry is shown in the table. The market price index is nearly 9 per cent higher than the factor cost index in 1955 (the reverse effect appeared in 1956 when output of television sets showed a substantial decline). The choice of the factor cost series in this instance would be necessary in a study involving resource allocation.

The use of market price weights in the expenditure approach and factor cost weights in the production approach leaves us open to criticism for conceptual inconsistency. We decided, however, to recognize the different needs of users and prepare the estimates in accordance with the two concepts. The available statistics lent themselves to this dual approach. In any case, for purposes of general economic analysis, where only broad groups of industries and of final demand components are involved, the choice of concept matters little in practice. In order, however, to enable users to assess the significance of differences in definition, the adjustments necessary to bring the two sets of estimates into conceptual agreement will be made explicit in published reports.

Real Output by Industry

As described earlier, the industry production approach aims at measuring changes in the volume of GDP at factor cost. In general the procedure consists of developing indicators of physical volume for each industry, expressing these as index numbers related to a common base period, and then combining the series into a composite total index by means of base-period weights derived from an industry breakdown of GDP at factor cost. Ideally, the industry indexes should reflect changes in real GDP at factor cost. Available statistics, however, do not measure this concept completely (none on purchases of business services by industry and insufficient detail on materials input for many industries) and each industry is represented by an indicator designed to approximate the desired concept as closely as available data permit.

Comprehensive annual census surveys for many industries make it possible to develop annual benchmark indexes which are extrapolated to the current period on the basis of monthly or quarterly data. Periodically, the current indexes are revised according to the latest obtainable data from the industrial censuses. The latest revision of the monthly Index of Industrial Production, for instance, incorporated the results of the most recent annual censuses of the mining, manufacturing, and electricity and gas industries. The more comprehensive and detailed data available for annual and decennial intervals permit the benchmark indicators to conform more closely to the desired concepts than do the current indexes.

CLASSIFICATION AND GENERAL PROCEDURE

The classification framework for the measures of industrial production, for the current dollar industrial distribution of GDP in the national accounts and for the input-output table, comes from the DBS Standard Industrial Classification. The three structures, however, are not forced into a rigid classification framework and sometimes the form of the available statistics or the particular uses to which the series are put require some rearrangement of the classification. For instance, the close integration of the nonferrous metal smelting and refining industry with the metal mining industry and the difficulty of accurately allocating profits and depreciation required that the two industries be combined under mining in the input-output table. However, for the production measures, GDP weights were

217

estimated separately for the two industries in order to allocate them respectively to the manufacturing and mining divisions.[25] Again, in the input-output table, all construction activity (including new construction and repairs by establishments with their own labor force) was classified in the construction industry. In the real output weighting system, estimated production arising from own account repairs was left with the industries originating the work. No data are available to measure this type of production on a current basis, and it is assumed that the amount of such repair activity is proportional to the industry's major activity. New construction by own labor force, however, is assigned to the construction industry to obtain a direct total measure for this important activity.

As noted earlier, the value of GDP at factor cost can be measured either directly by summing the factor incomes and capital consumption allowances for each industry or indirectly by subtracting all intermediate goods and services from the revenue (ex indirect taxes) arising from the production of goods and services in each industry.

In calculating indicators of real output by industry the first method is not practicable since no statistical measures have as yet been developed to express such factors as profits and depreciation in quantitative terms.[26] The second method (or an approximation thereto) whereby materials and service inputs in terms of base-year prices are subtracted from output also in terms of base-year prices, gives meaningful results and is the one generally followed. The series of net output in constant dollars derived in this way are so compiled that the relationship between the various primary inputs and output in each industry is kept constant (i.e., profits per unit of output, wages and salaries per unit of output, depreciation per unit of output, etc., for each industry are held fixed at base-period rates). Actually these rates are continually changing, so that a comparison between a measure of physical production and a measure of any or all factor incomes and depreciation (expressed quantitatively) would reveal changes in "productivity" over time. The most popular and, at present, practicable comparison is that between labor input and physical production whereby changes in output per man-hour are measured over a period of years. However, the direct method of summing primary inputs was followed in the derivation of the industry GDP weighting system.

FORMULA AND WEIGHTING SYSTEM

The formulae used throughout the production approach are of the base-weighted Laspeyres type, either averages of relatives or relatives

[25] See also the Alterman-Jacobs paper in this volume.
[26] See also possibility of a "difference deflator" sketched in the Phillips' paper.

of aggregates. And as for most of the major indexes, all output indexes are now compiled in terms of 1949 = 100. While other formulae (such as the Paasche, Marshall-Edgeworth or Fisher Ideal) possess some advantages over the Laspeyres type in certain circumstances, we have found the Laspeyres more practicable and easy to interpret when used over a reasonable period of years, and believe that we should concentrate our limited resources on developing more reliable indicators rather than devote extra time to the design and operation of more elaborate weighting systems.

Although the objective always is to measure changes in real GDP, in practice it is only possible to derive a complete measure for each industry in the base period and to project this ideal measure by means of indicators designed to approximate it as closely as possible. First GDP for each industry in the base period is expressed as a percentage to the total (weights). Then indicators of volume for each industry are constructed—index numbers with the base period equaling 100 (relatives). Finally, the relatives are combined according to their respective weights into a composite index representative of GDP in constant dollars.

The 1949 interindustry flow table made a major contribution to the industry production approach—a fifty-industry distribution of GDP at factor cost on an establishment basis. The distribution was based on the industrial breakdown of GDP at factor cost published in the national accounts after adjustment to achieve a complete establishment classification. Investment income and capital consumption allowances are hard to fit into an industry classification when the reporting unit is the multiestablishment firm whose establishments can be coded to different industries according to the nature of their principal products or types of activity. For instance, many major pulp and paper companies operate large wood-cutting establishments (forestry industry) as well as the pulp and paper mills themselves (manufacturing establishments). While salaries and wages recorded by establishment can be allocated, if necessary, to different industries, investment income and capital consumption allowances generally apply to a firm's total operations and any allocation by establishment must, of necessity, be rather arbitrary. For the input-output table, however, such adjustments were made. The 1949 method of distribution was crude, usually on the basis of value of output or salaries and wages. If data were available on services purchased by manufacturing companies (e.g., advertising, insurance, etc.), and if suitable cost accounting methods could be devised to allocate these costs between establishments of the same firm, GDP originating in each industry could be derived by deducting total intermediate input

219

from total output. The complete interindustry flow system would therefore not be required to provide the GDP weight structure, but the availability of the complete system would help verify its accuracy. It should be noted that the above method allocates profits residually, which is the correct procedure since profits are themselves a residual.

The interindustry flow table contained adjustments to the industrial breakdown of profits to remove any unrealized gains or losses on inventories which occurred as a result of compiling inventories at book value. To be consistent with the valuation of production, inventories should be valued by multiplying the physical change by weighted average prices during the year. Such an adjustment involves assumptions about the commodity content of inventory holdings, the normal turnover period for the industry, and the accounting methods used by the firms in arriving at book value. The difference between the value of the physical change and the reported book value is known as the "inventory valuation adjustment" which has recently been incorporated in our revised national accounts.

Below the level of detail obtainable from the input-output project, 1949 industry weights are distributed according to census "value added" (value of production excluding sales and other excise taxes less materials, fuels, and electricity consumed), net margins (for trade), gross revenues, or payrolls. Within industries, commodities or services are summed on the basis of unit selling value. In those industries for which census "value added" volume indexes were computed, the effect of "value added" weights for commodities is obtained residually in that the volume of materials, fuel, and electricity is subtracted in total from the volume of output. The implicit assumption that purchased services are proportional to the gross or census "value added" valuations within industries may not be unjustified since the general processing, distribution, and marketing characteristics tend to be similar for the majority of products in an industry.

In this connection, a test was carried out whereby the manufacturing industry indexes were reweighted with census "value added." The results, compared with those using the GDP at factor cost weighting system, are shown in Table 2 for total manufacturing, durables and nondurables.

Although the results do not reflect any changes over time in the relative proportion of business services purchased within industries (relationships are fixed at the 1949 base), they do incorporate the effect on the weights of the varying proportions of these costs as between industries. The effect was negligible on the composite durable manufacturing index. Even though the component indexes showed considerable dispersion, the proportions of GDP to "value added"

220

TABLE 2
The Effect of GDP at Factor Cost and Census "Value Added" Weights on Production
Indexes

| | Total Manufacturing | | Nondurable Manufacturing | | Durable Manufacturing | |
	GDP	Value Added	GDP	Value Added	GDP	Value Added
Weights (%)	100.0	100.0	53.915	56.960	46.085	43.040
1949	100.0	100.0	100.0	100.0	100.0	100.0
1950	106.2	106.3	106.0	106.2	106.5	106.5
1951	115.0	115.5	110.8	112.2	119.9	119.8
1952	118.5	119.0	113.2	114.8	124.8	124.5
1953	126.4	126.7	120.2	121.8	133.6	133.3
1954	122.9	124.0	121.2	123.4	124.8	124.8
1955	134.7	135.8	130.4	132.7	139.7	139.8
1956	145.1	145.8	138.1	140.0	153.3	153.5

varied little. For nondurables, however, the "value added" weights for chemicals and petroleum products (which recorded considerably larger increases in output than the composite nondurables index) were proportionately much higher than the GDP weights and accounted for most of the differences in the levels of the two series. These differences in the weights suggest that the costs of business services were particularly high in the chemicals and petroleum refining industries. No doubt such costs as advertising are relatively greater, but the difficulty of reporting proper factory product valuations (especially for refineries) was a factor. Many major oil companies operate oil wells, refineries, and distribution outlets; and their reported value of output is difficult to determine at each industry boundary thus affecting the comparability of the residual census "value added" with that of other industries.

MEASUREMENT APPROACH

As explained earlier, it is not at present possible to calculate a complete quantum measure of GDP at factor cost at the industry level, and efforts are concentrated in deriving the nearest approximation. The indicator that comes closest to measuring the desired concept is the volume of census "value added" (selling value of final products ex sales and other excise taxes plus the value of the change in goods in process less value of materials, fuel and electricity consumed) which will henceforth be referred to as "net" output for purposes of this paper. The concept can only be measured in years for which industrial census data on products, materials, and fuel and electricity are available, and then only in those industries for which the data are appropriate and sufficiently complete. As census material usually lags the current period by at least one year, the last available benchmark

221

indexes are projected forward by means of monthly or quarterly indexes based on less complete and precise data. The annual census of industry and other surveys which provide a considerable amount of information on both outputs and inputs are fully exploited in the development of the production indexes.

To construct annual benchmark indexes for individual industries, census data on recorded quantities and values of products or materials or both are first edited for inconsistencies and then compiled in terms of base-period (in this instance 1949) constant dollars. Within each industry there generally are some products and materials for which no quantity or price information is available. Each year the current value proportion is calculated of items for which quantities are available to the total value of output. This "coverage adjustment" is then divided into the sum of the constant dollar items and has the effect of deflating the total value of output or materials with a currently weighted unit value index based on the items for which quantity and value are recorded. Used with caution, this procedure is better than one which assumes that changes in the volume of reported items represent changes in the volume of all items. The proportion of represented items is often subject to wide variations because of the introduction of new products or sharp changes in output of particular items. The "coverage adjustment" device was not used when the coverage of represented products was less than half the total value of production in any industry. A higher coverage was generally required for materials used, since materials' prices tend to diverge more than products' prices. Certain important products or materials were handled individually because their unit values diverged significantly from those of the majority of products in the same industry.

Where both the constant dollar "blown up" aggregates of products and materials were judged accurate enough for the measurement of an index of "net" output, the materials, fuel, and electricity aggregate was deducted from the products aggregate according to the following formula:

$$\frac{\Sigma\,Q_i P_o - \Sigma\,q_i p_o}{\Sigma\,Q_o P_o - \Sigma\,q_o p_o}$$

in which Q and P stand for the quantities and unit values of products (output) and q and p stand for the quantities and unit values of materials, fuel, and electricity consumed in the production process (input).

Where the data were not suitable for the measurement of real net output, alternative indicators were used, such as the volume of gross output or revenue, the volume of materials used, values of output or materials deflated with available price or "cost of production" indexes, or labor input. In each case, the objective of net output was kept in mind and wherever possible appropriate adjustments were applied. It was possible in several cases to detect discrepancies arising from changes in the amount of duplication or processing or from incorrect reporting and to apply compensating adjustments to the gross series.

Rather than project the base-period GDP valuation by means of the volume indicators, we convert the aggregates to index numbers at the three-digit industry level and apply the GDP weights at this stage. Most analysis by users is conducted at this level, and the derived weighted indexes provide a more convenient means of determining the point contribution of each industry or industry group to the overall total.

TYPES OF INDICATOR

This section describes the measurement of net output (census value added), phsyical output, value of gross output deflated, labor input, volume of materials used, and other indicators. The relative importance of each type of measure is indicated in the following table.

TYPE OF INDICATOR—REAL OUTPUT INDEXES
(Showing 1949 percentage coverage of total G.D.P.)

	Benchmark Indexes	Quarterly or Monthly Indexes
Census value added	31	none
Gross output	20	42
Value deflation	37	32
Labor input (adjusted for output per unit of labor input)	—	10
Labor input (unadjusted)	6	10
All other types	6	6
	100	100

Net Output Indicators. Many factors influence the level of net output. Vertical integration of the manufacturing process, which occurs more often in industries turning out highly processed goods, is an important influence. And improved machinery may permit a higher output from a given amount of raw materials.

Our experience so far indicates that the most important factor is changes in "product mix" when an industry making a variety of products shifts some of its output to goods requiring a higher or lower degree of fabrication. During the war, for instance, in the meat packing industry, the production of canned and cured meats increased greatly relative to that of fresh meats, which require less processing. As a result, the net index rose substantially more during this period than the gross index. The opposite movement occurred immediately

223

after the war when foreign demand for canned and cured meats dropped to a more normal level. Another example is the dairy products industry, where the greater relative increase in ice-cream production and milk and cream bottling (products with proportionately higher net ratios than butter, cheese, and concentrated products) appears to account for most of the difference between the net and gross indexes over the period measured.

Not all industries, however, show a higher net output trend. Some, like the flour and feed milling industry, show an opposite movement, partly as a result of a progressively larger production of a cheaper type of flour and a relative decline in the output of better grades. In some years sharp changes in the volume of output of particular products had substantial effects on the movement of the net index.

Other factors which may have had an influence on the level of net output are the more efficient use of fuel and power or, as mentioned earlier, changes in vertical integration and in the yield of raw materials. But it is impossible now to assess how much the effect was. However, at least for industries with a high materials-products ratio, shifts in the type of products fabricated was apparently the main influence. (See Table 3 for comparison of net and gross indexes for selected industries.)

The measurement of the agriculture industry on the net basis is highly significant. A preliminary index has been developed (Table 3) which makes possible a more complete evaluation of trends in the farm economy. As expected, in years of large changes in crop size, changes in the net index were much sharper than in the gross series. Affecting the trend over the whole period, however, was the steady and rapid growth in the volume of materials used by farmers. Increasing mechanization over the past two decades and the trend towards larger farms and more scientific management of farms have resulted in sharp advances in utilization by farmers of commodities produced in outside industries. This trend has been accompanied by a steady decline in the agricultural labor force and the replacement of man power and animal power by mechanical energy.[27]

The degree of divergence between net and gross output often depends on the degree of homogeneity of the industry measured. All other things being equal, the net output index of a one-product industry will move parallel to its index of gross output. The more diversified the production of an industry, the more sensitive is the net output index to the influence of product mix. This is particularly true of industries in which materials account for a large proportion of the

---

[27] A similar trend was revealed in the first U.S. industry real product estimates, for farming, by Kendrick-Jones, reviewed in Phillips' paper in this volume.

TABLE 3

Indexes of Net and Gross Output for Selected Industries

(1949 = 100)[a]

	Agriculture		Flour and Feed Mills		Meat Packing		Dairy Products		Breweries		Tobacco Products		Sawmills		Steel Mills	
	Net	Gross	Net	Gross	Net	Gross	Net	Gross	Net	Gross	Net	Gross	Net	Gross	Net	Gross
1935	88.3	73.3	53.4	48.1	54.7	59.1	41.3	54.8	24.6	28.0	31.1	39.3	54.7	55.0	27.6	28.0
1936	80.8	67.8	56.4	52.9	66.6	70.7	46.0	58.6	25.1	29.0	35.7	42.3	60.1	60.9	32.8	32.5
1937	78.5	68.1	54.4	50.1	67.5	74.3	48.3	61.1	28.6	32.6	41.4	47.7	68.8	71.2	44.9	45.0
1938	99.8	84.0	52.6	49.0	70.7	70.7	48.7	64.0	28.5	32.1	45.9	51.5	65.4	66.1	36.8	35.5
1939	115.4	96.0	57.3	56.3	81.9	76.4	50.5	65.7	28.8	32.1	49.2	55.1	69.5	69.9	43.8	41.7
1940	118.4	98.1	63.8	62.5	91.8	91.5	55.2	69.7	33.8	37.5	53.1	59.0	81.9	83.1	65.0	64.1
1941	100.6	87.0	71.9	72.7	107.9	106.7	63.9	77.9	44.1	48.0	61.3	64.1	87.2	88.7	88.0	84.7
1942	150.2	124.2	70.0	74.4	126.2	111.5	72.9	86.5	54.9	59.2	76.0	77.1	89.5	90.5	121.6	111.8
1943	101.0	94.4	87.9	91.4	141.2	124.9	77.7	90.8	48.6	52.2	82.3	81.9	78.6	79.4	117.9	106.3
1944	124.5	111.8	97.7	100.5	153.4	146.8	79.2	92.2	58.5	61.5	89.6	89.3	79.2	80.4	104.3	95.0
1945	94.2	92.5	96.3	102.4	148.4	128.3	84.2	95.3	66.5	69.4	103.2	102.2	79.3	80.8	96.7	89.1
1946	104.4	102.6	112.2	114.6	134.1	111.4	83.1	92.3	77.9	80.9	90.6	91.2	88.2	89.1	71.7	68.6
1947	97.0	99.5	111.3	124.8	119.9	99.5	87.7	96.9	90.2	91.2	93.4	94.8	101.4	102.6	93.9	92.1
1948	103.8	102.9	98.2	105.8	100.4	104.2	101.7	99.4	98.5	98.7	93.4	94.9	101.1	100.4	99.1	101.5
1949	100.0	100.0	100.0	100.0	100.0	100.0	100.0	100.0	100.0	100.0	100.0	100.0	100.0	100.0	100.0	100.0
1950	109.7	108.1	99.1	98.7	104.3	100.3	97.8	97.9	99.6	99.5	103.4	102.1	110.1	109.8	109.4	107.2
1951	122.4	118.4	109.0	108.8	102.8	99.7	104.6	100.2	102.3	103.0	95.0	94.8	116.9	115.8	129.0	127.3
1952	137.3	131.1			122.6	118.9	103.2	104.4	116.3	115.0						
1953	126.8	123.1			119.7	116.1	111.5	110.9	122.3	120.3						
1954	92.1	97.5					120.4	115.9	120.5	118.3						

[a] These indexes incorporate two weighting systems: for 1935–46, average unit values in 1935–39 were used as weights within individual industries; after 1946 weights are based on 1949. The two sets of indexes were linked in 1946.

value of products, where even slight changes in the composition of production have a considerable effect on the net measure. Because for such industries the "net" aggregate is very sensitive to even small errors in either products or materials, the data were subjected to a careful scrutiny. Where the net index diverged markedly from the gross, and the movement could not be reasonably explained (for instance by changes in product mix or integration), the original establishment returns were examined and advice sought from DBS industry specialists. Often the data had clearly been erroneously reported and the errors missed in editing and it was possible to apply proper adjustments. Sometimes correspondence with major producers helped to correct important inconsistencies. When serious doubts as to the suitability of the data for purposes of the net indexes could not be eliminated, alternative indicators were substituted.

In an index of net output, when changes in the nature or quantity of raw materials are not reflected in the measurement of the resulting products, a problem arises similar to the problem of measuring changes in quality in the absence of sufficient detail in the tabulation of commodities or services. Changes in quality could be reflected in the volume of materials but not in the volume of output. While such changes will affect the level of the volume of materials, no compensating factor will be recorded in the measurement of the products unless an additional breakdown of commodities by types of materials used in their fabrication is available in census returns. This is often not practicable. In industries where discrepancies of this sort arose, computations of net output were not attempted.

For the revised manufacturing indexes soon to be released it was possible to develop net output indexes for industries representing 44 per cent of the 1949 weights for manufacturing. Net indexes were also compiled for electric utilities. Apart from industries covered by the Index of Industrial Production, net series are available for agriculture and, on a modified basis (deduction of fuel and major supplies only) for most components of the transportation division: railways, civil aviation, urban transport systems, interurban bus transport, and truck transportation. For railways and civil aviation the output measures consist of ton-miles and passenger-miles supplemented by the deflation of other revenues with appropriate price indexes. For railways, data are available on types of commodities transported, so a series reflecting changes in the type of freight handled could be developed. This series diverges significantly from one based on total ton-miles in periods of heavy bulk transport such as when grains or iron ore are shipped in relatively greater volume than items such as automobiles or appliances which are subject to higher tonnage charges. For truck and interurban transport, output measures are based on deflated revenues and for urban transport on number of passengers carried.

Those series for which net indicators could be calculated accounted for 31 per cent of total GDP in 1949. For purposes of comparison, they are shown in Table 4 along with the corresponding gross indexes for 1946–53.

TABLE 4

Comparison of Net and Gross Group Indexes for Selected Industries
(1949 = 100)

	Total Selected Industries		Agriculture		Manufacturing Total Selected Industries		Electric Utilities		Transportation Total Selected Industries	
	Net	Gross	Net	Gross	Net	Gross	Net	Gross	Net	Gross
1946	94.3	93.3	104.4	102.6	85.4	84.6	78.2	78.6	95.5	95.2
1947	96.0	97.0	97.0	99.5	93.6	94.0	89.3	88.8	101.1	100.5
1948	100.6	100.6	103.8	102.9	97.9	98.7	94.2	93.9	101.2	101.1
1949	100.0	100.0	100.0	100.0	100.0	100.0	100.0	100.0	100.0	100.0
1950	107.4	106.9	109.7	108.1	107.0	107,3	113.7	113.2	101.0	100.9
1951	117.7	115.6	122.4	118.4	114.7	114.0	131.1	129.5	109.4	108.7
1952	125.5	122.6	137.3	131.1	115.2	114.8	143.4	141.3	116.1	114.6
1953	123.7	121.7	126.8	123.1	120.2	119.7	151.0	151.0	116.3	114.5

In the manufacturing group, in which the industries represented by net indexes accounted for 12 per cent of the total GDP in 1949, the effects of deducting commodity inputs from the output aggregates are largely offsetting. Earlier, in 1940–45, however, increased demand by the armed services and foreign countries for goods requiring a higher degree of processing affected the input-output ratios of many industries with the result that, on average, the net indexes showed a somewhat greater increase than the corresponding gross series.

Because weather so affects the size of grain crops, which in Canada account for a large part of agricultural output, differences between net and gross indexes of farm production can be substantial. Consequently the indicator for agriculture (nearly 11 per cent of total GDP in 1949) should be calculated on a net basis. Unfortunately a more complete evaluation of the effects of using the value added formula is not possible at this time, but experience so far suggests that, in normal times, and barring any sharp changes in crop production, the use of gross output indicators will not, on balance, adversely affect the over-all measure of real GDP to any significant extent.

An important advantage of computing net output indicators apart from their use in industry output analysis and productivity ratios at the three-digit level is that they provide an excellent check on the adequacy of the basic data. When they are compared with indexes of labor input, materials used, and gross output, they permit a critical examination of related industrial statistics and play an important part in the improvement and integration of these basic data.

Gross Output Indicators. This type of indicator is used for industries where data on materials used are either unobtainable or not suitable for deriving net indexes. In most cases the total value of output or revenue is available from annual surveys so that the adjustment for total coverage can be applied in the calculation of the benchmark indexes. The series that can be measured by physical volume of output include the primary industries—forestry, fishing, trapping and mining, and gas and water utilities. Because materials used are not an important proportion of their total output, gross output indicators are a close approximation to net output. In manufacturing, nearly one-third of the GDP originating in this industry is represented by gross measures. In addition, shipping, stevedoring, pipelines, toll bridges, tunnels and ferries, grain elevators, telephone, telegraph and cable, motion picture theatres, education, hospitals, and undertaking can be represented by series indicative of physical volume of services performed. All of these series accounted for about 20 per cent of the total product in 1949 so that more than half of GDP can be measured directly with physical volume of output data (net and gross).

Value of Output Deflated. Deflation by either appropriate existing price indexes or derived cost of production indexes yields this type of measure. As will be explained below, series obtained by the second method can have serious limitations. Price deflation was used for the following series: manufacture of heavy electrical equipment, taxi service, storage and warehousing, postal services, wholesale trade, repair establishments, retail trade (value of sales by store-types are individually deflated with corresponding retail price indexes and weighted with net retail mark-ups in the base period), insurance other than life, real estate (including residential rents), stock and bond dealers, health services other than hospitals, barbering and hairdressing, dyeing and cleaning, hotels and lodging houses and restaurants, and cafes and taverns. These series accounted for about 27 per cent of GDP in 1949. Deflation by cost of production indexes was used for construction and for manufacturing industries representing 15 per cent of manufacturing GDP, about 10 per cent of total GDP in 1949.

Labor Input. Man-hours or deflated payrolls were used as output indicators for a few manufacturing industries, radio and television communication, government services, and armed forces and domestic service, about 6 per cent of GDP in 1949.

228

Volume of Materials Used. This type of indicator is used in manufacturing industries which accounted for 2.5 per cent of GDP in 1949.

Other Indicators. For the remaining 3 or 4 per cent of GDP consisting of life insurance, banks and other financial institutions, stock exchanges, religious and welfare services, business services, and miscellaneous personal services, indicators are designed to represent the desired concept of service as closely as available data will permit. Sometimes only population figures are obtainable. For life insurance and financial institutions, the measurement approach has not yet been completely explored, but the concept of service rendered suggests certain relevant indicators; in the meantime employment data are used.

PRESENT STAGE OF DEVELOPMENT AND FUTURE PLANS

Now that the revision of the Index of Industrial Production is completed, efforts will be concentrated on the further development of the production measures for the other industries in the economy. Most of the developmental work is already completed for the commodity industries and for the transportation, public utilities, trade, and government divisions. Research is still required in the other services and finance areas. Some of the new benchmark indexes for the commodity industries and for the public utilities, transportation, trade, and government divisions, appear in the tables shown earlier. But these have not yet been incorporated in our experimental total real output series. Although the total series is used only for internal purposes at present, it is shown beside the deflated expenditure series in the last section of this paper.

This experimental series is compiled quarterly for purposes of current analysis, and the data used in its calculation are necessarily more crude than annual data. Employment data are used more extensively in the current series, especially in the manufacturing division. In the revised manufacturing monthly indexes, however, adjustments for changes in output per man-hour have been projected from past trends based on the benchmark series for those industries represented by man-hours in the monthly series. These adjusted series should more closely approximate the benchmark levels than they have in the past. Eventually we expect to publish the quarterly production series along with the deflated expenditure estimates already contained in the current national accounts bulletins.

Since most of the data available to measure production by industry on a quarterly basis are already available by months, we intend to experiment with a monthly measurement of total nonagricultural production. Such a series would be extremely useful for detecting trends and turning points in advance of the quarterly national accounts. The monthly Index of Industrial Production is valuable in this connection, but it is more sensitive to short-term influences than the more comprehensive and stable GDP. Moreover, the seasonal adjustment of the current series can be carried out more accurately and conveniently on a monthly basis than by quarters. There are, admittedly, many additional problems of data and timeliness, but in view of the usefulness for current economic analysis of such a monthly series, we think the effort is well worth while.

Deflation of Final Expenditure Categories

The object of the deflation process is to revalue each of the quanitties currently produced in the prices of the base period, preferably by associating a price relative with the value of each individual commodity or service appearing as final product. Given the limitations of available data, one must select or construct price indexes which will approximately describe the price movements implicit in the value series. For some expenditure groups a large amount of detailed price information is available, but it must be used in a combined index because there is no corresponding breakdown within the value data (e.g., personal expenditure on food, at intervals between consumer sample survey benchmarks). For other series final product price information is lacking, although the value detail may be more or less refined, and deflators to approximate the product price movements must be constructed from data on the cost of labor and material inputs into the product (e.g., nonresidential construction).

It is desirable that the deflated estimates of GNE approximate a base-weighted or Laspeyres volume index, to match the measures of industrial real output. Such a volume index will result if the value series is deflated by a currently weighted or Paasche type of price index. To approximate the price index the value series are usually deflated at a fine level of detail, within the limitations of price and value data. Occasionally a currently weighted price index is specially constructed for deflating, as for exports and imports. The currently weighted subgroup price deflators which emerge from the process of summing both current and constant dollar items and dividing one into the other are known as implicit price indexes. They are only currently weighted to the extent that they incorporate the changing current item weights. If an item is composite, however, like food, the deflators cannot be currently weighted.

230

A description of deflation procedures was published recently in co-nection with the historical revision of the national accounts.[28]

REFINEMENTS FOR USE IN CURRENT ANALYSIS

The development of seasonally adjusted quarterly constant dollar data has been given a high priority in Canada as well as in the United States.[29] These data are necessary if cyclical changes are to be inter-preted in terms of physical volume and price changes, but the price and volume estimates required must be highly accurate. Some loss of accuracy can occur when the base period is remote in time, and a more recent time and weight base will provide a better answer for purposes of short-term analysis.

In general the weight base should be altered wherever there has been a substantial change in economic conditions. For current volume estimates these changes will appear as a significant dispersion of the prices which constitute weights in the volume index. For long-term comparisons, a period such as 1926–58 should perhaps be broken into time segments, each deflated with its own time and weight base, then linked and published either in constant dollars or as index numbers. We have published a long series on a 1949 time base, but the com-ponents were the 1935–39 based series from 1926–47, and the 1949 based series, from 1947–58, both linked at 1947. The industrial output index followed a similar procedure.

The single published series cannot satisfy requirements of all users. Periodic rebasing will partially satisfy the requirements of current economic analysis.[30] If rebasing is done following significant changes in price structure, the weights will be sufficiently representative of the current period, and the results will adequately approximate those that would be obtained if the deflators were continuously rebased to the period immediately preceding the current period.

Certain tests have been made recently of this procedure. A Laspeyres type price index of GDP, with a time and weight base of 1955, was constructed. It was used at its aggregate level to deflate the seasonally adjusted value series in order to derive a rough estimate of

[28] *National Accounts, 1926–1956, op. cit.,* pp. 176–85. (A similar statement appears in the U.S. National Income Supplement, 1954.) For more detail see *Problems and Tech-niques of Measuring the Volume of National Output* by George Jaszi and John W. Kendrick (Inter-American Seminar on National Income, Santiago, Chile, 1953).

[29] "The National Economic Accounts of the United States," Hearings of the Sub-committee on Economic Statistics of the Joint Economic Committee, Washington, 1957, p. 161.

Quarterly seasonally adjusted constant-dollar final products were published in the *Survey of Current Business,* U.S. Department of Commerce, December 1958, p. 10.

[30] If rebasing were to make a substantial difference in results, there would be a case for altering the base of the volume measurements also.

the volume changes from quarter to quarter. For the second and third quarters of 1957 additional comparisons were made, involving the rebasing of deflators to the base of the preceding quarter equal to 100. The rebased deflators were then used to construct both a Paasche (currently weighted) and a Laspeyres (fixed weight) index (both with the seasonally adjusted quarterly values used as weights). The results for the second quarter of 1957 were as follows:

	Estimated Price Change from the Preceding Quarter GDP excluding inventories
Laspeyres (1955=100)	+0.69 per cent
Laspeyres (1st Qtr., 1957=100)	+0.76 per cent
Paasche (1st Qtr., 1957=100)	+0.74 per cent

The results indicated that current rebasing was not required; use of a fairly recent base, 1955, was adequate.

Seasonal Adjustments. Seasonal adjustment of deflated quarterly expenditures can be carried through by dividing seasonally adjusted values by seasonally adjusted prices or by direct seasonal adjustment of constant dollar quarterly expenditures. The former method takes less resources, since not many prices have to be seasonally adjusted and the values are already adjusted in their own right. Direct seasonal adjustment is onerous, since many quantity series have to be adjusted directly. We are trying it both ways for one period only, 1947–57, and will perhaps discover that the simpler method can be used henceforth.

Problems of Measurement

CHANGES IN QUALITY

Most production measures fail to reflect intrinsic changes in quality. A 1958 television set, for instance, has a sharper picture, more automatic features, and is generally a more efficient instrument than its 1948 counterpart. To the extent that quality has improved, the output series will have a downward bias, since there appears to be no satisfactory statistical procedure to reflect intrinsic changes in quality. The only consoling fact is that there probably are often some offsetting features, such as less durability.

The use of price deflation, as in the Canadian expenditure approach, can sometimes take account of quality changes. In the compilation of retail price indexes, for instance, efforts are made to reflect measurable changes, as in the thread count in men's shirts or the number of shelves in a refrigerator. These efforts, however, are limited to differences in visible specifications and cannot extend to gradual, long-term changes in the efficiency, design, comfort, or durability of the great mass of consumer and investment goods produced by a highly industrialized economy.

A closely allied problem is caused by the lack of sufficient detail in many commodity and service classifications where data are often collected in statistical classes such as men's dress shirts, railway passenger-miles, etc. No problem would exist if it could be assumed that the relative proportions, within such classes of goods, of different types and qualities remained constant over the period covered by the series. However, consumers' tastes and living standards change, and producers are governed accordingly. If, for instance, the proportion of expensive shirts has risen, then the quality of the class "men's dress shirts" may be said to have improved, but the production series based on the total number of men's dress shirts would not reflect this change. However, the value series can be deflated by an appropriate price index. Changes in specifications are reflected in value totals. If the value total is deflated by a price index based on the more popular specifications of the item in question, the resulting aggregate will reveal the true change in physical output, assuming that the prices of all the different types of the product move in the same way as those represented in the price index. This assumption is recognized to be more valid than that of the constant composition of commodity classes.

The problem of using price deflators in the industry approach is to obtain price indexes corresponding to the various industry valuation levels and based on sufficient detail. Most existing price indexes are based on prices at the primary production and final distribution levels and often do not include either the intermediate or the more complex final products of industry. Particularly in secondary manufacturing, existing deflators are often not suitable for deflating the detailed industry values that form the basis of the industry approach. Most physical output measures in this area are therefore based on available commodity production detail. In the primary industries, commodities, in general, are more amenable to quantitative measurement so that the problem of handling variations in "group" quality is less likely to occur. Another problem is that the industry classification system may subdivide what is, in practice, a continuous integrated operation into two or more separate industries. This makes it difficult to obtain market valuations of output for the separate classifications and in these cases, the commodity approach is more practicable.

The development by the Prices Division of the DBS of special manufacturers' price indexes, based on a wide range of products cross-classified according to the Standard Industrial Classification, will soon be completed. These series will provide much more suitable price information for use in conjunction with industrial values of production and a more extensive use of the deflation method in the measurement of manufacturing production will then be possible.

SHORTCOMINGS FOR PRODUCTIVITY ANALYSIS

In the absence of proper physical output data or deflators in some areas neither approach takes account of changes in productivity. In the production approach, proper quantity or price data were not available for certain industries in which output and prices are difficult to determine in unit terms, a problem characteristic of industries producing investment goods such as industrial machinery, railway rolling stock, aircraft, shipbuilding, and building construction where output is more of the custom type and generally not organized on a mass production basis. The same problem is encountered in the expenditure approach where the same items appear as components of gross fixed capital formation or of government expenditure on goods.

This lack of price and quantity series for finished products has made it necessary to rely on a cost approach for deflating current dollar figures. The usual procedure is to construct a deflator based on prices of the major materials used and on average hourly earnings for each industry or expenditure component. This approach assumes that prices of the finished product will move in the same way as a weighted average of material prices and wage costs, and no adjustments are made for the effects of productivity changes on unit labor costs or for changes in profit margins and overhead.

Prices of raw materials are generally believed to change earlier and fluctuate more widely than prices of finished products, partly because wage costs are relatively rigid but also because profits and overhead per unit of output vary. Industries where there is some degree of monopoly tend to keep prices fairly rigid whether demand and production are falling or rising. However, when demand is rising and operations are at capacity, prices may move fairly well in line with costs. This probably means that in such industries between periods of general recession and expansion a price index based solely on wage and material costs will fluctuate more widely than the true price index of finished products. However, insofar as competitive conditions prevail in some sections of the industries or that escalator clauses are included in long-term contracts, the time sequence of price changes for materials, wages, and finished products will be more in line. The development of new price indexes for manufactured products noted

234

above will improve the deflation of machinery and equipment items. Further research is required to develop more satisfactory deflators for nonresidential building construction. Both approaches, however, follow the same general procedure, and although the technique is questionable it is at least consistent.

MEASUREMENT IN NONMARKET AREAS

The two approaches are aimed at arriving independently at the same global measure of real GDP. Therefore, the same basic guiding principles must be common to both. The production boundary, the point across which all goods and services are measured as they pass from the production process to final disappearance, must be clearly determined and measurement should neither fall short of, nor extend beyond, this boundary. Moreover, definitions of output in both approaches must be mutually consistent, i.e., the concept of output implied by the indicator selected in the production approach should be the same as that used in the expenditure approach.

Usually these principles are not difficult to follow, and definitions and procedures are quite clear. Where a market transaction takes place between a buyer and a seller a good or service (or bundle of goods and services) is exchanged for money or claims on money. Thus each value is implicitly composed of a physical good or a service at some market price defined as the average unit value of the item involved in the transaction. The nature of the commodity or service involved is quite clear, though data may not always be available to measure the transaction in the ideal way. Where no clear market transaction takes place, as in the case of government services, the quantity of output may be difficult to determine.

For most government departments, concerned mainly with administration and defence, measurement of output is, at present, impractical. Much effort and expense would be involved in attempting to devise proper indicators, although some acceptable measures immediately come to mind such as the number of unemployment insurance claims handled or the number of income tax returns processed. Such statistics would be readily available, however, for only a few departments and agencies, and at present we treat all public administration and defence services on the physical cost basis in the interests of uniform treatment in this sector. Although productivity is assumed to be constant, the implications of this procedure are considered less damaging for purposes of general economic analysis than any attempt to measure or arbitrarily estimate changes in real output in nonmarket sectors largely devoid of appropriate data.

The current official expenditure estimates use the cost approach for the measurement of school and hospital services, while the experimental production estimates follow the output concept. Those responsible for the deflation of the expenditure estimates would like to keep the national accounts valuation and deflation system intact for purposes of price and quantity breakdowns of existing concepts and have been reluctant to accept the output measurement. At the present time the problem of consistency in this area is under discussion. Ultimately, however, the main objective must be to achieve consistency between the two approaches.

INTERMEDIATE SERVICE COSTS AND "AREA DIFFERENTIATION" OF PRODUCTS

Theoretically, in the measurement of industry net output, the volume of purchased business costs, along with materials, fuel, and electricity, should be deducted from gross physical output. While Canadian annual census surveys provide sufficient data on materials, fuel, and electricity for a considerable number of industries, no statistics are at present collected, by industry, on purchases of business services such as advertising, insurance, transportation, and communications. Therefore, it is not possible to carry the calculation of real value added down to gross domestic product originating, and the resulting indicators still contain the duplicating effect of these service costs which are counted elsewhere as the output of the service industries concerned. To the extent, for instance, that the use of these services has increased proportional to "census" value added (gross output less materials, fuel, and electricity) the derived indicators of net output will show an upward bias. The possibility is being explored, however, of deducting these business services in total from the all-industry aggregate. The advisability of doing this would depend on how much effect any relative increases or decreases in these costs have on the indicators. This problem can best be illustrated by an example.

Suppose that there is a Canadian population shift from the central regions to the west coast and that there is a corresponding shift in the regional pattern of automobile sales. The retail price of cars is considerably higher in Vancouver than it is in Toronto which is close to the point of production, mainly as the result of the difference in the cost of transport. Let us assume that all other elements in the situation remain the same but the value of total retail sales rises simply because of the increase in transportation costs.

If the current value of sales is deflated by a retail price index of passenger cars, the result would be larger quantum even though there has been in fact no change in the total number of cars sold in both periods. Thus the result obtained by deflating the value of sales differs

236

from the measure derived from the total quantity of sales. To get identical results, in this case, the total quantity of sales approach would have to differentiate between cars sold in different areas; they would have to be treated as different products, with the numbers sold in each area weighted by their respective unit values in the base period.

If, in the production approach, the total quantity of sales had been used as the projector of base-period gross revenues of automobile retail dealers, and the physical cost of supplies and services subtracted from this figure to derive constant dollar net output, the deduction of the higher total outlay for transportation charges in the current period would result in a relative decline in net output of automobile retailers. This would nullify the corresponding increase of production in the transportation industry and be inconsistent with the deflation of final sales. In this case it would be preferable not to deduct the transportation input of car dealers and allow the increase in transportation output generated by Vancouver car buyers to be reflected in the real output of the transportation industry.

Thus, when the effect of changes in the input of services can be clearly appraised and measured at the final products stage (in other words, when the value of the service content of goods can be distinguished, and the consumer is, in effect, purchasing a separate service), the effect must be incorporated in the measure of the quantity of production before the deduction of commodity and service inputs in the same way that any changes in the physical input of commodity materials (affecting size and quality of a manufactured article) must be reflected in the output measure before deriving the residual net output aggregate. In the example, the deflation method will give the correct gross figure allowing net output of car dealers to remain relatively unchanged after the deduction of the higher transportation input, and the increase in total output will be reflected in the transportation industry.

Because of differences in development costs, proximity of markets, and available supplies, both the production and distribution price of natural gas is much higher in Ontario than in the Prairie Provinces. Although the products extracted in both regions are intrinsically the same, their relative importance on a value basis is quite different, and, consequently, they were treated as separate commodities. Otherwise, the rapid relative increase in Prairie gas production and distribution in recent years would have resulted in a substantial upward bias in the production indexes.

INSURANCE

The measurement of insurance requires special treatment. In the expenditure account the cost of all types of insurance purchased by

237

persons (except fire and other insurance on immovable property which is bought by persons in their capacity as landlords, not as consumers, and is therefore treated as business expenditure) cannot be measured by simply taking the payments (premiums) for such insurance as equal to the price of the service, since the premiums include moneys to be disbursed (claims) either in the same year or in future years to claimants. A portion of premiums and claims constitutes merely a redistribution of income within the personal sector, so premiums and claims are ignored. The cost of the service of the institutions which facilitate this process of redistribution is measured by their administrative expenses (including profits), i.e., premiums minus claims. At the present time both real output approaches use deflated administrative expenses.

Life insurance companies and fraternal societies have an additional characteristic. They not only protect, but also invest for their policyholders. The administrative expenses of life insurance companies include their investment expenses, i.e., a "fee" which policyholders pay as part of their premiums for the management of their investments. The real-output measures should reflect these two types of service provided to purchasers of life insurance. To represent the protection service, life insurance in force could be deflated with a general price index. The investment service could be represented by funds held by the companies on behalf of policyholders likewise deflated. However, this approach has not yet been incorporated in the real output series since we feel that further study of the functions of insurance companies and of methods of measuring these functions is necessary.

RENTS

In the national accounts' industrial distribution, nonresidential net rents are treated as operating revenue and shown as income originating in the industry which owns the property, thus reflecting the actual institutional arrangements in the economy. Capital consumption allowances are included in the industry using the property. Another viewpoint is that renting is merely an alternative way of securing the use of capital equipment and that all returns to such capital equipment should be shown as GDP originating in the industry in which the equipment is used. This is the treatment used for interest and dividends. For rents, however, data problems associated with the industrial allocation of renting expenses make it difficult to adopt this treatment. In the interindustry flow table, in order to keep industrial output free of investment income, nonresidential rents were set up as a "dummy" industry within the real estate division which would receive all rents and purchase all inputs associated with the

238

rental of buildings. For example, if a chemical manufacturer invests in a building and in turn rents it to a department store, the net rental income plus depreciation is allocated not to the chemical industry but to the real estate industry. In the real output approach the statistical convenience of the "dummy" industry device was adopted for all paid rents.

The operation of owner-occupied residential dwellings was treated in a similar manner. Owner-occupants are considered for national accounts purposes to be operating a business enterprise and are treated as landlords who rent houses to themselves as consumers. Imputed net rents plus capital consumption allowances on residential property are thus shown as a "dummy" component of the real estate industry.

A rent is also imputed on government-owned buildings used by the government. Here again the governments are considered as landlords renting to themselves. In this case, however, the imputed rents (net rents plus capital consumption allowances) can be treated as a factor of production along with salaries and wages and included as product originating in the public administration and defence industry. An alternative, of course, would be to handle this government renting activity as an additional "dummy" component in the real estate industry. The estimate of rent on government buildings is a recent replacement in the Canadian accounts for interest on the public debt used to finance productive assets and its treatment for purposes of industrial output is still undecided.

BANKS AND OTHER FINANCIAL INSTITUTIONS

The procedure by which industries are not shown as receiving interest means that the measure of output of financial institutions excludes the receipt of interest. The output of banks and similar institutions is measured by their income, other than interest, from the services they provide. Part of this service is measured by the charges made for bank services (cashing checks, issuing money orders, buying and selling foreign exchange, etc.). Part of the services to depositors, however, is paid for by the depositor allowing the use of capital without interest or at a lower rate of interest. Accordingly, imputations are made in the national accounts to represent the value of these services provided to persons and to governments; otherwise product originating in the banking industry would be negative or too low. Since no imputation is made in the national accounts for services provided to other industries, profits of other industries are overstated and banking output is understated to that extent. For real output purposes, the industry weights incorporate estimated adjustments to offset these biases. For measuring service to depositors in real terms, deposits deflated with a general price index appears to be an appropriate indicator.

Appraisal of Results

When two measures should theoretically give identical results but, in practice, give different results, it becomes important to determine which of the two measures is the more reliable. One cannot assess the reliability of the two measures of real output in mathematical terms. The best that can be done is to make a qualitative appraisal of their accuracy. Until developmental work on the production measures has been completed, however, such an appraisal would be inconclusive. As noted earlier, while the real expenditure estimates are published regularly in the national accounts quarterly bulletins, the industry production series are still preliminary and require further research and development work before they can be released for general use.

The results achieved so far are given below in Tables 5 and 6. Table 5 presents the annual results of the deflation of GDE and of the industry approach to the measurement of GDP, both at market prices, for 1949–56. The production measures incorporate the latest revised series for the industries covered by the Index of Industrial Production, and the expenditure estimates are the latest amended annual figures based on the series published in the recently revised national accounts reference document.[31]

TABLE 5

Annual Estimates of Real Gross Domestic Product at Market Prices
(1949 = 100)

	Production Approach	Expenditure Approach
1949	100.0	100.0
1950	106.4	107.2
1951	113.4	113.1
1952	120.0	121.6
1953	124.9	126.2
1954	123.4	122.7
1955	134.9	133.3
1956	146.2	144.9
1957	145.5	144.9
1958	146.4	145.9

Table 6 presents the quarterly results for 1953–58 as percentage changes between each quarter and the corresponding quarter of the preceding year. In this table, the expenditure estimates are at market prices while the production series are at factor cost.

[31] *National Accounts, Income and Expenditure, 1926–1956, op. cit.*

240

TABLE 6

Quarterly Real Gross Domestic Product,
Percentage Changes from Same Quarter of Preceding Year

		Production Approach at Factor Cost	Expenditure Approach at Market Prices
1953	1	+5.9	+7.5
	2	+6.8	+5.9
	3	+2.7	+1.1
	4	+0.2	+1.7
1954	1	+0.2	—
	2	−0.2	−1.2
	3	−8.2	−9.4
	4	+4.4	+2.1
1955	1	+4.7	+3.9
	2	+9.5	+7.8
	3	+14.4	+13.3
	4	+7.8	+8.1
1956	1	+9.3	+10.4
	2	+7.8	+6.7
	3	+9.3	+8.5
	4	+7.5	+9.6
1957	1	+4.9	+3.9
	2	+1.4	+2.4
	3	−4.8	−4.0
	4	−3.6	−0.9
1958	1	−1.7	−2.4
	2	−0.5	−0.6
	3	+0.1	+1.8
	4	+4.5	+3.6

The fairly close agreement between the two series suggests that an average of the results may be nearer to the actual level than either of the estimates. As noted above, however, until our appraisal of the two estimates is completed, any conclusion would be highly tentative.

The two approaches are largely independent. In fact, industries in the production approach which are represented by the same indicators used in the expenditure approach account for only about 20 per cent of GDP and consist mostly of government and defense services, construction, paid and imputed rents, and some recreational and personal services. The production series are therefore useful not only as an independent check on the deflated expenditure estimates but also in focusing attention at times on the underlying value figures. Occasionally an important difference occurs between the two real output series. This calls for a re-examination of the basic data especially in those areas where the estimates are relatively weak and where compensating adjustments would more likely be needed.

A complete reconciliation of the two approaches is, at present, impossible. Ideally the deflation of final products should be carried out at such a fine level of detail that all individually specified commodities and services could be identified as the final products of particular industries, subject only to the addition of distributive margins. Countries in which the consumer goods expenditure estimates are built up on a commodity flow basis, by adding transport and distributive margins to factory shipments of individual commodities, are fortunate in having developed this method, for it lends itself to the integration of industry and final product estimates. The Canadian estimates of consumer goods expenditure are based on retail sales, which do not provide commodity detail at other than decennial census benchmarks. Currently we have only the store-type totals. We have quarterly commodity flow estimates of machinery and equipment and of course the export and import figures contain a wealth of commodity detail, but in general the possibilities of easy integration are quickly exhausted.

In practice, we find ourselves confronted with two completely different classification schemes: on the one hand the industrial classification of establishments and on the other the sectors consuming final products, namely consumers, government, business on capital account and rest-of-world. These two separate classification schemes come together only at the total level and only occasionally do the two measures of output use the same indicators. In these circumstances, we are far short of the ideal set of data as portrayed by the commodity flow worksheets underlying the input-output table. To do an input-output table each year or quarter is, of course, quite beyond our resources even if the data were all available. All that can be entered here is a plea for the extension of work on commodity flow estimates entering the current final product totals. One suggestion already made is that the next input-output table should provide extra rows for important commodity details. What we really need is to develop a new table (e.g., for 1961 in constant 1949 dollars) and to pay attention, during its construction, to the selection of a set of the more important commodity flows.

We have already attempted consistency checks in a limited number of categories. In general, these checks involved cross-classifying final products by industry in some cases, while the opposite classification of industrial products by final expenditure components was done in others. The methods used were necessarily crude and the actual results

242

obtained were relatively inconclusive; they indicate, however, that further comparisons of the two series could prove very fruitful. For example, a detailed study of the automobile industry pointed up apparent inconsistencies in both current and deflated estimates of expenditures on automobiles, and indicated that commodity flow data are needed for the detail of consumer expenditure. Before starting these comparisons, we felt that such factors as trade margins and quality changes, which are extremely difficult to measure and trace through the two sets of estimates, might prevent any useful results being obtained. Our present feeling is that, although these may be important over time, most year-to-year discrepancies are caused by factors which can be isolated and measured—e.g., errors in prices, quantities, or values. In particular, if the comparisons are made on a current basis, with a knowledge of events fresh in mind, the task is much simpler.

COMMENT

MILTON MOSS, Board of Governors of the Federal Reserve System

It is clear from the paper by Berlinguette and Leacy that a very large and progressive effort on national accounting and related research is being undertaken in Canada. In their Division at the Dominion Bureau of Statistics (aptly named "Research and Development Division") the work done and in active preparation is considerable. More progress has been made in Canada than in most other countries in the estimation of total value of product—now amounting in Canada to a little over $30 billion. This progress is particularly evident in the estimation of total product in "real" terms. Canada was already in the forefront among countries developing their own factual record of economic growth with a regular quarterly publication of constant price estimates of Gross National Expenditures. With the announcement in the Berlinguette and Leacy paper that they are actively preparing to publish their estimates of real product classified by industry of origin on a quarterly basis, Canada's place among the leaders has been further advanced.

Certain aspects of the work in Canada on real output measurement suggest some implications for work in this area in the United States.

Canadian Program

The unique feature of Canadian national accounting work presented by Berlinguette and Leacy is the development of measures of value added in constant prices for all of the industry sectors of the economy. This has involved, essentially, expanding the scope of their

243

index of industrial production to include output of sectors in addition to mining, manufacturing, and electricity and gas, namely, agriculture, construction, trade, transportation, real estate and other services, and government enterprises.

Two aspects of this work are especially advanced: (1) the development of annual net output indexes (deflated output minus deflated input) for agriculture, electric utilities, nearly half of manufacturing, and to some extent for transportation, and (2) refinement of value added weights for manufacturing—that is, adjustment of Census value added data to exclude services purchased by manufacturing establishments from other establishments.

Coupled with this progressive effort has been a highly commendable flexibility of approach, particularly in connection with use of net output measures—i.e., using them only with considerable caution and only where differences between net and gross measures could be adequately explained. This flexibility is also evident in the recognition that for price analysis the implicit deflators in the net product estimates have shortcomings and that independent price indexes (with base year quantity weights) are also needed for price analysis.

With so large an effort in Canada, and strong emphasis on incorporating the newest concepts in their work, certain practical details may have been given less priority over the years. Thus, at the time of this writing, serious downward biases still exist in those areas of the production index based on employment data unadjusted for productivity change—biases which will be corrected in the forthcoming revision of their indexes. In addition, a prewar base is still being used in their presently published indexes. This also is to be corrected and the year 1949 incorporated as the base year in the revision. A final note on an important practical shortcoming is the rather late release of the Canadian production index involving a lag of over six weeks following the month covered. Maintaining a balance between implementing new concepts on the one hand and taking care of practical details on the other is a difficult task.

Brief View of Results

This paper presents little in the way of final results, and is chiefly concerned with describing the various problems faced in developing more or less consistent totals of real product by two approaches. Berlinguette and Leacy discuss such problems very well—particularly in pinning down the quantitative effect of use of market prices versus factor costs and net output versus gross output indexes.

Until the more complete over-all results appear, however, my discussion can deal with only a few fragments presented in the paper.

244

Two sets of annual indexes—one based on the expenditure approach, the other on the production approach—are shown in the paper for the 1949–56 period. They are shown as indexes in constant prices of the year 1949. The two measures should give conceptually the same results. Indeed, with complete information on the quantity and value of the flow of goods and services, they need not be considered as two separate approaches. But, as should be expected, the estimates differ for statistical reasons.

The increase in Canadian real output for the seven-year period, as measured by the two approaches, is about 45 per cent, or approximately 5 per cent per year. As the accompanying chart shows, the production measure indicates more growth over the whole period than the expenditure measure. For the earlier part of the period shown the expenditure approach yields the faster rise. But subsequently the production figures rise much faster. From 1952 to 1956 the production figures rise nearly 22 per cent compared with 18 per cent for the expenditure figures. Fluctuations in rate of growth are more evident in the expenditure measure and in the first postwar recession in Canada—in 1953–54—the expenditure measure shows the sharper decline.

Not enough information is provided in the paper to determine the basis for the differences indicated in the period. Perhaps the presentation of more detailed results upon publication of the quarterly figures will provide clues as to why the production figures tend to show larger growth and the expenditure figures more fluctuations during the 1949–56 period.

Implications for Real Output Measurement in the United States

Regularly published official measures of real output are widely diffused in the United States. The Federal Reserve monthly index of industrial production covering manufacturing and mining represents the longest effort in regular publication of a measure of real output for the United States. In its present general form it was introduced in 1927. Beginning in 1956 a monthly index of electric and gas utilities was published and in 1959 was incorporated into the production index. The Department of Commerce since 1951 has regularly published measures of constant dollar GNP on an annual basis, and since 1958 on a quarterly basis. The Department of Agriculture began publication in 1945 of an annual measure of total real farm output. In 1956 the Bureau of Mines published an annual index of mineral production carrying forward work begun much earlier. The Bureau of Labor Statistics has developed annual measures for various sectors of the economy in connection with its productivity work, notably net output measures for manufacturing. Estimates presented for this conference by Alterman and Jacobs reflect in good part the work of the Bureau of Labor Statistics in experimenting with real output measures by industry of origin for the total economy. Measures compiled by private and public agencies, apart from regular publication, have been available for various industry sectors for a long time.

In examining Canada's joint publication of an industry of origin measure (production approach) as well as a GNP type measure

CHART 1

Two Estimates of Canadian Real Product

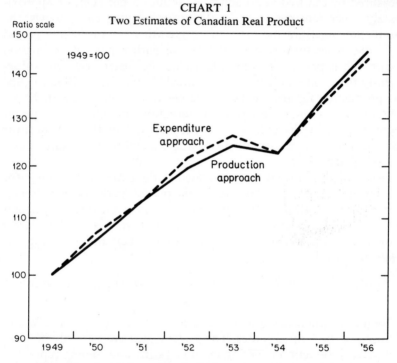

NOTE: Based on indexes given by Berlinguette and Leacy in this volume

(expenditure approach), it seems useful to me to reflect on the objectives to be served by these two measures, both for short-run and long-run analysis. This reflection should provide perspective on the work ahead in the United States.

Ideally the industry of origin approach provides data for analyzing supply problems and also problems of industrial performance. Ideally the expenditure figures would provide a framework for the analysis of changes in demand. I emphasize the word "ideally" because under the present conditions of data availability the production

246

figures and the expenditure figures may be used in ways that are somewhat different from those for which they are uniquely designed to serve. Thus, for example, the production figures tend to be more detailed than the expenditure figures. As a result, they often give better indications of changes in demand in commodity markets than do the less detailed expenditure figures. The production figures tend to be more prompt and more frequent. It is no accident, therefore, that the analysis of the economy's cyclical position tends to be centered around such indicators as the index of industrial production.

A chief advantage of the industry of origin approach is that it permits analysis of productivity developments in more depth than is provided by the expenditure figures. When matched with various resource use categories such as manpower, electric power, or fuel, the expenditure figures can be analyzed only in very broad terms. In the industry of origin approach, however, the comparison can be as detailed as the industry figures permit.

The wealth of data on quantities and values of product available from the production side of the economy is worth emphasis. Compare, for example, the detail available in the United States Census of Manufactures with the Census of Retail Trade. In the 1954 Census of Manufactures, for example, data are available on quantities and values for some 7,000 products. In the Census of Retail Trade for the same year, although seventy-five different kinds of stores are shown, no data on quantity and value are available for any single product.

An interesting consequence of the availability of product detail for the manufacturing sector is its use in the United States, through commodity flow procedures, in providing benchmark estimates of final sales of finished goods for the GNP expenditure figures.

In the industry of origin *concept*, the product detail so unique to industry statistics may be lost. This is because in the net output approach the deflation of outputs minus the deflation of inputs gives rise to a total net value for an industry. No similar subtraction can be made for individual products. Perhaps it would be helpful if the national accounts provided gross product listings even though the gross measures for products may not add to the net output for industries. With appropriate assumptions about input-output relations and value-added weights for products the product detail could probably be shown together with the net output measures for industries.

Product detail of course needn't be lost. It disappears only if the net output approach is strictly followed. In short-run measures, such as the quarterly figures proposed by Canada, gross output measures combined with value added weights are used. But they are used as a compromise device until such time as it becomes possible to develop

247

net output measures. Similarly, in the annual estimates prepared by Alterman and Jacobs, gross output measures were unavoidable for the later years shown.

The industry of origin approach—as a net output concept—is useful for long-run rather than short-run analysis. This is true at least under present conditions of data availability. Changes in the industrial composition of the total economy, which this approach can reveal so usefully, come about slowly. Changes in relations between output and usage of materials, fuel, electric power, and capital occur in ways that cannot yet be measured monthly or quarterly. Changes in the relation between input and output prices—in margins—may be more volatile than is sometimes thought. But the painstaking effort required for measuring these changes for all industry sectors of the economy is a long-run or benchmark type affair. Short-run changes in output per man-hour are measurable, if at all, only in the commodity producing sectors of the economy, notably manufacturing.

A final point on the relation between the expenditure and production approach: i.e., the need to show consistent results below the total level for at least three important areas of activity. These three areas, retail trade, equipment production, and construction are essentially common to both approaches. Retail trade figures are used in the expenditure approach for measuring changes in personal consumption expenditures and in the industry of origin approach for measuring changes in the gross output of the retail trade industry. In the case of equipment, including defense equipment, the production figures should be very similar to the expenditure figures, after adjustments for imports and exports, because for most large equipment items inventory changes in the finished product tend to be small. In the case of construction the industry and expenditure concepts may differ because of force account work but if the industry of origin approach is flexible enough to show this separately, the expenditure and industry figures should be essentially the same.

Now, these three areas are major gaps in our data needs for current analysis. When they are adequately taken care of the industry of origin and expenditure approaches will be far more useful for current analysis in the United States. Perplexities in other areas, namely, services, households, and government enterprises will probably continue to be unsolved and will be useful as challenges to graduate students and other philosophers.

JACK ALTERMAN, Bureau of Labor Statistics

The paper by Berlinguette and Leacy on the Canadian output measures and the paper which Mrs. Jacobs and I prepared on the

United States sector output measures both indicate that one of the main uses of such estimates is the development of measures of productivity. It may be of interest, therefore, to compare the rate of change in output per man-hour for the two countries. The paper by Berlinguette and Leacy does not provide estimates of output per man-hour but does indicate that estimates based on methods similar to those described in their paper are presented in a recent book by W. C. Hood and Anthony Scott, *Output, Labor and Capital in the Canadian Economy, 1958*, Appendix F, Chapter 5, p. 397. A comparison of the figures contained in that volume with our paper indicate that between 1947 and 1955 output per man-hour in the total private economy showed almost exactly the same annual rate of increase for both Canada and the United States—approximately 3.6 per cent. These estimates further indicate a substantial rate of increase for the farm sector—approximately 6.5 per cent for both countries. This sharp rate of increase for the postwar period in output per man-hour for the farm sector was a major factor in the over-all change in output per man-hour.

The rate of increase in the nonfarm sector was 3.0 per cent per year in the United States, compared to 2.5 per cent in Canada. This seeming paradox—approximately the same rates of change for total private and farm sectors but a higher rate in the United States for the nonfarm sector—is due to the greater effect of the farm-nonfarm shift in Canada than in the United States.

The effect of this shift in the United States has already been indicated in our paper. These estimates indicate that approximately 8 per cent of the total increase could be attributed to this shift during this period. The effect of the shift was of more importance in the Canadian economy, accounting for approximately 15 per cent of the total overall increase in output per man-hour. The greater effect of the farm to nonfarm shift in the Canadian economy is due to the fact that the farm sector accounts for a higher proportion of both man-hours and output in the Canadian economy than in the United States.

International Comparisons of Real Product and Productivity by Final Expenditures and by Industry

MILTON GILBERT AND WILFRED BECKERMAN
ORGANIZATION FOR EUROPEAN ECONOMIC COOPERATION

THE GROSS national product per capita (or per unit of labor input, if that is more suitable to the purpose), adjusted for price changes, provides a convenient over-all measure of intertemporal variations in the productivity of an economy. We in the OEEC have worked along these lines to obtain comparable indexes for our various member countries and for the OEEC area as a whole, so that the rates of change among the countries may be compared. The essential problem, of course, is to construct measures of real gross national product and of the labor force for the various countries that are conceptually and statistically similar. Our annual reports and publications on national product and expenditure show that considerable progress has been made in this work, although improvement of the data for some of the countries is still needed.

In this paper, however, we are concerned with another type of work designed to yield, not international comparisons of rates of change, but international comparisons of the absolute level of real GNP per capita or per unit of labor input. The essential idea is to provide the same type of basic data as that yielded by intertemporal comparisons, but with the indexes relating to a given point of time and the index numbers showing the comparative standing of various national economies.

We have approached this work by two methods. In the first, the basic datum for the construction of the indexes is the GNP broken down by final expenditures. Two reports have been published using this method. One in 1954 covered five countries and gave data for 1950 and 1952; one in 1958 covered nine countries and gave data for 1950 and 1955.[1]

In the second method, the basic datum is the GNP broken down by industry of origin or net output. This study, by Deborah Paige and

[1] Milton Gilbert and Irving Kravis, *An International Comparison of National Products and the Purchasing Power of Currencies* (OEEC, Paris, 1954); and Milton Gilbert and Associates, *Comparative National Products and Price Levels* (OEEC, Paris, 1958).

251

Gottfried Bombach, was published in June 1959 as a joint project of the OEEC and the Department of Economics of Cambridge University under the title of *A Comparison of National Output and Productivity of the United Kingdom and the United States.* In addition, two papers dealing with this method have been issued.[2]

Needless to say, the work with both these approaches was undertaken in an experimental spirit and intended to show the kinds of problems encountered, as well as the character of results that could be obtained. In this paper we intend to focus more on the problems that have not been dealt with adequately in previous papers or reports.

The Conceptual Basis of the Comparisons

THE CONCEPT OF PRODUCTION

The conceptual basis of the expenditure comparisons has been discussed in some detail in the first of the OEEC publications mentioned above. The following discussion will be confined mainly to those aspects of the conceptual problems that have been questioned or which have been the subject of further work since the publication of that study. It was said that the primary aim of the study was "to compare the flow of goods and services made available for the purposes of consumption, gross investment, and government by the country's own production resources."[3] It was emphasized that such comparisons are subject to well-known limitations. Most of these limitations, which are of various kinds, apply also to measures of the changes over time in a country's real national product. They are such that comparisons of real national product must not be confused with comparisons of well-being or happiness in a wider philosophical sense.

Nevertheless, measures of relative real national product are of considerable significance. Other things being equal, the size of the real national product is a component of well-being in a wider sense, and is the component about which economists and politicians are able to do something. Other elements of happiness, particularly those of a spiritual nature, are no doubt very important, but economists are not supposed to be responsible for them and, in any case, they are not subject to measurement. Whatever reservations may be attached to the concept, people do happen to be closely interested in the size of the

[2] Deborah Paige and S. Adler, "International Comparisons of National Products: An Approach by Industry of Origin," *Income and Wealth*, Series IV (1955), and Milton Gilbert, Gottfried Bombach, and Deborah Paige, "The Real Product of the United Kingdom and the United States in 1950," paper presented to the Fourth Conference of the International Association for Research in Income and Wealth at Hindsgavl (1955).

[3] Gilbert and Kravis, *op. cit.*, p. 61.

national product, its growth, and its composition. As economists our duty includes both the satisfaction of this interest and the provision of the statistical measures of this concept, which are indispensable tools of economic analysis. However, there are divergent views regarding the appropriate concept of output to use in productivity comparisons and, in fact, a question in some minds as to whether international comparisons can have a firm foundation at all.

For purposes of "real" comparisons of total national output, there are three concepts to consider:

1. The consolidated output of domestic establishments. This is the gross domestic product which includes exports but excludes imports.

2. The output of domestic establishments plus net income from abroad. This is the gross national product, including exports but excluding imports.

3. The gross national product made up of private consumption, government consumption, domestic capital formation—all including imports but excluding exports—and net foreign investment (including net income to or from abroad). This concept is identical to concept 2 at current prices, but for comparisons over time or between countries at constant prices they are not necessarily so. Concept 3 corresponds, in intertemporal comparisons, to GNP adjusted for changes in the terms of trade. It has been suggested that this concept be called the gross national income.

We have used this third concept in the OEEC studies and believe strongly that it must be considered the basic concept of aggregate production for both intertemporal and international measures. The reason for this view is that it measures the final output of the national economy in consumption and investment.

Technical and analytical objections have been raised against this viewpoint. The technical argument in favor of the first concept is that any index of production must be made up only of goods (i.e., commodities and services), the quantities and prices of which are the basic data for the calculation of the index. No purely financial flows, such as net income from abroad or net foreign investment, should enter into the index as these do not have specific flows of goods behind them. Such flows can only be deflated by attributing a flow of goods to them which would introduce an arbitrary element into the whole index. Thus the only logical concept of aggregate real output is the gross domestic product.

While this argument has formal validity, we do not believe it to be decisive. It may be more straightforward to determine how much the gross domestic product differs from situation A to situation B, but

253

this is not the question we want answered. We want to know how the national product, adjusted for any changes in the terms of trade, differs in the two situations because only that tells us what the residents of the nation are getting out of the economic process. If, in fact, the domestic product differs significantly from the national product, then it yields a result that cannot be interpreted, either from a productivity or from a welfare standpoint, as one cannot say either who produced the output or who received it.

Hence, we must try to find an acceptable technique for deflating net foreign income or investment, as the case might be. This can readily be done by using an import price index for net income received from abroad and for net foreign borrowings, or by using an export price index if the signs are reversed. This method is certainly appropriate since imports and exports are the real flows that correspond to the financial flows. The defect that remains is that one cannot specify which imports or which exports and is forced to use a general import or export price index. But this defect does not seem great in the light of the many compromise techniques that must be used to deflate aggregate output altogether. Moreover, one can say that the larger the financial flow is proportionately and the more important it is to deflate it to get a meaningful result, the more will the general indexes of export or import prices approximate the real flow of goods that should be measured.[4]

The analytical argument in favor of the gross domestic product is that the idea of productivity itself is only relevant to a specific flow of goods and services from a specific group of establishments. Presumably, productivity in this context, being conceived of as a kind of measure of industrial efficiency, would only be distorted by the addition of net income from abroad or by differences in the terms of trade.

This point of view seems to us to be wide of the mark essentially because a measure of overall productivity (either intertemporal or international) is not simply a measure of the difference in industrial efficiency narrowly defined. One of the main elements in its variation is differences in the industrial composition of output in the two situa-

---

[4] In some discussions of this problem, the impression is given that the choice of the real flow to represent the financial flow depends upon the purpose of the measurement. For example, it is said that net foreign investment might be deflated by import prices because the economy gives up the opportunity of obtaining additional imports by the act of investing abroad. Or, that net foreign investment might be deflated by an index of consumption goods prices because the investors forego additional consumption by the act of investing. However, when the real gross national product as a whole is being calculated, such considerations are irrelevant; each component of the gross national product can only relate to a particular category of real output. Net foreign investment can equally be called net exports and, hence, the only appropriate deflator to make the total result meaningful is export prices.

tions being compared. Foreign investment and foreign trade are essential parts of the economic process and a comparison of two situations leaving out these elements is incomplete.

So far as net income to or from abroad is concerned, we see no reason for omitting it from the calculation and consider that results without it are generally not very useful. Suppose, for example, that an economy has substantially increased its output with the help of a large import of foreign capital resulting partly in a flow of income to abroad. To measure the increase in productivity of this economy without allowing for this import of capital would be like measuring the increased productivity in agriculture without allowing for the increased use of fertilizers and machinery. While this may have some meaning in isolation, it has no meaning as part of a measure of overall productivity.

With regard to the effect of differences in the terms of trade, this has considerable independent significance, particularly in intertemporal comparisons of a single economy. This significance largely revolves around the analysis of year to year changes. However, the idea of productivity tends to lose much of its relevance in periods of cyclical change. From a longer-term standpoint when productivity is compared at the same stage of the business cycle, say at full employment, then the difference in the terms of trade cannot be considered an aberration. For example, the British economy produces less of its food requirements because it finds it advantageous to get these from abroad in exchange for manufactured goods. To say what the productivity change of the British economy has been after this shift in its structure, it is surely essential to include foreign trade as part of the productive process. Similarly, if the United States and British economies are being compared, only the final products available to the two economies will give a meaningful result.

DIFFERENCES IN TASTES AND INCOME DISTRIBUTION

Following the first of the OEEC studies mentioned above, J. L. Nicholson raised certain considerations relevant to the question of how far the comparisons provide valid indicators of relative economic welfare or productivity. He stated that "the problems involved in comparing the national products of two different countries are essentially different from those involved in comparing the national products of a single country at two points of time."[5] He notes that the main considerations are differences in tastes and in income-distribution between countries.

[5] J. L. Nicholson, "Official Papers: The International Comparison of National Products," *Economic Journal*, June 1955.

Nicholson also mentions that, between countries, "capacities for enjoyment" of a given collection of goods may differ and that "the enjoyment of economic goods depends to a large extent on uneconomic factors—the proximity of friends and relatives, the life-long associations of a particular part of the world, etc."[5]

It is necessary to specify what is meant by differences in tastes in comparing two countries. For purposes of the welfare theory of index-number comparisons, it is essential that the community preference fields, described by indifference surfaces relating quantities of goods purchased to their relative prices and to varying levels of income, be very similar. In this context, differences in tastes must be interpreted as the action of variables other than prices and incomes which result in different collections of goods being purchased at a given level of relative prices and incomes.

Thus we are not concerned with differences in, say, the style or design of the goods purchased. If one country has a greater preference for coffee than for tea—quite apart from differences in incomes and relative prices—such a taste difference is only significant if the two products require different types and quantities of real resources. In such a case, whether tea and coffee are treated as separate products or whether they are combined (after making appropriate quality adjustments), the quantities consumed would show differences between the countries beyond those that may be due to differences in incomes and relative prices. In other words, the indifference curves of the two countries cross whether or not tea and coffee are treated as separate products and, strictly speaking, no valid welfare comparisons are possible.

From the point of view of productivity comparisons, however, even this sort of taste difference may, in practice, be of minor importance. This would be the case when the *relative* real resources required to produce the same competing goods were the same in both countries. For example, suppose that, as a result of "taste" difference, relatively more radios were purchased in the U.S. than in the U.K., but U.K. purchases of sewing machines were relatively greater than in the United States. Then suppose that in both countries a given number of sewing machines could be produced by the resources required to produce some other given number of radio sets. (This is assuming there would be no change in relative costs if the proportion of the two goods produced were changed.) The relative positions of the exchange lines in the two countries tells us nothing about the relative positions of their indifference curves but it tells us something about the relative positions of their production transformation curves. Given the above

[5] Nicholson, *op. cit.*, p. 255.

256

assumption of a constant rate of production substitution between sewing machines and radios, these are parallel straight lines when drawn in two dimensions only (i.e., when relating only possible output of sewing machines to possible output of radio sets). For example, at the same level of aggregate consumption of radios and sewing machines, the exchange lines would coincide, even though the relative proportions of the two goods purchased in the two countries would differ.

From the welfare point of view, two questions arise: (a) whether there are likely to be greater differences in tastes between countries than between two years in a given country and (b) whether in any particular comparison, the differences are likely to be so great as to invalidate conclusions that might otherwise be reached. It does not seem to the present writers that any definite general answer can be given to the first question, nor does it seem that, with regard to tastes, there is any essential difference of principle between international comparisons and intertemporal comparisons—it is purely a matter of how far apart the two situations being compared are. Comparisons between two periods of time which are far apart (in terms of the scope for changes in tastes) may be just as limited as comparisons between two countries. It could be argued, however, that comparisons over very long periods of time are invalid as measures of changes in welfare, but that this does not make the international comparisons any less invalid, since these too will break down on the obstacle of large differences in tastes.

But what is the evidence for the assumption that, in general, international differences in tastes are greater than intertemporal comparisons involving, say, similar differences in income levels? In the second of the OEEC studies, an experimental analysis was made of the variations in consumption patterns among the nine countries covered in the study, with reference to differences in their incomes and their relative price structures.[6] In spite of the fact that in 1950 the play of consumer preferences was still far from free in some of the countries, or was subject to special distortions arising from postwar recovery, it was remarkable how greatly the observed international differences in consumption patterns appeared to be explained by differences in incomes and relative prices. These results suggest that international differences in tastes are not so important as is sometimes alleged, on the basis of no emiprcal evidence of which we are aware. This result is not particularly strange. If the average Frenchman buys more wine than the average Englishman, it is more likely because wine is relatively cheaper in France than in England, rather

[6] Gilbert and Associates, *op. cit.*, Chapter V.

than because every Frenchman is born with a taste for it or that every Englishman is born with a preference for beer. It is true that a low price of wine would result in a habit of wine consumption and that a subsequent rise in the price might take a long time to have its full effect. But this is merely a defect in the statistical methods of demand analysis employed which the use of more dynamic demand functions would eliminate. Furthermore, such failures of demand to adapt itself to sharp changes in relative prices or incomes affect only an insignificant minority of the products concerned.

There may be, in fact, reason to believe that international differences in taste are *less* important than differences over long periods of time in one country. Countries are, after all, connected by international trade and by many vehicles of communication so that the average Frenchman knows perfectly well that the average American has a big car, a television set, and drinks whiskey. It was much more difficult for the American of 1900 to know what the American of 1950 would consume, or to consume it if he had wished to. It is not out of ignorance that the average Frenchman drinks relatively little whiskey, and it is not for climatic reasons that the average Italian has no refrigerator. It is largely because their incomes are lower and because whiskey is relatively expensive in France and refrigerators are relatively expensive in Italy. Thus, there seems to be no *prima facie* reason for believing that international differences in tastes are particularly marked; such empirical evidence as is available suggests that they are not.

There remains the question of whether small differences in tastes invalidate the comparisons as indicators of relative economic welfare. According to the present state of the theory of welfare economics, the greater the difference between the two situations with respect to their real national products (or levels of consumption) the greater the certainty, other things being equal, that the apparent statistical difference reflects a real welfare difference. As I. M. D. Little has put it: "If one (person) wishes to maintain that consumption has risen and the other (person) that consumption has fallen, neither can possibly *prove* his case. Nor could he prove it however perfect the statistical techniques might be. Of course, if the index number showed a terrific rise, the person who maintained that consumption had fallen would look silly. One might cease to trust his judgment, but he could never be proved wrong. If, however, the index number showed only a small rise, it really becomes quite meaningless to say that consumption has either risen or fallen."[7]

It has been argued above that there is no reason in principle to

[7] I. M. D. Little, *A Critique of Welfare Economics* (Oxford, 1950), p. 218.

believe that there are greater differences in tastes between countries than there are over long periods of time within a given country and that, in fact, there are reasons to believe the contrary. Furthermore, the magnitude of the apparent differences in real levels of GNP or consumption as measured in the studies concerned are very large in some cases. Even the U.K. appears to have had (in 1955) a *per capita* consumption level about 50 per cent below that of the U.S. If value judgments have to be made—as they inevitably must in this type of comparison—it would be a bold man who could maintain that such apparent differences in *per capita* GNP's are likely to be significantly invalidated by differences in tastes between the average Englishman and the average American.

Similar considerations apply to the question of income distribution. It is true that to make welfare comparisons, some value judgment has to be made concerning income distribution. In the OEEC studies, abstraction has been made from the question of income distribution. The comparison of the relative products of the countries indicates the relative welfares that could be achieved if income distribution were no better or worse in some countries than in others. Given the magnitude of the differences found between the national products of the countries concerned, however, it would again be a bold man who would assert, as a value judgment, that they were significantly affected, from the point of view of welfare, by offsetting differences in the goodness of the income distributions.

QUALITY DIFFERENCES AND UNIQUE PRODUCTS

The main conceptual obstacle to the validity of the comparisons thus seems to be the question of unique products (products appearing in one situation but not in the other) and of quality differences. As Mr. Little has stated, "the introduction of a new good formally prevents us from saying that welfare has increased, and, similarly, if a good ceases to be produced, it would prevent us from saying that welfare has decreased. Quality changes also can obviously invalidate the analysis."[8]

In practice, of course, techniques can usually be found for assimilating the unique products into other commodity classes by means which do not appear to do too much violence to the rationale of the calculation or to the actual statistical results. Nevertheless, there is a limit, and when unique products become too numerous there may not be much of substance left in the comparison. On this point we have said, that "the necessity of having prices or costs of unique goods for both markets as data for the index-number equations point to the

[8] Little, *op.cit.*, p. 218.

fundamental difficulty involved in comparing the national products of very primitive and advanced economies. This difficulty has often been seen primarily in terms of the difference in tastes and needs. From the point of view adopted in this report, however, the difficulty is rather the large amount of unique goods in the national expenditure of the advanced society for which no meaningful price or cost can be imputed to the primitive society. The primitive society has no possibility of producing the good itself; an estimate of relative costs would be fictitious. Moreover, it has no possibility of importing the goods in significant quantities without a complete upheaval in its domestic price structure, assuming that this possibility exists at all. Hence the index number equations can be computed only on the basis of the price weights of the advanced society. This result may tell us something either from the standpoint of productivity or economic welfare."[9]

Quality differences give rise to a similar conceptual problem. They must be treated in practice partly by abstracting from them and partly by adjusting for them. There seems to be general agreement on how adjustments for quality differences should be made, so we may here discuss only what quality differences must be neglected in a quantitative measure of a change in production.

First, it is essential to draw a distinction between what we have called economic and non-economic differences in quality. Statistical adjustments can be made for the former whereas none can be made for the latter since they are essentially non-quantitative in character. We can define a non-economic change in quality as one which comes about through the general improvement of science and the arts but which does not involve any increase in production costs. For example, a physician of today can render a better quality of service to his patients than one of twenty-five years ago, simply because medical science has advanced (leaving aside drugs, medical equipment, and hospital services, which are products separate from the physician's services). There is no way to bring this improvement of quality of medical services into an index of production, just as there is no economic aspect of it that can serve as a basis of measurement. Hence, as in an international comparison, indexes of production must abstract from such non-economic quality changes.

Second, the whole question of what constitutes an improvement in quality involves an element of judgment and, therefore, the process of constructing an index of real production consists partly of an appraisal of what is or is not significant. If one takes the view that every difference between a given product in the two situations is a

[9] Gilbert and Kravis, *op.cit.*, p. 87.

COMPARISONS OF REAL PRODUCT AND PRODUCTIVITY

quality difference, then the whole task becomes hopeless. And this is the case even if the differences exist in the base year (or country) with differences in prices attaching to them. For example, consider the case of an identical product which sells for a different price in chain stores and in independent stores, or the case of a product of identical physical specifications which sells at a different price packaged and unpackaged. We believe that as a matter of judgment, these products must be considered to be without difference in quality and that the price differences represent imperfections of the market. Of course, it can be argued that the consumer gets something extra from the convenience of packaged goods or from the convenience of buying in a neighborhood store. But it seems more reasonable to consider such differences as changes in the process of production and distribution which are undertaken as a matter of business efficiency and not as affecting the consumer's economic welfare. Without a simplifying assumption of this kind, it really becomes physically impossible to construct any index of overall production.[10]

When one abstracts from the two kinds of quality differences mentioned above the task of dealing with the quality problem is statistically manageable. Nonetheless, the resulting index of production is subject to additional conceptual limitations from the standpoint of both welfare and productivity. We do not feel that it is necessary to throw out the baby with the bath water, but there are evidently extreme situations in which there is not much of a baby left.

PROBLEM OF WEIGHTS

It has been argued above that, given a substantial difference in the real national products of the two situations compared, valid conclusions may be drawn since other conceptual limitations (tastes, income distribution) will, in most cases, be relatively unimportant. Unfortunately, the greater the disparities in real national products, the greater the differences between the price (and quantity) structures of the two situations tend to be, and hence the greater the effect of the choice of weights on the measure of the disparity in real products (or in purchasing power equivalents). For example, as can be seen in Table 1, the relative position of the United Kingdom's *per capita* GNP on U.S. price weights is 29 per cent above its relative position on its own price weights, whereas for Italy it is 67 per cent above. How

---

[10] The whole matter of what constitutes a change in quality is not very clearly treated in the literature. For example, in the generally excellent book of Erland von Hofsten, *Price Indexes and Quality Changes*, Stockholm, 1952, there does not appear to be a precise definition of what a quality change really is. Evidently he believes it is of very frequent occurrence from the perspective of constructing a cost of living index. We believe a much more restrictive view is necessary for production indexes.

TABLE 1

Indexes of per Capita Gross National Product of Eight European Countries in 1950
(United States per Capita GNP = 100)[a]

Country	At U.S. Price Weights (1)	At National European Price Weights (2)	Ratio of (1) to (2) (3)
United Kingdom	62	48	1.29
Denmark	61	48	1.27
Norway	59	44	1.34
Belgium	57	48	1.19
France	53	39	1.36
Netherlands	52	37	1.41
Germany	44	30	1.47
Italy	30	18	1.67

[a] Gilbert and Associates, *op. cit.*, Table 4, pp. 28 and 163.

serious this weighting spread is depends, of course, on the particular question posed. Clearly, if one is interested in giving precise quantitative expression to the disparities in real product (or the subsidiary aggregates) the magnitude of the weighting spread constitutes a serious handicap, and the use of geometric means, for example, however unsatisfactory these may be from the conceptual point of view, is no doubt essential. However, this handicap accurately reflects the underlying economic meaning of comparisons between very different consumption patterns or price structures, and any method, such as that proposed by Nicholson, for example, for overcoming this handicap merely involves disguising, rather than solving, what is after all an insoluble problem.[11]

In the OEEC studies, the important difficulty arises from the desire to attach ordinal, if not cardinal, relationships between the pairs of countries compared in the binary comparisons (comprising separate comparisons of each of the eight European countries with the United States, both on U.S. weights and on the weights of each individual European country concerned) as well as among the various European countries themselves. The problem was whether to derive such relationships among the European countries from the set of eight binary comparisons. The objections to this procedure have been discussed by Gilbert and Associates,[12] who point out that this involves

[11] Nicholson proposes to base the comparison on an initial selection of goods which have the same relative prices and the same quantities of consumption in both situations. Apart from the impossibility of knowing what "relative prices" are until the over-all price level has been established, this method involves pretending that the two situations are nearly the same in order to avoid the problems arising out of the fact that they are different.

[12] Gilbert and Associates, *op. cit.*, pp. 153–5.

comparing pairs of countries on the basis of a set of weights which is common to neither. For this reason an alternative procedure was adopted which involves "Average European Weights," representing a weighted average of the price structures of all the European countries covered in the study.

This procedure is still subject to important limitations. "It is perfectly possible, for example, that Average European Weights, which are relatively heavily influenced by the weighting structures of the larger countries, including Italy, will have even less in common with the weighting structure of, say, Norway and Denmark, than would United States weights, or perhaps Australian weights (or even some imaginary set of weights). But while this may be the case for one or two European countries, it is not likely to be so for the eight European countries taken as a whole, not only because they are all represented to some extent in the computation of the Average European Weights, but also because, as is mentioned above, the United States income level lies far outside the range of income levels in the eight European countries."[13]

In fact, to compare any pair of European countries, the only solution is to make separate binary comparisons between them using the weights of both. This technique has been adopted in a recent study by the European Coal and Steel Community in which a complete matrix of binary comparisons between the six member countries of the Community has been established.[14] As the authors of this study would acknowledge, even this procedure does not provide any unique overall ranking of all the countries concerned, as the impossibility of doing so in a manner which provides a satisfactory set of common weights for the whole ranking is inherent in the nature of the index-number problem.

As far as questions of conceptual or theoretical principle are concerned, we conclude that the conceptual limitations on intercountry comparisons of national product are no greater, and may be even less, than those which apply to intertemporal comparisons. In both cases limitations exist on account of differences in tastes, income distribution, quality differences, etc. But it does not seem to the present writers that these considerations seriously affect the order of magnitude of the results that may be obtained. This is particularly so on account of the fact that even if there were no differences in tastes, some degree of uncertainty must be attached to these results on

[13] Gilbert and Associates, *op. cit.*, pp. 154 and 155.
[14] See publications by the European Coal and Steel Community, Luxembourg, *Informations Statistiques*, July–August 1957, and *Comparaison des Revenus Réels des Travailleurs des Industries de la Communauté: Analyse Statistique*, 1957.

account of the weighting problem, not to mention purely statistical problems.

The Expenditure Approach and the Industry of Origin Approach

ARE THERE TWO INDEPENDENT METHODS?

Mention has been made in the introduction to this paper of the comparison between the real products in the U.K. and the U.S. on the basis of the net outputs of the various sectors contributing to GNP. The preceding studies compared the prices and volumes of the goods and services entering into final demand. The industry of origin approach involves comparing, sector by sector, the value added by the sector concerned, first at the prices ruling in one country and then at the prices in the other. In principle, the comparison at, say, country A's prices, is made by estimating value added in the various sectors in country B at country A's prices, which involves, again in principle, deducting from the total output of each sector in country B valued at country A's prices for the products concerned, its total inputs of materials, etc., also valued at country A's prices. In practice, the complete quantity and price data necessary to apply this technique were not available and various simplifications had to be adopted. First, though, it is useful to consider the extent to which the expenditure approach and the industry of origin approach are independent.

If one conceives complete input-output tables for two situations being compared, and if all the transactions shown for situation 1 are valued at the prices prevailing in situation 2, the sum of the value added, shown in the first table, will still be equal to the sum of the final demands in that table—both being at the prices of situation 2. This is simply a mathematical identity, because all intermediate products cancel out, whatever prices one uses. In both cases all that is left is the value of the transactions entering into final demand, even though, by the industry of origin method the aggregate value of these transactions appears as distributed among the sectors in the form of their net outputs.[15] The industry of origin approach thus produces the same answer that would be obtained by the expenditure (i.e., final demand) approach since it is this answer which remains after all intermediate transactions are cancelled out. In this sense, therefore, the industry of origin approach is in no way independent of the expenditure approach, since if the answer by the latter were not already put into the calculation to start with, the cancelling out of

[15] For a formal exposition of this result see Richard Stone, *Quantity and Price Indexes in National Accounts* (OEEC, Paris, 1956), pp. 39–44.

all intermediate transactions would not necessarily leave behind an aggregate equal to GNP.

In order to value the net output of sector A in country A at country B's prices, it is necessary to include in the valuation of sector A's output its sales to final demand at country B's prices. To make such a valuation for all sectors, one has to include the sales by all sectors to final demand, each valued at country B's prices. But these constitute all that is necessary in the expenditure approach.

This point is stressed here because its implications are considerable in practice since one usually does not have all the data necessary to carry out a complete deflation of all outputs and inputs in the manner described above. This applies to both international and intertemporal comparisons.[16] In that case, the problem is to know what significance can be attached to comparisons based on net outputs when gaps in the data have to be overcome, particularly by use of the assumption of constant input coefficients. It would appear that the industry of origin approach gives a "correct" answer only insofar as it gives the same answer as the expenditure approach.

Now it is frequent in practice (e.g., in indexes of industrial production) to overcome the absence of complete data on inputs and outputs by assuming constant input coefficients. For if input coefficients were to remain constant, then net output at constant prices would move parallel to gross output or to gross inputs (whichever indicators are used). But insofar as this assumption is not realized (and, in general, it is not) any comparison of GNP's by the industry of origin approach based on this assumption will give an answer which is "wrong" in the sense that it is not the same as that which would be given by an expenditure comparison, if one could be made.

This raises the question of the advantages of the industry of origin approach. Either the data enable a complete deflation to be carried out, in which case one has to have all the data necessary for the expenditure approach, or one does not have the full data, in which case the practical expedients adopted to overcome the deficiencies will tend to introduce errors. The answer lies, in fact, largely in the sphere of the relative statistical problems encountered in the two approaches. One particular analytical advantage of the industry of origin approach arises from the fact that it is usually desirable to obtain not merely a comparison of aggregate GNP, but also of its components.

[16] The results of intertemporal comparisons made in the U.K. have appeared in various issues of the *Bulletin* of the London and Cambridge Economic Service (published quarterly in *The Times Review of Industry*). The methodological problems are discussed in W. B. Reddaway, "Movements in the Real Product of the United Kingdom, 1946–49," *J.R.S.S.*, Series A, 1950, Part IV, and "Some Problems in the Measurement of Changes in the Real Geographical Product," in *Income and Wealth*, Series I (1951).

In the expenditure approach, for example, the analytical value of the comparison is not limited to the results concerning relative aggregate GNP's. It is particularly interesting to compare also, in real terms, the structures of the GNP's both in respect to quantities and to prices. For example, one important aspect of the two OEEC studies was the light the expenditure comparisons threw on the relative "real" contribution made by the different countries to the common defense effort.

From this point of view, it is obvious that even though the result for aggregate GNP given by the industry of origin approach is logically dependent on expenditure data, the additional information on the contribution of individual sectors and the derived information on relative productivities may be of considerable value.[17]

Unfortunately, this advantage may be exaggerated. The industry of origin approach is only correct if full allowance is made for every sector for the differences in input coefficients. But this will produce results for the individual sectors which, while giving a correct total for GNP, may have limited economic significance in themselves. In the extreme case, the valuation of outputs and inputs in one situation by the prices of another situation can give negative value added. And if constant input coefficients are assumed, then while the results for the individual sectors appear more definite, the GNP will be distorted.

This feature of the industry of origin approach, however, is not entirely absent from comparison of individual items in the expenditure approach. In the former, the limitations on the results for individual industries arise not only because one is dealing with balancing items, valued at the prices of different situations, but also because there may be several inputs into one sector and the pattern of inputs varies with their relative prices. In the expenditure approach, insofar as a given item is not perfectly homogeneous and includes several subitems, the comparison between the aggregates for the item valued in the prices existing in only one of two situations is also subject to limitations of the type discussed in the preceding section of this paper. In other words, wherever there is a lack of homogeneity, there is no simple answer to the question of what are the relative aggregate amounts used in two situations. The use of index numbers provides only a limited answer, whether it is a problem of adding together consumers' inputs of eggs and cheese or of adding together the steel industry's inputs of pig-iron and coal.

The flexibility of the input structure in some industries may be very

[17] For an excellent study of production by this method, see J. B. Heath, "British-Canadian Industrial Productivity," *The Economic Journal*, December 1957.

limited on technological grounds. Smooth iso-product curves are abstractions and in many important industries the range of production techniques available may be restricted to very few combinations of inputs.

RELATIVE MERITS OF THE TWO APPROACHES FOR STATISTICAL REASONS

The relative conceptual merits of the two approaches may be considered both from the standpoint of the extent to which each gives a "correct" measurement of relative aggregate GNP's and from the standpoint of the analytical value of either on the breakdown of expenditures or the contribution to total value added by individual sectors. The former type of information is more interesting for demand analysis, the latter for the analysis of productivity. The reliability of the results realized in practice, however, depends on the statistical problems encountered in each approach.

For the industry of origin approach, the basic information required is the GNP in a breakdown by industry, with appropriate quantity indicators of output and inputs for each industry. The expenditure approach, on the other hand, requires the GNP in a breakdown by final expenditure with appropriate quantity indicators for each category of expenditure. Both approaches draw upon the same basic data for all sectors and types of output, except for manufactured goods. Hence, from the standpoint of reliability, the choice of method for any pair of countries must depend largely on whether the industry or the final product data for manufactured goods are better.

So far we have studied only two countries by both methods—the United Kingdom and the United States. The results are shown in Table 2.

TABLE 2

Gross National Products of the United Kingdom and the United States, 1950, by the Expenditure and Industry Methods
(Quantity Index: U.S. = 100)

| | Per Capita GNP | |
	U.K. Price Weights	U.S. Price Weights
Industry method	55	65
Expenditure method	48	62

The United Kingdom comes out better in the industry study, its *per capita* output being 15 per cent higher (relative to the United States) than in the expenditure study on United Kingdom weights and 5 per cent higher on United States weights. While we consider these differences to be reasonably small, given the nature of the two

267

calculations and the fact that they are both first attempts, they are not negligible—particularly on the U.K. price weights.

We must confess to having no firm view on which of these two sets of results is statistically better. The industry study was done later, and thus some improvéments of both data and method could be brought to it, but this does not do much to reduce the differences. The best we can do is to list elements of weakness and strength of the two methods, given the basic data that were available for both calculations.

There was available for both countries an excellent census of manufactures. A lot of work was required to make the industry classifications comparable and this reshuffling is a possible source of error. Nonetheless, the mass of detailed information on manufacturing gave a firm base to the industry study. (Anyone who has done this kind of work will know the feeling of confidence one gets from having a good census as a point of departure).

For the expenditure approach, on the other hand, a much less detailed breakdown was available. The major components of final expenditures were available in value form, of course, in the usual GNP data. But for many of these categories the detailed quantity and price data required for the comparisons had to be obtained by various inquiries and estimation procedures.

From this point of view, the industry approach seemed to offer two advantages. First, a much greater weight in the comparisons is borne by relatively good quantity indicators for fairly homogeneous semi-finished products—steel, cloth, paper, rubber, etc. Secondly, for certain important categories of final manufactured products, quantity indicators could be obtained from census material for a large part of the aggregates, whereas in the expenditure approach virtually no direct quantity indicators were available. This applied particularly to producers' durables, household goods, and clothing. Consequently, the quantity indicators had to be derived in aggregate from the original value data by means of price comparisons. This involved both the difficult task of collecting representative price data for as many components as possible of the categories and also estimating the appropriate weights with which to combine the price data. In the industry approach, of course, the latter part of the work was relatively unimportant in view of the detailed quantity data available for many of the components. However, the absence of the readily available detailed price and quantity data in the expenditure approach is not a difficulty of principle, and can be overcome according to the time and resources at one's disposal.

Against these advantages must be set its disadvantages. The chief

268

disadvantage of the industry approach is that in principle a correct result can only be obtained by a complete deflation of all the inputs and outputs of the various sectors. In practice, however, the census of production data which have been used do not include sufficient information on inputs for such a complete deflation, and compromise solutions have had to be adopted. For certain non-manufacturing sectors, particularly agriculture, fuel, and transport, it has been possible to treat inputs and outputs separately (i.e., to use the "double indicator" method), but this has not been possible to any significant extent for manufacturing, the sector on which the relative statistical merits of the two approaches really depends. Only two adjustments have been made for differences between the two countries in input coefficients. One was applied to manufactures in aggregate; this is the adjustment for differences in the relative fuel inputs. It was not possible, however, to make this adjustment for the individual component sectors of manufacturing. The other adjustment made was for differences in transport input; here the correction could only be applied globally to all transportable goods (including manufacturing, agriculture, and fuels).

Thus the inability to allow fully for differences in input coefficients in manufacturing will give rise to error, and unfortunately it is not possible, *prima facie*, to be sure which way the error will lie.

The other disadvantage of the industry approach is its treatment of quality differences. In the expenditure method, an attempt was made to obtain price data for goods of equivalent quality or, where these did not exist to adjust for the difference in quality through an estimate of cost. There is no reason, in principle, why this method should not be fairly satisfactory, in spite of various practical difficulties. The limiting factor is again largely the time and resources available for the investigation. With the industry approach, as carried out so far, it might appear that one aspect of quality differences may be adequately accounted for, namely those arising from differences in inputs of materials (since these will be reflected in the outputs of the sectors producing the materials). But it is not known how far greater inputs of a certain raw material are reflected fully in higher quality rather than in a greater degree of wastage. This problem probably does not apply to many sectors (assuming that, as between countries even more than over time, knowledge of production techniques is fairly similar), but it will no doubt apply to some.

In addition, quality differences that are not due to differences in inputs but to the amount of value added cannot be allowed for in the industry approach without making the same kind of quality evaluations as in the expenditure approach, and, in principle, for a much greater variety of transactions. As, in fact, a greater part of manu-facturing output in the industry method could be covered by direct quantity indicators, there was necessarily less adequate consideration given to quality differences than in the expenditure method.

We hope that more experience will give greater insight into the relative reliability of the two approaches.

C O M M E N T

TIBOR SCITOVSKY, University of California

There is a tug of war between the more imaginative statisticians and the more rigorous—or should I say more pedantic—theorists. The former have occasionally discovered interesting correlations, estab-lished significant rates of growth, and found suggestive international differences. All too often, however, the rigorists have attacked their methods, questioned their results, and even denied the meaning of the problems they posed. Such criticism is useful if it leads to a better understanding of the underlying concepts and the development of better statistical methods. If it is purely destructive and defeatist, however, then it is largely self-defeating, for it is hard to find a statistical series that has been discontinued owing to its methodologi-cal condemnation by the theorists. Indeed, the field of economics is littered with such live corpses: concepts, laws, and statistics that mathematical economists have condemned to death and the rest of us continue to use because we find them useful.

International comparisons of standards of living are among the very few examples of statistical work that have been abandoned under the methodological onslaught of the theoretical economist. Gilbert's work is the first in this field in almost two decades. Although I have been cast for the role of the pedant for which I am temperamentally ill-suited, I have the greatest admiration for Gilbert's excellent work and for his temerity in doing it at a time when the rigorists have the field.

I agree with Gilbert's and Beckerman's choice of the gross national income concept for international comparisons. I also agree with their analysis of the difference between the final expenditure and the in-dustry of origin approach. I should like, however, to discuss further the meaning of international product comparisons.

As an example, take the finding of Gilbert and his various as-sociates[1] that in 1950 the U.S. *per capita* GNP was 61 per cent above

[1] I am referring not only to the paper here under discussion but also to the two OEEC volumes: M. Gilbert and I. B. Kravis, *An International Comparison of National Products and the Purchasing Power of Currencies* (OEEC, Paris, 1954) and M. Gilbert and Asso-ciates, *Comparative National Products and Price Levels* (OEEC, Paris, 1958).

the British figure, taking U.S. prices as weights, and 108 per cent above the British figure, taking British prices as weights.

This can be given either a welfare or a productivity interpretation; I propose to deal with both. As for welfare, the two indexes are estimates of the distance between two levels of consumer well-being, or rather between two indifference surfaces. It is unfortunate that this can be measured at different points, in different directions, and with different results. The 61 per cent can be shown to underestimate the distance between John Bull's and John Doe's indifference surfaces when travelling from the point and in the direction of the British product mix. The 108 per cent is an overestimate, unfortunately not of the same distance along the same route, but of the distance between the two indifference surfaces in the direction and to the point of the U.S. product mix. That the two indexes are estimates of distances along different routes is unavoidable. The best one can hope for is that the two distances are not too dissimilar; and economists usually regard as the best guarantee of this that the two indifference surfaces belong to the same system of integrated wants. Unfortunately, international comparisons offer the greatest scope for the nonfulfillment of this condition.

I suspect, however, that such pessimism is partly a matter of one's frame of mind. Economists, traditionally cast for the role of Voltaire's Pangloss, go to the opposite extreme when they deal with index-number problems; and they usually assume the worst imaginable conditions for comparisons of real income. Perhaps the first to strike a more optimistic note are J. R. Hicks[2] and, to some extent, Gilbert and Beckerman in the paper under discussion. I should like to rationalize the Gilbert-Beckerman approach.

If it were not for differences in the product mix in different countries and at different dates, I think economists would not worry about differences in different people's preference functions but would instead proclaim the basic similarity of human wants. International differences in the product mix can be explained not only by differences in preference functions but also by differences in production possibilities and in standards of living. Indeed, the more the difference in product mix can be explained by these other factors, the more confidently can one assume the similarity of preference scales.

This seems to be the approach followed by Gilbert, Beckerman, and their associates. They use partial regression analysis to explain international differences in product mix by differences in income levels and relative prices, presumably imputing the price differences to

[2] J. R. Hicks, "The Measurement of Real Income," *Oxford Economic Papers*, N.S., Vol. X, June 1958, pp. 125–62.

differences in production possibilities.[3] Having thus explained 85–90 per cent of the differences in product mix, they feel justified— and I think rightly so—in assuming that what they call the average consumer's long-run indifference map is not very different in the different countries. In other words, they assume that the two indifference surfaces belong more or less to the same integrated system of preference scales. All this means, strictly speaking, is that the indifference surfaces will not intersect, although it is customary to read into it the meaning that the distances between the two indifference surfaces will not be too dissimilar along the two routes.

Now, the productivity interpretation. Here we seem, especially at first, to be on firmer ground. We avoid altogether the slippery concept of consumer's welfare and concern ourselves with production and productivity. On this interpretation we want to know the distance between the British and the American production frontiers. The Paasche and Laspeyres quantity indexes now become estimates of this distance measured at different points and in different directions. This looks like the same awkward situation that we faced on the welfare interpretation, but it is not because now the difference between the distances measured along the two routes becomes not only not awkward but also highly significant. The superiority of the U.S. economy over the British is bound to be very different in different fields and industries and these differences are expressed by the shapes of the two countries' production frontiers. The difference between the distances along the two routes is one indication of the nature and extent of these differences. The 61 per cent difference between the British and the American *per capita* GNP now becomes an *over-*estimate of the distance between the two countries' production frontiers in the direction of the British product mix; the 108 per cent figure now becomes an *under*estimate of the distance in the direction of the U.S. product mix. In other words, U.S. *per capita* output would be less than 61 per cent greater than the British if Americans insisted on consuming it in the form the British do. It is more than 108 per cent greater than the British only because Americans have adjusted their expenditure pattern so as to consume more of the goods the American economy is especially good at producing and thus make better use of the latter's special advantages.

I think this interpretation is more meaningful, since it makes use of the discrepancy between the two estimates, a piece of information that is left unused by the welfare interpretation. But unfortunately it, too, has its shortcomings. In the absence of perfect competition, the the production frontiers to which the price planes are tangential

[3] Gilbert and Associates, *op. cit.*, Chap. V.

certainly cannot be given the interpretation of technologically deter-mined production possibility surfaces. They can, however, be given the meaning of Graaff-type production feasibility surfaces, which express the limitations imposed by technological and institutional conditions.[4] The trouble with these production feasibility surfaces is that one cannot assume that they are convex. Indeed, these short-comings of the productivity interpretation explain the preference of most economists in the past for the welfare interpretation.

I should like to point out two things in favor of the productivity interpretation. First of all, the shortcomings of this approach seemed formidable in the past because we felt overconfident about the wel-fare approach. Now that we have fully realized the limitations and shortcomings of the welfare approach, the productivity approach looks, by comparison, more promising. Secondly, I feel much sympathy with Hicks's position[5] that for making real income comparisons we need not know the shape of production frontiers or indifference sur-faces throughout their entire extent but only within the range bordered by the two product mixes; and this range is likely to be fairly narrow.

PAUL STUDENSKI, Special Legislative Committee on the Revision and Simplification of the Constitution

Gilbert has effectively demonstrated that the difficulties in making international comparisons of national income are not necessarily greater than the difficulties in making intertemporal comparisons of it. I wish, however, that he had made one point more clear, namely that the international comparisons in question can be made precisely only between countries that are similarly advanced economically. Such comparisons are misleading when made between economically advanced and economically underdeveloped countries whose pro-duction and consumption are wholly different. Gilbert suggests this, but he does not state it in so many words.

The Gilbert-Kravis international binary comparisons of national income published by the Organization for European Economic Co-operation in 1954 were limited to some five economically advanced countries. I recently asked Gilbert whether in his new work (which I have not seen) he still limited his binary comparisons to economi-cally advanced countries, or had extended them to the undeveloped countries. Gilbert answered that his binary comparisons were still limited to the economically advanced countries; that at one time he had hoped to include Turkey and started work upon it, but had given up because of the lack of sufficient price data and of sufficient staff.

[4] Cf. J. de V. Graaff, "On Optimum Tariff Structures," *Review of Economic Studies*, Vol. XVII, pp. 47–59, where they are called efficiency loci.   [5] Cf. *ibid.*

Estimates of Real Product in the
United States by Industrial Sector, 1947-55

JACK ALTERMAN AND EVA E. JACOBS
BUREAU OF LABOR STATISTICS U.S. DEPARTMENT OF LABOR

THE output of the economy can, in theory, be measured as the total value of final goods and services (gross national product in constant prices) or as the sum of the unduplicated output (real gross product) by industry of origin. The first approach is based on expenditure by major categories of final demand, e.g., household purchases of consumer goods and services and business investment in plant, equipment, and change in inventories. The second approach reflects the difference between deflated values of production and purchased intermediate products, calculated on an industry basis. Only the former method is currently used to develop the official estimates of United States GNP.[1]

This paper presents the results of some exploratory work on annual indexes of national production for the 1947 to 1955 period based on the latter method, i.e., the development of real product measures for major industrial sectors. These estimates were the outcome of a special study undertaken at the request of and in cooperation with the Interagency Subcommittee on Production and Productivity, Office of Statistical Standards, Bureau of the Budget.[2] The paper also includes a general analysis of sector trends in output per man-hour, based on the results of the interagency project but representing the views of the authors.

There has long been a need for sector real product measures that would be consistent with an aggregate measure for the total economy. Such data would provide information on the growth or decline of individual sectors, relative to each other and to the trend of total

[1] A description of the methods and sources used to develop both the current and constant dollar estimates of gross national product is given in the *National Income Supplement, 1954, Survey of Current Business.*

[2] The following agencies were represented on the Subcommittee: Bureau of Labor Statistics, Department of Labor; Office of Statistical Standards, Bureau of the Budget; Office of Business Economics, Department of Commerce; Bureau of the Census, Department of Commerce; Federal Reserve Board. The chairman was John Kendrick of the Office of Statistical Standards. Along with the Subcommittee, a member of the staff of the Council of Economic Advisers participated in the development of the sector real product estimates.

activity. In conjunction with matching man-hour data, sector estimates could yield output per man-hour measures which would indicate the net effect of differential movements in sector productivity and shifts between low and high output per man-hour. Sector productivity estimates might also be usefully correlated with related variables. Finally, if sufficient data were available, the aggregation of sector real product measures would provide an independent check on the published GNP estimates derived from deflated expenditures.[3] This was not a purpose of the present study, but to the extent that independent sources were used, a check is provided.

Since the project aim was to explore the feasibility of estimating sector production and productivity on the basis of readily available data, there was no intensive consideration of alternative methods or data sources. Further work is needed to improve the estimating methods and to clarify the theoretical problems involved in defining output and output per man-hour in areas such as finance, insurance, real estate, business and personal services, and communications. Therefore, the estimates derived should be regarded as tentative.

The limitations of the individual sector estimates are not considered in this paper. Many of the data limitations for specific sectors are covered in Leon Greenberg's paper prepared for this conference, "Data Available for the Measurement of Output per Man-Hour."

Concept of Real GNP by Industrial Origin

Real GNP is implicitly the sum of the real gross products of the component industries, each industry product thus encompassed representing gross output minus purchased intermediate goods and services. Since the output values involved are net, in that the contribution of other industries is excluded, aggregation provides an unduplicated measure of the value added at each stage of the productive process.

Industry gross product can theoretically be obtained by either a product or an income approach. In the national income accounts, income by industrial origin is estimated by an appropriate allocation of labor and property shares. GNP originating could be estimated by adding to the factor payments, the nonfactor charges (capital consumption allowances, indirect business taxes, and miscellaneous items). However, such estimates are not regularly prepared because of

---

[3] John W. Kendrick in "Measurement of Real Product," *A Critique of the United States Income and Product Accounts*, Studies in Income and Wealth, Volume Twenty-Two (Princeton University Press for National Bureau of Economic Research, 1958), used industry output estimates primarily for purposes of checking aggregate real product estimates.

276

special problems involved in the distribution of the latter, particularly indirect business taxes and, in any event, estimates thus derived cannot be readily deflated.

Gross product originating does not measure the total output of an industry but only the portion attributable to the activity in question. Since the usual type of price indexes are not directly applicable to the deflation of value added, industry real gross product must be obtained by deflating gross output and intermediate purchases separately and then subtracting deflated inputs from deflated output.[4]

Derivation of Real Product Estimates

Only for agriculture and manufacturing have estimates been developed by methods which are technically consistent with the concept of "double deflation," and data are not readily available for the development of similar real product measures for other sectors. Therefore, the estimates prepared for this paper were based on the more conventional gross output concept. This approach assumes that there was relatively little change in input-output relationships within each of the sectors from 1947 through 1955 and that, therefore, changes in gross output approximate changes in net output.

The sector indexes were combined with value added or net output weights to provide an approximation at the national level of the conceptually correct measure. The output measures entering into the sector indexes were similarly weighted wherever possible. 1947 was selected as the base year because, when the study was started, the published real GNP figures were in 1947 dollars.[5]

SECTOR WEIGHTS

The weights used in this study are 1947 gross national income weights derived by estimating capital consumption allowances and indirect business taxes by sector and adding these items to the published figures of sectoral national income. It was not possible to distribute the other components of GNP consisting of subsidies, less the current surplus of government enterprises, business transfer payments,

---

[4] Almarin Phillips, in his paper "Industry Net Output Estimates in the United States," this volume, develops Kuznets' suggestion that value added can be directly deflated by an index formed by taking a weighted average of the difference between a gross output price index and an input price index

[5] Since completion of this study, the constant dollar GNP figures have been modified due to revisions in the data and shifting of the price weights from 1947 to 1954. (See *Survey of Current Business*, July 1958.) However, no attempt has been made to revise the estimates shown here since the original purpose of the project was to explore the feasibility of constructing sector real product estimates.

277

and the statistical discrepancy. These items represented about 1 per cent of GNP in 1947.

The total capital consumption allowance for each sector was obtained as the sum of separate estimates of (1) depreciation, (2) capital outlays charged to current account, and (3) accidental damage to fixed capital. Similarly, the estimate of sector indirect taxes was based on separate estimates of (1) federal excise taxes, (2) state and local sales taxes, (3) state and local property taxes, and (4) miscellaneous indirect taxes and nontax liabilities. The distribution of the various categories of capital consumption allowances and indirect business taxes was based on various data including Internal Revenue tax returns and data from the Office of Business Economics, Department of Commerce.

One major adjustment was made to the distribution of gross national income as originally derived. In certain branches of manufacturing, particularly petroleum and steel, the activities of parent companies frequently include the operation of captive mining operations, e.g., petroleum drilling and extraction, iron ore and coal mining. In order to be consistent with manufacturing and mining output data which reflect activity on an establishment or product basis, the estimated part of manufacturing gross income derived from captive mining activities was transferred to the mining sector. This modification primarily affected nonlabor charges because the estimates of wages and salaries used in the national income accounts were already on an establishment basis. The same statistical problem (captive operations in sectors other than that where the parent company is located) exists elsewhere but not so seriously as to require modification of the gross national income weights.

There is an additional problem of relating output to gross national product which occurs in almost all sectors but is particularly important in utilities, communications, and railroads industries. The problem is that sector output data usually do not include the output of new construction workers on payroll of utility, etc., whereas the gross national product originating weight for each sector does reflect these activities. No adjustment has been made for this factor in the estimates prepared for this paper.

The procedure employed in deriving sector weights is described in greater detail in Section I of the appendix. The weights themselves are presented in Table A-1.

SECTOR INDEXES

The sector real product estimates were prepared in approximately the same industry group detail as that shown in Table 13, National

278

Income by Industrial Origin, *National Income Supplement, 1954, Survey of Current Business*. However, the following modifications were made in order to achieve consistency with the available output and man-hours data:

1. Separate estimates were made for general government and government enterprises. This change was made because the real gross output measure for government, based on the National Income concept and methodology, is limited to the output of general government employees. The output of government enterprises, e.g., Post Office and TVA, is considered part of the private economy. Productivity measurement considerations were another reason for showing general government product separately.

2. "Agriculture" was separated from "agriculture, forestry, and fisheries" and shown separately as farming to be consistent with the coverage of the net output index for agriculture. "Agricultural services, forestry, and fisheries" were added to the services sector to be consistent with the BLS man-hour estimates.

3. "Radio broadcasting and television" was separated from "communications and public utilities" and added to the services sector to be consistent with man-hour estimates.

4. "Real estate" was removed from "finance, insurance, and real estate" and shown separately because of statistical and conceptual problems in relating output and man-hours.

5. "Private households" was removed from "services" and shown separately for the same reasons as in the case of real estate.

Sector real product indexes are shown in Table A-2. Net output indexes derived by the separate deflation of output and intermediate inputs were available for agriculture and manufacturing. The former series was developed by the OBE; the latter by the Division of Productivity and Technological Developments of the BLS. For the remaining sectors industry gross output indexes were combined with national income originating weights or value added weights to obtain approximate net output measures. National income weights were obtained from the national income accounts; industry value added data were obtained from unpublished detailed charges against final product prepared in connection with the BLS interindustry relations study, which also referred to a 1947 base year. The industry output indexes were derived either by deflating current output values or by measurement of physical quantities, such as ton miles and kilowatt hours. Where current output data were not available, substitute measures were employed.

279

A wide variety of sources and methods were of necessity involved in the derivation of the sector real product estimates and these are described in Section II of the appendix. In general, the data differed from those used in the development of the official constant dollar GNP measures but the detail of the Commerce Department estimates provided the basis for estimates of general government, finance and insurance, real estate, households, services, and rest of the world.

Comparison of Sector Real Product Aggregate with Published GNP

Data other than that used by the Commerce Department for estimating gross national product were used to measure the change in output, wherever such data were readily available. However, overlap is inevitable where the output of an industry consists almost entirely of a product that becomes a component of personal consumption expenditures, such as local transportation. In such cases the project estimates may be independent and still identical with the Commerce figures. Duplication is also present because limited resources for investigating the possibilities of alternative methods of estimation or deficiencies in primary data made it necessary to substitute the movement of appropriate components of personal consumption expenditures for industry output. In all, about 25 to 30 per cent of the total weight of the combined index represents industries for which the output estimates were not independent.

With this limitation in mind, the index derived by aggregating the sector real product estimates can be compared with that based on the published GNP in constant dollars for 1947–55. These indexes are given in Table A-2. The average difference between the two is less than 1.5 per cent, and the largest difference between them in any one year is less than 3 per cent. Although the derived index is consistently lower than the published index, the difference does not increase over the period; if anything, it decreases in the latter years.

The two indexes can also be compared in terms of average annual change over the period. The average annual change of the published private GNP index was slightly higher than that of the derived GNP, 4.2 per cent as compared to 4.1 per cent. The closeness of the results of both comparisons may have been due to offsetting movements of net-gross ratios in various industries.

On the basis of this comparison, the Subcommittee concluded that it was feasible to use existing data, to construct a largely independent sector output aggregate that coincided closely with the published deflated GNP. This conclusion does not imply endorsement of the

280

particular methods and sources used. Much work remains to be done and the estimates must be considered as primarily exploratory.

Derivation of Estimates of Real Product per Man-Hour

One of the major uses of the sector real product measures is in the development of sector real product per man-hour measures. The remainder of this paper is devoted to a brief description of some of the problems involved in the development of such estimates and an indication of how they may be used to analyze trends for the economy as a whole and major components of the total.

"Productivity" can be defined as the ratio of output to any related input or combination of inputs. However, most existing measures relate output to labor input. As we all know, such measures do not represent the unique contribution of labor to production but the interaction of many factors, such as changes in technology, capital per worker, scale of output, utilization of capacity, etc. Within the general concept of productivity, defined as output per unit of labor input, there are several alternative measures which can be developed. First, there are gross physical productivity measures which show the change in labor time required to produce a fixed composite of goods and services. Second, there are the measures which reflect shifts in the relative importance of industries with different levels of value of output per man-hour, in addition to changes in physical productivity. These measures can record an increase in productivity for a sector even if there is no change in the productivity of component industries. Third, there are the net measures which reflect not only physical productivity changes and interindustry shifts but also changes in labor requirements due to changes in materials consumed per unit of output, e.g., less coke per ton of steel.

RELATIONSHIP TO BLS MEASURES OF PRODUCTIVITY

Most of the work of the BLS in the field of productivity measurement has been based on the concept of physical productivity but more recently two sets of estimates have been developed based on the net output concept. The two sets of net output productivity estimates cover the man-hours of all persons, including the self-employed, unpaid family workers, and wage and salary workers, but are distinguished by the fact that they are based on different man-hour data sources.

One set was based primarily on Census Bureau figures which attempt to measure hours worked. The other set was based primarily on BLS employment and hours data which refer to hours paid for,

281

including hours paid for but not worked, such as vacations, holidays, and sick leave. The latter cover the total private economy with breakdowns between agriculture and nonagriculture, and manufacturing and nonmanufacturing for 1947 to 1957.

The BLS-based man-hour data were used in conjunction with the sector output indexes derived for this paper to develop measures of sector real product per man-hour. In concept these measures are net but because the real product estimates for most sectors were developed by combining industry gross output measures with fixed net output weights, they do not adequately reflect changes in labor requirements due to changes in materials consumed per unit of output. In most cases they were not developed in as much detail or with quite the same intensive statistical analysis as the productivity measures previously published by the BLS. Therefore, they must be regarded as exploratory and not official.[6]

SPECIAL PROBLEMS

Certain areas of the economy involve special problems from the viewpoint of productivity measurement.

1. *Government.* In the national income accounts, the output of general government is approximated by employee compensation, implying no change in productivity. Although there are other areas where output is measured by labor input, this is, from the viewpoint of employment, by far the most significant. Since the concept of productivity in government is without meaning, most estimates of national productivity such as those developed by John Kendrick, and by the staff of the Joint Economic Committee, have excluded general government. In this paper, as in the *1958 Economic Report of the President*, the estimate of productivity is limited to the private economy.

2. *Rest of the World.* GNP includes income from abroad accruing to U.S. residents. Since this income is not related to domestic labor input, it should be subtracted so that domestic employment is related to gross domestic product. The detail shown in Table A-2 provides the basis for such an adjustment.

3. *Households.* In the national income system, this classification includes the output of domestic employees and net interest received by

[6] The BLS estimates of net output in 1947 dollars per man-hour for the years 1947 to 1957 are published in the *January 1958 Economic Report of the President* (Appendix E, Productivity Statistics). These estimates, revised to be consistent with constant dollar GNP in 1954 dollars and extended to 1958, are published in *Trends in Output per Man-hour in the Private Economy, 1909–58*, BLS Bulletin 1249, December 1959. A detailed analysis of these estimates and a description of the methods and sources employed is presented in this Bulletin.

individuals. Since the former is measured by labor compensation and the latter has no labor input, it was felt that no meaningful measure of productivity could be derived for this area.

4. *Real Estate.* In the national income accounts, the real estate industry includes the imputed rental of owner-occupied homes as well as income from commercial operations. For homes that are rented through real estate agencies employment involved in managing and maintaining the property is reflected in the industry total. However, the time thus spent by owner-occupiers cannot be calculated. Consequently no productivity estimates were prepared for this sector.

5. *Services.* This sector also includes a number of business and personal service industries where output is measured by payrolls. Since it is difficult to separate these industries from those where the data are more adequate, the effect of this limitation cannot be quantitatively evaluated. The effect is probably a downward bias since some productivity increase has probably taken place and the measurement of output through employment assumes no change in productivity.

Analysis of Changes in Real Product per Man-Hour

SECTOR TRENDS

Estimates of the average annual change in real product per man-hour between 1947 and 1955 for the total private economy and major sectors are presented in Table 1. Whether or not these percentages represent trends that can reasonably be expected to continue or whether the period is a "normal" one that can be compared, without further analysis, with prior periods or some "long-run" average is not at issue here. These estimates, however, may not be indicative of secular rates, since 1947 was below trend and represented a decline in total private output per man-hour from the peak level reached in the last year of the war, 1945.

The average annual increase of 3.6 per cent shown for the total private economy compares with a rate of 3.7 per cent derived from the productivity indexes (based primarily on BLS man-hour data) published in the *1958 Economic Report of the President.* This is not surprising since the aggregate of the sector real product measures is quite close to the constant dollar GNP estimated from the expenditure side and the man-hours are consistent with those used in the published estimates. Excluding the "Rest of the World, Real Estate, and Households" from the private economy has no effect upon the estimate because the excluded sectors account for less than 10 per cent of total private output, and their implied change in productivity,

TABLE 1

Average Annual Change in Real Product, Man-Hours, and Real Product per Man-Hour, by Sectors, 1947–55
(per cent)

	Real Product	Man-Hours	Real Product per Man-Hour
Total private	4.1	0.6	3.6
Total private, excluding rest of the world, real estate, households	4.2	0.6	3.6
Total goods	4.2	−0.2	4.4
Farm	1.8	−4.2	6.3
Mining	2.1	−2.7	5.0
Construction	5.6	3.0	2.5
Manufacturing	5.0	1.6	3.3
Total services	4.1	1.2	2.8
Trade	3·9	1·3	2·6
Finance and insurance	6.8	4.4	2.3
Transportation	2.8	−1.5	4.3
Communication and public utilities	8.7	1.9	6.7
Business and personal services	2.6	1.6	1.0
Government enterprises	3.9	2.8	1.1
Addendum			
Private nonfarm (goods and services)	4.4	1.4	3.0
Private nonfarm (goods)	4.8	1.6	3.1

Source: The underlying real product estimates are presented in Table A-2 and described in Section II of the appendix. The man-hour data, mostly from the BLS, are described in the Appendix, Section III. The average annual per cent change is based on the least squares trend of the logarithms of the three sets of indexes.

which has little meaning in itself, is little lower than the average for all other sectors combined.

The sectors producing "goods" showed a considerably higher rate of increase than the "service" sectors, 4.4 versus 2.8 per cent. Much of this difference, however, was due to the 6.3 per cent gain in the farm sector. The increase for nonfarm goods sectors combined was about 3.1 per cent, which is not much higher than the average gain for services, and about the same as the increase for the total private nonfarm economy. This indicates that the popular belief that increases in output per man-hour in services have been lagging behind goods producing sectors must be qualified and, in fact, services such as transportation, communications, and public utilities showed better than average increases.

There seems to have been more variation within the goods and services groups than between these groups. Within the goods group, the increases ranged from 2.5 per cent for construction to 6.7 per cent for farm, with manufacturing at 3.3 per cent. The increase within services ranged from about 1 per cent for business and personal services to 6.7 per cent for communication and public utilities. It is

284

difficult to estimate how much of the relatively modest increase indicated for business and personal services is due to the conceptual and statistical problem of measurement and how much to the inherent nature of the industries involved. In either case, the small gain here tended to dampen the rate of increase for the private economy as a whole.

INTERSECTORAL SHIFTS

Besides providing information on the differential movement in productivity for individual sectors, the sector estimates can be used to determine how much of the over-all increase in output per man-hour was due to increases in physical productivity and how much to shifts in the relative importance of sectors. Methods of accomplishing such a breakdown are described in section IV of the appendix.

The estimates indicate that changes in the relative importance of all private sectors accounted for only about 4 per cent of the total increase in output per man-hour between 1947 and 1955. (The result is about the same whether relative importance is considered in terms of output or man-hours.) Conversely, 96 per cent of the total increase is accounted for by productivity advances within the sectors.

When the farm and nonfarm sectors are considered as units the effect of internal shifts are eliminated and the effect of the shift between these two groups can be isolated. The preliminary estimates indicate that about 8 per cent of the total increase in output per man-hour of the private economy was accounted for by a shift in man-hours from farm to nonfarm activities. This positive effect arises because the farm sector, with a relatively lower level of productivity, constituted a declining proportion of total man-hours.

Since the farm-nonfarm effect was higher than the "all sector" effect, shifts within the nonfarm segment must have had a dampening effect on the change in total output per man-hour because the only difference between the two analyses was the treatment of shift among nonfarm activities. Actually, the effect of shifts within the nonfarm group was minus 5 per cent. Thus, as a result of the increasing importance within the nonfarm group of sectors with lower than average productivity, the total change in output per man-hour of the nonfarm group was 5 per cent lower than the average of the increases within the sectors.

These results led to an attempt to relate the data to the belief that the relatively faster growth in man-hours of the service industries has had and may continue to have a depressing influence on productivity in general.

The data show that the service industries as a whole comprise a steadily increasing proportion of total man-hours, but that this shift

285

in man-hours has not been the factor responsible for the dampening effect of the nonfarm total. The shift in man-hours from all goods to all services has had practically no influence on the change in output per man-hour of the nonfarm economy, but the shift within each group has been to lower output per man-hour industries. This analysis can be summarized as follows:

1. For the period 1947–55, increases in output per man-hour within sectors were responsible for almost all of the increases in real product per man-hour of the total private economy.

2. The effect of changes in relative importance of sectors with differing levels of real product per man-hour was positive but minor.

3. A shift from the less productive farm segment to the more productive nonfarm segment accounted for all of the positive effect. The latter was somewhat offset by the negative effect of shifts within nonfarm goods and services.

These conclusions must be qualified because the analysis of shifts is limited to the sector level. More work is required at the industry level to determine the full effect of changing resource allocation.

Another major qualification to the estimated effect of shifts on the change in output per man-hour is the price level underlying the real product estimates, i.e., whether the real product is stated in 1947 dollars or the dollars of some other period. Some exploratory work done based on the revised GNP in 1954 constant dollars indicates that the effect of farm-nonfarm shift is higher because the difference in the relative productivity levels of the farm and nonfarm sectors was greater in 1954 prices than in 1947 prices.

APPENDIX

Derivation of Sector Weights

The weights for combining the sector indexes are 1947 gross national income weights, as shown in Table A-1. National income originating by sector and total capital consumption allowances and indirect business tax are from the *National Income Supplement, 1954, Survey of Current Business*. Estimates of sector capital consumption allowances and indirect business taxes were derived by distributing the totals for these items as follows:

FARM

Capital consumption allowances for this sector were computed from data compiled by the Agricultural Marketing Service (AMS) of the Department of Agriculture. Depreciation was built up from the

286

TABLE A-1

Gross National Income by Sectors, 1947

(millions of dollars)

	National Income Originating	Capital Consumption Allowance	Indirect Business Tax	Total
Gross national product				232,228
+Subsidies less current surplus				−227
−Statistical discrepancy				1,383
−Business transfer payments				674
Gross national income	197,168	14,118	18,658	229,944
General government	16,663	—	—	16,663
Gross private national income	180,505	14,118	18,658	213,281
Farm	17,777	2,444	610	20,831
Mining[a]	5,445	1,119	384	6,912
Contract construction	8,401	301	187	8,889
Manufacturing[a]	57,463	2,723	6,543	66,729
Trade	37,341	1,562	4,595	43,498
Wholesale	11,651	365	567	12,583
Retail	25,690	1,197	4,028	30,915
Finance and insurance	4,949	133	258	5,340
Real estate	10,301	2,795	2,691	15,787
Transportation	11,498	984	1,355	13,837
Railroad	6,294	362	901	7,557
Other	5,204	622	454	6,280
Communication—tel. and tel.	2,077	304	490	2,871
Utilities	2,811	544	461	3,816
Electric and gas	2,709	544	461	3,714
Local utilities	102	—	—	102
Households	3,272	—	—	3,272
Services[b]	16,340	1,209	1,120	18,669
Government enterprises	1,956	—	—	1,956
Rest of the world	874	—	—	874

[a] After "Establishment-company" adjustments. See notes.

[b] Excludes households; includes agricultural services, forestry and fisheries, and radio broadcasting and television.

annual charges to the replacement value of durable goods adjusted to exclude the amount allocable to nonfarm landlords. Capital outlays charged to current expense were selected from appropriate items included in the AMS farm production expenses. Indirect business taxes were also derived from AMS expense data.

The gross national income of the farm sector equals national income originating plus these two items. It is less than published farm GNP by the amount of government payments to farm landlords. However, the difference is insignificant and has no effect on the weighted output measure.

NONFARM

Capital Consumption Allowances. For each sector, separate estimates of depreciation, capital outlays charged to current account, and accidental damage to fixed capital were added to arrive at the total capital consumption allowance. Much of the basic data were obtained from the Office of Business Economics (OBE).

Depreciation, which accounts for 85 to 95 per cent of capital consumption allowances, was distributed by industry largely on the basis of tax returns data. Within each sector, corporate and noncorporate segments were estimated separately.

The components of capital outlays charged to current account for which separate estimates are available are oil and gas well drilling, and "producers' durable equipment." The former was allocated entirely to mining. The latter was distributed mainly on the basis of the sector proportions of total corporate and noncorporate nonfarm depreciation after the exclusion of real estate, where this item appeared insignificant. Accidental damage to fixed capital was similarly distributed, with real estate included.

Indirect Business Taxes. "Indirect business tax and nontax liabilities" were classified into four main categories and allocated as follows:

1. *Excise taxes.* Federal excises on manufactures of liquor and tobacco were obtained from the published National Income tables, which in turn are based on Internal Revenue Service (IRS) data adjusted to an accrual basis. Federal exercises paid by manufacturing excluding liquor, tobacco, communications, and retailing firms were taken from Federal budget documents with fiscal year estimates averaged to derive calendar year estimates. Taxes on transportation of persons and property from IRS collections were allocated between railroads and other transportation on the basis of corporate sales.

2. *Sales taxes.* The published total was distributed largely on the basis of 1947 sales by sector after assigning those known to be paid by specific industries such as tobacco and liquor.

3. *Property taxes.* The nonfarm total was distributed in general on the basis of relative industry capital assets from IRS data.

4. *Miscellaneous indirect taxes and nontax receipts* were allocated in general on the basis of sector sales.

Mining-Manufacturing Adjustment. The above estimates of capital consumption allowances and indirect taxes were derived on a basis consistent with national income classification structure. The resulting gross national income estimates for mining and manufacturing were then adjusted to put both sectors on an establishment basis.

1. Gross national income of the mining sector on an establishment basis was estimated through the use of data from the BLS 1947 Interindustry Relations study. Table 1 of the 192 order matrix of that study

provided for each mining industry the items that generally cover the income and other charges contained in the concept of gross national income.

2. It was assumed that the difference between mining GNI on an establishment basis (interindustry derivation) and on a company basis (national income derivation) was solely the result of mining activities classified under manufacturing in the national income accounts. The difference was therefore subtracted from manufacturing gross national income as originally estimated to derive estimated gross national income on an establishment basis.

3. National income originating and the intervening items were then adjusted to conform to the adjusted GNI.

The sources and methods employed in arriving at the various output indexes presented in Table A-2 are described below.

TABLE A-2

Sector Indexes of Production, 1947-55
(1947 = 100)

	1948	1949	1950	1951	1952	1953	1954	1955
Total GNP—published	105.0	104.0	114.0	121.8	126.5	131.5	129.8	139.0
Total GNP—derived from weighted sector output indexes	104.4	101.4	112.9	120.4	124.2	129.7	128.3	138.2
Private GNP—published	105.4	103.9	114.4	120.5	124.7	130.2	128.6	138.7
Private GNP—derived	104.7	101.2	113.3	119.0	122.3	128.3	127.1	137.8
Farm	118.9	109.7	117.0	109.7	112.1	115.5	122.3	126.7
Mining	105.0	92.2	103.5	113.4	111.5	113.0	108.4	118.6
Contract construction	108.9	109.2	125.1	138.0	139.7	139.1	145.6	155.9
Manufacturing	102.0	94.8	110.9	121.2	124.8	135.6	127.4	142.3
Trade	101.8	101.2	114.8	116.7	121.4	125.8	125.0	135.2
Finance and insurance	106.1	111.9	125.0	131.9	140.6	150.2	156.8	167.9
Real estate	104.5	106.1	111.5	117.4	119.5	119.9	122.4	126.2
Transportation	100.1	91.0	103.8	113.8	112.3	115.5	110.5	121.4
Communication and public utilities	111.0	117.0	129.6	143.9	154.2	165.7	176.5	197.3
Households	104.9	112.0	129.1	131.0	132.1	143.6	144.1	166.3
Services	103.5	104.5	107.5	109.5	113.3	116.4	119.3	124.0
Government enterprises	107.8	112.9	117.0	123.9	128.6	130.4	133.6	138.3
Rest of the world	112.2	117.2	127.5	124.8	124.4	132.7	163.6	180.4

Derivation of Sector Indexes

FARM

This is an index of net output derived by deflating gross output and subtracting deflated intermediate inputs. The estimates are from the *Survey of Current Business*, June 1957 and November 1957. The procedure is described in the August 1954 issue.

289

MINING

The index on an establishment basis was estimated by combining Federal Reserve Board indexes of production for coal, crude oil and natural gas, metal mining, and stone and earth minerals with estimated gross national income weights derived from BLS interindustry data.

CONTRACT CONSTRUCTION

The production index was derived by deflating estimated GNP originating in current dollars. The implicit deflator was derived by dividing the value of new construction minus the value of building materials used, both in current dollars by the value of construction minus building materials, both in constant dollars. The estimates of building materials used in new construction are from an unpublished study of the Commerce Department's National Income Division which was benchmarked on BLS Report No. 2, *Construction in the 1947 Interindustry Relation Study*, and *Census of Manufactures* product detail for 1947 and 1954.

MANUFACTURING

1947, 1949–53. Estimates for these years were based on the previous work of the BLS on net output indexes for manufacturing industries.[1] They were obtained by subtracting the cost of materials, parts, components, etc., in constant dollars, from the constant dollar value of output (sales adjusted for changes in inventories). The data on dollar value of shipments, inventories, and cost of materials were obtained from the *1947 Census of Manufactures* and the *Annual Survey of Manufactures*, 1949–53. These data were supplemented by unpublished tabulations and special estimates. Totals for manufacturing cover virtually all of the approximately 450 Census industries. The deflators were specially constructed by arranging the BLS wholesale price series for commodities into industry groups.

1948, 1954–55. The detailed value data required for calculating the desired net output index for 1948 were not available since there was no Annual Survey that year. Detailed data for 1954 and 1955 have become available only recently. Therefore, a gross measure based on the deflation of manufacturers' sales, adjusted for change in inventories of finished products and goods in process was substituted for these years. The data on sales and inventories are from the published estimates of the OBE. The adjusted sales at the total manufacturing level were deflated separately for total durables and nondurables and then

---

[1] For a detailed description see BLS Report No. 100, "Trends in Output Per Man-Hour and Man-Hours Per Unit of Output-Manufacturing, 1939–53," 1955.

combined with value added weights. The deflators were special unpublished BLS price indexes for durable and nondurable manufactures.

TRADE

1947–52. The same procedure was followed for both wholesale and retail trade for this period. Indexes for the wholesale and retail components of the trade sector are shown in Table A-3. Base year margin

TABLE A-3

Trade Sector—Industry Production Indexes
(1947 = 100)

Year	Wholesale Trade	Retail Trade
1948	100.7	102.2
1949	98.8	102.2
1950	114.1	115.1
1951	119.9	115.4
1952	124.0	120.3
1953	125.2	126.0
1954	122.1	126.2
1955	130.8	137.0

ratios were computed from the Interindustry input-output table as the ratio of the value of wholesale and retail margins to manufacturers' shipments for each industry. These ratios were then applied to the deflated value of manufacturers' shipments in each year. The shipments were obtained as one stage in the process of computing net output for the manufacturing sector. The constant dollar value of margins were then summed and an index derived.

1953–55. The retail trade index was extended by an index obtained by deflating total retail sales by a retail price index, both furnished by the OBE. The wholesale trade index was extended by a series derived by deflating total wholesale sales from the OBE by the total BLS Wholesale Price Index.

FINANCE AND INSURANCE

Industry indexes were combined with national income originating weights. Indexes for banking, security brokers, etc., and insurance are shown separately in Table A-4. The index for banking was imputed to "finance, n.e.c." and the index for insurance carriers was imputed to "insurance agents."

Banking. National income originating in current dollars was deflated. The deflator was derived by dividing the current value by the constant dollar value of the personal consumption expenditures (p.c.e.) for

291

TABLE A-4

Finance and Insurance—Industry Production Indexes
(1947 = 100)

Year	Banking	Security Brokers, etc.	Insurance
1948	103.5	103.3	109.2
1949	110.6	93.9	114.4
1950	131.5	145.1	127.8
1951	131.0	127.0	133.3
1952	140.0	105.3	143.4
1953	148.4	108.2	154.6
1954	156.8	138.1	158.0
1955	168.4	155.7	168.1

(1) bank service charges, (2) imputed bank services, and (3) interest on personal debt.

Security Brokers, etc. This is the index of deflated p.c.e. for brokerage charges.

Insurance. Separate indexes were derived for life and nonlife insurance and these were combined with estimated national income weights from the Interindustry study.

The life insurance index was derived from the sum of p.c.e. for life insurance (expenses) and hospital and health insurance. (According to the BLS interindustry report, life insurance companies are large sellers of health and accident insurance.)

The nonlife index was constructed by combining auto, casualty, and health and accident (sold by nonlife companies) indexes with output weights derived from the interindustry reports. The indexes for auto and health and accident insurance represent deflated p.c.e. for these items. The index for casualty insurance (other than auto) is derived from premiums earned data from Best's insurance volumes. Indications are that there were no rate changes in this area and the value was not deflated.

REAL ESTATE

This index was derived by deflating estimated GNP originating in current dollars by the NID deflator for nonfarm residential space rent adjusted to exclude repair and maintenance. For this purpose repair and maintenance expenditures included in space rental values were deflated by the cost price index for new residential construction.

TRANSPORTATION

A separate index was derived for each industry as shown in Table A-5. The index for transportation other than railroads was computed

292

TABLE A-5
Transportation Sector—Industry Production Indexes
(1947 = 100)

	1948	1949	1950	1951	1952	1953	1954	1955
Railroads	96.5	79.9	87.4	95.9	91.5	89.7	81.5	91.1
Other transportation	104.4	104.4	123.6	135.3	137.3	146.6	145.3	157.8
Highway and local passenger	98.7	87.2	80.9	77.1	73.8	71.0	64.6	61.7
Highway freight	113.7	124.0	169.3	184.2	190.6	212.7	210.2	221.5
Water	93.6	85.8	91.5	108.5	100.7	96.8	94.2	116.5
Air	106.1	120.5	137.7	169.5	195.7	223.9	255.1	294.0
Pipelines (oil)	111.0	108.7	126.1	151.0	157.4	167.7	175.4	198.9
Services	99.3	96.7	108.1	128.0	128.2	133.5	137.3	159.8

by combining the component industry indexes with national income originating weights from National Income Table 13. "Other transportation" was combined with railroads with estimated gross national income as weights to obtain the sector index.

Railroads. Ton miles and passenger miles were weighted by 1947 revenue per ton mile and passenger mile. Data from Interstate Commerce Commission (ICC), *Statistics of Railways*, and Statement M-220.

Local and Highway Passenger Transportation. Indexes of deflated p.c.e. for intercity bus, taxi, and local transportation were combined with estimated national income weights derived from the Interindustry Division tabulation of charges against final product.

Highway Freight. Index of vehicle ton miles of intercity freight traffic as estimated in ICC, Statement No. 568 and seventieth annual report, p. 43.

Water. The index for U.S. water transportation companies for 1947 to 1953 was built on estimates presented in Harold Barger, *The Transportation Industries, 1889–1946* (NBER, 1951). Separate indexes were prepared for freight and passenger traffic.

The freight series was extended to 1953 by using essentially the the same sources and methods described by Barger. The sources are various reports of the Maritime Commission, Army Engineers, and the Census Bureau. Except in the case of inland and Great Lakes traffic, the series are derived from separate tonnage and average haul estimates.

In the case of passenger traffic, the Barger series for international trade from 1939 was extrapolated by the numbers of arrivals and departures from and to foreign countries on American flag vessels reported in the annual reports of the Immigration and Naturalization Service, Department of Justice. Estimates of other passenger travel were made from the gross tonnage of vessels engaged in the coastwise and internal trade of the United States.

293

The 1947–53 series was extrapolated to 1954–55 by a weighted index of inland waterway and ocean transportation. Weights are estimated national income as derived from interindustry data.

The estimate for ocean transportation is an index of freight and passenger traffic weighted by 1947 revenue. Freight traffic consists of tons of dry and tanker cargo, exports and imports, carried by American operated vessels. Tons of each type and 1947 revenue are from the *Survey of Current Business*, March 1956, pp. 19 and 20.

Passenger Traffic for 1953 and 1954 is index of arrivals on U.S. flag carriers. The 1955 index was derived by applying the change 1955/1954 in total arrivals in the United States. Passenger revenue is from the interindustry report.

The estimate for inland waterways is an index of ton miles of freight traffic on inland waterways as estimated in ICC Statement 568.

Air. Index of ton miles of passenger, excess baggage, mail, express and freight of domestic and international scheduled air carriers, weighted by 1947 revenue per ton mile. Data from Civil Aeronautics Administration, *Statistics of Aviation.*

Pipelines (Oil). For 1947 through 1954, barrel miles of crude and refined oil were weighted by 1947 revenue per barrel mile, on the basis of data from ICC, *Statistics of Oil Pipeline Companies.* The index was extended to 1955 by the change 1955/1954 in intercity ton miles carried by oil pipelines from the ICC annual report, 1956.

Services Allied to Transportation. This industry consists of numerous miscellaneous activities. Indexes for the major ones were imputed as follows: (1) Services incidental to water transportation, i.e., docks, piers, stevedoring and other terminal operations—production index for water transportation; (2) Forwarding and arranging of transportation—weighted average of trucking and railroad freight; (3) Flying, except common carriers, and operation of airports and flying fields—production index for air transportation.

Output weights for each activity, obtained from the interindustry reports, were used to combine the indexes.

COMMUNICATIONS AND PUBLIC UTILITIES

Communications. Separate indexes were computed for the Telephone and Telegraph industries as shown in Table A-6 and these were combined with estimated national income weights derived from the interindustry table of charges against final product.

Estimates for the Telephone industry were based on deflated revenues rather than the number of calls, as has sometimes been used.

TABLE A-6

Communications—Industry Production Indexes
(1947 = 100)

Year	Telephone	Telegraph
1948	112.7	90.0
1949	119.4	83.0
1950	128.4	85.5
1951	139.9	87.1
1952	148.5	76.1
1953	156.6	80.0
1954	163.6	76.9
1955	188.0	78.3

It was felt that the latter understated industry output because of the change in the classification of calls since 1948.

Revenue data were obtained from the Federal Communications Commission (FCC). Local service revenues were deflated by the unrevised BLS Consumer Price Index for telephone service (1939 =100). Toll message revenues (excluding private line service) include intrastate and interstate revenues. Intrastate revenues were deflated by the Consumer Price Index. Interstate revenues were not deflated through 1952 because there were no rate changes. In 1953 and 1954 they were deflated by the estimated effective rate increases determined in consultation with the FCC. A similar procedure was followed for 1955 but certain estimates were made because all the necessary FCC data were not then available.

For the telegraph segment the number of messages, domestic, ocean cable, and radio telegraph were weighted by 1947 revenue per message. Data was from the FCC, *Statistics of the Communication Industry of the U.S.*, 1956.

Utilities. Separate indexes from the Federal Reserve Board, as shown in Table A-7, were combined with FRB value added weights. The

TABLE A-7

Utilities—Industry Production Indexes
(1947 = 100)

Year	Electricity	Gas	Total Electricity and Gas
1948	111.3	112.1	111.5
1949	118.1	118.7	118.2
1950	132.6	138.5	134.2
1951	148.7	159.3	151.6
1952	162.0	172.5	164.9
1953	178.8	181.3	179.5
1954	192.4	198.9	194.2
1955	213.5	216.5	214.4

published weight for electricity was reduced to reflect the private sector alone.

The index for electricity (private) is a weighted combination of seven series, including six series on energy sales by Class A and B utilities by type of customer for residential, general industrial, Atomic Energy Commission, commercial and other; and one series for energy sales of cooperatively owned utilities.

Gas is a component of the Federal Reserve Index of Electricity and Gas Output, as described in the *Federal Reserve Bulletin*, October 1956. The gas index is a weighted combination of four series by class of customer for residential, industrial, commercial, and other. Separate indexes are not available for private and public (municipal) utilities. In 1955, it is estimated that the latter accounted for 4 per cent of total therms sold to ultimate consumers. This percentage is somewhat higher than in 1947.

For local utilities the index represents deflated p.c.e. for water.

HOUSEHOLDS

Deflated domestic service payrolls and net interest on consumer debt from NID estimates of GNP in constant dollars. Other interest, such as that on brokers' loans, equals less than one-third of one per cent of total income (and product) originating in households and was not deflated.

SERVICES

Indexes were derived for each industry (excluding private households) in the services sector as shown in National Income Table 13 and combined with national income originating weights from the same table. The industry indexes are presented in Table A-8. Many of them were derived by combining appropriate items of constant dollar p.c.e. The detailed unpublished expenditures were obtained from the OBE. The assignment of the expenditures to the various industries was made on the basis of an examination of the content of each industry in terms of the Standard Industrial Classification, 1942 edition. The reconciliation of the national income and SIC classification is shown on p. 66 of the *National Income Supplement*, 1954. The notes accompanying Table 30 of the same publication were also helpful in making industry assignments.

Hotels and Lodging Places. Constant dollar p.c.e. for housing in hotels and clubs were combined with estimated expenditures by business for hotels. The latter 1947 weight was estimated on the basis of data in the interindustry report. The index imputed to it was the index for clubs because it was lower than the hotel index. The latter

296

TABLE A-8

Services Sector—Industry Production Indexes
(1947 = 100)

	1948	1949	1950	1951	1952	1953	1954	1955
Services	103.5	104.5	107.5	109.5	113.3	116.4	119.3	124.0
Hotels and lodging places	103.6	101.8	102.9	106.0	109.1	112.4	116.1	120.9
Personal services	99.5	97.4	97.5	96.1	97.3	100.1	102.2	105.4
Commercial and trade schools	103.7	106.8	118.6	121.1	123.0	109.3	108.1	109.9
Business services n.e.c.	106.7	104.8	111.8	122.5	132.0	139.4	146.0	157.8
Miscellaneous	109.7	118.0	134.0	138.0	145.1	148.8	153.3	163.5
Motion pictures	93.5	88.9	84.8	80.2	76.3	69.5	67.9	65.2
Amusements, excluding motion pictures	98.1	97.4	94.5	95.0	97.5	98.1	98.9	102.1
Medical and other health services	104.1	108.6	113.5	114.8	118.7	123.1	125.9	129.7
Legal services	112.6	114.1	114.1	112.9	109.3	113.3	111.1	112.1
Engineering and other professional services	111.1	107.6	109.0	127.1	144.4	151.4	152.8	167.4
Educational services n.e.c.	106.0	112.6	119.8	124.3	131.6	133.3	142.3	149.1
Nonprofit membership organizations n.e.c.	100.6	102.5	103.3	100.0	105.6	109.0	113.9	115.7

includes motels, the index for which is known to be increasing faster than that for hotels. The industry index was computed from the sum of the deflated expenditures.

Personal Services. An index was derived from the sum of constant dollar p.c.e. for shoe cleaning and repair, cleaning, dyeing and pressing, laundry, barber and beauty parlor, other personal services, and funeral services.

Commercial and Trade Schools and Employment Agencies. An index was derived from the sum of constant dollar p.c.e. for commercial business schools, correspondence schools, and employment agency fees.

Business Services, n.e.c. This industry includes advertising and miscellaneous activities such as credit bureaus, duplicating services, and building services. An index was derived by deflating national income originating in this industry by the implicit deflator for services (National Income Supplement, Table 41).

Miscellaneous Repair Services. Constant dollar p.c.e. for these services were combined with an estimate for business expenditures for repair services. An estimate of the 1947 value of business use of repair services was derived from the interindustry report. The index imputed to this segment was the deflated p.c.e. for care of electrical equipment. The items represented by p.c.e. include upholstery repair,

297

rug repair, care of electrical equipment, radio and TV repair, and watch and jewelry repair.

Motion Pictures. Included are motion picture production and distribution as well as theaters. The index of constant dollar p.c.e. for motion picture theater admissions was imputed to the entire industry.

Amusements, except Motion Pictures. An index was derived from the sum of constant dollar p.c.e. for legitimate theaters, spectator sports, commercial participant amusements, and pari-mutuel net receipts.

Medical and Other Health Services. An index was derived from the sum of constant dollar p.c.e. for physicians, dentists, other professional services, and hospitals.

Legal Services. The index of deflated p.c.e. was imputed to this industry.

Engineering and Other Professional Services. This is the index of persons engaged in this industry from National Income Table 28.

Educational Services, n.e.c. An index was derived from the sum of constant dollar p.c.e. for higher education, elementary and secondary schools, other instructions, foundations' expenditures for education and research, and museums, libraries, etc.

Nonprofit Membership Organizations. An index was derived from the sum of constant dollar p.c.e. for clubs and fraternal organizations, labor union net payments, religious bodies, and social welfare.

GOVERNMENT ENTERPRISES

Production indexes were estimated for Post Office and public power operations as shown in Table A-9. The Post Office index was

TABLE A-9

Government Enterprises—Production Indexes
(1947 = 100)

Year	Post Office	Public Power
1948	107.3	117
1949	112.0	130
1950	115.2	151
1951	120.7	184
1952	124.6	203
1953	125.7	217
1954	128.5	229
1955	130.7	279

imputed to all government enterprises except public power. The two indexes were combined with estimated national income originating (employee compensation) weights. Data from OBE on wages and salaries for the Post Office and TVA provided a basis for making a crude allocation of total government enterprise compensation.

Public Power. The index was obtained by subtracting the output of privately owned utilities from that total utility output of electricity. This index approximates a directly computed index weighted by class of customer. Unweighted total kilowatt hours sold by publicly owned utilities are available from the Federal Power Commission.

Post Office. The index represents a weighted aggregate of the number of pieces of mail handled or number of transactions performed by the Post Office, by type. The weights are based on the estimated amount of labor involved in performing a unit of each of the various services.

REST OF THE WORLD

These estimates represent investment income received from abroad deflated by an index of the value of U.S. imports of goods and services, and investment income paid to foreigners deflated by an index of U.S. exports. The deflators were based mainly upon the published indexes of unit values of merchandise compiled by the Bureau of Foreign Commerce. Wages and salaries, which represent a fractional part of the total, were not deflated.

Man-Hour Data Underlying "BLS Based" Productivity Estimates

BLS DATA

Estimates of nonagricultural employees by industry, and hours of workers were taken from the BLS "Employment and Earnings" monthly reports. The BLS statistics are based on payroll records from a sample of establishments. Changes from one month to the next in the employment reported by the sample respondents are applied to benchmark totals based primarily on unemployment compensation returns made by employers.

Average hours data are available only for production workers in manufacturing and nonsupervisory workers in certain nonmanufacturing industries. In computing the total hours for industries except for manufacturing, the hours of supervisory employees were assumed to be the same as for nonsupervisory workers. Thus, estimates of employees were multiplied by the average hours of nonsupervisory workers. For manufacturing, production workers were multiplied by production worker weekly hours (estimates of both being readily available) while nonproduction workers were assumed to work a forty-hour week. The average hours data refer to hours paid for.

299

Since the BLS data are limited to nonfarm employees (excluding domestics), estimates for farm employment, nonfarm self-employed, unpaid family workers, and domestics were obtained elsewhere. Data from other sources were also used to supplement BLS average hours data in certain areas. The Census *Monthly Report of the Labor Force* provided estimates of agricultural employment and hours. In computing total hours, average hours data were applied to estimates of all employees instead of just those "at work," for comparability with the BLS concept of hours paid. This procedure implies that persons who held farm jobs but were absent from work were paid. The same procedure was used for other areas, e.g., finance, insurance, and real estate, where average hours from Census labor force data were used.

Although the BLS statistics cover government employment, separate data are not shown for government enterprises which sell their "product" (Post Office, TVA) and are therefore considered in the National Income framework to be part of the private economy. For this series, estimated employees of government enterprises as shown in the *National Income Supplement* and the average hours of public administration workers from the *Monthly Report of the Labor Force* were used.

Active proprietors in unincorporated enterprises were derived from the National Income Supplement by subtracting the full-time equivalent employees from the total number of persons engaged in production, by industry. The number of domestics were obtained from the same source. The average hours for these groups were obtained from unpublished Census data on hours worked. Unpaid family workers included in this measure, are persons working without pay in family businesses for at least fifteen hours a week. The number of such workers and the average hours worked were taken from the Census *Monthly Report of the Labor Force.*

In evaluating the estimates, it must be remembered, that assumptions and imputations have been made, and that the data come from different sources and reflect different concepts. For 1955, one-fourth of the total employment figure was taken from non-BLS sources, and the hours of one-half of the employees were either obtained from other sources or imputed from other BLS data. Of the nonfarm total (i.e., excluding farm, self-employed, and unpaid family workers), only 7 per cent of the employment estimate was derived from other sources, and the hours of only one-third of the employees were either imputed from other BLS data or derived from other sources.

Methods of Determining the Effect of Intersectoral Shifts on the Movement of Total Real Product per Man-Hour

In analyzing the change in total private real product per man-hour it is useful to determine the respective rates of (1) changes in the productivity of individual sectors and (2) changes in the relative importance of sectors with different levels of productivity. In this context, relative importance can be measured in terms of either sector output or man-hours, depending on the purpose in view.

An accepted analytical procedure involves holding each contributory factor constant in turn while the direct effect of the other is measured.[2] The sum of the effects so measured will not generally equal the total change in real product per man-hour because the two factors do not in fact remain constant over time and the interaction between them also affects the result. Also, the effect of each factor on the total change will vary depending on the weight base period, that is whether the factors are held constant at the beginning or the end of the period being measured.

One method of eliminating the differences in results due to differences in weight base period and at the same time allocating the effect of the interaction to the two directly measured factors is to average the alternative measures of change for each direct factor. The average change in sector productivity plus the average change due to shifts, obtained by this method, will equal the total change in real product per man-hour, the effects of the interaction being distributed equally between the two factors.

Another approach, suggested by Frederick C. Mills,[3] is to allocate the effect of the interaction equally to each of the two direct factors as measured by either the beginning or end year base weighted alternatives. This procedure will yield the same result as the previous method, the difference being that in this case the effect of the interaction is allocated explicitly.

The results of a productivity analysis of this type may be affected to some extent by the particular set of price weights used in constructing the sector output measures because the relative levels of sector output and consequently sector output per man-hour may be affected differently by the price weights of different years. The output

---

[2] See the Technical Appendix to article by Harlow D. Osborne and Joseph B. Epstein, "Corporate Profits since World War II," *Survey of Current Business*, January 1956. For a more detailed and technical discussion of the alternative methods and problems of decomposing total change into the additive contributions of various input factors, see Irving H. Siegel, "Concepts and Measurement of Production and Productivity," Working Paper of the National Conference on Productivity, 1952, pp. 86–92.

[3] *Productivity and Economic Progress*, National Bureau of Economic Research, Occasional Paper 38, 1952, pp. 31–6.

301

measures used in this report to compute real product per man-hour are based on 1947 price weights.

COMMENT

CHARLES L. SCHULTZE, Council of Economic Advisers

Instead of attempting a critique of the concepts and methodology of the Jack Alterman's and Eva Jacobs' sector output measurements, I have combined them with current income data to indicate how they might be used to construct an integrated set of price, output, and unit cost measures.

Concepts

PRICE INDEXES

From the standpoint of income distribution, a price is the sum of all charges against output calculated per unit of product. In the case of sector value added, which is Alterman's concern, the relevant price deflator is the sum of income and other charges per unit of "real" value added. Since real value added is defined in terms of constant base period prices, the division of total income paid out by real value added automatically yields a Paasche price index with the constant dollar base year (1947) as 100.

In each sector the index of value added price can be converted into unit cost components—labor, property, and indirect tax.

Let L_i = Compensation of employees in sector i

R_i = Sum of gross property income—net rent, interest, profits, and capital consumption allowances

I_i = Indirect taxes

P_i = Price deflator

Z_i = Value of output, expressed in constant 1947 dollars

Y_i = Total gross income (charges against product) originating in sector i.

Then
$$\left[\frac{L_i}{Z_i}\right]_t + \left[\frac{R_i}{Z_i}\right]_t + \left[\frac{I_i}{Z_i}\right]_t = \left[\frac{Y_i}{Z_i}\right]_t = P_i(t).$$

The ratios L_i/Z_i, R_i/Z_i, etc., can be considered as "points" in the price index. Hence a given price increase may be allocated to the cost elements which benefited therefrom as follows:

$$\Delta P_i = \Delta L_i/Z_i + \Delta R_i/Z_i + \Delta I_i/Z_i$$

(where the Δ's are expressed in percentage points). The meaning of the $\Delta L_i/Z_i$, etc., is somewhat ambiguous since the individual sectors are themselves aggregates of industries, encompassing many different products. This does not, however, affect the character of the P_i as standard indexes of the Paasche form, since we have defined them as

$$P_i = Y_i/Z_i = \Sigma p_1 q_1 / \Sigma p_0 q_1.$$

The change in the price index between the base year and a given year does not incorporate the effect of "mix" changes since the weights are constant. The indexes of output and price are also internally consistent since the price index is Paasche and the output index, Laspeyre: multiplying the price index by the output index yields a value index identical to that derived by dividing given year aggregate value by base year aggregate value.[1]

UNIT COST INDEXES

Movements in the sector unit cost indexes, however, even between the base year and a given year are not pure measures of changes in unit costs. A unit labor cost index, U, in sector i, with given year quantity weights (quantity equaling constant dollar output in base period prices), would equal:

$$U_i = \frac{\Sigma \left[\dfrac{L_1}{p_0 q_1} \cdot p_0 q_1 \right]}{\Sigma \left[\dfrac{L_0}{p_0 q_0} \cdot p_0 q_1 \right]}$$

$$= \frac{\Sigma L_1}{\Sigma \left[\dfrac{L_0}{p_0 q_0} \cdot p_0 q_1 \right]}$$

where the L, p, and q are the wage bill, price, and quantity of the commodities produced in sector i. This unit labor cost index is thus the given year total wage bill divided by the wage bill which would have existed had given year quantities been produced at base year unit labor costs.

The unit labor cost index, derived from L_i/Z_i which we shall use as a component of the sector price deflator, is however:

$$U_i = \frac{\Sigma L_1}{\Sigma p_0 q_1} \bigg/ \frac{\Sigma L_0}{\Sigma p_0 q_0} = \frac{\Sigma L_1}{\Sigma L_0} \bigg/ \frac{\Sigma p_0 q_1}{\Sigma p_0 q_0}.$$

This is simply the index of the aggregate sector wage bill divided by the index of the aggregate sector output. The $\Delta L_i/Z_i$, $\Delta R_i/Z_i$, etc., consequently reflect not only changes in the unit costs of producing each product, but changes in product mix as well. Comparing changes in unit costs by this method is somewhat analogous to comparing Paasche indexes between years other than the given year and the

[1] Cf. Richard Stone, *Quantity and Price Indexes in National Accounts*, Organization for European Economic Cooperation, December 1956, pp. 37–8.

base year, although here one cannot strictly compare the given year even with the base year.[2]

The sensitivity of the cost indexes to intrasectoral shifts probably does not invalidate these measures since changes in product mix seldom seem to be so large in the short run as to make a substantial difference in the results. For example, a comparison of Paasche and Laspeyres GNP price indexes, using sector quantity weights showed that from 1947 to 1955, the two indexes were never more than $\frac{1}{2}$ of 1 per cent apart, and that the differential change in any one year was even smaller. While not conclusive proof of the minor impact of intrasectoral shifts on "true" unit labor cost measures, this finding is indicative of the usually narrow range of variation imparted by changes in product mix to indexes incorporating quantity weights.

The equation allocating a given price change to the cost elements involved reveals "ex post" relationships only. If money wages rise more than productivity, unit labor costs increase. The latter development is often associated with a price rise, but whether the wage advance or the price increase is the causal factor can never be discovered from ex post price and cost data alone. Usually, changes in costs and prices are mutually determined by interacting changes in supply and demand schedules, a fact which is generally recognized when profits per unit of output are at issue but often neglected when unit labor or material costs are discussed.

SECTOR PRICE INDEXES

Just as the price index of sector value added can be separated into cost components, the price index for total GNP can be decomposed into the "points" contributed by each sector. In this case, however, the appropriate price index is not the GNP deflator, which incorporates given year quantity weights, but a base year weighted index. If $P_{g(t)}$ is the base year weighted price index for GNP in year t, then

$$P_{g(t)} = \sum_{i=1}^{n} \frac{Y_{i(t)}}{Z_{i(t)}} \cdot \frac{Z_{i(0)}}{\sum\limits_{i=1}^{n} Z_{i(0)}},$$

remembering that the $Z_{i(t)}$ are sector outputs valued in constant base period prices. Thus a change in the GNP price between any two periods can be allocated to the sectors responsible, as follows:

$$\Delta P_g = \Delta Y_i/Z_i \cdot W_i + \Delta Y_j/Z_j \cdot W_j, \text{ etc.},$$

[2] See the Appendix to this comment for an exposition of this point.

where
$$W_i = \frac{Z_{i(0)}}{\sum\limits_{i=1}^{n} Z_{i(0)}}.$$

Despite its ex post nature, such an analysis can be a useful research tool.

While the measures described above suffer from the shortcomings inherent in defining changes in real economic output as changes in physical production, and from the further difficulties presented by product heterogeneity, they do provide internally consistent data on incomes, output, prices, and unit costs. Unit costs equal unit price and the latter rises as incomes per unit increase. Also, the movement of the "price" of GNP can be specifically related to price movements in each sector, and within sectors to changes in specific incomes per unit of output.

Construction of Estimates

Construction of price and unit cost indexes requires, in addition to the measures of real sector output provided by Alterman, corresponding measures of current dollar *gross* charges against product, by major components. The Department of Commerce publishes series on income originating by sector. To these data must be added estimates of capital consumption allowances and indirect taxes. The Alterman-Jacobs paper describes the method of estimating the latter in the base year, 1947. Essentially the same methodology was followed in deriving estimates for succeeding years.[3] In the mining and manufacturing sectors, the nonwage components of gross income were changed from the company basis used in the Commerce data to an establishment basis.[4]

With this information and the Alterman-Jacobs estimates of "real" gross product, consistent price and unit cost indexes for the total private nonfarm economy (less real estate) and for some of the major sectors were constructed. These are not presented here because (1) they represent a first attempt at quantifying the concepts discussed above and require additional refinement, and (2) they do not as yet incorporate the important recent revisions in the income accounts.[5]

[3] I wish to acknowledge the cooperation of the National Income Division of the Dept. of Commerce, in making available certain unpublished estimates. Harlow Osborne of the Division also furnished some of the calculations behind the article, written in conjunction with Epstein, "Corporate Profits Since World War II," *Survey of Current Business*, January 1956. The division bears, of course, no responsibility for the particular results obtained from the use of their data.

[4] The procedure for this redistribution is described in the Alterman-Jacobs paper.

[5] Since this paper was written, some of the sector price, cost, and output indexes have been published. See, Charles L. Schultze, *Prices, Costs and Output*, Committee for Economic Development (Washington, 1960); and Charles L. Schultze and Joseph L. Tryon, *Prices and Costs in Manufacturing Industries*, Study Paper No. 17, Joint Economic Committee, U.S. Congress, 86th Cong., 2nd Sess. (Washington, Govt. Printing Office, 1960).

However, some derivative calculations of changes in prices and unit costs are presented in order to illustrate the possible uses of the data.

Illustrative Analysis

1951–55 PRICE STABILITY

One interesting application of the data is in the interpretation of postwar cost-price behavior. Table 1 shows the percentage change in

TABLE 1

Percentage Changes in Selected Deflators and Price Indexes, Intervals, 1947–55

Deflator or Index	Percentage Change		
	1947–55	1947–51	1951–55
All industries: deflator: given year weights	22.2	16.2	5.2
deflator: base year weights	22.8	16.7	5.2
Manufacturing: deflator: given year weights	26.1	23.1	3.3
wholesale price index, manufactured products[a]	18.2	18.9	−.6
Retail trade: deflator: given year weights	10.4	11.3	−.8
Farm products: wholesale price index[b]	−10.4	13.4	−21.0
Crude industrial raw materials: wholesale price index[c]	22.1	30.0	−6.1

[a] Table 39, *Productivity Prices and Incomes*, Joint Economic Committee, 85th Congress, 1957.

[b] Bureau of Labor Statistics, Wholesale Price Index.

[c] January 1958, *Economic Report of the President*, Table F-37.

Source: With the exceptions noted above, developed from data described in the text.

selected deflators for intervals from 1947 to 1955. The deflator for private nonfarm GNP (less real estate) rose at a rate of about 1 per cent per year from 1951 to 1955.[6] It appears from Table 2, which shows the points attributable to movements in sector indexes, that about one-half of this increase was contributed by the steady upward trend in "all other industries," consisting mainly of services, finance, and insurance. The deflator for value added in manufacturing increased only 3.3 per cent over the same four years, while that for retail trade declined slightly.[7]

[6] Whether one uses a standard deflator with implicit given year weights, or weights the individual sector deflators by base period values makes little difference in the results, as can be seen from the first two rows of Table 1.

[7] Since the changes in "real" retail trade value added are essentially measured as the change in the physical throughput of commodities, this implies a decline in retail sector charges per unit of commodities sold. Such a measurement ignores changes in the volume of "services" rendered per unit of retail sales. This omission is also generally implicit in the currently used measures of real GNP (except where such changes take place through a shift from one kind of store to another, e.g., from department stores to discount houses). Hence these indexes are at least consistent with the underlying GNP data.

TABLE 2

Relation between Changes in the All Industries and Sector Deflators, Intervals 1947–55

Sector	Per cent Change			Sector Point Contribution			Base Period Weight[a]
	1947–55	1947–51	1951–55	1947–55	1947–51	1951–55	
All industries[b]	22.8	16.7	5.2	22.8	16.7	6.1	100
Mining	21.0	21.7	−.6	.8	.8	0	3.9
Construction	28.6	20.8	6.5	1.4	1.0	.4	5.0
Manufacturing	27.1	23.1	3.3	10.2	8.7	1.5	37.5
Wholesale trade	24.5	16.1	7.2	1.7	1.1	.6	7.1
Retail trade	10.3	11.3	−.8	1.8	2.0	−.2	17.4
Railroads	40.3	33.2	5.3	1.7	1.4	.3	4.1
Highway freight	3.0	−12.6	17.9	.1	−.1	.2	1.4
Telephone and telegraph	29.0	15.4	11.8	.4	.2	.2	1.6
Electric and gas utilities	3.3	4.2	−.9	.1	.1	0	2.1
All other industries	23.4	7.5	14.8	4.7	1.5	3.2	20.0

[a] Sector gross charges against product as a per cent of total gross charges for all industries during 1947.

[b] Excludes farm, government, and real estate sectors.

Source: Developed from data described in the text.

Table 3 provides information on the behavior of various elements of cost. In contrast to prices, unit labor costs and indirect taxes increased substantially from 1951 to 1955. In manufacturing, the movement of these two items alone represented a rise of about seven points in the deflator, other things being equal, while in retail trade, they represented over two points of increase. Had not "property" costs (net rent, interest, profit, and capital consumption allowances) declined in some areas, and increased far less than labor costs in others, the impact on the value added deflators would have been much more significant. In manufacturing, the small rise in the deflator of value added that did occur was offset by sharp declines in the price of raw materials, so that the index of product prices remained stable.

A review of earlier developments clearly indicates that from 1951 to 1955 the economy was living off the "fat" of the immediate post-Korean inflation. In 1950 and 1951 rapid increases in demand led to price advances far in excess of increases in unit labor and indirect tax costs so that gross property charges against product were lifted well above normal in most sectors. Between 1947 and 1951 the latter absorbed about one-half of the increase in unit prices (in the all industry average and in manufacturing), although they constituted only between a quarter and a third of total charges in the base period. Aggregate data on functional income distribution reveal the same phenomenon. By 1951, for example, corporate profits before taxes

307

TABLE 3

Relation between Changes in Price and Unit Cost, Indexes, Selected Industry Sectors,
Intervals, 1947–55

Sector	Per cent Change			Factor Point Contribution			Base Period Weight[a]
	1947–55	1947–51	1951–55	1947–55	1947–51	1951–55	
All industries[b]							
Total charges per unit (=deflator)	22.3	16.2	5.2	22.3	16.2	6.1	100
Labor	22.1	13.3	7.8	13.3	8.0	5.3	60.3
Property	24.3	23.9	.3	7.5	7.4	.1	30.9
Depreciation	78.0	42.0	25.3	3.9	2.1	1.8	5.0
Other	13.9	20.5	−5.4	3.6	5.3	−1.7	25.9
Indirect taxes	17.0	9.1	7.3	1.5	.8	.7	8.8
Manufacturing							
Total charges per unit (=deflator)	27.1	23.1	3.2	27.1	23.1	4.0	100
Labor	24.1	15.6	7.4	16.1	10.4	5.7	66.7
Property	39.1	51.5	−8.7	9.2	12.1	−2.9	23.5
Depreciation	90.2	39.0	36.8	3.7	1.6	2.1	4.1
Other	28.4	54.1	−16.7	5.5	10.5	−5.0	19.4
Indirect taxes	18.4	6.1	11.5	1.8	.6	1.2	9.8
Retail trade							
Total charges per unit (=deflator)	10.3	11.3	−.9	10.3	11.3	−1.0	100
Labor	15.5	13.1	2.1	6.7	6.5	1.2	49.7
Property	−4.3	4.6	−8.5	−1.6	1.7	−3.3	37.3
Depreciation	69.2	43.6	17.9	2.7	1.7	1.0	3.9
Other	−12.9	0	−12.9	−4.3	0	−4.3	33.4
Indirect taxes	32.3	23.8	6.8	4.2	3.1	1.1	13.0

[a] Factor charges against product as a per cent of total charges against product during 1947.
[b] Excludes farm, government, and real estate sectors.

Source: Developed from data described in the text.

were 22 per cent of corporate gross product as compared to 18.5 per
cent in 1947 and a post war average of 19.5 per cent.[8]

For several years after 1951, the cushion of abnormally high gross
profit margins permitted sizeable increases in unit labor costs and
indirect taxes, without either a full pass-through of such costs or a
decline of profit margins to subnormal levels. This is brought into
even sharper relief when net property margins are examined. While
gross property costs per unit declined from 1951 to 1955, capital consumption allowances per unit increased rapidly. Part of the increase
reflected the post-Korean accelerated amortization program, and
should be reallocated to profits but even after such an adjustment,

[8] Profits were adjusted to reflect straight line nonaccelerated depreciation in order to
make the postwar years comparable with each other. I am indebted to Alterman for his
permission to use some unpublished estimates as the basis for this comparison.

the decline in net property margins was substantial, although not excessive.

The behavior of raw materials prices also contributed to price stability. The prices of farm and industrial products in this category rose rapidly during the Korean inflation only to decline sharply from 1951 to 1955, thereby providing an offset to rises in labor costs indirect taxes and depreciation charges.

Demands for goods and services were not generally excessive during the period. The rate of increase in aggregate demand slackened significantly after 1951, as declining inventory investment and consumer durable purchases offset the rise in defense spending.[9] The handsome profit margins enjoyed by most industries gave rise, however, to an excess demand for factors of production. The result was an exceedingly low rate of unemployment and a continued advance in unit labor costs. This "factor demand" inflation is the inevitable aftermath of a sharp increase in profit margins in an economy characterized by substantial downward rigidity in prices. Even when aggregate excess demand in the commodity markets has been eliminated, the combination of high profit margins and downward rigidities in the prices of finished goods practically guarantees a further inflation in factor prices. A new floor is erected beneath the price level reached in each burst of inflation. Paradoxically, then, an analysis of the period between 1951 and 1953, when commodity prices were generally stable, provides a good insight into the process by which a secular upward bias is imparted to the general price level.

1947–55: SHIFTS IN DISTRIBUTION OF UNIT COSTS

By 1953 price-income relationships had returned to a more normal pattern. Although a typical cyclical shift in functional income distribution occurred in 1954 normality was restored by the middle of the 1955 recovery. Considering 1947 to 1955 as a whole, Table 3 shows that for all industries, unit labor costs accounted for 13.3 points or 60 per cent of the total 22.3 point rise in the price index. This is the same proportion which labor costs were of total costs in the 1947 base period. Thus the increase in price relative to labor costs in the first subperiod was exactly offset by the increase in labor costs

9 In "The Lull that Came to Stay," *Journal of Political Economy*, February 1955, John P. Lewis, examines the major demand factors in the 1951–55 period, and comes to much the same conclusion reached here. Lewis' major objective is to point to the special features which make it impossible to generalize the possibility of the coexistence of full employment and price stability solely from the experience of these years. Somewhat similar conclusions may also be found in Bert Hickman's *The Korean War and United States Economic Activity*, National Bureau of Economic Research, Occasional Paper 49, 1955.

relative to price in the second period. Gross property costs accounted for 7.5 points, or 34 per cent of the change in price, compared to a base period weight of 30 per cent. Again the sharp rise in property costs relative to total costs in the first subperiod was offset by their subsequent decline.

Manufacturing presents a similar picture. Between 1947 and 1955, labor costs accounted for 60 per cent of the rise in total charges per unit compared to a 67 per cent base period weight. The less than average contribution of labor costs before 1951 (10.4 points, or 45 per cent of the total 23.1 point rise) was not quite offset by their more than proportional rise thereafter (5.7 points compared to a 4.0 point rise in total charges). Property costs accounted for 52 per cent of the rise in total unit charges in the first interval and declined absolutely in the second.

Retail trade does not appear to have shared the experience of "all industries" and manufacturing. From 1947 through 1955 labor and indirect tax costs per unit rose by 10.9 points, while the over-all price increase was 10.3 points. Gross property charges actually declined during these years. In the first subperiod the latter contributed only 1.7 points out of a total 11.3 point price increase. During the second subperiod, while price declined 1.0 points, unit gross property charges fell 3.3 points, and net property charges 4.3 points.

Gross property margins may have failed to rise more than proportionately during the 1947–51 period because they were initially quite high. In 1947 net property margins were approximately 33 per cent, while depreciation charges were only 4 per cent of unit value added. The corresponding ratios for the all industry average were 26 and 5, and for manufacturing, 19 and 4. Net margins were 5 times depreciation in the latter two areas and 8 times depreciation per unit in retail trade. If depreciation per unit is used as a crude measure of capital investment per unit, then profits in retail trade appear to have been relatively high. While retail net property charges had fallen to 4.5 times depreciation by 1955, the ratio for both the all industry average and for manufacturing had declined to 3.2. However, because the meaning of book depreciation is so vague, particularly in a transition period like 1947, such comparisons can only be suggestive.

POST 1955: INFLATION

The increase in aggregate demand after the end of 1955 was not substantially greater than that between 1951 and 1955, but it was accompanied by a significant rise in prices. This is not surprising in view of certain contrasts between the two periods. The price stability between 1951 and 1955 was in part the result of a distorted income distribution built up in the prior inflation. Although the rapid upsurge of demand which occurred during 1955 lifted profit margins somewhat above the postwar average,[10] the abnormality was substantially smaller than in 1950 and 1951 and the "cushion" of a distorted set of price-income relations much less. Also, raw materials prices appeared to have reached a lower turning point in 1955. Hence increases in labor and raw material costs—whether of an autonomous nature or stemming from excess demands in particular sectors—had their main impact on prices rather than on profit margins.

Conclusion

This analysis illustrates one potential use of an extension of the concepts in the Alterman-Jacobs paper. While this particular analysis might have been based on aggregate income distribution data alone, the use of sector unit cost data provides a direct link between price behavior and income distribution changes. It also illuminates the relationship between price movements in general and trends in individual sectors. So long as the analyst remembers that he is dealing with ex post facto data, and does not try to impute simple causality between associated developments, this type of data can be a significant aid to aggregate price analysis.

The particular body of data used in this paper requires substantial further refinement. In particular the segmentation of the manufacturing area would provide much needed information. Further, matching man-hour data with the unit labor cost and output data would shed some light on the determinants of unit labor costs.

This type of analysis shares with all attempts to deal with price-output relationships to the problem of suitable definitions of terms. Unequivocal measures of the magnitude or interrelationship of prices, costs, and output cannot be achieved; the necessary information on utility functions (or preference fields) and on production functions will never be available. Recourse must be had to "a basis of comparison in pragmatic terms which can be given an operational significance."[11] It is because the measures developed by Alterman and Jacobs and elaborated here may provide insights into certain important economic problems, that they promise to be of operational significance when further refined and developed.

---

[10] This tendency appears in sharper relief in the recently revised GNP data, which raise the 1955 estimates of corporate profits about $2 billion above the earlier estimates incorporated in our data.

[11] Richard Stone, *op. cit.*, p. 12.

APPENDIX

The sector unit cost measures used, assuming for the purpose of exposition only two components of costs—labor (L) and property (R) —are:

$$\frac{\Sigma L_1}{\Sigma p_0 q_1} + \frac{\Sigma R_1}{\Sigma p_0 q_1} = \frac{Y_1}{\Sigma p_0 q_1} = \frac{\Sigma p_1 q_1}{\Sigma p_0 q_1} = P_1 \qquad (1)$$

With appropriate weighting, "true" unit cost indexes can be also made to add up to a Paasche price index:

$$\frac{\Sigma L_1}{\displaystyle\sum \frac{L_0}{p_0 q_0} \cdot p_0 q_1} = \text{"true" unit labor cost index} = \bar{L}_1 \text{ in period 1} \quad (2)$$

$$\frac{\Sigma R_1}{\displaystyle\sum \frac{R_0}{p_0 q_0} \cdot p_0 q_1} = \text{"true" unit property cost index} = \bar{R}_1 \text{ in period 1} \quad (3)$$

$$\frac{\Sigma L_1}{\displaystyle\sum \frac{L_0}{p_0 q_0} \cdot p_0 q_1} \cdot \frac{\displaystyle\sum \frac{L_0}{p_0 q_0} \cdot p_0 q_1}{\Sigma p_0 q_1} + \frac{\Sigma R_1}{\displaystyle\sum \frac{R_0}{p_0 q_0} \cdot p_0 q_1} \cdot \frac{\displaystyle\sum \frac{R_0}{p_0 q_0} \cdot p_0 q_1}{\Sigma p_0 q_1}$$

$$= \frac{\Sigma L_1}{\Sigma p_0 q_1} + \frac{\Sigma R_1}{\Sigma p_0 q_1} = \bar{P}_1 \text{ (by equation 1).} \quad (4)$$

Hence by weighting our "true" unit cost indexes (which themselves have given year quantity weights) with the base year unit cost of producing given year quantities we can sum to a Paasche price index. The sum of the changes in the aggregates derived by weighting our "true" unit cost indexes thus equals the change (in terms of per cent points) of the price index. But these changes in the unit cost aggregates are a combination of changes in the index of unit costs and in the product mix, $p_0 q_1 / \Sigma p_0 q_1$ which enters into the weights.

The per cent point difference between a Paasche price index in a given year and its value in the base year $(=1.00)$ does not, of course, involve the problem of changing product mix. The point difference in the unit cost aggregates as used in this paper—which sum to the price index—does, however, involve a change in product mix, even when taken against the base year. For the difference in points is:

$$\Delta \frac{\Sigma L}{\Sigma Z} = \frac{\Sigma L_1}{\Sigma p_0 q_1} - \frac{\Sigma L_0}{\Sigma p_0 q_0}; \qquad \Delta \frac{\Sigma R}{\Sigma Z} = \frac{\Sigma R_1}{\Sigma p_0 q_1} - \frac{\Sigma R_0}{\Sigma p_0 q_0}. \quad (5)$$

In both the base year and the given year these aggregates add to the price index, which is of course 1.00 in the base year. On the other

312

hand, the unit cost aggregates in the base year which have the same weights as in the given year are:

$$\bar{L}_0 \cdot \frac{\sum\left[\dfrac{L_0}{p_0 q_0} \cdot p_0 q_1\right]}{\Sigma p_0 q_1} + R_0 \frac{\sum\left[\dfrac{R_0}{p_1 q_0} \cdot p_0 q_1\right]}{\Sigma p_0 q_1}. \tag{6}$$

Since both $\bar{L}_0$ and $\bar{R}_0$ equal 1, the expression is:

$$\frac{\sum\left[\dfrac{\bar{L}_0}{p_0 q_0} \cdot p_0 q_1\right] + \sum\left[\dfrac{\bar{R}_0}{p_1 q_0} \cdot p_0 q_1\right]}{\Sigma(p_0 q_1)}. \tag{7}$$

which *does not* equal $\Sigma(p_0 q_1)/\Sigma(p_0 q_1)=1.00$, the Paasche index in the base period. Only if the $p_0 q_1/\Sigma(p_0 q_1)$ in equation (6) are replaced by $(p_0 q_0/\Sigma(p_0 q_1))$ will equation (6) reduce to

$$\frac{\Sigma L_0}{\Sigma(p_0 q_0)} + \frac{\Sigma R_0}{\Sigma(p_0 q_0)} = \frac{\Sigma Y_0}{\Sigma(p_0 q_0)} = 1.00.$$

Hence the aggregates of unit costs, which can be made to add to the price index in all periods, are not free from the effects of changing product mix, even when we are comparing a given year with a base year.

Industry Net Output Estimates
in the United States

ALMARIN PHILLIPS

UNIVERSITY OF VIRGINIA

THIS paper reviews three recent measures of United States industry net output (or input) which have been done within the framework of, or by methods consonant with, national income and product statistics. The studies, taken chronologically, are Simon Kuznets' "Long-Term Changes in the National Income of the United States of America Since 1870,"[1] John W. Kendrick and Carl Jones, "Gross National Farm Product in Constant Dollars, 1910–50,"[2] and the Bureau of Labor Statistics' "Trends in Output per Man-Hour and Man-Hours per Unit of Output Manufacturing, 1939–53."[3] Each is first described and then evaluated.

Estimates of net output by industrial origin should be an integral part of a complete system of national accounts. Economic change involves shifts in the allocation of resources and changes in the efficiency of their application within and among industries. The description and analysis of this process require empirical knowledge of the industrial composition of the aggregate national output. However, unlike certain other nations, the United States boasts no regularly published official estimates of industry net output.[4] The closest approximation is the Department of Commerce series on

[1] *Income and Wealth of the United States, Trends and Structure*, Income and Wealth Series II, Cambridge and Baltimore, 1952.

[2] *Survey of Current Business*, September 1951. See in addition John W. Kendrick, "National Productivity and Its Long-Term Projection," *Long-Range Economic Projection*, Studies in Income and Wealth, Volume Sixteen (Princeton University Press for National Bureau of Economic Research, 1954), where Kendrick compares farm net output and productivity with gross private national product and productivity; also, L. Jay Atkinson and Carl Jones, "Farm Income and Gross National Product," *Survey of Current Business*, August 1954, and "Note on Farm Gross National Product," *Survey of Current Business*, October 1958.

[3] BLS Report No. 100.

[4] At least twelve countries publish estimates of net production by industrial origin in constant prices. For description of techniques see W. B. Reddaway, "Movements of the Real Product of the United Kingdom, 1946–49," *Journal of the Royal Statistical Society* (Part A, 1950) and V. R. Berlinguette, "Measurement of Real Output," *Canadian Journal of Economics and Political Science* (February 1954), and Berlinguette and Leacy, "The Estimation of Real Domestic Product by Final Expenditure Categories and by Industry of Origin in Canada" (in this volume).

national income (factor payments) by major industries in current dollars. There is no official attempt to deflate these data due to the lack of an appropriate factor price index. The works reviewed here are the forerunners of what many hope will soon be a permanent addition to United States social accounts.

Study Coverage and Methods

THE KUZNETS ESTIMATES

The Kuznets' study is the only one which takes a factor payment rather than a market price approach. "Since," says Kuznets, "industries are not complexes for the production of final goods, it is difficult, if not impossible, to identify any specific final product magnitude with any specific industry's activity. Industries contribute the efforts of the factors of production engaged in them . . . Since the industries are interlocked in the production of any group of final goods . . . an industrial distribution of the national product must be based on the general assumption that the contribution of each industry is proportional to the economic magnitude of the resources engaged in them."[5]

The factor payment approach raises immediately the problem of deflation. Kuznets rejects a deflator based on the prices of goods purchased by the factor owners since this would reflect changes in the "terms of trade" of the factors in one industry vis-à-vis the rest of the economy rather than the unique value of their contribution. Instead, he would, conceptually, employ an index based on a weighted average of the difference between the prices of goods bought and sold by firms in the industry.[6] Actually, while this deflation technique is illustrated for agriculture,[7] Kuznets' final allocation of national product in constant dollars is based on indexes of physical output, most of which were presented in previous publications of the National Bureau of Economic Research.[8]

The translation of indexes of physical output into a percentage distribution of real national product is typical of Kuznets' ingenuity in treating data. A percentage distribution of national income by industry of origin in current dollars was available. Total national product, in 1929 prices, was converted to index form for overlapping decades with the average value for the decade 1919–28 as a base.

[5] Kuznets, op. cit., p. 92.

[6] Ibid., p. 93. See also his earlier statement of the same method, "Income Originating in Nine Basic Industries," National Bureau of Economic Research, Bulletin No. 59, May 1936, p. 5.

[7] Ibid., pp. 93–8.

[8] Ibid., pp. 99–103.

Indexes of the physical output of the respective industries for over-lapping decades were converted to the same base, and these were divided by the index of constant price total national product for each decade. The quotient indexes were then multiplied by the relative shares of the respective industries from 1919 to 1928 to obtain esti-mates of percentage shares of national product in 1929 prices for each of the other decades. Thus any industry whose physical output grew more rapidly than deflated national product shows an increasing share, and vice versa. Kuznets was able to obtain such estimates for agriculture, mining, manufacturing, contract construction, and trans-portation and public utilities. Output indexes for trade, service, finance, and government were unavailable; hence, their combined share was obtainable only as a residual.

THE KENDRICK-JONES ESTIMATES

These estimates of net farm output are apparently the first expressly to use the Geary approach[9] for a major sector of the United States GNP. Gross output in current market values for each of several classes of farm products was found by summing sales (i.e., cash receipts from farm marketings), Commodity Credit Corporation loans, home consumption of farm products, net change in farm in-ventories, and the rental value of farm homes. The current value of intermediate products consumed was derived by totalling Bureau of Agricultural Economics data on production expenses other than con-tractual factor costs. Rents paid to nonfarm landlords, unlike rents accruing to farmers, were included in intermediate purchases rather than in factor costs of farming and are thus not included in the final estimates of net farm output. In line with the Commerce Depart-ment's treatment of financial intermediaries, the value of commercial banking services was measured by imputed interest on farmers' deposits in commercial banks. Net farm output, or GNP originating on farms, is the difference between gross output and intermediate purchases.

Kendrick and Jones also estimated current capital consumption by subtracting estimates of depreciation allocable to nonfarm landlords from BAE data on total farm depreciation, in order to derive farm net national product in market prices.

Deflation of output and input was done at the detailed product level with BAE price series converted to a 1939 base. Special deflation

---

[9] See R. C. Geary, "The Concept of Net Volume of Output with Special Reference to Irish Data," *Journal of the Royal Statistical Society* (New Series), 1944. Solomon Fabricant discussed the same concept previously in *The Output of Manufacturing Industries*, National Bureau of Economic Research, 1940, pp. 23 ff.

techniques based on moving the 1939 values were necessary for banking services and rents paid to nonfarm landlords. With ideal indexes, the deflation would yield a series of net outputs composed of given year quantities of output less given year quantities of intermediate purchases, both valued in 1939 prices.

In subsequent presentations the Kendrick-Jones constant dollar net farm output estimates or revisions of them are compared with larger aggregates of output and residual nonfarm output measures are presented. Kendrick utilized Commerce Department deflated private gross national product data to obtain gross private nonfarm product.[10] Atkinson and Jones later compared farm GNP with both private nonfarm and government GNP in constant dollars.[11]

The Kendrick-Jones estimates were used to derive productivity measures. In the original article, net farm product was compared with BAE man-equivalent hours to obtain output per man-hour. An index of composite labor, capital, and land productivity was also shown. The series for durable capital was prepared by deflating annual capital outlays, subtracting deflated annual depreciation, and successively adding the difference to the sum of fixed capital in the base year. Changes in constant dollar farm inventories were added to obtain estimates of total capital. The series for land was obtained by moving the value estimate for the base year by changes in acreage. A composite factor input index was constructed by combining the labor, capital, and land indexes with weights reflecting the distribution of income payments in the period 1940 to 1949.

Kendrick compared output per man-hour for the farm, private nonfarm, and total private sectors, and provided an analysis of the effects of interindustry shifts on productivity. The Atkinson-Jones revision of the original series changed the productivity measure from output per man-hour to output per worker, probably because of conceptual difficulties in the BAE man-hour series.

THE BUREAU OF LABOR STATISTICS ESTIMATES

These estimates for manufacturing are the first large-scale attempt to measure the net output of a major non-agricultural sector of the United States economy with the Geary method. They were made as part of a continuing study of man-hour productivity based sometimes on physical output and sometimes on value added.

The BLS study works from the details of the four-digit industry classifications of the *Census of Manufactures*, 1939 and 1947, and the *Annual Survey of Manufactures*, 1949 through 1953. Each industry's

[10] "National Productivity and Its Long-Term Projection."
[11] *Op. cit.*

value of shipments was adjusted for changes in inventories of finished goods and goods in process to obtain figures for gross output. Primary and secondary products were added together. The value of output reflects sellers' net receipts rather than market prices since indirect taxes paid by manufacturers are not included in shipments figures in the 1947 and subsequent census and surveys. The gross output of each industry contains not only the usually conceived intermediate purchases but also substantial amounts of double-counting due to interplant transfers within each industry.

Intermediate purchases were also taken from Census figures. These purchases include interplant transfers within industries so that double-counting, referred to above, is eliminated by subtraction in the calculation of net output. However, Census purchases cover only materials, supplies, containers, fuels, contract work, and purchased electrical energy. The omission of items such as legal and accounting services, insurance, telephone and telegraph, repair work, etc., leaves much in the Census and BLS value added figures which is foreign to the national product concepts.

The gross output of each industry was deflated by an average of the BLS Wholesale Price Indexes for products primary to that industry. The weights used in averaging were the relative values of the several products in 1947 as shown by the *Census of Manufactures*. Except for 1939 and 1953 when purchases were deflated for the aggregate of industries, each four-digit industry's purchases were deflated by an average of the price indexes for the supplying industries, the weights being the relative values for such industry purchases shown in the BLS Interindustry (input-output) Chart for 1947.

The price indexes available were of the Laspeyres type with base year quantity weights. These were used in two different ways to produce two indexes of net output. The first technique was to divide both gross output and intermediate purchases by their respective price indexes to obtain:

$$\frac{\sum_{1}^{n} P_1 Q_1 \left(\dfrac{\sum_{1}^{n} P_0 Q_0}{\sum_{1}^{n} P_1 Q_0} \right) - \sum_{1}^{m} p_1 q_1 \left(\dfrac{\sum_{1}^{m} p_0 q_0}{\sum_{1}^{m} p_1 q_0} \right)}{\sum_{1}^{n} P_0 Q_0 - \sum_{1}^{m} p_0 q_0}, \tag{1}$$

where P and Q represent prices and quantities of n items of gross output, p and q prices and quantities of m items of intermediate purchases, and the subscripts 0 and 1, the base and given years, respectively. Since the BLS lacked the necessary Paasche price

319

indexes, this provided the best approximation to the generally preferred Laspeyres production index. The second method was to
"inflate" 1947 gross output and intermediate purchases by the price
indexes for given years and to divide the result into the given year
value of net output to yield the index:

$$\frac{\sum_{1}^{n} P_1 Q_1 - \sum_{1}^{m} p_1 q_1}{\sum_{1}^{n} P_1 Q_0 - \sum_{1}^{n} p_1 q_0}. \tag{2}$$

This results in a straight Paasche production index in which each
year's index is comparable only with that of the base year. The labor
productivity indexes were prepared by simple division of a man-hour
index into the relevant net output index.

Evaluation

THE KUZNETS ESTIMATES

These estimates of net output by industry of origin are certainly of
the "rough and ready" variety. With the exception of the agricultural
estimate, they are not net at all. Their validity depends on the
generally untested assumption that the ratio of real net output to real
gross output is constant.[12] Other issues could be raised—Kuznets'
concept of national income, the very limited level of disaggregation,
the use of overlapping decades rather than individual years in some of
the initial computations, the failure to distribute rent by industrial
origin, index number biases—but a discussion of them seems
inappropriate here. This was a pioneering study and its positive contributions far outweigh its apparent shortcomings.

Kuznets' analysis of his estimates illustrates the value of industry
net output data. The insights he derived from a comparison of industry product shares through time and from the observation of
productivity changes within and among industries constitute a strong
argument for devoting greater effort to the development of a continuing series of this nature.

More specifically, Kuznets' method for deflating factor incomes
may have more merit and applicability than is currently recognized.
The most widely recommended approach to measuring net output is

[12] The same criticism applies to the method of combining indexes of gross output with
value added or net output weights. See Jack Alterman and Eva E. Jacobs, "Estimates of
Real Product in the United States by Industrial Sector, 1947–55," this volume, p. 227.
Berlinguette and Leacy, *op. cit.*, pp. 222–223, suggest that it is sometimes necessary to
adjust gross output indexes for Canadian industries before they can be used as substitutes for indexes of net output.

to use the Geary formula usually with a Paasche price index.[13] However, where the necessary data on purchased materials and services are lacking, or where the definition of output is problematical, deflated gross dollar output or some "representative" physical production series are usually substituted.[14] Resort to Kuznets' factor payments approach in such cases may be preferable. There is a simple algebraic relationship between one variant of the Kuznets' deflation technique and the Geary formula which seems to have gone unnoticed.

The Census gross industry output data exclude indirect taxes, while the industry purchase data include such taxes. When value added is computed by subtracting purchases from gross output, indirect taxes are eliminated and what is left, except for purchases not collected by Census, is factor income plus capital consumption allowances. Thus, the OBE estimates of income originating in an industry plus their unpublished estimates of capital consumption allowances are *conceptually* identical to Census value added, again ignoring uncollected items of purchase. This makes it possible to estimate net output in any given year, $\sum_{1}^{n} P_1 Q_1 - \sum_{1}^{m} p_1 q_1$, with OBE data.

Given-year net output can be deflated directly, without the separate deflation of gross output and inputs, by applying a price index formed by taking the weighted average of the difference between the gross output and the input price indexes. The weight for the gross output index is unity (i.e., the ratio of gross output to gross output) and the weight for the input price index is the ratio of inputs to gross output in the base year. This index appears as:

$$\frac{\dfrac{\sum_{1}^{n} P_1 Q_0}{\sum_{1}^{n} P_0 Q_0} - \left(\dfrac{\sum_{1}^{m} p_0 q_0}{\sum_{1}^{n} P_0 Q_0}\right)\left(\dfrac{\sum_{1}^{m} p_1 q_0}{\sum_{1}^{m} p_0 q_0}\right)}{1 - \dfrac{\sum_{1}^{m} p_0 q_0}{\sum_{1}^{n} P_0 Q_0}}, \tag{3}$$

which reduces to

$$\frac{\sum_{1}^{n} P_1 Q_0 - \sum_{1}^{m} p_1 q_0}{\sum_{1}^{n} P_0 Q_0 - \sum_{1}^{m} p_0 q_0}. \tag{4}$$

[13] "Index Numbers of Industrial Production," *Studies in Methods*, Statistical Office of the United Nations (September 15, 1950).

[14] For illustrations, see Reddaway, *op. cit.*, and Berlinguette and Leacy, *op. cit.*, pp. 222 ff.

321

The index of net output (factor incomes plus capital consumption) before price correction is:

$$\frac{\sum_1^n P_1 Q_1 - \sum_1^m p_1 q_1}{\sum_1^n P_0 Q_0 - \sum_1^m p_0 q_0}, \tag{5}$$

and deflation of (5) by the price index in (4) yields:

$$\frac{\sum_1^n P_1 Q_1 - \sum_1^m p_1 q_1}{\sum_1^n P_1 Q_0 - \sum_1^m p_1 q_0}, \tag{6}$$

the Paasche variety of the Geary formula.[15] This is precisely the algebraic result of the second BLS deflation technique shown in (2) above, but the need for deflating output and inputs separately is avoided.[16]

This method was checked, using the BLS price indexes for gross output and inputs for manufacturing as a whole. Since Census does not publish gross shipments for all manufacturing, the $\sum_1^n P_0 Q_0$ value was estimated by multiplying total manufacturing value added in 1947 by one and a half on the strength of a statement in the *1947 Census of Manufactures* that value added tends to be two-thirds of gross shipments.[17] The value for $\sum_1^m p_0 q_0$ was derived by subtracting OBE income originating in manufacturing plus manufacturing depreciation from the estimated gross output value.[18] This produced a weight for the input price index of .451.

Table 1 compares the BLS current year weighted net output index for manufacturing with the net output index derived by deflating Census value added in manufacturing directly by the price index

[15] The Laspeyres type of the Geary formula results if Paasche price indexes of gross output and input are used, the weights being unity and the ratio of input to gross output in the given year valued in base year prices. These price indexes will be negative under the same circumstances as those which produce negative results for the Geary formula.

[16] Alterman and Jacobs, *op. cit.*, state that the net output of an industry "must be obtained by deflating output and intermediate goods and services separately and then subtracting deflated inputs from deflated output." This is an apparent denial of the point made here. Their position is based, however, on the lack of a satisfactory index for the prices of the factors of production which might be used to deflate income originating, not on a refutation of the possibility of using price index (3), above.

[17] Vol. I, p. 20.

[18] At the time this was prepared the data on depreciation were the only part of total capital consumption allowances available from the OBE on an industry basis.

in (3) above. The difference is slight and appears to be wholly attributable to differences in the underlying data, as follows. First, the BLS index is a weighted average of the component indexes of the individual four-digit industries while aggregate manufacturing value added was deflated by the direct method. Second, the BLS adjusted inventories to change shipments to production. Data to make a similar adjustment to Census value added were not available. Finally, the weights used in deriving the value added deflator may be inexact. Whatever the reasons for the differences, it is clear that precisely the same index would result if identical data were used with the same level of disaggregation.

TABLE 1

Comparison of Variously Derived Indexes of Net Output for Manufacturing, 1947–55
(1947 = 100)

Year	BLS Current Year Weighted Index (Geary Method) (1)	Index Based on Direct Deflation of Census Value Added (2)	Index Based on Direct Deflation of OBE Income Originating Plus Depreciation (3)
1947	100.00	100.00	100.00
	—	—	—
1949	94.51	94.92	100.96
1950	109.37	110.49	116.52
1951	120.40	115.40	127.15
1952	124.09	122.85	129.86
1953	136.13[a]	135.87	140.67
1954	123.36[a]	128.69	130.60
1955	138.36[a]	142.58	147.17

[a] Cost of materials was deflated for total manufacturing rather than at the four-digit industry level.

Source: Col. (1)—Bureau of Labor Statistics Report No. 100. Derivation of the indexes in cols. (2) and (3) is described in the text in the section evaluating Kuznets' estimates.

Table 1 also presents a net output index prepared by deflating value added estimated by summing OBE income originating and depreciation for manufacturing industries. If there were a constant relationship between value added thus computed and Census value added, this index would be identical with that in column (2). However, the two series are markedly different.

Manufacturing has been used in these illustrations only because the necessary price indexes were at hand. The alternative proposed for the Geary formula is not designed for industries such as farming and manufacturing where annual estimates of both output and input are available. Instead it should be useful for those industries where factor

323

payments and capital consumption estimates are available annually but where input data are known only occasionally.

These estimates and the subsequent revisions are careful work but immediately apparent is the inadequacy of the deflation techniques and the sensitivity of the findings to alternative deflation processes. The estimates based on 1939 prices used price indexes converted from an original 1910–14 base. The Atkinson and Jones revision used the newer 1947–49 based price indexes with pronounced differences in the results. Based on 1939 prices, net farm output grew at an average annual rate of about 0.6 per cent between 1910 and 1950. In 1947–49 dollars, the annual rate of increase was 0.9 per cent between 1910 and 1953. This is a considerable difference, especially if the output measures are to be used in ratio to make productivity estimates.

Regarding this disparity, Atkinson and Jones point out that the prices of products produced were higher in 1947–49 than in 1939 relative to the prices of products consumed. Since gross output rose less rapidly than intermediate consumption, this explanation seems correct. There were also some revisions in the underlying USDA output and input estimates which may have affected the two rates of growth. Atkinson and Jones also point out that there was a shift between 1939, and 1947–49 in the mix of purchased materials, relatively cheaper items becoming more important and vice versa. Whatever the full explanation, it is apparent that alternative weight bases can change the output estimates significantly.

The comparison of deflated net farm output with deflated private GNP raises other problems. First, certain components of GNP which are not easily deflated are glossed over when one or a few industries are deflated individually and the remainder treated as a residual between these and GNP. Kendrick recognized one such problem area when he excluded general government from GNP prior to comparing farm and nonfarm net output. However, the rationale for this deletion was not the difficulty of deflating general government. Rather it was that the inclusion of this sector would dampen nonfarm productivity, since the index of government productivity would be constant at one hundred for all years.

The same reasoning which leads to government's exclusion would seem to apply with equal force to many areas in the private economy. The output values for households and some of the service industries such as the medical, legal, and insurance professions, can hardly measure more than real factor input after deflation. Kendrick himself

324

estimates that 20 per cent of real GNP is thus constituted.[19] The industries where net output is measured through inputs should be separated from those where net output is measured directly.[20] Then a particular industry, say farming, could be compared with aggregates similarly derived: all private commodity producing industries, all private business production, etc.

Another issue concerns the validity of the comparison of net farm output with private GNP. The net production of an individual domestic industry includes all domestic and foreign demand on the output side, and all factor payments to nationals and nonnationals on the input side. Since factor payments from abroad are in no way included, the sum of the net outputs of private domestic industries equals gross private *domestic* product rather than gross private *national* product.[21] Hence, the former provides a better basis for comparison and for the computation of a residual from the output of specific industries.

Had Kendrick and Jones been able to show subgroups of net outputs within farming, such data would have provided much more knowledge about how the growth in farm output has occurred. It would have been possible to study the effects of shifts within agriculture as well as shifts between agriculture and other activities. However, agricultural data do not readily lend themselves to such calculations.

THE BLS ESTIMATES

BLS has noted many of the limitations to their net output measures and most of them need only be mentioned. For example, a full listing of intermediate purchases is not available. For use in national product accounts it obviously would be preferable if such data were provided. Similarly, the industry output estimates should include indirect taxes levied at the manufacturing level if these data in the aggregate are to coincide conceptually with gross national or gross domestic production valued in market prices.[22]

[19] "Measurement of Real Product," *A Critique of the United States Income and Product Accounts*, Studies in Income and Wealth, Volume Twenty-Two (Princeton University Press for National Bureau of Economic Research, 1958), p. 414.

[20] For a similar suggestion see Kendrick, "Measurement of Real Product."

[21] See "A System of National Accounts and Supporting Tables," *Studies in Methods* (No. 2), Department of Economic Affairs, United Nations, 1953; G. Stuvel, "A System of National and Domestic Accounts," *Economica* (New Series), August 1955; Kendrick, "Measurement of Real Product;" and Berlinguette and Leacy, *op. cit.*, pp. 212–13.

[22] It is not impossible to distribute indirect business taxes by industry from existing U.S. data. Alterman and Jacobs, *op. cit.*, distribute indirect taxes by major sector in order to obtain weights for combining the sectors' production indexes which are consistent with the concept of GNP in market values. Neither the manufacturing net output series nor the wholesale prices indexes used for deflation contain these taxes, however, so they remain somewhat inconsistent with the GNP concept.

Paasche price indexes would yield Laspeyres production figures but these are nonexistent. In certain industries where product heterogeneity is great and secondary production bulks large in the aggregate, deflation of industry output by indexes of primary products may be quite crude.[23] Deflation of the output values of the individual products of an industry in each year would be a preferable procedure. It would take care of secondary production and automatically allow for the effects of a varying product mix.

An analogous argument applies to the deflation of intermediate purchases. The prices of products actually purchased may be quite different from the average price of the products of the supplier industry. Again, if individual items purchased could be deflated separately, the effects of changes in the purchase mix would be included in the deflated total of intermediate purchases. Reliance on the fixed weighting scheme of the Interindustry Chart probably causes an overstatement of intermediate purchases and, hence, an understatement of net output since the impact of price-induced materials substitution is not incorporated.[24]

Unfortunately, the BLS has not presented their detailed industry figures for net output. Although the composite index for manufacturing is formed by aggregating 453 Census industries and both production and man-hour indexes could be shown for each of them, the only breakdown given is between durable and nondurable goods. This lack of detail makes it impossible to study the structural aspects of growth within the manufacturing sector. Presumably, detail was omitted because of the likelihood of error in individual industries. Granting that this is a good reason for not showing four-digit industry data, it is less valid in the case of two-digit or even three-digit data.

Conclusion

These studies clearly demonstrate that estimates of industry net output are possible when adequate resources are applied to the task. An even clearer demonstration is provided by the Alterman and Jacobs and the Berlinguette and Leacy papers in this volume.

It is significant that all three estimates are virtually devoid of conceptual error. Measurement of net output has progressed to the point where everyone is generally agreed on what should be measured. Disagreement is largely confined to questions of procedure, and it exists here principally because of data limitations. More and better price

[23] BLS provides a test for this (see Report No. 100, p. 332). The test is inappropriate for individual industries, but seems acceptable for large aggregates.

[24] This indicates a need for periodic interindustry flow data so that the weighting of intermediate purchases can be up-dated fairly often.

indexes, more and better information on the industrial origin of capital consumption, etc., are needed.

Estimation of net output by industry of origin cannot await improved data, however, and the latter are apt to be provided only as demanded. It is encouraging to learn[25] that progress is being made in the development of an official series on net output and productivity for the whole economy. The three studies reviewed here form a solid foundation for the future work. Closing the residual area of national production will entail some crude techniques in estimation but knowledge of the operation of the economy requires that the effort be made. Also, we can expect continuous refinement once a program is underway.

[25] See *Economic Report of the President*, January 1958, p. 91.

PART III
The Estimation of Real Factor Inputs

Some Difficulties in the Concept of Economic Input

KENNETH E. BOULDING
UNIVERSITY OF MICHIGAN

THE concept of economic activity as an input-output process is perhaps the most basic concept of economics. Nevertheless it is vague, and curious difficulties emerge when an effort is made to specify the inputs and outputs involved and to define the nature of the transformation implied. These difficulties may arise because the general concept is necessary in the statement and solution of many different, though not wholly unrelated, problems. Each problem requires a tailormade set of concepts and it is unlikely that a general definition will cover the range of needs.

There are four major problems where the concept of an input-output process is important. First, there is the problem of income distribution. Aggregate real income is equated in some sense to aggregate output, and the latter has to be allocated to participants in the system. The pertinent question concerns the extent to which the individual's income share measures his "contribution," or input. Second, there is the problem of the allocation of resources among different occupations. Inputs are conceived of as distributed among different "industries," with their distribution determining the structure of output. Interest focuses on changes in the composition of output when inputs are shifted from one "use" to another. The third problem is that of the relations between the stocks and flows of the system. Input and output are regarded as flow variables rates per unit of time. Input flows into the capital stock, output emerges later. The set of problems associated with the Austrian theory of capital are involved in this concept. The fourth problem is that of gauging efficiency. Efficiency is always measured in some sense as a ratio of output to input; the higher the ratio the more efficient the production process.

In all of these problems, most of the difficulties arise because of the extreme heterogeneity of both inputs and outputs; a property which is not accidental, but basic. A system with only one kind of input and output would lack most of the significant features of actual economic organization. Some sort of production function could be postulated

331

(though it is difficult to see how it could be anything but linear), and an efficiency ratio calculated, but the problem of income distribution, if it is not to be trivial, calls for at least two kinds of input. Similarly, the problem of resource allocation requires at least two kinds of output. Actually, there are numerous kinds of input and output, and it is the condensation of this multidimensioned structure into manageable proportions without loss of essential information which constitutes the major problem. Situations that arise because of the uncertainty of economic events make the problem of abstracting from reality yet more difficult. The same is true when the complex time relationships of input and output—the fact, for instance, that today's input may be associated with the output of many future dates while today's output may be associated with a series of earlier inputs—are taken into account.

The reduction of the many dimensions of input and output to a single measurable dimension can only be done by multiplying each diverse quantity by a valuation coefficient or "price." Here the familiar index number problem of the most appropriate set of valuation coefficients is encountered. But even if this problem is avoided by assuming no change in the price structure, there are serious difficulties connected with the "dollar value" concepts of input and output. From the point of view of the income distribution and allocation problems, input and output should be defined so that their measure is the same. The aim is to allocate all output as income to the providers of input, possibly with some provision for "surplus value" and transfer payments, and to allocate all input, however employed, to the various forms of output. In this context, therefore, it is important that input and output be construed as equal.

This concept is modified, though not drastically so, in the "simple" stock-flow or river model. The process is defined by some segment of a "river"—input is the substance (water) which enters the segment, output is the substance which leaves. Input now need not equal current output, though each unit of input can ultimately be tagged as output, just as each drop of water that enters a segment of a stream eventually leaves it. Any imbalance between flows implies an adjustment in stock. Thus, if in a year 100 million bushels of wheat are produced (input) and 90 million consumed (output), 10 million bushels have necessarily been added to the stock. This model becomes more complicated if an effort is made to apply it to the whole economy and to separate out profit or surplus value, as did Ricardo and Böhm-Bawerk. Input becomes restricted to "original factors" such as labor, or labor and land, and the value of output exceeds the value of the input *which gave rise to it*, because of the accrual of profit or interest. To revert to the river analogy, it is as if profit or interest were fed into the stream from underground springs, and represent a form of input that is added in the course of time.

When we turn to the efficiency concept, we find now that if the concept is to mean anything, input and output must be defined so that they are *not* equal. If all input is conserved as output, and all output originates as input, the efficiency ratio (output per unit of input) is always unity, and there can be no way of comparing the efficiency of alternative processes. For the concept to be useful, it is necessary to differentiate between significant and nonsignificant input or output. When an engineer measures the efficiency of an engine by the ratio of output of kinetic or other available energy to input of chemical energy, he is implicitly assuming that the output of non-kinetic energy is not significant or valuable. On this basis, a fundamental input-output equality, following the law of conservation is expressed thus:

Energy input
$$= \text{Available energy output} + \text{Unavailable energy output}.$$

A "price system" indicative of significance is then applied to the output. Since the valuation coefficients are 1 for available and 0 for unavailable energy, the value of the output is equal to the amount of available energy and the efficiency measure becomes:

$$\text{Efficiency} = \frac{\text{Value of output}}{\text{Value of input}} = \frac{\text{Available energy output}}{\text{Energy input}}.$$

An effort to express this concept in terms of accounting data encounters serious difficulties. Insofar as all revenue is imputed back to some expenditure, measuring efficiency by the ratio of revenue (value of output) to cost (value of input) involves the conservation problem again. To circumvent this problem, expenditure is divided into cost and profit, and the measure of efficiency becomes:

$$\text{Efficiency} = \frac{\text{Revenue}}{\text{Cost}} = \frac{\text{Cost} + \text{Profit}}{\text{Cost}} = 1 + \frac{\text{Profit}}{\text{Cost}}.$$

Even from the point of view of the individual firm this is a curious and unsatisfactory measure. The investor sees an investment as a series of payments into and out of a capital account, the in-payments being just that, the out-payments consisting of dividends, interest, and capital distributions. If the process involves a single in-payment C and a single out-payment R one year later, then the efficiency ratio is R/C, or $1 + (R-C)/C$, which again is $1 + \text{Profit}/\text{Cost}$, or the "force" of interest. In this simple case $(R-C)/C$ is the rate of interest. However, if the in- and out-payments are spread along the time scale, the ratio of out-payments to in-payments neglects the time-position of these quantities. For example, an investment of $100 which returned $105 after one year would not be regarded as equally efficient with one that yielded $105 ten years later. Of course, no matter how complex the series of in- and out-payments, it is always possible to derive an internal rate of return which is essentially the average rate of growth of capital over the life of the investment.[1]

The tendency here is toward the "Austrian" notion of input as that which grows into output, and of the rate of growth as a measure of efficiency. However, great difficulties arise when this notion is applied to the economy as a whole. Is labor the only "significant" input, the only "original" factor, or is it necessary to construct, as Böhm-Bawerk tried to do, a melange of labor and land? Is capital merely an intermediate product, the embodiment of original factors on their journey toward realization in final product, or should it be included in an input measure? There are no single or simple answers to these questions; the concept must fit the task.

When per capita income is used to measure the economic efficiency of the system, the whole population is regarded as an input productive of the whole output. As a rough measure of performance this makes sense; if per capita income with a given price structure is $100 in country A and $1,000 in country B, it is likely that A is much poorer than B. However, per capita income is not the only test of economic efficiency and a rise in per capita income achieved by undesirably hard work and sacrificed leisure might represent a worsening of economic welfare. Furthermore, population efficiency is not the only significant resource-efficiency concept, although it is the most important. Land-efficiency (output per acre) is also of interest in certain cases; with a given population on a given land area an increase in per capita income implies an increase in per acre income, whether stemming from increased yield per acre of crops or a shift to more productive industrial employment. The concept of capital-efficiency is more difficult, but not meaningless: if the same income can be obtained with a smaller capital stock this is a clear gain. Here, capital efficiency is measured by the reciprocal of the average period of production, and a capital-saving improvement is one which shortens the production period, or enhances the capital-income ratio, for a given income.

These relationships can be illustrated by means of the familiar production function. In Chart 1 labor and capital are measured along OL and OC respectively, and product or income vertically

[1] See K. E. Boulding, "The Theory of a Single Investment," *Quarterly Journal of Economics*, May 1935, p. 475.

along ZY. If land or natural resources is a limiting factor, the production surface $OCYL$ will not be linearly homogeneous, but will exhibit diminishing returns to scale—that is a curve such as OY, which represents the relation of income to equal proportional increases in

CHART 1

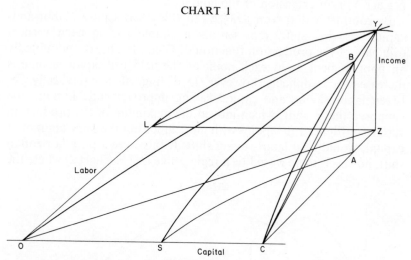

both land and labor, will curve downwards and eventually decline (income increases at a decreasing rate with increasing doses of labor and land in constant proportions). The curves LY and CY exhibit the usual diminishing returns to capital and labor respectively.

In Chart 2 three kinds of "pure shift" in the production function are distinguished. $OY_1M_1N_1$ is a section of the production surface of

CHART 2

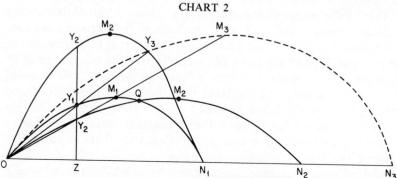

Chart 1 in the plane OZY. M_1 is the maximum output (income), assumed to be the maximum of the production surface of Chart 1. A shift from $OY_1M_1N_1$ to $OY_2M_2N_2$ is a pure horizontal shift. It is hardly an improvement, since between O and Q it results in a lowering

335

of per capita income. However, it does push the maximum outwards and postpone the diminution of total output or the increase in labor and capital. It might be described as a pure land-saving shift; as far as the figure goes, it could represent either an increase in yields (income per acre) or an extension of the land area

By contrast a shift from OM_1N_1 to OM_2N_1 is a pure "labor-and-capital" saving shift, representing a simple rise in each vertical originate of the production function of Chart 1. This is undoubtedly an improvement as at each point of the field per capita income is increased. It is difficult, however, to distinguish unequivocally between labor saving and capital saving improvements. It might be supposed that a shift, which moved the maximum of the production surface of Figure 1 to a point with more labor but the same amount of capital, would be a labor-saving shift. If this were a pure horizontal shift, however, there would be a region (like OQ in Chart 2) where the

CHART 3

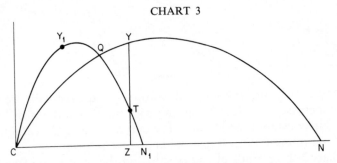

shift was actually a "disimprovement" with lower labor and capital efficiencies. Thus in Chart 3, CY, CZ are as in Chart 1: CYN is the section of the production surface in this plane. A pure labor-saving shift then means a shift to CY_1N_1: each quantity of product can now be produced with less labor than before. Now it is at large amounts of labor input, beyond the point of intersection of the two curves at Q, that the improvement becomes a "disimprovement." At the old position Z, output, and therefore the efficiency of both labor and capital, has actually fallen, from ZY to ZT. The difficulty arises because it is impossible to raise the production surface of Chart 1 without raising both labor and capital efficiencies. Thus at point Y in Chart 1 the labor efficiency (per capita income) is ZY/LZ and the capital efficiency (income-capital ratio) is ZY/CZ. Increasing ZY obviously increases both these fractions and in exactly the same proportion.

A third type of shift might be called a pure scale shift, represented by the move from $OY_1M_1N_1$ of Chart 2 to $OY_3M_3N_3$. Here a constant proportion, OY_1/OY_3 is maintained, meaning that if there is a pure scale improvement in the ratio k, then both labor and capital can be increased in the proportion k without change in the efficiency of either. Thus a pure scale shift might be thought of as equally saving of all three factors.

This conceptual apparatus may illuminate the significance of the input concept from the point of view of efficiency studies. Suppose that history reveals, as it has in the United States, a rise in the total output of the society: to what extent can this be attributed to a rise in input, and to what extent is it attributable to a rise in the efficiency of the production process? The answer depends largely on the concept

CHART 4

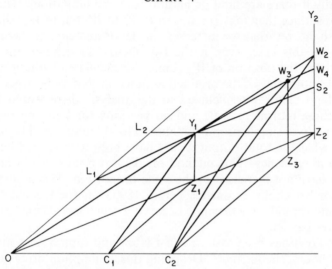

of input employed. In effect, a comparison between two dates involves a comparison of two points on two different production functions, like Y_1 and Y_2 in Chart 4. If the production function was known, one could say with some confidence how much of the rise in total output between state Y_1 and state Y_2 was due to a change in the inputs and how much to a change in the production function itself. Thus if OY_1W_2 is a line on the production surface cutting Z_2Y_2 in W_2, of the increase in output S_2Y_2, S_2W_2 is due to an increase in inputs and W_2Y_2 to an increase in efficiency. If the production function is linearly homogeneous in the case of the two inputs, and if the input increases in the same ratio, as from Z_1 to Z_2, the answer is wholly unambiguous. Whether some measure of the sum of the inputs is used, or each is taken separately, the result is the same. For

337

example, labor efficiency at point Z_1 is $Z_1 Y_1/C_1 Z_1$. If the labor efficiency had remained constant, output at state Z_2 would have been $Z_2 W_2$, and the increase due to increased efficiency would again be $W_2 Y_2$.

In practice, of course, inputs rarely increase in the same proportion. If capital, for instance, has increased faster than labor, the second position may be at a point such as Z_3, where $OZ_1 Z_3$ is not a straight line. Now even if the production function is linearly homogeneous, the point W_3 on the old production function cannot be found by simple geometric constructions; it is necessary to know the formula of the production curve $C_2 W_3 W_2$. Another complication is that the production surface itself is unlikely to be linearly homogeneous, especially if there are land or natural resource limitations. The production surface then may run not from Y_1 to W_2 but to W_4, showing diminishing returns to increases in labor-and-capital taken together. In this case, even if the two factors increase in the same proportion, the position of W_4 cannot be calculated without mathematical knowledge of the production function. It may be argued that if the land factor was included in the analysis there would be no diminishing returns to scale and no necessity for knowing the production curve: simple proportionality to total inputs could be used to decide what the total output would have been if there had been no change in efficiency. This method breaks down, however, when the factors have not increased in the same proportion. This assumption may not be wholly erroneous before 1890, but for the most part, labor and capital have expanded against a much less elastic land and resources barrier.

Thus far it has been assumed that labor and capital were measurable in homogeneous units. Dropping this assumption brings up the formidable problem of the significance of aggregate measures of labor and capital. In the case of labor it seems reasonable to start with hours of work performed but even this simple measure involves difficult decisions when it comes to separating labor from leisure. For instance, should the labor of the housewife and the self-employed be counted? If not, then a shift of these individuals into wage labor will lead to seriously misleading statistics. (The Russians seem frequently to have been guilty of this error.) On the other hand, assessing the "labor" time of a housewife necessarily involves difficult matters of judgment. The enormous rise of "do it yourself" projects suggests that an appreciable proportion of the labor input of this country is leisure time activity. Thus estimates of national input or product should ideally include the cooking or dinner of the housewife and the carpentry or furniture of her spouse. This is a difficult area where

338

accuracy can be purchased only at the cost of coverage: the choice is between accurate figures for wage labor and less accurate figures for the more significant concept of total labor input.

The problem of how to measure the *intensity* of labor has plagued theorists from the time of Adam Smith and the labor theory of value. Wages are a notoriously poor measure of labor intensity and many other factors have to be allowed for before there would be even a positive relation between hard work and high wages. Yet everybody senses a distinction between hard and light work—a distinction which cannot be measured merely by calorie output, for information throughout may be just as exhausting—and the observation that Americans work harder than the Portuguese or Ceylonese is not meaningless, however difficult it may be to quantify. Currently the most promising approach would seem to be to pursue some physiological leads: if a fairly simple measure of fatigue could be obtained and applied over a large population, the results would be interesting despite the fact that fatigue depends on many subtle psychological factors not necessarily closely related to physical exertion. In any event, the question "has an increase in output come about because of a rise in efficiency or because of a rise in the intensity of labor" deserves serious attention in view of the Marxist tendency to attribute an increase in product under capitalism to an increase in labor-intensity, and in view of the recurrent difficulties in industrial relations as a result of real or imaginary speed-ups.

Aggregate capital is even more difficult to measure than aggregate labor input. The composition and physical nature of capital changes constantly, and any measure of its aggregate becomes increasingly arbitrary as time goes on. How, for instance, can horses be compared with tractors, abacuses with IBM computers, cotton plants with nylon spinners? The most that can be done is to estimate the dollar value of the existing capital stock and compare this with a dollar estimate of national income. This capital-income ratio, however, is a measure of the period of production only in stationary equilibrium; in a dynamic society there may be wide divergences between the number of years of current income required to total the capital stock, and the average production period. Thus in the case of human capital (the population), the ratio of the total population to annual births or deaths is equal to the average age at death only in a static situation; if the population is growing or declining, or if the age distribution is changing rapidly, annual births (input) may differ from annual deaths (output), so that the capital-income ratio depends on the measure of income selected. Also, the capital-income ratio, however computed, will not in general correspond to the average age at death.

Nevertheless, the latter figure (the period of production) is of great importance not only for the human population but also for the population of goods. Generally speaking, the more durable the product of a given input, the better off the society. Of course this formulation disregards the problem of the optimum flexibility of structure: if either people or goods are too long lived, it is hard to replace them with younger and possibly superior items!

This argument has been inconclusive, and not perhaps much help to the statistician. However, the problems are very difficult, and the context, very general. In all problems of measurement, the fundamental question is, *what questions can be answered better* as a result of the measure devised. There is perhaps a tendency among statisticians to devise measures for their own sake, rather than with a particular purpose in view. The danger of the information system controlling the questions instead of vice versa is to be taken seriously.

COMMENT

MURRAY KEMP, McGill University

Kenneth Boulding's chief concern is the problem of allocating changes in output to changes in factor inputs and to shifts in the production function. He insists that nothing can be inferred from the data unless special assumptions are made about the form of the production function and the market structure. Even if constant returns to scale and perfect competition are assumed, it is impossible to allocate changes in output, except conceivably where factor proportions remain unchanged, or changes in input and output are very small. The production function may, of course, shift in any number of ways, and each type of shift produces its own effect on total output and on the relative marginal productivities of the factors. Boulding selects for detailed discussion three "pure" types of shift. He defines each one diagrammatically and then advances several statements, apparently intended as theorems, concerning their individual factor-saving (or factor-wasting) properties. Several of these theorems seem to be weak or at least in need of a more careful defense than Boulding has provided.

It is necessary at the outset to clarify the meaning of a factor-saving shift (innovation). Boulding remarks that "A pure labor-saving shift then means . . . each quantity of product can now be produced with . . . [less] labor than before." It is not clear whether this is intended as a definition or as a theorem based on some alternative but unstated concept of a labor-saving shift. However, it is the nearest that Boulding comes to a definition and I shall accept it as such. Then similar definitions of capital- and land-saving shifts can

340

easily be formulated. The three shift types can be illustrated with some elementary algebra. Imagine that a single output P is a function of labor L, capital K, and land A:

$$p \cdot P(lL, kK, aA).$$

The lower-case letters stand for shift parameters which initially are set equal to unity. Then it is in keeping with Boulding's definition to associate a pure labor-saving shift with an increase in l and to identify capital- and land-saving shifts with increases in k and a, respectively. Three properties of pure factor-saving shifts are analytically important: (1) if P is a maximum, it is invariant under such shifts, (2) maximum (P) is attained after a shift with less of the factor economized but with the same quantities of the other factors. It follows from (1) and (2) that (3), a factor-saving shift, does not necessarily result in an increase in the output associated with a given vector of inputs, since the efficiency of the latter may be reduced. In particular, the preshift product-maximizing vector will be less efficient after the shift than before.

A pure output-increasing innovation, on the other hand, may be identified with an increase in p. For *any* vector of inputs the postshift output exceeds the preshift output and the efficiency of all inputs increases. In the special case when constant returns to scale prevail over the relevant range of input values, an output-increasing innovation is equivalent to a factor-saving innovation which is general and uniform in its incidence, that is, for which

$$\varDelta l = \varDelta k = \varDelta a = \varDelta p.$$

Boulding's analysis is in terms of a series of two-dimensional diagrams with "output" measured vertically and "labor and capital" measured horizontally. Four variables are collapsed into two by supposing that labor and capital are combined in fixed proportions and that land is fixed in amount.

His first type of shift, the "pure horizontal," involves increases, in the same proportion, of the amounts of labor and capital needed to produce a given output. This is the opposite of a labor- and capital-saving shift and might be called labor- and capital-*wasting*, with

$$\varDelta l = \varDelta k < o.$$

Boulding's discussion is confusing largely, I suspect, because he is undecided whether it is total or per capita output that is being measured along the vertical axis. For example, he states that "... between O and Q [a pure horizontal shift] results in a lowering of *per capita* income. However, it does push the maximum outwards and postpone the diminution of *total output* . . ." (my italics). Assuming

341

that total output is at issue, income per capita must fall uniformly and not simply between O and Q. I had also difficulty with the description of this type of shift as "pure land-saving" and with the remark that "as far as the figure goes, it could represent either an increase in 'yields' (income per acre) or an extension of the land area." In the scheme of definitions set out above, a land-saving shift is not equivalent to a labor-and-capital-wasting shift. A horizontal shift is land-saving only in the sense that, for given output and given land input, the ratio of land input to labor-and-capital input falls as the result of the shift.[1]

Boulding's second type of shift is described as "pure labor and capital saving" and is represented diagrammatically by "a simple rise in each vertical originate." However, a pure labor-and-capital-saving shift should be represented by a leftward compression of the curve, and while the latter usually implies an increase in the output associated with any particular input of labor-and-capital, such an increase is not inevitable. In particular, the increase will not take place for those values of capital-and-labor input in excess of the preshift output-maximizing input (where the latter exists).

Boulding describes his third type of shift as a "pure scale shift" and depicts it diagrammatically as a radial projection, in constant proportion, of all points on the total product curve. In symbolic terms:

$$\Delta p = -\Delta l = -\Delta k > o,$$
$$\Delta a = 0.$$

Thus, it is a combined output-increasing and labor-and-capital-wasting shift and involves a horizontal extension of the *average* product curve for labor-and-capital. To describe it as a "pure scale shift" is a little misleading; to infer, as Boulding does, that it is equally saving of all factors is incorrect.

I am sure that the propositions discussed here are regarded by Boulding as tangential to his major theme, with which I am in complete sympathy. Also, my comments may be unjust for they are based on definitions which I have read into a single paragraph which occurs *after* the section of the paper that I have criticized. I hope, therefore, that Boulding will make clear (1) whether the definitions are acceptable to him, and, if so, (2) the stage of his analysis at which they are to be adopted.

---

[1] A land-saving shift, in the sense of the above definition, involves: (1) for given output and given labor-and-capital input, a decrease in the ratio of land to labor-and-capital, but (2) for given output and given land input, an increase in the ratio of land to other inputs. Further, for given output and given land input, a land-saving shift does not call for an increase in labor-and-capital.

KARL BORCH, European Productivity Agency

The main utility of a conference like this is probably that it makes one re-examine long-held beliefs. Thus I have asked myself, *what* is this productivity we want to measure, and *why* do we want to measure it?

Circular definitions are an obvious danger. Productivity is a ratio between output and inputs, but as Kenneth Boulding and others have pointed out, the value of all inputs must be equal to the value of total output. Similarly, the price paid for new capital equipment must be related to the prospective profits, and under certain reasonably plausible assumptions one can prove that the capital output ratio must be constant. If it fluctuates, it is because the expectations of the entrepreneurs have not been fulfilled.

I have gradually come to take a more pragmatic view, and to ask if the results obtained by measurement are useful—more specifically, do they enter into any conceivable decision models? Is there really any such justification for trying to find out the number of hours worked by a farmer, his wife, and children?

I discussed these questions in Yugoslavia awhile ago. The Marx-Lenin-Tito concepts of productivity are different from those that have been discussed here. In making productivity indexes, the Yugoslavs seek to allow for every disturbing factor; quality of the man-hour, investments in vocational training, etc. They arrive at an almost perfect index, the only drawback being that this paragon could go up even if the cruder index of output per man went down. We agreed that a productivity index was useful only if it measured the output per capita available for consumption and investment. We further agreed that the Yugoslav index was ideal if you wanted to reward efficient workers, managers, and officials with medals or titles like "hero of socialist labor," but entirely unsuitable if the rewards were to take the form of increased real wage income.

In twenty years European GNP per capita in constant prices will be about 50 per cent higher than it is today. Does this information have any real meaning or practical value? All that is signified is a gain in utility—which is not measurable. Since a 50 per cent increase in GNP will mean a substantial change in the composition of the total output, knowledge of the behavior of the aggregate can tell us nothing about capital requirements and the distribution of labor between sectors twenty years hence. Data like the trend of bushels of wheat per acre and tons of coal per man-shift are obviously useful in predicting and preparing for the future but I see no use for an aggregate estimate.

Over-all productivity clearly plays a fundamental part in economic analysis, but that does not mean that it is possible or necessary to measure it. As a parallel, look at the velocity of circulation of money in the Quantity Theory. A generation ago economists thought this concept was of supreme importance, and tried to measure it. This turned out to be not only fruitless, but unnecessary to an understanding of the relationship between prices and monetary policy.

I am probably the only one here working for an institution which has "productivity" in its title, so it may seem strange that I should try to minimize the importance of this concept. However, I am less certain today than five years ago that productivity is the best approach to the complex problems of economic growth and technical progress. In this connection it may be worth mentioning that we are seriously considering renaming our institution, "The European Development Agency."

REPLY, MR. BOULDING

Kemp raises some interesting problems which, since they are peripheral to the main concerns of this conference, must receive much briefer treatment than they deserve. In part the difficulty is one of language. The terms "labor saving," "capital saving," or "land saving" correspond to very vague—though important—notions. Attempts to impart precision to these notions inevitably result in a multiplication of concepts. Such proliferation is necessary and useful as long as it does not provoke controversy about which of the proposed substitutes is the most "correct"; one precise concept may be useful for one purpose, one for another.

Kemp's definition of a factor-saving change in the production function—which amounts to a rescaling of the factor axis—is not the only way of sharpening a vague concept. Also it evades the basic difficulty that no change in the production function is possible which does not change the amount of product produced by a given combination of all factors, and which therefore changes, in a different sense at different points, the product-factor ratio for all factors. Furthermore, if the production function exhibits a maximum, there will be some combinations of inputs for which, say, a labor-saving change according to Kemp's definition, actually produces a diminution of product and hence a diminution of product per unit of labor. Thus while the type of change which Kemp describes is interesting, I am not sure that it deserves the appellation of factor-saving. I am not sure either that I am prepared to defend my substitute definitions. The real difficulty is that a factor-saving change can be defined only in relation to a given price or market structure; it cannot be adequately defined as a property of the production function alone. Thus a change in the production function which might be "labor saving"

344

at one set of relative prices of labor and land might be "land saving" at another set, as defined by its impact on the proportions of factors actually used.

Turning to a general problem relating to the topic of this conference, I feel it is time for statisticians in general, and economic statisticians in particular, to recognize more explicitly the sociological, as well as the arithmetical, basis of their art. A statistic is an interesting number. For the most part this meeting has considered how one interesting number can be expressed as the product of two others— a value index as a price index times a quantity index, or an output index as an input index times a productivity index. There are infinite ways of achieving multiplicative disaggregation, but very few of these are interesting. If statistics is the science of interesting numbers more investigation is needed into what it is that makes numbers interesting, for interest is a property of the reader, not of the number. The attempt to find purely internal, mathematical justifications for statistical procedures is doomed to frustration, as it abstracts from the essentially sociological nature of the subject.

Measurement of Labor Input:
Some Questions of Definition
and the Adequacy of Data

EDWARD F. DENISON
COMMITTEE FOR ECONOMIC DEVELOPMENT

THIS paper is mainly concerned with the relative merits of employment and man-hours as measures of labor input in the measurement of productivity, and with the adequacy of the statistical sources for each. However, choice of an input measure cannot be wholly divorced from the measurement of output, nor from one's general approach to the meaning of productivity changes. Hence, this brief introductory section.

Discussion of changes in either economic welfare or the efficiency with which a society satisfies wants and needs is facilitated by distinguishing between changes in the external environment in which the individuals live, and changes in their tastes, likes, and dislikes (even though these may be influenced by the external environment). Insofar as I am aware, no one has attempted to adjust measures of output or productivity for the latter type of change, while efforts have been at least proposed to take account of changes in the external environment.

Conventionally, I shall ignore the fact that, given the same environment, different individuals at different times will not necessarily derive the same satisfactions from any given quantity of goods and services, and also will not be alike in their aversion to work and saving. Unless this is done, quantitative comparisons of the economic performance or economic welfare of a community at different times are not possible. Experience has shown the pragmatic value of such comparisons at least for large groups.

There has been less readiness to make welfare or productivity comparisons that ignore changes in the environment. Unless we do so, a reasonably full appraisal of changes in the performance of an economy and in the economic welfare of individuals requires, in addition to population data, at least four aggregate measures whose general character is as follows:

1. An index of the requirements of the people that would change as needs imposed by the physical or institutional environment or the relations of the society with other peoples change. This index would

347

move with changes in such things as differences in the costs of urban as against rural living as the population becomes more urbanized, weather changes (such as a shift in the hurricane belt), new diseases, and national defense requirements. It would not take account of changes in the tastes or wants of individuals such as may arise from better education or becoming accustomed to a higher living standard— that is, changes in the individual's own perceptions rather than in his environment. An index of this type has never been attempted. It would have to be subjective to an undesirable and probably pro- hibitive extent.[1]

2. A measure of the national product, representing the quantity of goods and services produced each year.

3. A measure of the real costs incurred in producing the national product.

4. The ratio of the economic resources actually used to those avail- able to the economy, including involuntarily unemployed resources.

Each of the four measures is informative in itself.[2] In addition, the relationships among them are interesting. The ratio of 2 (national product) to 1 (requirements) would indicate changes in the extent to which wants and needs are satisfied, once the general qualification concerning changes in tastes is accepted. The ratio of 2 to 3 (real costs incurred) would show changes in the efficiency of the economy in using resources actually employed. The product of this ratio and the fourth series would provide a broader measure of efficiency, reflecting both the success of the economy in making full use of resources and its efficiency in utilizing those actually employed.

These four measures, regardless of whether they can be statis- tically measured, are a minimum that cannot be reduced. The attempt to do so is responsible for much of the debate that has characterized the development of national product measurement, and particularly so in two respects that are crucial for our purpose.

1. Kuznets' recommendation that measures of the national pro- duct should omit provision for what he calls "maintenance of the fabric of society," including national defense, police and courts, as well as certain expenditures like travel to and from work that he views as intermediate products, in my opinion amounts to an attempt

---

[1] Suppose, for instance, that in the base year (1) national product of 100 were divided 60 for consumption, 30 for capital formation, and 10 for national defense and (2) that this represented the public's free choice in full knowledge of the dangers of foreign aggression. Suppose that in a different year, all other things being unchanged, it would cost twice as much to provide the same degree of security from foreign aggression. The index would then rise to 110, regardless of what was actually done about defense expenditures.

[2] Each also has difficult problems of exact definition that I shall ignore here.

to eliminate the need for the first measure, changes in requirements imposed by the external environment, by adjustment of the second, national product.[3] In effect, he would omit from the measurement of output provision for the satisfaction of all needs that change over time because of changes in individuals' external environment, and count as output only those products that satisfy wants that have not in recent centuries been greatly affected by such changes. His procedure thus attempts to eliminate the necessity for a measure of requirements by narrowing the scope of the output measure. But it fails precisely *because* of the narrowing of scope. No account is taken of provision to satisfy needs that have changed. Hence, it gives the unacceptable result that with the same output of "admissible" consumer and capital goods, and the same population, we are equally well off whether we must walk or can ride to work, or regardless of what we do to forestall thermonuclear destruction by the Communist world. The procedure thus fails as a device to obviate the requirement of a measure of wants and needs for welfare comparisons. It has the positive disadvantage that elimination of part of current output destroys the national product as a measure of the total output that actually is available to satisfy wants and needs.

From the standpoint of productivity measurement, the relation of output to real costs (the ratio of series 2 to series 3), such an omission from output is disastrous. It would destroy the significance of comparisons of output with those of real costs or inputs unless resources devoted to the production of "excluded" output were omitted from the latter series.[4] If they were omitted (which would require very difficult allocations), we would have comparable data, but their coverage would be only a fraction of the economy. In this paper, which is devoted to the labor portion of series 3, we shall assume that labor and other inputs are to be related to an equally comprehensive measure of national product.

2. The frequently advanced proposition that inputs should be measured in units of constant quality, as determined by their ability to contribute to production, is tantamount to making the index of series 3, the economic resources used in production, identical with

---

[3] See Simon Kuznets' "Discussion of the New Department of Commerce Income Series," *Review of Economics and Statistics*, August 1948; "On the Valuation of Social Income—Reflections on Professor Hicks' Article," *Economica*, February 1948; "Government Product and National Income," *Income and Wealth, Series I* (Cambridge, England, 1951); and "Quantitative Aspects of the Economic Growth of Nations," *Economic Development and Cultural Change*, October 1956.

[4] Kuznets, of course, would not accept this statement. From his standpoint, I think, diversion of resources to protect ourselves, with a consequent reduction in goods contributing directly to consumer welfare, would properly show up as a reduction in the productivity of the economy.

that of series 2, national product. For if a unit of input is defined in terms of its contribution to production, then total input must move in proportion to total output, and the ratio between the two, productivity, can never change.[5] Also, to measure the quantity of input of any one factor, such as labor, it would be necessary to identify the output specifically attributable to it. Since efficiency, or productivity, is the topic of this conference, it seems wise to deal with measures that do not eliminate changes in productivity in the economy as a whole by definition, and to concern ourselves with input measures that are not adjusted for quality change.

Measures of Labor Input

As a practical matter, the units of measurement of labor input that are available for comparisons over time may be reduced to the average number of persons employed and the total number of hours worked. (There are, of course, variants of each, but these need not concern us at this point.) Differences between the movements of the two arise from changes in average hours of work. Intelligent choice, or even discussion, requires information concerning two aspects of working hours about which we unfortunately know too little. First, what is the relationship between hours of work and real costs—"disutility"—of labor? Second, what is the relationship between hours of work and output?

HOURS AND REAL COSTS

Does the movement of total man-hours worked or of employment better approximate changes in the real cost, or disutility, of labour? If we waive the problem of aggregation, we can rephrase the question to ask how disutility varies with hours of work for typical individuals. We concentrate upon the range of hours prevalent in the past and possibly prevalent in the not-completely-remote future—say over thirty hours a week.

[5] Under one scheme, economies of scale might be construed as introducing changing productivity in the economy. Under this scheme, movement *along* a production function represents a productivity change, while movement from one function to another does not, since it can be interpreted as resulting from a change in the quality (and hence in the quantity, adjusted for quality change) of one or more inputs. I agree with Nicholas Kaldor ("A Model of Economic Growth," *The Economic Journal*, December 1957, p. 396) that such a distinction is entirely artificial. Also if, as seems quite arbitrary, the qualities of entrepreneurship and labor are not interpreted to include the knowledge of the entrepreneur or worker (distinguished somehow from the technological state of capital goods), a divergence might appear on that account. This does not seem to me either a valid or workable distinction. For a discussion of the general point that adjustment of inputs for quality change is equivalent to measuring total inputs by output, see my "Theoretical Aspects of Quality Change, Capital Consumption, and Net Capital Formation" in Volume 19 of *Studies in Income and Wealth*.

If disutility varied proportionately to hours worked, man-hours would provide an appropriate index of the real cost of labor. If disutility did not vary at all with hours of work (above thirty) employment would provide such an index. Only if the percentage increase in the total disutility of work is less than half the percentage increase in working hours as hours increase would employment be the better measure of changes in total disutility. Is this likely?

Usually it is supposed that, after only a few hours' work a week, the marginal disutility of an hour's work increases as hours are increased; certainly it is never assumed that it declines. On the other hand, the disutility of the first hour's work in the week and, possibly to a lesser extent, in each day is certainly high, since the mere necessity of going to work interferes most with one's freedom to do as he will, and also carries with it a heavy overhead in time spent going to and from the work place, changing clothes, etc.[6]

If the disutility of the first hour were sufficiently high relative to subsequent hours, the condition in which employment represents total disutility better than do man-hours would be met; the most important distinction would be between working and not working, rather than in the number of hours worked. If, for example, the disutility of the first hour in the day were twelve times that of every subsequent hour, not until the twelfth hour of the day was reached would the total disutility of work increase by half as large a percentage as working hours, and man-hours therefore move more closely than employment with total disutility of work.

Most people seem to feel intuitively, however, that, within the range experienced in the past or likely to be met in the near future, a reduction in hours does mean something like a proportional reduction in disutility or real cost. I shall assume here that man-hours represent better than employment the real cost, or disutility, of labor input.[7] This assumption is not so firmly based, however, as to

[6] We can, of course, conceive of distributions of working hours over the year, or even a lifetime, in which these initial costs would be minimized; longer vacations, more holidays, and earlier retirement are current examples of a trend in this direction. However, for the past, at least, hours have mainly been reduced by shortening the workweek. Elimination of Saturday work was one general characteristic of the change, and thus eliminated one of the onerous "first hours."

[7] Evidence as to the shape of the real cost curve based on the decisions of individuals facing choices as to how many hours they will work is impossible to obtain. All that can be observed is, at best, the marginal rate of substitution between effort and income, not absolute changes in disutility. Further, individuals are not necessarily in equilibrium because they cannot get the combination of hours and earnings that would suit them best, or do not know the available alternatives. Even for groups of individuals, standard hours have rarely been set by any real comparison of leisure gained with income lost, or even with knowledge of the income actually sacrificed for shorter hours.

351

warrant the current overwhelming emphasis on output per man-hour to the near exclusion of output per man.

It is obvious that, in this context, the relevant series is that for man-hours actually worked, not man-hours paid for.

HOURS AND OUTPUT

Do man-hours or employment better measure effective labor input, the contribution that labor makes to production? We conclude that, at least where changes in standard hours are under consideration, the evidence favors employment.

We consider first wage and salary workers. It is customary (and I believe correct) to depict the relationship between the length of the workweek of employees and total output as follows. Starting from just over zero hours, as the workweek is lengthened total output rises by a larger percentage than hours (output per man-hour increases) to a point at which output per man-hour is at a maximum; thereafter total output rises less than hours to a point where total output is at a maximum; and thereafter both total output and output per man-hour decline.[8]

Such a theoretical relationship is the same if one moves to left or to right. And it applies to the condition in which skill of management and the quantity of capital are unchanged (although in the long run the form of capital goods may change). Hence the shape of the curve is governed by increasing fatigue of workers as hours are lengthened (which is accompanied by deterioration in the quantity and quality of output, increased losses of work time due to accidents and sickness, etc.) and by other factors (such as opening and closing time, and absenteeism that results from workers' need for time to conduct personal affairs) that are more or less specific to labor.

The historical development, however, has been such that shortening of hours has also had a very decided and immediate impact on the quality of management and, perhaps to a lesser extent, the form and quantity of capital. Shortening of standard hours has come (1) at different times in different establishments and industries; (2) by large discrete amounts (typically from 72 hours to 60, 60 to 48, 48 to 44 or 40, or 84 to 56); and (3) without reduction in the weekly wage. As a consequence, firms faced much higher unit costs unless output per man-hour could be greatly increased, while in many cases other firms producing the same product, and in all cases producers of other products, did not simultaneously face increased costs. Hence firms affected had no assurance that prices could be raised correspondingly

---

[8] Such a diagram is shown, for example, in Lloyd G. Reynolds, *Labor Economics and Labor Relations*, second edition, p. 254.

without a calamitous loss of sales. Under these circumstances hours shortening usually led to radical tightening up of operations and reorganization of production to increase efficiency, and often also to increased mechanization.

At least to the point where reduction did not bring daily hours below eight, it was typically possible for firms or industries shortening hours to maintain the previous rate of output per man, or at any rate, fully to restore it within a year or two, implying a huge and sudden increase in output per man-hour.[9] The proper apportionment of credit for this result among the reduction of fatigue and similar factors, improved organization and management, and mechanization is not at all certain.

The results of the further shortening of standard hours below 48 a week have not yielded a clear pattern, perhaps because they have not been systematically collected and analyzed.[10]

Lloyd Reynolds, apparently assuming the quality of management and quantity of capital to be constant, has suggested that the maximum total output week in the United States at present is between 40 and 50 hours for most occupations. For purely illustrative purposes, he supposes further that a reduction in hours from 40 to 30 would cause an increase in output per man-hour of 20 per cent and a decline in total weekly output of 10 per cent. With this pattern, it is clear that output per man will vary less than output per man-hour with a change in hours at all points above 30 hours. Others concerned with the subject have often feared the shortening of hours from present standards would reduce output more than this.

The impact of a reduction of standard hours—occuring in different firms at different times, and without reduction of weekly pay—upon the efficiency of operations and mechanization is not obviously related to the length of the workweek from which hours are shortened, but only to the size of the percentage reduction. Hence, it is possible that in the future much, or even all, of the decline in total output that would otherwise result from shorter hours can continue to be offset by better management and mechanization resulting from the shortening. (General hours' shortening throughout industry—as by a change in the wage-hour law—might be expected to provide less stimulus

[9] The widely quoted studies of H. M. Vernon, P. Sargent Florence, and Josephine Goldmark provide much of the basis for this statement.

[10] Bureau of Labor Statistics studies of wartime experience were not concerned with standard hours but with changes in actual hours (mostly overtime) without an offsetting change in wage rates. They showed that, in dealing with actual hours, the results of increasing hours are not simply the opposite of decreasing them. Results also varied according to the physical labor involved, the sex of workers, whether the pace of operations is machine-determined or worker-determined, the weekly pattern of hours, and other factors.

since the chances of passing on increased costs in higher prices would be much greater.) If these effects of hours shortening are considered, in addition to the quality of nonmanagerial labor as such, the case for greater stability in output per man than in output per man-hour is greatly strengthened.

These pressures are not felt when *standard* hours are unchanged but *actual* hours are shortened as a consequence of a cyclical reduction in demand, or increased in periods of rush business, without an offsetting change in hourly wages. Such fluctuations in hours, consequently, are likely to be accompanied by more stability in output per man-hour, and less in output per man, than are changes in standard hours. Standard hours are mainly relevant to long-term trends, while changes in actual hours are chiefly of short-term interest.

This discussion has referred to the relationship between the hours of work of full-time wage and salary workers and their output.[11] For proprietors of unincorporated businesses and unpaid family workers, the considerations are rather different. Generally, wage and salary workers are laid off or put on short time when, to the firm, their output is not worth its cost. Hence it can be assumed that firms are always seeking to maximize employees' output during the time that they are working. Proprietors, on the other hand, remain employed as long as the enterprise is in existence, and their hours are often conventionally set, regardless of the amount of work to be done.

For our purpose, active proprietors fall into three classes. First is a group whose total output is limited by the time available to them. These are the proprietors of the larger establishments and farms, who typically hire workers to do what they cannot perform themselves, and proprietors selling their individual skills—professionals, repairmen, barbers, etc.—when demand keeps them fully occupied. For this group the relationship among employment, hours, and output is much the same as for hired workers, so that, at least when changes are in standard hours, employment is a better measure of effective labor input than man-hours.

Second is a group—notably professionals with offices—whose hours are conventionally set but who could do more within those hours if the volume of business waranted. If the customary hours change, it is likely to have little effect on their total output, so that employment is again the better measure. Also, if hours are unchanged, changes in their output per unit of labor input respond to demand conditions whether input is measured by man-hours or by man-years.

---

[11] Part-time workers, as discussed later, usually work very few hours and are not affected by changes in standard hours.

Third is a group that is also under-employed but whose working hours (assuming they are accurately measured) adjust to the amount of work available. This group consists largely of farmers with insufficient land to occupy their time and of construction workers, not in establishments, whose working hours are governed by the work available. Hours may be a better measure of effective labor input than employment, but are still deficient since there is little incentive to maximize output per man-hour.

Unpaid family workers fall into the same categories as proprietors, though with possibly a greater tendency for employment and hours to respond to work requirements in the individual establishment.

If one may judge by the low total output of some millions of farms, and by the predominance of very low incomes among nonfarm proprietors even in prosperous years, the second and third groups, among whom output is mainly demand-determined rather than limited by available labor time, each may easily be as large as the first even under conditions of general business prosperity. There is also some shift from the first group into the others when business declines, although this shift may not be large. (Agricultural production does not typically decline, and proprietors of larger nonfarm establishments may both take over work from paid employees and face more difficult management problems.)

We may also mention the well-known tendency for the number of proprietors and family workers (particularly in agriculture and construction) to respond inversely to sharp changes in employment opportunities for paid workers. Very little output is associated with these marginal proprietors and family workers so that changes in their numbers help to impart a cyclical pattern to series on output per man or output per man-hour.

It is apparent that any meaning attached to either output per man or output per man-hour for proprietors and unpaid family workers must be heavily qualified, but it appears that for long-term comparisons, involving changes in standard hours, the choice again favors employment as the better measure of effective labor input.

From the foregoing discussion of employees and proprietors, I conclude that when we are dealing with reductions in *standard* hours in the economy as a whole (increases have not been and are unlikely to be important), employment, though defective, is a better measure of effective labor input than is man-hours. Changes in standard hours have dominated long-term changes. Whether the same conclusion is applicable to changes in actual hours unaccompanied by changes in standard hours, the situation generally dominant in cyclical swings, there is not sufficient evidence to judge.

The evidence on which I have relied for the crucial wage-and-salary group is based on the experience of individual firms and industries. It might be supposed that comparison of actual changes in output per man-hour and output per man-year in the private economy as a whole as hours have changed in the past would provide additional evidence on these points. It does not because changes in hours, taking place at different times in different industries, have been so gradual that noticeable departures from trend in the economy as a whole invariably appear in both output per man and output per man-hour. A choice between the two based on continuity in years prior to 1929 or subsequent to World War II is impossible for this reason. Between these periods both series show a dip in the depression of the thirties and a bulge during World War II. Each deviation from trend is more pronounced in output per man than in output per man-hour.[12] However, since forces making for deviations were sufficient to affect both series, although their strength is unknown, this is of little assistance in deducing the separate effect of changes in actual hours.

CHOICE OF A MEASURE

The preceding two sections sketched my reasons for assuming (1) that man-hours are a better measure than employment of changes in the disutility or real cost of labor; and (2) that employment is a better measure than man-hours of effective labor input.

From the first proposition, I conclude directly that man-hours is the better series to use as the labor input component of a series representing the total real cost incurred in producing the national product, and hence in computing output per unit of real input as a measure of the efficiency or productivity of the economy.

From the second proposition, I conclude that the difference between changes in output per man and output per man-hour may be thought of as measuring, though very crudely, that part of the increase in output per man-hour that is the result of shortening hours (whether because of the stimulation it provides to improved management or of its effects on the efficiency of other types of labor). Output per man may accordingly be viewed as a measure of labor input (including management labor) that is adjusted for one type of quality change.

If I am correct in supposing that much of the past increase in output per man-hour is simply the result of shortening hours, it follows that, for long-term projections based on historical experience, projection of output per man will be preferable to that of output per man-hour if the future rate of hours shortening is different from that

[12] I rely here upon John Kendrick's series.

356

in the past. It may also be preferable in that it forces explicit consideration of the question whether future hours shortening will have the same effect as in the past. My view about other feasible adjustments for specific types of quality change in labor input is identical. John Kendrick, for example, has weighted man-hours in each industry by base-year average hourly earnings to obtain a measure of what he calls "labour input," which is then combined with "capital input" to obtain "total factor input," the series used to measure overall productivity. I would argue that to *measure* changes in productivity this is not appropriate; the shift of resources from industries in which labor is less productive to industries in which it is more productive is one source of greater productivity in the economy, not something to be eliminated. The calculation is nevertheless valuable. Comparison of output per man-hour with output per unit of "labor input" in Kendrick's sense (or broader input measures of which these are a part) provides a useful measure of the contribution of industry shifts to past increases of productivity, and hence also a useful tool for projections.[13] Other similar calculations, based on such factors as occupation and education, would be useful in the same way (although the results would not, of course, be cumulative except to the extent that available data permitted cross classification).

I do not mean to suggest that one or more such feasible adjustments could really hold the quality of labor input substantially constant. Too many elements enter into the quality of labor to make reasonably complete adjustment for quality change feasible.

Adequacy of Data

This section discusses the adequacy of labor input data for obtaining total output per man-hour worked, and total output per person engaged in production (or some other employment measure). The appraisal would be the same if labor input measures were combined with other imputs to obtain a broader measure of productivity. Two important general points are immediately obvious.

THE SHORTER THE PERIOD, THE GREATER THE NECESSARY ACCURACY

It is customary to express changes in output per man-hour (or per man) in terms of the average annual rate of change between two dates. The farther apart these dates are, the larger is the percentage error in the estimate of man-hours (or employment) that we can tolerate.

[13] If the labor input measure is to be used separately to obtain output per man-hour, the weights should, of course, be value (GNP) added rather than wage rates. It will be evident that I prefer the calculations to be based upon employment, rather than man-hours, so as to facilitate separate treatment of the effects of hours changes.

Suppose, for example, that the true average annual rate of increase in output per man-hour is 2 per cent (approximately the accepted estimate of the long-term rate) and the measures of output at both dates, and of man-hours at the earlier date, are correct. We would then arrive at a rate of increase within one-fourth percentage point (12.5 per cent) of the true (2 per cent) figure if the man-hour estimate for the second date did not deviate from the true figure by more than the percentage shown, for varying periods, in the following table.

Number of Years	Percentage Deviation from True Figure
$\frac{1}{4}$	− 0.06 to 0.06
1	− 0.25 to 0.25
2	− 0.49 to 0.49
3	− 0.74 to 0.73
4	− 0.98 to 0.98
5	− 1.23 to 1.22
10	− 2.48 to 2.42
20	− 5.02 to 4.79
30	− 7.62 to 7.10
50	−13.02 to 11.55
100	−27.74 to 21.76

The numbers in the table would be practically the same if a different true rate of increase—say 1 or 6 per cent a year—were assumed, although in that case a quarter percentage point error would appear more, or less, serious.

More generally, the error in the man-hour estimate that we can afford roughly approximates the product of (1) the error, in percentage points, that we are willing to tolerate in the annual rate of increase in output per man-hour and (2) the number of years separating the two dates of comparison. Because of compounding, this is not literally true, and for comparisons over long time periods an underestimate of the later man-hour figures is (by the criterion used) slightly less serious than an overestimate. However, unless we deal with extremely long time periods and large margins of error, this rule of thumb will suffice. It follows that, in computing annual average rates of change, short-period comparisons require far more accuracy in man-hour or employment estimates than do long-period comparisons. The extent to which the data are in fact more accurate for short periods is considered later.

The previous discussion has been phrased in terms of an error in the man-hours (or employment) estimate for the later date when that

358

for the earlier date is correct. Actually, of course, what is significant is the percentage error in the index of man-hours in the second year when man-hours in the first year are taken as 100. If man-hours are understated by 10 per cent in both years, no error results.

ADVANTAGE OF STATISTICAL CONSISTENCY BETWEEN INPUT AND OUTPUT ESTIMATES

There is, similarly, no error in the change in output per man-hour (or per employed person) if the indexes of output and of man-hours (or employment) have the same percentage error, or bias. There is an enormous advantage, consequently, in achieving maximum statistical interdependence between the measures of labor input and of output.

For output per man, this advantage can be maximized by use of the Office of Business Economics series for gross national product, measured from the income side, with its series for "persons engaged in production." The former series should be regarded simply as a statistical alternative to the published GNP series, not as something conceptually different. It is not published in constant dollars, but it can readily be obtained by applying to the published constant-dollar series the ratio of current-dollar GNP less statistical discrepancy to current-dollar GNP. Future references to GNP will be to the estimates based on the income side. For short-period comparisons this adjustment often introduces a worth-while improvement.

Data for the employment of wage and salary workers and of payrolls are drawn from the same sources and, to the modest extent that estimation is required, based on similar methods. The same is true of the main components (about 4/5 by value) of employer contributions for social insurance. The opportunity for statistical inconsistency between wage and salary worker employment, on the one hand, and payrolls and employer contributions, on the other, is consequently slight. Since payrolls and employer contributions comprise 56 per cent of the GNP (based on 1956 data), and full-time equivalent employment comprises 85 per cent of "persons engaged in production," the gain from this interdependence of sources and methods is very great.[14] In addition there is some, though much less, interdependence between the estimates of the number of nonfarm proprietors (10 per cent of persons engaged) and nonfarm proprietors' income (7 per cent of GNP), and in the longer run between farm

[14] Data cited throughout this paper are estimates published in July 1958 or the supporting detail published in "U.S. Income and Output," November 1958.

proprietors and their income. For proprietors, interdependence is much greater over longer periods than for year-to-year changes.[15]

Such interdependence of estimates is extremely helpful, but it should not be understood to mean more than it does. In particular, it must be stressed that errors in the deflation of GNP have no counterpart in the employment estimates. Also, the "persons engaged" series measures full-time equivalent employment, while the interdependence refers to average monthly employment. However, I believe there is little likelihood of much error—insofar as movement over time is concerned—in the conversion to full-time equivalence.

Two characteristics of the OBE series on persons engaged in production require brief discussion.

First, in industries where part-time work is important, the figures for wage and salary workers are reduced to full-time equivalence. This seems to me clearly desirable. In most industries the average weekly hours and earnings of part-time workers are only about one-sixth or one-seventh those of full-time workers. Inclusion of part-time workers at full weight in the employment total could consequently badly distort productivity measures if their proportion in the total changed. It is true that the ratio of full-time equivalent to total employment in individual industries seems in fact to be quite stable. Indeed, were this not so, the full-time equivalent employment estimates would be suspect, since in most industries data for an adequate correction are available only when the Census of Business is taken. But such stability need not always prevail, and in addition changes in the relative importance of industries affect the ratio for the all-industry employment totals. A result similar to full-time equivalence in employment is sought for proprietors by the effort to count only those who receive the major fraction of their income, or devote the major portion of their time, to their business or profession.

Second, the OBE series excludes unpaid family workers. The reason is the unsatisfactory state of the data, and particularly the enormously greater figures (roundly in the ratio of 3 to 1) that are reported in establishment censuses than in the Census of Population or the Monthly Report on the Labor Force.[16] Until the reason for this is cleared up, the omission cannot be made good nor its importance even appraised. For estimates running back no farther than

---

[15] Interdependence carries over to productivity data by industry, if GNP by industry is obtained by adding the necessary adjustment items to national income originating. Because of the problems involved in classification by industry, the advantage of using statistically interdependent employment and output data is, in fact, even much greater in industry than in aggregate productivity measurement.

[16] See my comment on the paper given by Edwin Budd in Volume 24 of *Studies in Income and Wealth.*

1929, I believe the least objectionable procedure is to follow OBE practice and simply omit unpaid family workers. For earlier periods, when family workers were presumably more important, it may be preferable to follow Kendrick's procedure and to include a series tied to the Census of Population or MRLF level, but it should be recognized that this may be little more than a token inclusion if the establishment censuses are correct.

The general OBE procedure, somewhat oversimplified, for estimating employment in industries covered by social insurance laws is (1) to obtain average monthly employment for establishments covered by state unemployment insurance laws or reporting to the Interstate Commerce Commission; (2) to add employment in firms with fewer employees than are required for unemployment compensation coverage, based on special Old Age and Survivors Insurance tabulations; and, until recently, (3) to adjust the resulting aggregate by the ratio of payrolls based on taxable wages under the Old Age and Survivors Insurance and Railroad Retirement Board programs plus nontaxable wages based on unemployment compensation data, to a preliminary estimate of payrolls based on procedures paralleling those described for employment in steps (1) and (2). The last step was designed to correct for inconsistencies between actual size-of-firm exclusion from unemployment compensation coverage and presumed exclusions, based on BOASI size-of-firm tabulations for a single month, and to pick up firms (chiefly new firms) in covered industries that are omitted from unemployment compensation coverage for reasons other than small size.

In the last decade, the source data have improved in one respect and deteriorated in two. The improvement has been the reduction in size-of-firm exclusion in state unemployment compensation laws. The deterioration, which seems to me more important, stems from (1) discontinuance in 1950 of final annual tabulations from the state unemployment compensation agencies that include late-reporting firms, so that the only reports now submitted are quarterly statements including actual data for firms reporting promptly and estimates for those reporting late; and (2) changes in the definition of taxable wages under the BOASI program such that these no longer correspond to taxable wages under the unemployment compensation laws. This has forced substitution of a direct estimate of delinquency in BOASI small-firm tabulations for the third step described in the previous paragraph. Correspondence between the adjustments for employment and payrolls is preserved, however.

Estimates of employment in uncovered industries, and of proprietors, are obtained from a variety of sources we need not describe here.

In general, the annual estimates for 1939 on are of excellent quality, slightly better for 1940 through 1949 or 1950 than in the other years.

HOW GREAT AN ERROR CAN WE AFFORD?

From 1929 to 1957 GNP per person engaged in production, based on OBE data, increased at an average annual rate of 1.6 per cent. Output per man-hour, according to available estimates, has increased at a long-run rate slightly above 2 per cent. In these trend figures, it is apparent that an error of even a fraction of 1 per cent is large relative to the quantity being measured.

We shall also be concerned with year-to-year changes. A distribution of year-to-year changes in output per person engaged since 1929 is shown in the first column of Table 1. It is apparent that the range is

TABLE 1

Distribution of Annual Percentage Changes in Real Gross
National Product per Person Engaged in Production
(number of cases)

Percentage Change from Previous Year	All Years 1930–57	Years 1948–57
6	3	0
5	5	2
4	0	0
3	3	1
2	2	2
1	7	4
0	2	1
−1	2	0
−2	1	0
−3	0	0
−4	1	0
−5	1	0
−6	0	0
−7	1	0
Total	28	10

Source: Computed from Office of Business Economics data.

very large, and that if an error of no more than, say, 2 or 3 per cent in the data is assumed, we could still distinguish twelve to fourteen of the twenty-eight annual changes as being distinctly above or below the trend average of 1.6 per cent. The period is decidedly abnormal, however, in that it is distorted by the great depression and World War II. Of the ten years from 1948 to 1957, a more normal period, for only two could we conclude that they differed from the trend level

362

if we admitted an error of as much as 2 per cent, and assuming accuracy within 1 per cent would add only two more to the list. More refined analysis would require very accurate estimates.

It is against this background that we must appraise the accuracy of employment and man-hour estimates.

APPRAISAL OF EMPLOYMENT ESTIMATES

We come now to an appraisal, which can represent only my own judgment, of the adequacy of data for "persons engaged" for use in productivity measurements. I make no allowance for the omission of unpaid family workers since I do not know how to judge its importance.[17]

My judgment is that, for the period since 1939, the error introduced, by errors in the persons engaged series, into the year-to-year percentage change in GNP per person engaged in production is not likely to exceed 0.2 percentage points. I have in mind a range corresponding to one standard deviation, which means that two changes out of three would be less, and one out of three would exceed (usually slightly) 0.2 percentage points, while errors of as much as 0.4 percentage points would be rare.

This is not an estimate of the error in the persons engaged series itself, which would be larger. It is reduced by the interdependence between employment and income figures. Moreover, a similar reduction is allowable in the error for GNP. Indeed, the meaning of the 0.2 estimate (or guess) may most easily be made clear by indicating the types of error in GNP that would have to be allowed for, in addition, to obtain a complete appraisal of the reliability of year-to-year changes in output per person engaged. These are: (1) the errors in the sum of current-dollar estimates of rental income, corporate profits, net interest, farm proprietors' income, "other labor income," indirect business taxes, business transfer payments, capital consumption allowances, subsidies, and the current surplus of government enterprises; (2) errors in employee compensation and in nonfarm proprietors' income that have no counterpart in the employment series (for employee compensation, I believe this would be a minor fraction of the total error, but for nonfarm proprietors' income it would comprise the bulk of the total error); (3) all errors in deflation, except for

---

[17] In Table 5, MRLF estimates of unpaid family workers (which may be far too low) are shown in absolute numbers and as a percentage of OBE "persons engaged" in private industries as far back as 1940. The reader may judge the difference that their addition to the OBE series would make to productivity estimation, but this says nothing about their reliability. In addition to the question of level, the earlier years can scarcely be considered comparable with those for the later period in view of a change in questioning procedure in 1945.

deflation of the compensation of government employees and of domestic servants.[18]

The errors in employment that concern me tend to be random rather than cumulative. In addition, the interdependence between proprietors and proprietors' income is greater over longer time periods than short. Hence, for the period since 1939, I would not increase by much the error margin introduced by the employment estimates in comparing estimates that are not adjacent. This means that, in computing an average annual increase in output per person engaged over a two-year period, the error from this source drops to about 0.1 percentage point and for longer periods becomes negligible.

Were no errors introduced by output measurement, the employment estimates since 1939 would suffice for measurement of year-to-year changes in productivity. The estimates from 1929 to 1938 are less reliable, but given the large productivity changes of that period, probably are good enough for meaningful year-to-year measurement, and should certainly be adequate for average changes over three or four years. Also, an average rate of change from 1929 to, say, 1957 should be as good as from 1939 or a later year if the advantage of a longer time period is considered.

Table 2 indicates my approach to the appraisal of reliability of year-to-year comparisons since 1939. The "persons engaged" total is divided into the four groups shown.

Since the deflation of GNP expenditures for general government employees and domestic servants assumes no changes in productivity, employment there may be considered a "wash" item introducing no error into the productivity estimate (provided, of course, that the deflation convention is accepted).

Estimates of farm employment (proprietors and employees) are statistically independent of year-to-year changes in the income measure (for proprietors and employees combined). Hence the error margin of 1.5 per cent (within which two-thirds of the changes are assumed to fall) carries over entirely into the error in output per person engaged.

For other employees I have put the error in the annual change at 0.3 per cent, but this has almost no effect on the error in productivity since I have taken only 2 per cent of this amount as the portion that

[18] It is not my assignment to appraise the output measures. However, if we admit an error of as much as 2 per cent in the items covered in (1) and (2)—and this does not seem exorbitant at least for preliminary estimates prepared prior to the availability of Internal Revenue Service data—this is equivalent to 0.9 per cent of GNP. The error margin in deflation can scarcely be supposed less than 0.5 per cent. It would be hard luck if the errors (0.2, 0.9, and 0.5 per cent) should be cumulative, but should this happen they would total 1.6 per cent, which is the same as the average annual increase in output per person engaged since 1929.

TABLE 2

Categories of Persons Engaged	1956 Number of Persons Engaged (000)	Assumed Margin of Error (per cent)	Assumed Degree of Independence of Corresponding Employee Compensation or Proprietors' Income (per cent)	Independent Error in Persons Engaged Series (per cent) (000)	
General govt. and private households	10,545	a	0	0	0
Farms (proprietors and employees)	5,269	1.5	100	1.5	79
All other employees	43,830	0.3	2	0.006	3
Nonfarm proprietors	6,538	1.5	85	1.28	84
Total of above	66,182				166
Allowance for errors in conversion to full-time equivalence and in weighting	66,182			0.1	66
Total	66,182			0.35b	232

a Not estimated.
b Computed from first and last columns.

would not affect employee compensation proportionately. Either figure could be changed considerably without much effect on the end result.

For nonfarm proprietors I have used the same error margin, 1.5 per cent, as for farm proprietors, but have assumed that 15 per cent of such an error would carry over into the estimate of proprietors' income.

Finally, I have allowed 0.1 per cent for errors in the conversion to full-time equivalence, and to cover errors that might arise because errors in the levels of any of the series affect the weights, and hence the movement of the aggregate.

Summed up, this would give an error margin of 232,000, or 0.35 per cent, in year-to-year movement of "persons engaged" at the 1956 level. However, given the probability that errors of the various types will not be in the same direction, this must be reduced to, roundly, 0.2 per cent.

Again, I must stress that the values in the table represent no more than moderately informed guesses. Different guesses for farm employment and for proprietors, particularly, would change the result appreciably.

Preliminary estimates of full-time equivalent employment, prepared without benefit of annual unemployment compensation statistics, have been published in the February issues of the *Survey of*

Current Business since February 1953. A comparison for private industries of changes shown in February with those shown the following July and with the latest estimates is given for six years in Table 3. At best, these advance estimates, although rather good by ordinary standards, have been accurate enough to warrant their use (supplemented by preliminary estimates of proprietors) only in the early discovery of years in which productivity change departs sharply from trend.

TABLE 3

Comparison of Preliminary and Revised Estimates of Full-Time Equivalent
Employment in Private Industries
(preceding year = 100)

Year	Revised July 1958	Published in Following July	Published in Following February
1952	101.1	101.3	100.0
1953	102.5	102.8	103.2
1954	96.6	96.5	96.5
1955	103.4	103.7	102.5
1956	102.9	103.4	102.7
1957	100.4	100.4	100.8

Source: Computed from Office of Business Economics data.

There is now no quarterly series for "persons engaged." One could be constructed, but the error introduced into current quarterly productivity changes by errors in the employment (and GNP) estimates could not be reduced nearly as much as we have reduced that in annual changes to take account of statistical interdependence, and the actual quarter-to-quarter error in employment might well approach that in the preliminary annual estimates. Given the extreme accuracy required to say anything about quarterly changes in productivity (as indicated in the table on page 358), I see little prospect of obtaining a meaningful quarterly measure. Nor do I see any great need for it. Such estimates would have value only in constructing an advance estimate for the year.

Estimates of employment prior to 1929 have been prepared by several investigators. I have not reviewed these in detail. I judge, however, that at least back to 1880 their quality does not deteriorate much faster than is offset by the statistical advantage of a longer time period for computing an annual rate of change in output per man for periods ending with the present. They are probably good enough to establish, over periods of two or three decades, any sharp changes in productivity trends (if the same can be said for the deflated GNP figures). They are clearly inappropriate for short-term productivity comparisons.

Although the advantage of interdependence with the product

measure seems clearly to indicate the desirability of using OBE employment statistics with OBE national product data, employment estimates of BLS or Census are sometimes used in practice, so it is of some interest to compare them. The comparison will also prove useful when we turn to the man-hours data.

Office of Business Economics employment estimates are compared with those of the Bureau of Labor Statistics in Table 4. The comparisons here exclude government employment since productivity calculations have generally been confined to private industries, and since the government comparison has certain difficulties.

TABLE 4

Comparison of OBE and BLS Estimates of Private Wage and Salary Worker Employment
(full-time and part-time)

Year	OBE (excluding government, farms, and private households) (000)	BLS (excluding government) (000)	BLS as a Percentage of OBE
1929	28,066	27,975	99.7
1930	26,175	25,944	99.1
1931	23,299	23,119	99.2
1932	20,303	20,152	99.3
1933	20,397	20,299	99.5
1934	22,551	22,401	99.3
1935	23,453	23,315	99.4
1936	25,327	25,140	99.3
1937	27,210	26,969	99.1
1938	25,151	25,026	99.5
1939	26,570	26,316	99.0
1940	28,385	27,856	98.1
1941	32,246	31,560	97.9
1942	34,804	34,296	98.5
1943	36,303	36,026	99.2
1944	35,614	35,491	99.7
1945	34,172	34,093	99.8
1946	36,368	35,692	98.1
1947	38,260	37,988	99.3
1948	39,077	38,798	99.3
1949	37,531	37,459	99.8
1950	38,931	38,712	99.4
1951	41,480	40,958	98.7
1952	42,216	41,694	98.8
1953	43,370	43,036	99.2
1954	41,946	41,680	99.4
1955	43,301	43,142	99.6
1956	44,663	44,489	99.6
1957	44,861	44,536	99.3

Agreement of the OBE data for average monthly employment of private wage and salary workers, excluding farms and private households, with BLS data is sufficiently close that if the average annual change in output per man between each of the twenty-eight prior years shown and 1957 were computed on the basis of both employment series, the result would differ by more than 0.1 percentage point only in the two comparisons involving the two immediately preceding years. Differences in year-to-year changes are larger. Of twenty-eight cases, twenty differ by more than 0.1 per cent, fourteen by more than 0.2 per cent, seven by more than 0.5 per cent, and two (both including 1946) by more than 1.0 per cent.

Since 1939 a principal difference in methodology between OBE and BLS has been the handling of social insurance statistics in estimating employment. In the BLS procedure the third step noted in the description of OBE procedures is omitted, and the first two steps are utilized only for the first quarter of each year, the other quarters being estimated by interpolating these benchmark figures by employment in the BLS sample of firms.

Census Bureau estimates of employment of private wage and salary workers and proprietors and own-account workers are compared with OBE estimates of persons engaged in production in private industries in Table 5.

The series, which have largely independent statistical sources, also differ in definition. Probably the most important differences are (1) that the Census series counts part-time workers holding a single job at full value but does not account for second jobs, while the OBE series (in industries in which part-time work is common) counts all part-time jobs at a fractional value; and (2) that the Census series shown here, based on definitions prior to the 1957 revision, includes workers with a job but not at work, who are omitted from the OBE series.

From 1947 to 1956 general agreement of the two series is nonetheless fairly good, but year-to-year movements frequently differ enough to affect seriously short-term productivity comparisons. There is some suggestion of greater cyclical stability in the Census series. Prior to 1947 agreement is poor, although for the annual rate of productivity change from, say, 1940 to 1956 the difference is less than 0.1 percentage point.

APPRAISAL OF MAN-HOURS ESTIMATES

Output per man-hour cannot be estimated as accurately as output per "person engaged." For short-period comparisons the difference in accuracy is likely to be substantial. The error introduced into

368

TABLE 5

Comparison of Census Estimates of Private Wage and Salary Workers and Self-Employed with OBE Estimates of Persons Engaged in Private Industries

				Addendum	
Year	Census Labor Force (000)	OBE Persons Engaged (000)	Census as Per Cent of OBE (%)	Census Unpaid Family Workers (000)	Unpaid Family Workers as Per Cent of Persons Engaged (private) (%)
1940	45,520[a]	46,137[a]	98.7[a]	2,000	4.7
1941	48,110[a]	50,066[a]	96.1[a]	2,240	4.9
1942	51,100[a]	53,235[a]	96.0[a]	2,650	5.5
1942	46,050	48,141	95.7	2,650	5.5
1943	45,820	48,684	94.1	2,840	5.8
1944	45,410	47,552	95.5	2,770	5.8
1945	44,620	46,045	96.9	2,660	5.8
1946	47,640	48,583	98.1	2,300	4.7
1947	50,944	50,915	100.1	2,043	4.0
1948	52,134	51,776	100.7	1,957	3.8
1949	51,311	50,043	102.5	1,959	3.9
1950	52,308	51,346	101.9	1,831	3.6
1951	53,131	53,515	99.3	1,786	3.4
1952	53,026	54,054	98.1	1,773	3.3
1953	53,944	55,078	98.0	1,696	3.1
1954	52,884	53,529	98.8	1,675	3.2
1955	54,533	55,098	99.0	1,823	3.3
1956	56,141	56,398	99.5	1,904	3.4

[a] Includes government civilian employees (except work relief) since Census data for 1940 and 1941 are not available without them.

Source: Bureau of the Census and Office of Business Economics.

year-to-year comparisons of output per man-hour by errors in the man-hour estimates could hardly be put at less than several times the error that is introduced into output per "person engaged" estimates by errors in the estimates for the number of "persons engaged." For long-term trends the difference in accuracy may not be important because if the time period is long enough, even the error in man-hours may be quite acceptable. Were it not for the wide divergence between alternative estimates of the long-term trend of average hours in agriculture, we could be fairly certain that this is so.

We have been referring to output per man-hour worked, not output per man-hour paid for. This clearly is the concept appropriate for measuring the performance of the economy. Even for analysis of inflation I believe it is the more useful concept, since it shows the amount by which employee compensation could be increased in any form without giving impetus to inflationary pressures.

For the period since 1940 three general approaches can be used in estimating total man-hours worked in the economy as a whole, or in such broad branches as government, agriculture, and private non-agricultural industries.[19] For the period prior to 1940, only the third is available.

1. Total man-hours worked can be computed directly from the Census Bureau's Monthly Report on the Labor Force.

2. "Persons engaged," as estimated by the Office of Business Economics, can be multipled by average hours worked, as reported by the MRLF.

3. The various industrial components of average monthly employment and the number of active proprietors, as estimated by OBE,[20] can be multiplied by estimates from establishment sources of average hours of work paid for (or, in the case of agriculture, "required" for the work done); corrections to an "hours worked" concept can be attempted on the basis of scattered information; and the components can then be summed to obtain the desired aggregates. Data are collected on a sample basis for a number of large groups by the BLS, by the Census Bureau in certain industrial census and census surveys, by regulatory commissions, and by the Department of Agriculture. For others, average hours must be estimated from fragmentary sources, by imputing hours of groups for which data are available, or by use of MRLF data for them. These include salaried employees generally, all nonfarm proprietors, and employees in agricultural services, forestry, and fisheries; finance, insurance, and real estate; services (except year-round hotels, laundries, and cleaning and dyeing plants); transportation (except railroads and local transit lines) and government.

Some considerations that should influence the choice of method and appraisal of the error introduced into output per man-hour follow:

1. Regardless of which method is used, the error in the estimate of average hours worked, unlike that in "persons engaged," has no statistical counterpart in the production estimate, and hence creates directly a corresponding error in output per man-hour.

2. The second and third methods preserve for the man-hour series, while the first does not, the advantage of interdependence between employment and output data.

[19] None of these cover military employment, for which the whole concept of hours worked is vague.

[20] Different estimates of employment, particularly those of the Bureau of Labor Statistics, for the groups covered might also, of course, be used.

3. Even aside from this interdependence, the absence of a comprehensive establishment reporting system like that provided for employment by the social security system means that hours statistics are much less reliable. Hours reporting from establishment sources is less complete than employment reporting prior to 1939.

4. Strictly, the conceptual differences between "persons engaged" and MRLF "employment" make use of MRLF hours with OBE "persons engaged" inappropriate. The choice between using MRLF data directly for total man-hours (the first method) and using them only to obtain average hours (the second method) rests on the reason for the divergences shown in Table 5 between the movement of "persons engaged" and the most nearly corresponding employment data from the MRLF. If they result mainly from the conceptual differences in definition, use of MRLF aggregate hours is preferable. If, as seems much more likely, the greater part of the difference is statistical rather than conceptual, the second method is preferable. (Even so, some error resulting from inconsistent definitions must be allowed for.)

5. The MRLF data for "hours worked," dependent as they are on the respondents' knowledge and memory, subject to certain biases (such as the reported tendency to overlook hours worked on a secondary job), and based on a small sample, are inferior statistically to the available establishment data for "hours paid for." But there are huge gaps in the latter. Even if these are filled by use of MRLF data for the missing sectors, the presence of secondary job holders and probable inconsistencies in classification introduces a hybrid element into the resulting aggregate. An additional limitation on the third method is the need to convert "hours paid for" into "hours worked," an adjustment for which information is scanty. Fortunately, in the pre-1940 period, for which this is the only approach available, the distinction was much less important. For the later period, the choice between the second and third methods is a close one.

6. The trend of farm hours is in dispute. Department of Agriculture estimates imply no significant trend, but substantial fluctuations, in farm hours since 1910. John Kendrick, in measuring productivity, has used this series and continued the assumption of no trend in hours since 1869. MRLF data, on the other hand, show a reduction of farm hours since 1940, and the Twentieth Century Fund has assumed a reduction comparable to that in nonfarm occupations during the entire period since 1870. The difference is large and, because of the importance of agriculture in the earlier decades, of

371

some importance even in the long-run trend of output per man-hour in the economy as a whole. I am not in a position to resolve this question.

7. The accuracy of employment data is limited by the fact that reports are available only for one payroll period a month (or less), so that they represent a sampling of the year. Hours data are subject to a similar limitation, but for hours it is more serious because there is less continuity in hours than in employment. Indeed, estimation of annual averages of hours worked weekly requires careful examination to see that holidays and vacations are properly represented. Omission of a single holiday in a 260-work-day year represents a 0.4 per cent error in the annual hours figure. Use of a week including a holiday to represent a full month would involve a 1.1 per cent error. These are large amounts in the measurement of annual productivity changes.

8. Even rounding, a cause of error practically absent from employment reporting, cannot be ignored in hours estimation for productivity measurement. In MRLF data, average hours are computed from the nearest reported whole hour, and rounding on the part of respondents must also be assumed. An error in the resulting average of as much as 0.1 hours, or six minutes, on a forty-hour average is an error of 0.25 per cent, greater than the whole error we allowed in year-to-year movements in "output per person engaged" arising from errors in the employment estimates.

My estimate of that error margin at 0.2 per cent was cut markedly because employment and output data are statistically interdependent. The same statistical interdependence reduces the error that must be allowed for in the product measure. Estimates of changes in average hours, even when prepared as carefully as possible, must be assigned a much larger error margin than those for employment, and allow no reduction for statistical interdependence. The error likely to be introduced into year-to-year changes in output per man-hour by errors in the man-hour series, even if estimated so as to preserve the interdependence between employment and output, could hardly be put at much less than 1 per cent, at the two out of three probability level. The errors in output measurement that must be combined with this are the same as in the case of employment. If the methodology does not preserve the interdependence between employment and output, a much larger allowance for error must be made in both employment and output.

As with employment, but with an important possible exception for agriculture, errors are not likely to cumulate much over time, so that the error becomes unimportant in comparisons spanning long periods.

COMMENT

G. S. TOLLEY, North Carolina State College

I

Denison's judgments on employment series, in the form of subjective standard errors, probably are the best available on their reliability. It is made clear that the man-hours series are less reliable than employment estimates, but no similar numerical judgments on accuracy of man-hours is given. This lack is perhaps the main criticism to be made of this part of Denison's work. Those who prefer man-hours to employment as a labor input concept will particularly feel the lack.

Judgments like Denison's provide a beginning toward more rigorous data accuracy procedures. The paper concerns labor input for the U.S. economy as a whole, an area in which we are relatively well off. Percentage errors may be larger for inputs on a disaggregated basis. His footnote 17 emphasizes that output measures appear less accurate than those of labor input. The most serious errors of all may arise in measures of capital input.

A conjecture is that, unlike labor, capital introduces its most serious errors in productivity comparisons over an intermediate length such as five to twenty years. For a longer period, as Denison points out, there can be a great deal of error before estimated rate of productivity change is affected much. This is particularly true for capital, because its weight as an input for most industries is on the order of only a third to a quarter. For closely adjacent years of relative economic stability, errors introduced by capital measurement may be small enough to be neglected also. This is because errors due to conceptual and estimating problems may be of substantially the same bias over short stable periods. However, suppose that the estimate of capital were correct at the beginning of the period with a 10 per cent error coming in over five years. If true productivity growth was around 2 per cent per year, we could have the illusion that it was as low as about 1.5 per cent or as high as about 2.5 per cent.

II

In the other part of Denison's paper, which deals with conceptual issues in measuring labor input, he concludes that employment is a better measure than man-hours of effective labor input. The contrary view can be supported.

His contention that better management and mechanization result from shortening of hours seems to me to support use of hours rather than employment. What is being said is that capital and output per unit of input may have changed when hours shortened. Do we want productivity measures to obscure these effects?

For man-hours to be superior to employment as a measure of input would seem to me to require that the output of a worker be the same no matter how many hours he works. This would be a kind of Parkinson's law in economics surely not valid for the United States. Rather, qualitative considerations cited for any diminishing returns at all to hours strike me as having limited importance. Cited were increasing fatigue of workers as hours are lengthened, opening and closing time, and absenteeism that results from workers' need for time to conduct personal affairs. These may be minor enough to warrant being neglected altogether. That is, as a first approximation, we might safely assume the quality of a man-hour does not change with hours worked.

The choice between man-hours and employment in part depends on a conception of what productivity indexes should try to measure. No formulation is going to be perfect from every point of view, but my feeling is that we should be trying to get at shifts in firm production functions within the context of a market-oriented economy. Man-hours seem more consistent than employment with a firm approach.

If quality changes are in fact associated with hour shortening or if hour shortening induces productivity and capital changes, these adjustments can be made explicitly.

The use of man-hours is a straightforward measure of input. It is easy to understand, whereas the idea that employment is a measure of labor input "adjusted for one type of quality change" could be confusing to a wider audience.

III

In generally not allowing for changes in input quality, Denison is at one extreme of positions on how to construct productivity measures. He is against measures that eliminate changes in productivity in the economy as a whole by definition. At the other extreme is the view that measures should try to do just what Denison fears. According to this view, the total change in output cannot be understood unless inputs of some kind or other add up to total output. This again raises the question of what productivity indexes should try to measure. The no-quality-change approach and the explain-everything approach do not comfortably fit into a scheme for interpreting relative price movements and factor remuneration. The production function approach favored in the preceding section does fit into that scheme. My feeling is that such a scheme has the best chance of furthering our understanding of economic growth.

If productivity indexes try to get at shifts in production functions, adjustments will be made for some input quality changes, but the adjustments are unlikely to account for all the growth in output. For instance, changes in quality of labor that are the result of investments in education would be allowed for inasmuch as these may be expected to affect the return to that labor. But such things as economies of scale and easily copiable innovations, e.g., inventions and reorganizations of production such as the assembly line or automation, would not be adjusted for. The effects of the latter would show up as productivity increases.

Let us try to illustrate how this approach fits into an understanding of growth relations between agriculture and the rest of the economy. We will be concerned with the relative price of agricultural products and will bring in the role of inputs purchased by farms. A value added productivity measure is used, and the analysis suggests how this type of measure can fit into a total interpretation of growth.[1]

The demand for agricultural products is related to the total sales value of output, but on the production side we find this breaks down into value added and purchased inputs. Value added may be viewed as the agricultural output that is "produced" in the farm sector of the economy, whereas the purchased inputs are agricultural output "produced" in the nonfarm sector. Let k be the proportion of total agricultural output "produced" in the nonfarm sector, i.e., the ratio of intermediate products consumed to total agricultural output. Over the quarter century from 1929 to 1954, the proportion rose from 11 per cent to 23 per cent. A main reason is that more power is produced off the farm than previously in connection with widespread shift from horses to tractors. It can also be said that more soil is produced off the farm, as fertilizer has increased dramatically as a source of nutrients.

The following identity concerns the price of agricultural products relative to the price of nonagricultural products:[2]

[1] The ensuing is related to a study in progress by Seymour Smidt and myself on agriculture's role in economic growth.

[2] This is derived from the relation that total value of agricultural output=value of intermediate products consumed+value added on farms. Divide both sides of the relation by a constant dollar measure of total agricultural output. We then have: Implicit price deflator for total agricultural output=(Implicit price deflator for intermediate products consumed on farms) (k)+(Implicit price deflator for farm value added) $(1-k)$. To get the text expression, we then divide by the implicit price deflator for private nonfarm gross product. The numbers in the text are in terms of 1929 dollars and are derived from figures given in the *Survey of Current Business*.

$$\begin{bmatrix} \text{Relative price of agri-} \\ \text{cultural products} \end{bmatrix} = \begin{bmatrix} \text{Relative price of} \\ \text{purchased inputs} \end{bmatrix} \begin{bmatrix} k \end{bmatrix}$$

$$+ \begin{bmatrix} \text{Relative price of out-} \\ \text{put added by farms} \end{bmatrix} \begin{bmatrix} 1-k \end{bmatrix}$$

For the 1929 base this identity is

$$[100] = [100]\ [.11] + [100]\ [.89].$$

For 1954 it is

$$[95] = [86]\ [.23] + [98]\ [.77].$$

The slight decline in relative price of agricultural products, from 100 to 95, is probably best viewed as essential constancy.

For purchased inputs there was a fall of relative price from 100 to 86, and we have already mentioned the dramatic swing to these inputs. This swing had implications for farm adjustment problems, because it displaced farm resources. But the purchased inputs did not become important enough to be overriding in the explanation of the essential constancy of relative price of agricultural products.

The main reason for the essential constancy is the fact that the relative price for output added by farms changed very little. The change was from 100 to 98. In trying to relate this result to farm productivity, consider the assertion that movements in capital and labor rates of pay were nearly the same in agriculture as in the rest of the economy over the twenty-five year period. We will not take space to support the assertion except to say that real returns to labor appear to have risen secularly in similar fashion in the farm and nonfarm sectors, and relative returns to capital probably remained roughly the same also. If this is true, the relative price for output added by farms must primarily reflect efficiency in use of the factors.

Preliminary calculations of productivity change for the value added concepts, farm gross product and private nonfarm gross product, have been carried out on a comparable basis. They indicate an increase in output per unit of input in both sectors at an average annual rate of perhaps 1.5 per cent per year over this period. Thus the expectation of equal productivity change from the relative price analysis is fulfilled.

This illustrates how productivity measures can contribute to an understanding of changes in the economy. This ought to guide construction of the indexes. We can be even more explicit by emphasizing aims in productivity measurement that would be ruled out if this aim were accepted.

The ruling out of no-quality-change and explain-everything approaches has already been discussed. Another idea that sometimes

376

gets into discussions of productivity measurement is that indexes should measure changes in welfare. We come back to an old question: If our concept of utility is ordinal, what is the meaning of trying to measure it cardinally? Productivity indexes among other things throw light on welfare changes, but we need to avoid the pitfall of thinking that the indexes themselves can directly measure welfare changes.

This gives us a criterion for not trying to take account of such things as time spent going to and from work. While this unremunerated time is assuredly relevant to worker welfare its inclusion does not give a measure of *firms'* efficiency. How much disutility is involved in going to and from work is a question that productivity indexes cannot measure.

Still another idea is that productivity indexes should reflect projectable uniformities in the data. This idea seemed partly to motivate Denison's preference for employment over man-hours as a labor input measure. While projection is one of many uses of an understanding of economic growth, the projectionist may naturally also wish to find smooth trends that look extrapolatable—sometimes regardless of theoretical justification. To my mind, the latter type of trend should not have the name of productivity index.

IV

One source of changes in quality of labor input is changing skill associated with occupational structure. Denison mentions that it would be useful to have calculations showing this effect. Let me synopsize some calculations carried out in a broader study.

The calculations are made possible by the volume giving historical data on occupation by detailed groups published in connection with the 1940 census.[3] Suppose we take income differentials among the occupations in 1949 as a measure of relative quality.[4] A quality index can then be constructed, showing for each census year, what income per worker would have been in 1949 if the occupation mix of the given year had prevailed.

A report follows on quality indexes for the nonfarm and farm labor forces going back to 1910.[5] These are used to conjecture what has happened to quality of labor input for the economy as a whole.

[3] Bureau of the Census, *Sixteenth Census of Population: 1940, Population. Comparative Occupation Statistics for the United States, 1870–1940* (Washington: Government Printing Office, 1943).

[4] Bureau of the Census, *1950 Population Census, Characteristics of the Population, U.S. Summary* (Washington: Government Printing Office, 1953), Table 129.

[5] As part of the study by Seymour Smidt and myself on agriculture's role in economic growth the details of these and other related calculations will be described.

Numbers of persons are available by census year for the major socioeconomic groups: professional; proprietors, managers and officials; clerks and kindred; skilled workers and foremen; semi-skilled workers; and unskilled workers. About 150 detailed occupations form subgroups of these. Comparable data on numbers for each census year and income for 1949 are not available for all of the 150 subgroups. Subgroups for which comparable data were not available were put into an "other" category for each of the major socioeconomic groups. The quality indexes are based on the resulting fifty-five occupational groups, including the "other" groups.

Put on a 1910 base, the quality index for the nonfarm occupations is as follows.

1910	100
1920	102
1930	103
1940	102
1950	105

This lack of much quality increase between 1910 and 1950 is especially surprising if one looks at the relative decline in unskilled workers.

While there were large increases in the highly paid groups of professional persons, these still did not make up a large percentage of the labor force. Meanwhile there were numerically more important increases among groups of clerks and kindred workers with below-average incomes. Semiskilled workers also became more prevalent. These are the kinds of change that account for the apparent lack of quality increase, even though there were substantial changes in occupational composition of the labor force.

QUALITY OF THE FARM LABOR FORCE

Within agriculture there was a relative shift away from farm laborers to the managerial groups of owners and tenants. This made for a rise in quality.

The farm labor force may be incorporated into the analysis under two alternate assumptions. First is a low-quality assumption that uses the 1949 unadjusted income figures for farmers. The second, a high-quality assumption, uses nonfarm incomes within the same major socioeconomic classification as the measure of farmer quality. This second assumption is motivated by thoughts on why farmer money income may understate the desired measure of income. Low price levels may prevail for farmers due both to rurality and to concentration in the South. Moreover, income in kind is undoubtedly more important for farmers.

378

Under the low-quality assumption, the actual 1949 average income for farm laborers is $1,080 and for owners and tenants is $2,073. Under the high-quality assumption, the income for farm laborers is $2,002 and for owners and tenants is $4,621; these are average incomes for nonfarm laborers and nonfarm proprietors respectively.

The farm labor force quality indexes are as follows.

	Low-Quality Assumption	High-Quality Assumption
1910	100	100
1920	106	107
1930	104	104
1940	103	104
1950	105	107

The alternate assumptions do not much affect general movement of farm quality, but they are of importance in combining farm and nonfarm labor forces.

LABOR FORCE QUALITY FOR THE ECONOMY AS A WHOLE

For farm and nonfarm separately, the above indexes show hypothetical average income per worker, using a 1949 income measure in conjunction with occupation mix. An index of quality for the economy as a whole is obtained if we add the hypothetical farm and nonfarm total income and divide by total labor force to get hypothetical average income per worker.

	Low-Farm-Quality Assumption	High-Farm-Quality Assumption
1910	100	100
1920	106	102
1930	107	100
1940	108	99
1950	114	100

The alternate assumptions underlying these indexes are the same as described previously for the farm labor force.

The 14 per cent rise from 1910 to 1950 under the low-farm-quality assumption is principally due to the relative decline of agriculture and to the fact that farm quality is substantially less than nonfarm quality under this assumption.

The marked stability under the high-farm-quality assumption is due to the fact that farm quality here turns out to be somewhat higher than nonfarm. The farm decline then makes for a fall in quality that offsets the slight rise in nonfarm quality.

379

The indexes are hardly exact measures of quality. Too many questions can be raised as to the underlying classifications and the choices made in the index construction.

Yet the measures support several important conclusions. Changing quality of labor inputs associated with occupational mix seems to have been a minor source of U.S. growth from 1910 to date. While a positive increase in quality may be indicated, it is almost certainly very small on an average annual basis as compared with changes, say, in output per unit of input. If there has been a significant increase in quality at all, it is associated with the relative decline of agriculture. Possible lack of comparability of farm and nonfarm money income is a chief hindrance to accuracy in our estimation of changing quality.

Data exist for extending the calculations back to 1870. Preliminarily, it looks as if labor quality change was greater in the four decades prior to 1910 than it has been since.

MURRAY WERNICK, Board of Governors of the Federal Reserve System

Edward Denison has presented a useful discussion of over-all productivity measurements, relying primarily on OBE employment data to compute labor input. However, productivity statistics using manpower inputs have many uses and users and the fundamental question is, as Boulding has stated, "What questions can be answered better as a result of the measure we devise?"

From earlier concern over the labor-displacing effects of mechanization, interest has increasingly shifted to the relationships of labor productivity to wages and inflation, to expanding national industrial strength, to future manpower needs, to cyclical relationships, and to the distribution of the increments in real income among the factors of production.

Much has been said at this conference about the need to determine the effect of quality changes of inputs on productivity measurements. The impact of recent technological innovations, shifts in demands, and the increasing importance of research and development are accelerating shifts in the composition of employment. However, disaggregating the effect of such changes in specific quality variables as industry, occupation, and sex is difficult. Not only is there a question of adequacy of manpower input data, but even the presumption that we can ever obtain the necessary comparable real output data is suspect. Research, however, is indispensable if we are to obtain insight into periodic deviations from long-term trends in productivity or to analyze actual changes in the slope of the trend line for important industries and occupations, as well as the economy as a whole.

380

Denison is primarily concerned with a long-run measure of productivity which tends to incorporate all qualitative changes in manpower input into a single homogeneous quantity, either total employment or total man-hours. His series, he indicates, measures the efficiency with which an economy maximizes output while minimizing real costs. Other uses of productivity series are mentioned but it is clear that the over-all series he has constructed is not sufficiently versatile to meet the broader needs mentioned above. This leads to two problems: the validity of his suggested measures of manpower inputs in aggregate productivity series and the additional measures of input which are necessary to evaluate and answer questions, especially operational questions often imposed by public policy needs.

I believe that in the construction of labor productivity series, the preferable labor input measure is usually some man-hour measure. The number of persons employed is not satisfactory because of the wide diversity of hours experience and the sharp relative growth in recent years of part-time employment, particularly in service and trade industries. Denison implicitly acknowledges this and attempts to compensate for variation in the workweek and in the number of weeks worked per year by converting part-time employment into full-time equivalent employment in some major industry groups. This is accomplished by dividing total wages and salaries by average annual salaries of full-time workers. This conversion is, however, not performed for manufacturing, mining, construction, farming, or public utilities because of the estimating procedure used by Denison, although the Bureau of the Census' Current Population Survey reports a small but increasing number of part-time workers in these industries. Inclusion of full-time equivalents for the excluded industries would reduce the denominator and increase output per man.

Other objections can be raised to the full-time equivalent employment series. Annual data used by the Office of Business Economics to estimate full- and part-time employment and payrolls are available for selected industries only for years in which a Census of Business is conducted. Estimates of full-time equivalent employment are accurate only if the ratio of part-time workers to full-time workers and the ratio of average hours worked by part-time workers to average hours worked by full-time workers has remained constant since the last benchmark. During recent years, these ratios have shown sharp changes which are not reflected in the "persons engaged" series. Thus, for example, between 1950 and 1957, the number of part-time workers, primarily women engaged in service and trade occupations, rose by 40 per cent, while the number of year-round full-time workers increased by only 10 per cent. This shift in workforce composition has probably had some adverse influence on measures of output per unit of labor input which are not fully reflected in the "full-time" equivalent series.

Since average hourly earnings of full-time employees are substantially higher than earnings of part-time employees, the OBE series in effect implicitly makes a partial adjustment of employment for quality changes by weighting hours paid for by earnings. While it is at times desirable to adjust input factors for specific quality changes, such adjustments are most useful when done on a more systematic and comprehensive basis.

Denison buttresses his preference for employment rather than man-hour inputs by stating that reductions in standard hours worked have been a prime cause of increases in output per man-hour. He states that hours reduction has exerted an influence on productivity through two channels: reduction of worker fatigue and, more important, encouragement of greater managerial effort and of the substitution of capital for labor. These factors undoubtedly have played some role in past advances in output per man-hour, but probably were of less significance than Denison implies.

A real reduction in fatigue undoubtedly accompanied the shortening of the workweek, so long as average hours were considerably over forty. There is considerable evidence that since the end of World War II, fatigue is no longer a compelling reason for reducing the workweek. In many industries workers have willingly traded some leisure for additional income. In the Akron rubber industry, a standard workweek below forty hours led to a sharp growth in the number of persons holding two jobs and apparently to an actual increase in average hours worked per worker. When labor demands are strong multiple job holding tends to become more prevalent. Twice as many employees in 1957 held dual jobs than in 1950.

The more important aspect of Denison's position, however, rests on the fact that historically reductions in standard hours have usually been accompanied by a rise in hourly earnings. Denison argues that this rise in labor cost has been an incentive to more effective organization of the labor force and to mechanization of operations. However, it is well known that improvement in management practices and in the substitution of capital for labor have occurred during our entire industrial history. The high relative price of labor and the belief that hourly labor compensation would continue to increase relative to capital cost (irrespective of whether hours declined or remained constant) has, of course, provided an incentive for investment. Other related developments should not be overlooked: the constant advance of technology, the growing skill and education of the labor force, the

382

growth of scientific management, and the increasing use of engineers and other professional employees. It is true that in the past, hours reduction sometimes involved sufficiently large increases in cost to have some shock effect on managerial efficiency. Nevertheless, it seems more fruitful to view reductions in standard hours as one of the methods by which productivity gains are shared rather than as a specific cause of productivity advance.

The postwar trend has been toward more leisure. Longer paid vacation periods and more holidays, rather than reductions in the standard workweek, have become the major forms in which leisure has been extended. These developments make it increasingly important to use man-hours worked rather than man-hours paid as a measure of labor input. The older age of entrance into and earlier retirement from the labor force may also be conceived as adding to the leisure of persons in the working age population and a benefit of increasing productivity. This form of welfare gain is only implied in current productivity measures and to measure its significance probably requires an approach which relates man-hours worked to potential manpower resources available.

I now turn to current needs for more refined labor productivity data. I would urge in this connection the extension of manpower input measures in the following areas.

1. Disaggregation of over-all input data by industry. Substantial progress is being made, as indicated in Alterman's and other papers delivered at this conference. Output per man-hour series for individual industries should eventually permit us to compare rates of change between manufacturing and other sectors, and to determine the influence on economy-wide productivity change of the shift in manpower resources from commodity-producing industries to non-commodity-producing activities, such as government and private services, and distribution. It should also shed important light on wage-cost-productivity relationships among the industries. "Should" is used advisedly instead of "would" because the meaning of productivity measures outside the commodity-producing sectors remains unclear conceptually.

One of the major advantages of disaggregation may be a negative one. Industry detail tends to highlight the inadequacies of measures of real output for the noncommodity sectors. For instance, productivity gains have probably been substantial in domestic service, but if real output is measured by deflated payrolls then output per man-hour is shown as a constant over time. Constant dollars of personal consumption expenditure for medical services divided by the number of medical personnel may measure growth in overhead medical staffs and change in the number of patients a doctor manages to see in a day, but has little relevance to the real productivity factors, such as number of visits required for a cure, average length of illness, or proportion of patients surviving a particular disorder. Likewise, the validity of deflated personal consumption for educational services as a measure of output is questionable.

Generally, industry manpower input series are more inclusive than output data. Producers of productivity indexes have handled these problems in various ways. General government employment and output are excluded from most productivity measures, although the manpower input of this sector has become increasingly important. Professional workers are included in input series, although their product is only partly measured in current output data. Domestic servants are included, though under the asumption of constant productivity. These inconsistencies affect the validity of productivity measures as these sectors change in importance or as their rate of productivity change differs from that of the economy.

2. Further analysis is urgently required of the impact on output of shifts in the composition by occupation and sex of the employed labor force. In the past decade the number of salaried employees has risen sharply. At the same time the number of semi-skilled mechanical or hourly rated employees has shown no increase or possibly even a decline, despite a very large increase in total real output.

In manufacturing industries the rapid increase in employment of non-production workers relative to the increase in output in recent years has been reflected in at least a temporary retardation of the rate of growth in measures of output per man-hour of all employees and has been an important element accounting for a continuous rise in unit wage and salary costs between 1952 and 1957. However, if the man-hours input measure is limited to production workers, the rate of increase in productivity has been more in line with historical patterns, and unit wage costs show relatively small changes since 1952.

The sharp growth in the number of nonproduction workers in manufacturing reflects primarily expanded employment of professional workers, many of whom are engaged in research and development activities. Research and development, however, is not fully reflected in current measures of output either in the physical volume series or in GNP-based measures. A more realistic approach probably requires the capitalization of at least part of current research expenditures, rather than their present treatment as a current labor cost.

Women accounted for more than 55 per cent of the rise in employment in the past ten years and the proportion of employed women is at a record level. Female employment tends to be concentrated in certain occupations—salesworkers, clerks, nurses, and school teachers—and a high proportion is in part-time work. Their entrance into employment probably has some dampening effect on over-all productivity measures. The rapid and sustained rise in the participation rate of women in the work force is possibly due in large degree to the substantial reduction in labor input required in homemaking, but no present measure takes account of this factor. It is thus likely that the social output per woman worker has risen, a fact excluded from current productivity measurements.

3. Large variations in year-to-year changes in productivity pose important problems for current economic analysis, especially when public and government attention is focused on inflation. A case in point is the experience of 1956 and 1957, which in most computations show up as years of relatively small productivity increases. The 1956 Economic Report of the President states that "the smallness of the 1956 gain in productivity contributed to the rise in unit labor costs and, in turn, to the increase in prices."

Nowhere have I been able to find an adequate analysis of why productivity failed to make normal gains in these two years. On the manpower input side of the equation a rapid shift in the composition of the employed labor force can be shown to be one possible important short-run factor. The rather consistent pattern of change in productivity growth during the business cycle is also worthy of analysis.

Some interesting work on changes in productivity during the cycle has been done with existing data. Thor Hultgren of the National Bureau, using monthly BLS man-hours data and some of the monthly industry series of FRB Index of Manufacturing Production for which quantity data are available, has shown a definite relationship for the industry series between the stage of cycle and the rate of productivity change. Our own studies generally confirm the findings of an acceleration of productivity gains and a consequent decline in unit labor costs during recovery periods with the reverse development taking place in expansion periods.

Are the available data adequate for such detailed analysis of manpower inputs? The answer must be equivocal. A vast expansion has taken place in both the quantity and quality of available manpower statistics in the postwar period and such data are a basic part of our statistical area economic intelligence. A wide variety of cross-classified information relating to industry, occupation, sex, part-time work, and dual job holding are being produced from sample establishment reports, sample household reports, and from expanded social security programs. While progress is being made, much of this information

385

lies dormant and has not been exploited for experimentation in input-output measures and related problems of labor requirements and unit labor costs. In large part this is due to lack of appropriate comparable real output quantities. However, our preliminary studies using Bureau of Census data for the manufacturing industries leads to the conclusion that occupational and other data relating to quality factors can be meaningfully used as inputs when a real output series exists for an industry.

The rather stringent criteria which Denison has established for permissible error in manpower input measures, the need for inter-dependency between input and output data, and the greater relia-bility of long-term measures cannot be ignored. But, if current interests and frequently legitimate policy questions pertaining to labor productivity are to be taken seriously, then compromises with less precise measures—a not unusual operational practice—may have to be made.

386

Concepts of Real Capital Stocks and Services

RICHARD AND NANCY RUGGLES
YALE UNIVERSITY

THE measurement of productivity is one of the major purposes for which real capital stocks and services data are developed. The very concept of productivity implies that the contribution to output that a factor makes can differ for reasons other than differences in the quantity of that factor. The separation of such influences from quantity changes requires the development of indexes of factor inputs in quantity terms, which can be studied in relation to changes in output also expressed in quantity terms. This paper will consider the concept of capital in this context.

But the requirements of other uses of concepts of capital stock and services must not be overlooked. In the first place, the measurement of output in real terms requires a determination of the quantity of capital produced. Capital formation not only provides for future input into the economic system; it is also a major component of gross national product and national income, and valid output indexes for the economy as a whole cannot be obtained without considering the method of measurement of the capital produced in different periods. Second, there are some purposes for which a measurement of real capital stocks and services is needed that is based upon the concept of capacity to produce. In the comparison of two different economies, for example, steel capacity may be a good indicator of the relative amount of real capital available in the two countries for the production of steel. For individual industries within countries, also, changes in capacity and in the utilization of capacity provide information relevant to questions of output, employment and investment decisions. And for the guidance of governments spending for social capital, a much wider concept of this sort is needed. Finally, the effort to obtain data in constant prices should not blind us to the large number of uses for which constant price data are not relevant. In the analysis of the flow of funds, the financing of capital formation and decisions with respect to investment, the amortizations and revaluations engaged in by business are the realities of the situation. Deflation or other adjustments aimed at deriving "real" data may obscure relationships which have an important bearing on decision-making in the economy.

The Quantity of Capital as a Concept for Productivity Measurement

The concepts involved in measuring the efficiency of capital as a factor of production can be traced back to the basic notions underlying the theory of the production function. In the simplest case, the process is quite straightforward. For example, land, one form of capital, is considered to be one factor of production, labor another factor, and output the result of efficient combinations of varying quantities of these factors. Such a textbook presentation assumes a given state of technical knowledge and constant qualities of land and a constant quality of labor. No time period is involved, and both factors can be measured in physical units. Land can be measured in acres and labor in man-hours. Such a production function can illustrate the principle of diminishing returns as one factor is increased and the other is held constant. It can also be used to determine whether there are constant returns to scale. There are no ambiguities in any of these concepts.

The introduction of differing qualities of a factor does not complicate the problem very much if quantity is measurable along with quality, and an unambiguous transformation of quality differences into quantity differences is possible. Thus if one piece of land is twice as good as another under all circumstances, the analyst can still study the relationship between land and output with varying amounts of labor. He has a choice of two procedures. Land can be expressed either on a straight acreage basis, or in terms of its equivalent in acreage of a constant quality. In the first case, its varying quality will influence the capital-output ratios derived, but for many problems it is precisely this relationship which the analyst wants to study. The second case can also yield interesting results. It does not necessarily preclude productivity change, nor does it necessarily imply constant returns to scale, any more than the initial example cited.

Unfortunately, an unambiguous translation of quality into quantity is not always possible. It is more likely that as differing intensities of labor are applied to two pieces of land of different quality, different ratios of relative output will emerge. In other words, the marginal rate of substitution of one kind of land for the other is different with different quantities of labor. This general point is raised by both Joan Robinson and R. M. Solow in their discussions of production functions and the measurement of capital.[1] This presents the first so-called

---

[1] Joan Robinson, "The Production Function and the Theory of Capital," *The Review of Economic Studies*, No. 55, p. 95. R. M. Solow, "The Production Function and the Theory of Capital," *The Review of Economic Studies*, No. 61, p. 101.

index number problem in the measurement of capital. If we try to include quality differences in the measurement of the quantity of capital we are saying that the quantity of a given item depends not only on the item itself but also on how much labor is used with it. Thus the scale by which capital is measured shifts at different points on the production function.

But our problems have just begun. In this simple example no passage of time has been allowed, and thus no technical changes can take place. Also, we still have available a physical measure of the quantity of capital. Since the concept of a physical measure of capital simplifies the analysis so much, economists naturally try to extend it as far as possible. Thus when they turn from the discussion of land to capital goods they tend to talk about identical machines which can be used in different quantities. Such a framework, however, cannot provide a satisfactory conceptual basis for capital measurement where physical measurement is not possible or where different kinds of capital are expressed in different physical units. The only recourse in these circumstances is to measure capital in some sort of comparable unit in the same way we measure output—in value terms.[2]

Given this sort of measurement, and still staying within a single time period, there are again two alternatives. First, we can measure capital in terms of input costs. This would mean that an item which costs twice as much to produce as another item is twice as much capital. In terms of the allocation of resources this might be satisfactory, but it leaves one incongruous result. It assumes that in the production of capital there are constant returns to scale, and in some cases this is at variance with common sense reasoning on the basis of physical units. For example, if two pipelines of a given diameter were laid together over a desert, the cost would be less than twice that of installing a single pipeline, due to the economies achieved by putting them in simultaneously. Thus, measured in cost terms the two pipelines are not twice as much capital as one pipeline, even though they function identically. The question here is whether economies in the production of capital goods should reduce the output of capital. Solely for the purpose of analyzing capital as an input, however, the cost basis of measurement would seem to be internally consistent. The second alternative would be to base the measurement of capital on its ability to produce, i.e., either on output or on capacity. But this method also involves problems. An index-number question arises if the marginal rates of substitution between different kinds of capital are different in the periods being compared. Furthermore—and this more seriously impairs the usefulness of this measure for the study of

[2] This point is taken up by Boulding in his paper for this conference.

389

efficiency—since actual capacity or output is used as the measure of quantity, there can never be any change in the productivity of capital. Whereas the first of these alternatives attributes all increase in efficiency to the change in the productivity of capital itself, the second goes to the opposite extreme, attributing the increased efficiency to the greater economy with which capital can be produced.

By introducing time (i.e., technical changes and changes in prices), additional problems are raised. It is commonly held that technical change in the design of capital equipment should not be incorporated into the measurement of the quantity of capital, since this again would be attributing all quality change to changes in the efficiency of producing capital, leading to a productivity index in the use of capital always equal to unity. But it is extremely difficult and often unrealistic to abstract from technical change, unless one goes all the way in the other direction, as in the first of the two alternatives in the preceding paragraph. Although it may be possible to estimate what the capital stock of 1900 would cost in today's prices if the techniques, labor skills, and materials of today were used to produce replicas of the buildings and machines of 1900, the reverse is not possible. The techniques, labor skills, and materials of 1900 could not produce perfect replicas of today's plant and equipment, since the necessary technical knowledge and equipment would be missing. Thus even though the problem can be stated in index-number terms it cannot really be solved in these terms, since comparisons can only be made in one direction. In order to get around this difficulty, it has been suggested that standard labor units expressed in terms of product be used to evaluate the cost of the capital stock in each period.[3] But this leads to the anomaly that two identical plants would be assigned different capital values if they were produced at different times, although at one moment of time they would have the same cost and the same capabilities.[4]

There does not seem to be any satisfactory general solution to this problem. The basic fact is that capital in general has no physical units, and any arbitrary solution will predetermine the answers. It will therefore be useful to examine the measurements of real capital stock that are currently being made or proposed to see what assumptions they involve, and how these assumptions affect the analysis which is based upon these figures.

[3] Robinson, *op. cit.* p. 86.
[4] Solow, *op. cit.*, p. 101.

The Rationale of Existing Measurements of Real Capital Stock

In a very stimulating paper presented at the 1953 Conference on Income and Wealth, Edward Denison set forth three possible methods of measuring capital.[5] The first measures capital by cost. The second measures it by the capacity of the system as a whole to produce output. The third measures it by the contribution which the capital specifically makes to total production. Denison strongly favors the first method. He feels that the second, which makes the stock of capital proportional to total output, is essentially uninteresting, although it might be feasible statistically if certain arbitrary conventions were adopted. The third method, which involves evaluating the contribution to production of each kind of capital good, he believes to be completely beyond any hope of accurate independent measurement. Furthermore, as has already been suggested, method 3 would necessarily lead to an unchanging productivity of capital. Thus Denison settles on the first method, which corresponds fairly well to the current practice of the Department of Commerce in measuring gross capital formation in constant prices.

Even the valuation of capital at cost, however, is not simple and straightforward. If the price of producing capital goods did not change over a period of years, the gross addition to the capital stock in any year would be equal to the value of gross capital formation in that year. Unfortunately, however, the price of producing capital goods does change, so a price index for capital goods is needed to deflate the current price data. It is in arriving at appropriate price deflators that the most difficult conceptual problems of this method become apparent.[6] Although Denison wishes to exclude from his index of the output of capital those quality changes in capital goods arising from such things as improvements in design and serviceability, he does not wish to exclude changes in productivity in the production of capital goods. Thus even though a machine can be produced in period 2 at half the price of the identical machine in period 1, the amount of capital represented by the machine should be the same in both periods. The price index for capital goods, therefore, should not be simply a weighted index of the prices of the inputs used to produce them. In practice this may be done in some areas (notably

[5] "Theoretical Aspects of Quality Change, Capital Consumption, and Net Capital Formation," in *Problems of Capital Formation*, Studies in Income and Wealth, Vol. 19, pp. 215–61.

[6] The problem is somewhat similar to that which would be involved in determining changes in quantities of labor used, given only wage bills in current prices and no direct knowledge of wage rates, man-hours, or employment.

construction, where the price deflator is a weighted index of labor and materials costs), but Denison considers this an unfortunate defect since the deflated data obscure the productivity changes that occur within the construction industry.

The crucial problem is the separation of design improvements from changes in the cost of production; that is, increases in productivity of capital goods from increases in productivity in the production of capital goods. Design improvement in capital equipment often occurs through simplification. Welding may take the place of riveting, plastic parts may be substituted for metal, or stampings may be used instead of machined parts. Whether these are in fact identical machines (to be counted as the same amount of capital) or different machines (to be counted as more or less capital) can only be determined on the basis of function. If with such changes the machine serves the same function, Denison would probably consider any associated cost changes to relate to the production of capital; i.e., the price index would change but the quantity of capital produced would not. On the other hand, if an increase in the cost of producing the machine were accompanied by improved functioning of the machine, Denison would allow these increased costs to be counted as increased capital because of changed technical specifications. In this case, the machine would be considered a different one representing more capital, and the price index for producing capital might remain unchanged.

The most ambiguous problem arises in a situation where changes in the design of a machine both reduce its cost and improve its functioning. One is then faced with two alternatives: (1) the cost of producing the machine has fallen, but the quantity of capital is unchanged, or (2) the cost is unchanged but the machine is now a different one that represents less capital. Thus if there is any change in the functioning of the machine, we are forced to decide whether or not it is still the same machine. This decision in turn determines the behavior of the price index for capital, and this in turn determines the measure of the quantity of capital produced. Resort to important physical or performance specifications cannot avoid the consideration of function, since it is this that determines what specifications are important. In fact, since specification changes are basically changes in quality—which we wish to exclude from our measure of the quantity of capital—strictly speaking even the most minor changes should require that the machine be treated as a different machine. Pushed to its logical end, this argument leads to the measurement of price behavior by prices of input factors, rather than prices of units of capital output. In practice, this has happened in the construction industry; the problem of identifying units of output has proved so difficult that an output price index is recognized as unsatisfactory, and estimates of construction prices are based upon input prices instead.[7]

It should be noted that the index-number problem arising from cost-reducing technical change is different from the normal index-number problem; the latter would exist even in absence of technical change in the cost of producing capital. The problem arises because, although we might now be able to reproduce exactly the products made in 1900, the reverse is not true. The valuation of the capital stock in 1958 as if it could have been produced in 1900 therefore necessarily involves the assumption that price indexes for the cost of capital based on those particular capital goods that are present in unchanged form in both 1900 and 1958 are representative for products which did change.[8] This assumption is of course quite likely to be invalid, because the newly introduced capital goods tend to be those for which the cost of production has fallen fastest. The price index based on 1900 would therefore be relatively too high, and the resulting quantity of capital too low. Similarly, taking 1958 as a base, goods which have disappeared since 1900 tend to be ones for which production costs did not fall as fast as for the new capital goods which supplanted them. Thus, while the index using 1958 as base year may be very different from that based on 1900, it too will minimize the increase in the efficiency of making capital goods.

A further consequence, as Denison points out, of adherence to the cost concept for measuring capital goods is that the principles of valuation that would be used for the output of capital goods are different from those commonly used for consumer goods. In measuring the volume of consumer goods we attempt, at least in theory, to include quality change as a part of output, where this measure of capital output tries to exclude it. Denison, however, is inclined to minimize the importance of this consideration. He suggests that quality change excluded from the measurement of capital goods will

[7] Although it is possible to ask what it would cost to construct some standard structure, this would bias the price index in several ways. First, different indexes of change would be obtained for different standard structures; the cost of building an 1890 Victorian house would have changed differently from that of a simple colonial house. Second, as long as construction methods are different there will be differences in supposedly identical structures, and the importance of these differences can only be evaluated in terms of function. For instance, handmade trim for houses differs from machine-milled trim in significant detail. If one asks how much it would cost, given the technology of 1900, to produce trim with the same specifications as today's machine-milled trim, the cost of obtaining the same degree of regularity, in terms of man-hours, might be exorbitant. It would only be because regularity is not considered a very important aspect of the function of house trim that one could consider machine-milled trim and handmade trim the same thing.

[8] The use of chained indexes, etc., would perhaps diminish the statistical magnitude of this problem, but it could not eliminate it.

eventually show up as additional production of consumer goods, and that as long as changes in the quality of other factors of production cannot be taken into account, neglecting such changes in measuring the output of capital goods scarcely seems a critical weakening of the income estimates. For the purpose of the measurement of efficiency, there is a good deal of merit in this argument, but, as will be pointed out below, the qualification becomes more important when we consider other uses to which these estimates of capital stock are put.

A final problem in the interpretation arises in estimating the net value of the capital stock. The measurement of the capital stock not only requires valuation of newly produced capital goods; it also requires consideration of what has happened to the existing stock of capital. Denison would value capital consumption at base year cost for the particular types of capital goods used up. He argues that obsolescence should be charged at the time the capital good is discarded, and that it should be handled as a deduction from gross capital formation rather than as an addition to capital consumption. His rationale is that "net capital formation"—the net improvement in the capital position of the economy—should be equal to the difference between (1) the contribution to production by the new good (as measured by its cost of production), and (2) the contribution which could have been made by the displaced capital good (as measured by the obsolescence charge).

On the other hand, a different treatment has been proposed by John Kendrick. He suggests:

"... as nonpermanent assets age, their contribution to net output declines; this is the result of declining gross output capacity, increasing maintenance and repair costs, and creeping obsolescence. Obsolescence results in the reduction in the rate of return on old equipment, not only when the installation of new equipment leads to reduced product prices or higher factor prices, but also when the old equipment is utilized less intensively or in less productive activities. Empirical and theoretical considerations suggest that these effects may be assumed to occur gradually over the lifetime of groups of capital equipment."[9]

It might be questioned, however, whether such considerations are relevant to the concept of capital discussed here. In view of the decision to exclude productivity improvement (i.e., increase in efficiency) from additions to the capital stock, it seems incongruous

9 John W. Kendrick, "Productivity Trends: Capital and Labor," *Review of Economics and Statistics*, August 1956, p. 250.

that decreases in the efficiency of existing capital due to aging should be so carefully taken into account. Just as there is logic in saying that improved design of capital good is not more capital but an increase in its efficiency, so also it is perfectly reasonable to say that the efficiency of capital varies with its age, and that deductions from the quantity of capital to make the productivity of existing capital a constant over its life are not consistent with the desired concept.

Furthermore, as Kendrick implies by his inclusion of "creeping obsolescence," the ordinary capital consumption allowance would considerably exceed the actual physical deterioration in a capital good over its useful life. Charging such obsolescence against existing capital is allowing for quality changes that have not occurred but are only expected to—those resulting from changes in the technical design of capital goods to be produced in the future. The same technical change that improves the quality of new capital will make the old obsolete. Kendrick's treatment of additions to the capital stock does not count the quality increase due to technical changes in new equipment, but it does take into account the reduction in the relative quality of the existing capital stock because of the increased technical efficiency of new capital equipment which could be constructed. Again, therefore, the treatment of new and old capital does not seem to be parallel.

A more consistent treatment would seem to require that if efficiency increases are to be eliminated from the measurement of the capital stock, efficiency decreases must also be eliminated. Capital should not be deducted from the total stock until its retirement, despite the fact that producers may, for financial reasons and in order to derive a meaningful profit figure, amortize it over its life. This procedure would carry Denison's method 1 a little farther, deriving net investment in each period as gross investment minus discards. Such a concept was used by Evsey Domar in discussing a model relating changes in capital to changes in capacity.[10]

To summarize, conventional measures of real capital favor a concept based on the cost of production rather than on capacity, partly because of ease of measurement and partly because one of the major purposes of developing real capital data is the analysis of productivity changes. "Cost," in these terms, is not simply the deflated value of the inputs; it is not intended that increased efficiency in the production of capital should reduce the amount of capital produced. This means that changes in the cost of producing capital must be analytically and statistically separated from changes in the efficiency

[10] "Depreciation, Replacement, and Growth," *Economic Journal*, March 1953, pp. 1–32.

of utilization of capital. Such a separation, however, requires a physically measurable unit of capital, and this in turn cannot be established without a consideration of the quality and function of capital equipment. Any attempt to separate quantity and quality without considering function is doomed to be arbitrary and subjective. It would perhaps be possible to derive a real capital measurement independently in terms of the quantity of input factors (labor, resources, and savings), but this approach does not appear to have much support.

Time and technical change also create problems in the interpretation of the conventional measures of real capital stock. The thesis that real capital can be measured by what it would cost in the base year to produce the given year's stock is not meaningful if technical changes make the comparison an impossibility. If the most recent year is chosen as the base year, the comparison may be possible, but this may also produce a trivial and uninteresting measurement. Finally, in evaluating the *net* capital stock, one may question the practice of deducting a capital consumption allowance before a capital good is actually retired from service. Such an allowance is in fact an attempt to measure the decrease in the quality of the equipment, whether from physical deterioration or from potential technical obsolescence. Such changes in quality are intended to be excluded from this concept of the quantity of capital.

The Use of Capital Stock Measurements

Despite these theoretical objections, one cannot help being impressed by the intrinsic interest of the real capital stock series that are obtained by the usual cost deflation procedures. For example, the capital-output ratios for manufacturing from 1880 to 1948 as given in Creamer's study are most illuminating and give rise to a number of hypotheses.[11] One may reasonably ask why these results are so interesting if their theoretical structure is built on such shifting sands. In part the answer may be given by Creamer's effective demonstration that a number of variants of measures of capital and output yield the same general conclusion as to the pattern of change in capital-output ratios over the years. Creamer points out, for example, that the pattern of change of the capital-output ratios derived by measuring both capital and output in constant prices does not differ very significantly from that for capital and output expressed in the current prices of each period separately. This result would be expected if the

[11] Daniel Creamer, *Capital and Output Trends in Manufacturing Industries, 1880–1948*, NBER, Occasional Paper No. 41, 1954.

price index used to deflate capital did not differ substantially from the price index used to deflate output. Relative to the other changes that occurred during the period, these differences in the price indexes were, in fact, rather small.

Some of the alternative measures discussed above might well yield quite different patterns of change. One cannot say how the ratio of capital to output would be affected in these instances. If the price deflator for capital had been based on the price indexes of input factors alone, not allowing for the change in efficiency in the production of capital, the price deflator would have been raised and thus gross capital formation over time lowered. On the other hand, deduction of retirements instead of an allowance for depreciation and obsolescence would probably increase the volume of the capital stock. If quality changes in consumer goods and perhaps capital goods were reflected more fully, output would have been larger throughout the period. The net effect on the pattern of change of the capital-output ratio is highly debatable. Capital-output ratios measured this way would not necessarily be more meaningful than Creamer's, but they might be less arbitrary and more internally consistent.

Furthermore, capital-output ratios based on current price data may also be quite meaningful, because they measure the capacity of the economy to produce in relation to its current efforts. An economy with a small capital-output ratio in this sense could turn out the equivalent of its capital stock in a brief space of time, whereas one with a high capital-output ratio would take many years to build up the capacity needed for the current level of output. By studying current relationships, the difficult problem of price deflation could be avoided. Most dynamic problems concerning capital and capital formation, furthermore, can more usefully be cast in current than in constant prices, since it is the actual flows of income and values in the various periods which are related in a time dimension.

Thus before we attempt to solve the problem of measuring real capital, we should face the question of how to measure capital stock at a given moment in the prices of a single period. This is not nearly as perplexing as the measurement of capital over time, since many of the index-number problems are absent. It is still true that a concept of capital that will be useful in the analysis of efficiency should probably not be measured in terms of capacity. Nevertheless, it would be useful to know what it would cost, given existing technology and capacity, to reproduce the *function* of the various capital goods existing in the economy. This does not require that products of another period be reproduced in their exact technological form, but rather brings into play the concepts of capacity, function, and substitutability. In a normally competitive economy, this reproduction cost of capital goods (in terms of economic function) would approximate market value, so that we could also ask how a given increment in the volume of capital, valued at the cost of production, would affect annual rates of output. The relationship between the stock of capital thus measured, in current prices, and the current output or income of the economy in various periods would be somewhat similar to Creamer's measurements in current prices. Thus changes in capital-output ratios over time could be calculated without the use of indexes of the quantity of capital or of output.

The Measurement of the Real Services of Capital

In the analysis of questions relating to the efficiency of capital, it is of course the services of the capital stock rather than the capital stock itself with which we are really concerned. Many analysts, however, use capital stock data, on the ground that, although the measurement of real capital stock is open to question, the measurement of the real services of capital is even more difficult. As Denison points out, in measuring real capital services, production cost is not available as a principle of valuation.[12] One is forced to evaluate capital consumption in terms of the ability of capital goods to contribute to production in the future. For this reason it seems necessary here also, before evaluating real capital services, to consider how the services of capital can be valued in current prices.

When a producer purchases a capital good he expects to use it over a given period. At the end of its useful life he expects that it will have repaid in services at least its original purchase price. The apportionment of the cost over this useful life is a matter for philosophers and revenue agents. It may be argued, for instance, that the machine should be charged off in a manner which would equalize profit over the period, given no unexpected changes in prices, demand, or costs. It is on this basis that peak load facilities of power plants and local transit systems are charged off against their period of use. Alternatively, it may be argued that the services of equipment are greater in its early life when it needs less repairs and maintenance and is utilized more fully. The essential consideration, in either case, is that expected returns be separated from unexpected returns in order to differentiate between operating income and capital gain or loss. If a plant burns down this should be a capital loss, and not a charge against the operating income of the plant in the year it happens. Similarly,

12 Denison, *op. cit.*, p. 241.

unexpected obsolescence, or unexpected capital gain in monetary terms due to general price level rises, should be excluded from current services of capital and reflected instead as capital gain or loss. The services of capital thus should be valued (in current price terms) not in terms of original or historical cost but rather in terms of replacement cost, and the difference between historical cost and replacement cost should be considered capital gain or loss.

A problem does arise in relation to gains arising from expected price level changes, but even here it seems reasonable to distinguish operating income from the gain or loss arising from the producer's dealing in assets and liabilities. We follow this practice in national income statistics in adjusting the income concepts for inventory price changes, and it seems reasonable to make a similar adjustment with regard to capital consumption allowances.[13]

The problem of converting capital services in current prices to capital services in constant prices is not simple. The same dilemma in the construction of a price index faces us here as in the measurement of real capital stock. To include all quality changes as changes in the quantity of capital is to make the resulting index meaningless for the measurement of productive efficiency. On the other hand, the attempt to eliminate those quality changes due to the technical design of capital and to retain those due to changes in the efficiency of production of capital and in its economic usefulness leads to serious difficulties. Of course, if the index for deflating capital services is about equal to the GNP deflator (as seems to be the case in the actual calculations) the relationship between capital services and output in constant prices will be the same as that in the current price data. The results of such a calculation, therefore, may not be meaningless, but what they will reflect will be the relationships in the current price data.

Capital Goods Production as a Component of Output

In recent years the gross national product has steadily increased in favor as a measure of total output, and gross capital formation is a major component of GNP. In the valuation of capital formation as a component of output, certain problems arise in addition to those considered above.

Thus far in the discussion, we have considered only those forms of capital which have market value, and have been content to consider social capital in general as part of the setting within which

[13] See, for example, *The National Economic Accounts of the United States.* Hearings before the Subcommittee on Economic Statistics of the Joint Economic Committee, October 29 and 30, 1957, especially pp. 189–93, 153, and appendix tables A-1, A-11, and A-13.

self-liquidating capital is placed. It has long been argued, however, that certain government expenditures are of the nature of capital, and should be included in any general measure of capital formation. Such a procedure would result in (a) shifting some items from current government expenditures to gross capital formation, and (b) including the services of government capital on the expenditure side as part of product and on the income side as an addition to capital consumption allowances.[14]

In the most obvious case, where government enterprises sell their products on the market, such arguments are very persuasive; the form of industrial organization should make no difference in computing gross capital formation. In these cases the government has produced an asset which, like privately held assets, yields a stream of money income for future periods, and the parallel with the private producer is complete. The government may make a loss in the operation of the enterprise, but this situation is no different from the case where the government subsidizes a private industry. The extension of the argument to non-self-liquidating expenditures of the government on hard goods (i.e., goods made of wood, steel, or concrete) is less clear, however. This procedure would include roads and other public works as gross capital formation. To the extent that such assets are in fact directly revenue producing (other than by taxes) and it can be determined whether or not they are paying for themselves, such a procedure is legitimate. Thus toll roads might well be considered part of gross capital formation. Government buildings also could be set up as a sort of government enterprise, charging each agency rent at appropriate market values for the space it occupies, thus treating government buildings much in the same way that owner-occupied housing is. This has, in fact, often been suggested as a desirable budgetary reform.

On the other hand, the argument is much less clear for other government expenditures on durable goods. There seems little reason to treat non-self-liquidating roads and public works differently from government expenditures on research, education, and public health, all of which also improve the amount of social capital available in the economy. The fact that an expenditure is embodied in physically durable materials is not really relevant, and there would be considerable disadvantage in trying to develop a concept of government capital formation which covered all improvements in social capital, since this is a question not of objective fact but of political philosophy.

[14] It can be argued alternatively, with respect to government enterprises but not to general government, that the services of government enterprise capital goods should not be added to the market value of output but, instead, the surplus of government enterprises should be reduced by the amount of capital consumption taking place.

Expenditures by business on research and development, unlike those by government, are treated in the national income statistics as intermediate products, and so do not add to final product. Such expenditures are becoming increasingly important in changing the setting within which the economy operates, and they are not fully reflected in the changing market value of assets which are counted in output. It would seem highly desirable, therefore, to include research and development in the list of final expenditures on goods and services, even if we exclude it from the concept of gross capital formation. It could, for instance, be carried as a separate item of current expenditure.

Another serious omission from the list of final expenditures is the amount which producers spend on current account for the repair and maintenance of existing capital stock. If these expenditures were constant or were proportional to output this omission would not be serious, but in fact they vary considerably over time. When producers are making high profits they often take that opportunity to refurbish their plant and equipment. Conversely, in periods when they are having difficulty in paying dividends or even in meeting payrolls, they may postpone maintenance and repair expenditures. In the housing industry this cyclical fluctuation in repair and maintenance is well known. By omitting changes in repair and maintenance from our measure of gross production we may be neglecting something that is just as important as changes in inventories. Overmaintenance unquestionably adds to the value of the capital stock, and undermaintenance reduces it.

In view of the importance of these two elements—research and development expenditures and repair and maintenance expenditures —serious consideration might be given to the development of a grosser concept of total output than we now have. This need not mean altering the present concept of GNP, but perhaps we could include information on research and development and repair and maintenance in a grosser concept of output which we might term "gross national expenditure."

In deriving indexes of real output of capital from the measure of output in current prices (however the latter is defined), many of the problems of deflation considered above are still relevant. If we adopt the solution proposed by Denison, changes in the quality of capital goods would be excluded from output. Output of capital goods would therefore be measured quite differently from that of consumer goods. If we are trying in measuring output to approach some sort of welfare index, it seems reasonable to argue that the well-being of a nation is related to its ability to sustain or raise its standard of living in the

401

future, and that omitting the quality change in a nation's productive facilities drastically understates its real progress in this respect. Especially in the case of underdeveloped countries, where a great deal of effort is being put into developing productive capacity, a measure which grossly understates the change in this dimension does considerable violence to the basic purposes of the measurement.

As a final point in the discussion of capital as a component of output, consideration must be given to the derivation of net, as opposed to gross, product. The concept of net product is commonly assumed to be based upon the principle of keeping capital in some sense intact. But there are ambiguities in this concept too. In the first place, if real capital is measured by the cost method, the conventional concept of keeping capital intact is inapplicable. However, as Denison points out, from many points of view the concept of net product remains interesting and meaningful. Second, if, as suggested above, we extend the concept of gross investment to include repair and upkeep, it is necessary to consider the various levels of both maintenance and replacement required to maintain productive efficiency. But there is no unique level that will "maintain capital intact." Finally, a concept of real capital which includes reductions in the relative quality of existing capital (obsolescence) but does not include increases in the quality of additions to capital does not appear to be internally consistent. As Domar has pointed out, our concept of net capital formation as it has conventionally been handled assumes that depreciation equals replacement, and to the extent that this is not true models based upon such a thesis may not be fully relevant to the questions they are designed to answer.[15]

Capital and the Measurement of Capacity

Denison rejected his method 2—measuring capital by capacity—not only because it made the concept of productivity of capital tautological but also because it posed serious problems of measurement. There are many circumstances, however, in which capacity is an extremely useful tool of analysis. Industry studies have long worried about capital coefficients, asking what amount of capital would be required, with existing technology, to obtain a given increase in capacity. Such studies are important for problems of economic development and for developing the capital portion of input-output matrixes. They are also useful in analyzing the effect of a change in demand for specific products on the capital goods industries. For growth models, also, capacity measurements are extremely important

[15] *Op. cit.*, footnote 10.

since such models involve an estimation of the impact of an increment of saving and investment on the future stream of income, saving, and investment. Recently, capacity measurements have also been used in analyzing short-run fluctuations in income and employment. The underutilization of capacity for the economy as a whole has serious repercussions on the level of investment, which in turn affects the level of income and employment. Both private and government agencies are now engaged in making capacity estimates for various parts of the economy, and in view of the obvious usefulness of capacity as a basic concept in economics, it does not seem reasonable to suggest that efforts to obtain better capacity figures should be abandoned.

This does not, of course, mean that changes in capacity can be identified directly with what we have considered to be capital formation in this paper. Changes in capacity also can result from such things as research and development expenditures, government expenditures on education and health, and other expenditures which may carry with them a social product conducive to quality improvement.

Financial Flows and Integrated Economic Accounting

Before concluding this discussion, attention should be drawn once again to the desirability, in any measure of capital stocks and services, of maintaining consistency and comparability with other forms of economic accounting. In studying the financing of capital formation, for instance, it would be useful if capital formation were measured in such a way that it could be assigned directly to decision-making units and financing institutions, so that financial flows and real output could be related to one another empirically as well as theoretically. There are no serious conceptual problems standing in the way of such an integration. The measurement of the capital stock could very well be embodied in the national balance sheets developed for various institutional sectors of the economy. These balance sheets in order to be useful in studying financial flows, must of necessity extend beyond the concept of national wealth (the capital stock), embracing in addition the financial assets and liabilities held by each sector, but this poses no special problems of integration. The objective of valuing capital in current prices set forth above could be met simultaneously with the maintenance of a record of actual historical financial flows, by carrying assets on each of the balance sheets at market value but showing in addition both realized and unrealized capital gains and losses.

403

COMMENT

EVSEY D. DOMAR, Massachusetts Institute of Technology

My strongest reactions to the Ruggleses' paper were feelings of relief for having been spared myself, and of gratitude to them (if a paper on this subject had to be written) for having done the job. For the Ruggleses' theory of capital measurement grew in soil where harvests, at least in recent years, have been meager in relation to the effort and ability of the workers.[1] An attempt to work out the definition of the capital stock in general seems to me hopeless. But several useful definitions can be designed, each to fit a particular problem.

This conclusion is reached sooner or later in most aggregations of heterogeneous items. If we were satisfied with a microstudy of industrial processes, engineering specifications would be required of the various pieces of participating capital (including their age, condition, etc.) but not with their aggregate value in real or money terms, at original or replacement cost. But so much disaggregation might overwhelm even the most microminded economist.

As an object for aggregation, capital possesses several particularly nasty attributes:

1. Longevity, so that aggregation involves items of different vintage, bought at different prices and produced under different technological conditions.

2. Impermanency, hence the depreciation and replacement problems.

3. Technological change, both in its production and in the quality of the finished product. The second attribute is particularly important because new capital is a major source of technological change in industries where it is an input.

4. Future income. This affects both its cost of production and, of course, its present value.

5. A limited secondhand market (most examples usually consist of automobiles, trucks, and farm machinery) with an unhealthy fondness for brand-new items. Evaluation of the existing stock of capital is therefore of limited use.

But why bemoan the defects of capital? Labor also possesses longevity but not permanency, and is also subject to depreciation (as

---

[1] This is true even of the fine paper given by Edward F. Denison on "Theoretical Aspects of Quality Change, Capital Consumption, and Net Capital Formation," given at this Conference five years ago (Volume Nineteen, pp. 215–61), and also of Joan Robinson's *The Accumulation of Capital* (London, 1956), and a paper by J. R. Hicks on "The Relation Between the Measurement of Capital and the Measurement of Other Economic Aggregates" delivered at a meeting of the International Economic Association in Corfu, Greece, September 4–11, 1958.

shown by the life cycle of earnings in various occupations) and retirement. The cost of its training, let alone of reproduction and upbringing, also changes. The heterogeneity of labor is striking; it is also a source of future income.

All these difficulties do not prevent our labor friends from merrily aggregating man-hours among industries and over time. They are, it is true, helped by several circumstances, unfortunately not available to students of capital. The first is the feeling of shame which would arise if they began depreciating the labor force (including themselves), treating labor merely as a source of earning power. The second is the well developed and evidently reliable secondhand market for labor. While some companies prefer to buy brand-new college graduates, used labor carries no stigma (unless the person changes jobs too often), and with some exceptions is thought to be more valuable than new. For that matter, the secondhand labor market is practically the only one there is; the wages it sets are not questioned, which relieves labor statisticians of having to estimate the value of labor power. They don't even try to evaluate the existing stock of labor. But perhaps we can take a lesson from them and try to minimize the use of the stock of capital. For many problems only increments in the capital stock are needed. Why then not leave the devil alone whenever possible?

But if the stock of capital must be measured, let me suggest two thoroughly unoriginal approaches. The first would define the problem with some precision, and then select the proper definition of capital. Thus for one type of production function it may be desirable to eliminate changes in the quality of capital itself; for another this painful method may not be needed. Similarly, if the stock of capital is treated as a source of future productive power, depreciation of a one-hoss shay should be deducted, even if this wonderful instrument is equally useful to its very end. But from the capital productivity point of view, no such change should be made.

The second approach is even more pragmatic. Let us take existing figures, manipulate them, and then look around for suitable uses for them. Here are a few examples.

1. The stock of capital at original value of acquisition (not necessarily new), with or without depreciation. This will not do for estimates of capital productivity, but it is a standard measure of capital in accounting, financial, and legal circles.

2. The stock of capital deflated by a price index of inputs. Technological progress either in the production or in the quality of capital goods is not eliminated (though much will depend on the definition of

405

the inputs). For the study of capital productivity this concept may not be useful, but it can estimate the magnitude of social effort going into capital formation.

3. The stock of capital deflated by the price index of capital goods (Denison's method 1).[2] This would eliminate changes in the production of capital goods, but not in the quality of capital goods themselves.

Both methods 2 and 3 have their place in the evaluation of Soviet capital formation, as an example. The fraction of Soviet gross national produce, expressed in current prices, invested in the interwar period was 20 to 25 per cent. Prices of capital goods, however, were rising less rapidly than other prices. Hence if each sector of gross national product were deflated by its own price index (method 3), the fraction of Soviet product invested would be much higher.[3] Capital formation as a source of productive capacity can be estimated more meaningfully by method 3, but as a measure of effort or sacrifice method 2 is proper, though I wish that investment were charged with the cost of technological progress (education, training, and research) from which Soviet capital formation benefited more than any other sector of the Soviet economy.

4. Stock of capital deflated by a price index in which quality changes of capital itself have been accounted for. The result would be a "pure" input of capital, very useful from the productivity point of view, but as shown by Denison, quality changes are hard to define, let alone measure.[4]

5. Capital stock as an inventory, in which new goods are weighted more heavily than old ones. The proper weighting could take care of almost anything, including technological change, depreciation, and obsolescence, but where would these weights come from? A well developed second-hand market could give a set of weights, but in its absence (is it really as bad as we usually think?) this method remains merely a good wish. This is unfortunate, because, among other things, it could give a good estimate of the stock of capital as a source of future earning power.

There must be many other examples. Instead of citing them, let me mention only three fields in which further research seems desirable.

1. Evaluation of publicly owned capital. Comparisons with privately owned capital can be misleading. A new highway saving transportation cost will appear in such a comparison as an increase in

[2] Denison, *op. cit.*, pp. 222–7.
[3] See my *Essays in the Theory of Economic Growth* (New York, 1957), pp. 236–40.
[4] Denison, *op. cit.*, pp. 217–22.

the productivity, while in reality it is merely an increase in capital input.

2. Investigation of the role played by current capital formation in the introduction of technological change.

3. Investigation of the accumulation and use of knowledge, that is of research, education, and training (but not necessarily of economics of education).

MILTON GILBERT, Organization for European Economic Cooperation

The Ruggleses have carefully probed the conceptual difficulties of measuring the stock of real capital. I feel they have left a few matters unclear, however, and would like to make some points which I hope they will find acceptable.

The stock of capital consists of a variety of goods (and structures) produced over a series of years, during which prices have changed. The only way to measure this stock in real terms is to view the goods as a series of outputs that must be combined by the same rationale and the same procedures used in constructing any index of real product. Of course, the annual figures for the real capital stock are aggregated, while the indexes of production are expressed as relatives, but they are still conceptually the same.

Also, there is no conceptual alternative to this index of production approach for measuring the total stock of capital; what may seem like alternatives are either meaningless or impossible.

A measure derived from inputs of factors of production is not possible because quantity units for all the factors of production cannot be conceived of. This would be similar to trying to deflate the national income by distributive shares independently of output; it cannot be done, and not merely because of lack of data.

A measure derived independently on the basis of output, such as by making the stock of capital proportional to total output, is by definition not a measure of capital at all, but only a measure of output.

A measure in terms of capacity, while it may yield interesting information for particular industries, is not possible for total capital. There is no common denominator for adding up the parts, even assuming that it can be applied to all categories of capital goods separately.

In the index number approach, the data needed are quantities (or quantity indicators) of the various kinds of goods and unit value or price weights for combining the quantity data. Quantities often have to be determined indirectly as a practical matter—by deflating current value figures with an appropriate price index or by using material input as an indicator of the quantity of output. These tricks, however, do not change the conceptual basis of the process. In fact, if the

407

quantities are known, as in the Ruggleses' pipeline example, that settles the matter. In that example, two pipelines must be taken as twice as much quantity as one pipeline. If it costs less per unit to construct two than one, this can only affect the price weight, not the quantity indicator.

In this connection, cost and price at the time of production are the same thing; differences between cost and market are only significant for different periods of time.[1] Furthermore, the unit cost or price weight must be taken as the average for all the units produced. Prices for identical units may differ because of market inperfections, trade practices with regard to quantity discounts, differences in mark-ups for different kinds of outlets, etc. But this can affect only the average price weight, not the quantity indicator.

The crux of the Ruggleses' argument is that capital in general, presumably because of technological changes, has no physical units, and that any arbitrary solution will predetermine the result. It is always possible to reach this dead end by focusing attention on the worst cases, that is, new products—and equally so for consumption goods as for capital goods. But it seems to me that quantity units can be established for a very wide variety of capital goods, enough to make a production index (or a capital stock measure) possible. Locomotives, freight cars, trucks, ships, motors, standard machine tools, textile machinery of various kinds, office buildings, standard factory space, dwelling units of various categories, thermal electricity capacity, hydro-electricity capacity, blast furnaces, etc., all have recognizable quantity units. The real problem is to adjust for quality changes, and this becomes possible once it is recognized, as I believe it is by the Ruggleses, that quality improvements arising from better knowledge, but not requiring increased costs, cannot be given an economic value and therefore cannot be included in a quantity index or aggregate. The rest is a matter of data and statistical estimation. In the end, one will obtain some number of quantity indicators covering some percentage of the universe. It is only at that point that one can say whether a meaningful measure for the total is possible. And it usually is.

The Ruggleses are disturbed by the fact that it may not be possible to compute Laspeyres as well as Paasche indexes over a long period of time because the new products of the current period may not be able to be priced in the earlier period. I mentioned the same problem in comparisons between developed and underdeveloped countries, and am in favor of making comparisons with more than one set of weights whenever possible. However, to conclude with the Ruggleses that

---

[1] I am referring to "cost or market" as bases for valuation—not to factor costs or market prices as alternative price weights.

using only current weights may produce a trivial and uninteresting measurement seems extreme.

The Ruggleses may be right in their view that the gross capital stock will correlate better with output than the net. This is an empirical question and to answer it one needs both the net and gross figures.

Finally, I must insist that current price data alone will not do. This illusion seems reasonable sometimes when prices are not moving much. But as soon as prices move significantly, we distrust every inference made from the data unless we feel we know the distortion introduced by changing prices.

G. WARREN NUTTER, University of Virginia

I disagree with the Ruggleses' argument that depreciation of capital should be ignored if improvements in quality are also ignored. The rationale in weighting capital at base-year cost is that capital should be standardized in efficiency units of the base year. Unit costs in the base year are assumed to measure both cost and efficiency: there is an implicit assumption of competitive equilibrium. New capital items should be expressed only in base-year efficiency equivalents, and this is done by translating the new item into an equivalent number of base-year items that could have been produced at base-year costs. The point of this exercise—leaving aside the technical difficulties—is to keep the capital stock from reflecting changes in efficiency of *existing* capital. Depreciation should certainly be deducted as it occurs, though obsolescence should be charged only on replacement of the obsolete item. On this matter, Denison seems to be entirely correct; Kendrick and the Ruggleses seem to be half wrong—taken together, I suppose entirely wrong, since each is wrong about the other half.

On a more trivial matter, I am not swayed by the reasons given for the relevance of capital-output ratios in current prices. I don't see the usefulness of such estimates of periods of production, since they all depend on a stable technology, constant returns to scale, and so on. Calculation of capital-output ratios is useful in showing that they are not very useful.

EDWARD F. DENISON, Committee for Economic Development

Richard and Nancy Ruggleses' instructive article treats most generously the paper I presented to this Conference in 1953. Although they appear to agree with most of my analysis, they do reach some quite different conclusions or judgments upon which I should like to comment.

I find puzzling their sharp distinction between the difficulties of estimating the current value of the capital stock and capital consumption and those of estimating constant dollar series for the same items.

It is true, as they note, that the current value of the capital stock can be construed as its market value—if one can forget all the valuation problems associated with lack of organized markets, transfer costs, and specialization and indivisibility of capital goods—but a method of establishing the current market value of the capital stock directly is yet to be found, and the authors suggest none. Unless market value can be estimated directly, some variant of the perpetual inventory method is necessary, and the problem of estimating current value for any year is identical with that of obtaining deflated series in prices of the same year. Both involve trying to get some common denominator between capital produced this year and that produced in all prior years. Further, the constant dollar series that corresponds to a market valuation of current value is a method 3 solution in the terminology of my 1953 article, which I think the authors agree is the most difficult of all to apply.

While present methods of measuring capital stocks or services are certainly crude, the authors' appraisal of them, when they are construed as measuring capital in terms of base-year cost, seems unduly harsh. Also, the criticism that only a recent-year base can be used seems only moderately disturbing. In practice, deflated series are *usually* presented only on a recent-year base. I wonder whether the authors might have been less critical if they agreed that a flight to current-dollar comparisons provides no escape from the problems of equating capital goods produced at different times.

The recommendation to substitute retirements for capital consumption in measuring the net capital stock, while correct with respect to obsolescence and perhaps tenable with respect to deterioration in the quality of services provided, does not meet the problem of the simple exhaustion of service life. I don't see how this can be ignored in measurement of net capital formation. The authors appear to reach their position as a result of the rejection of the argument that the ratio between output and capital consumption, not output and the capital stock, is the one that would be expected to have some degree of regularity and is relevant for the measurement of productivity or capital capacity. The reason given for preferring the gross capital stock to capital consumption for these uses—that it is less difficult to measure—is not persuasive since the movements of the two series usually differ only because of changes in average service life. For measurement of net capital formation, capital consumption appears clearly to be the appropriate offset to gross capital formation.

I continue to have doubts as to the meaning of capacity (as measured by capital stock or capital consumption) for the economy as a whole. Capital capacity, in terms of physical units of output, makes sense for a single plant or product in some few highly capitalized, mostly continuous-process, industries. But I don't see the sense of adding up capital stock figures, in dollar terms, to obtain the "capacity" of the economy. And if one did do so, I should think he would add up the values of the products that could be produced with existing capital, not the capital stock figures, since capital-output ratios vary so widely among industries. But in reality the capacity of an economy has real meaning only in terms of all the factors of production available to it, and measurement is best approached in terms of the national income or product. If a single-factor measure of under- or overutilization of the capacity of the economy is essential, it seems to me that labor force and hours data are much more appropriate, since for the economy as a whole labor probably provides the limiting factor on total output at any point in time and is much more transferable. I find it hard to reconcile the authors' relative enthusiasm for the amorphous capacity concept with their disparagement of the capital stock estimates of the type now being prepared.

An Appraisal of Long-Term Capital Estimates: Some Reference Notes

DANIEL CREAMER
NATIONAL INDUSTRIAL CONFERENCE BOARD

JUST as the quality and character of wealth and capital estimates are limited by available data, so is their appraisal. One facet of an appraisal, for example, would compare the concept demanded by theory with the concept that is actually measured. However, I think that the theorists have not provided a fully formulated set of concepts that could test the concepts underlying the capital estimates. If these questions are difficult for the theorists, as Boulding states, how much more so for a worker in the empirical vineyard. So I shall not attempt this aspect of an appraisal.

Other facets of an appraisal would indicate how well the estimates measure what they purport to; whether there is agreement between estimates of the same concept and industrial scope, but independently arrived at; and, lastly, whether the indications of the estimates appear to be reasonable. A comprehensive discussion of all three facets is beyond our resources. We have chosen instead to restrict the discussion primarily to explorations of the first two. Moreover, we have not examined all wealth estimates for the U.S. economy but only those sector estimates prepared for the NBER in the course of its investigations into "Trends in Capital Formation and Financing."

One of the research objectives of the NBER in this area is to provide some building blocks for those in need of long-term series of capital estimates, either by industry sectors or for the entire economy. The contents of the estimates must be known before a judgment can be made as to whether the sector estimates may be added to reach larger aggregates and whether a sector estimate is sufficiently independent in terms of data and methodology to be checked against another estimate of the same sector. The annotations that follow are meant to provide a basis for these judgments.

A major part of the NBER's program in this area has been concerned with the development of capital estimates for those sectors of the economy that have been large demanders of capital; viz., agriculture, mining and manufactures, the regulated industries (transportation, communications, and public utilities), and nonfarm residential

413

real estate. Each is the subject of a monograph and it is the estimates in these four monographs that are described here.[1]

Wealth Estimates for Agriculture

These estimates were prepared by Alvin S. Tostlebe and presented in his monograph, *Capital in Agriculture: Its Formation and Financing Since 1870* (Princeton University Press, 1957).

Period Covered: 1870 through 1950. Restricted to years covered by the Census of Agriculture: 1870 and decennially until 1920 and quinquennially thereafter to 1950.

Definition of Agriculture: Agriculture is the aggregate of all farms and a farm is defined as it is in the Census of Agriculture. Despite an essentially similar definition of a farm throughout the eighty-year span, there was nevertheless enough variation in minor aspects of the definition, in instructions, and in interpretations, judgment, and zeal on the part of enumerators and their supervisors so that the count of small farms probably varied considerably more than their actual number from census to census, and from one region to another in the same year.

"As most of the error was in the enumeration of the smallest farms, the effect on the comparability of acreage, value of real estate, machinery, livestock, and production was far less serious than on number of farms. Except for number of farms, the damage to comparability was perhaps not very significant, at least insofar as national and regional totals are concerned" (p. 42).

Definition of Capital: Financial and physical capital used in farming.

a. Financial capital is the working balances of currency and demand deposits held by farmers. Estimates for years before 1900 are not presented.

b. Physical capital is the sum of farm land and buildings, including farm residence; implements and machinery, including automobiles, motor trucks, and tractors; and livestock and stored crops. Excluded are inventories of mill feed, insecticides or other supplies that farmers may have on hand.

Wealth Components Estimated:

a. Financial capital: Separate estimates for currency beginning with 1900 and demand bank deposits beginning with 1925.

[1] The monograph on agriculture and the one on nonfarm residential real estate have already been published. The other monographs in this series probably will appear in 1959 or 1960. Much of the description is in the words of the authors, although quotation marks are seldom used.

b. Physical capital: Separate estimates for land, buildings, implements and machinery, livestock (with a separate estimate for horses and mules), and crop inventories.

Estimates of each component of physical capital are presented for the United States and for each of ten regions comprised of arrangements of states frequently used by the Bureau of Agricultural Economics to emphasize type of farming. The following regions are distinguished: Northeast, Appalachian, Southeast, Lake States, Corn Belt, Delta States, Great Plains, Texas-Oklahoma, and Mountain and Pacific.

Price Valuation in Source: Current prices.

Sources of Basic Data and Method of Estimation:

a. Physical capital: The value in current prices of the two major classes of physical assets—land and buildings, and implements and machinery—were obtained by states from published reports of the Census of Agriculture.

The values of livestock in current prices were, with minor exceptions, obtained from published reports of the BAE. The census has regularly reported the number and value of various classes of livestock on farms, but as successive enumerations occurred at various times of the year, the data are not really comparable. The BAE's published estimates for January 1 of each year are therefore much to be preferred.

The values of crops stored on farms, in current prices, were estimated by the author in the following fashion: the census figure for the amount of crops produced in the year preceding the census was multiplied by factors relating production to the amount stored at the beginning of the following year. Estimates were made for years for which both types of data were available.

b. Financial capital: Estimates of currency for 1900–40 are taken from R. W. Goldsmith, *A Study of Savings in the United States, 1897–1949* (Princeton University Press, 1954); for 1945 and 1950 from *Balance Sheet of Agriculture*, Department of Agriculture, 1953.

Estimates of bank deposits for 1900-20 from Goldsmith, *op. cit.*; for 1925-35 from *Impact of the War on the Financial Structure of Agriculture*, Department of Agriculture, 1945; for 1940–50 from *Balance Sheet of Agriculture, 1953, op. cit.*

Adjustments for Price Changes:

a. *Reference base:* Average prices 1910–14 for national and state total; for comparative purposes and for national total only the value of physical assets are shown also in 1929 prices.

415

b. *Components of capital shown in constant prices:* Same components as are shown in current prices.

c. *Derivation of physical assets:*

1. Land: For each state the procedure consisted of multiplying the estimated 1910–14 prices of improved and unimproved land by census-reported acreage of each type. This was worked out separately for the thirty-seven humid states and for the eleven western states for which additional distinctions were made involving irrigated, dry-farming, and grazing land.

2. Farm buildings: Before 1900, the value of farm buildings was not reported separately in the census. To estimate constant price values of farm buildings for 1870, 1880, and 1890, it was assumed that the physical inventory of buildings per farm in each state was the same in each of the three preceding census years as it was in 1900. The value of buildings per farm in each state as reported in the 1900 census was multiplied by the number of farms in the state in 1870, 1880, and 1890.[2] These values, together with those reported in the 1900 census, were then raised 26 per cent, an adjustment indicated by the rise in cost of construction on farms from 1900 to 1910–14.

The values of farm buildings for the census years 1910–50, calculated in 1910 prices by the BAE, were raised 1 per cent to place them on the 1910–14 level. This slight increase was suggested by the BAE's farm construction cost indexes. In calculating the value of farm buildings, the BAE started with the value of buildings reported in the 1910 census and extended the series by adding each year expenditures on buildings, wells, windmills, and fences, and subtracting depreciation, each in terms of 1910 prices. Rates of depreciation, based on average length of life, are 3.6 per cent for operators' dwellings and 6 per cent for other farm structures.

3. Implements and machinery: Current values reported in the census divided by an index of prices paid by farmers for machinery. Latter compiled by the BAE beginning with 1910. This is extended backward by linking with F. C. Mills' "Index of Wholesale Prices of Processed Goods Entering into Capital Equipment," which in turn is

---

[2] This may have resulted in some overstatement of the physical inventory of buildings for the earlier years, especially in regions that were relatively newly settled in 1870. In these areas it is likely that some service buildings were added on established farms, or that some smaller temporary buildings gave way to larger, more substantial ones. On the other hand, such additions and improvements were probably somewhat restricted before 1900 because of the persistent and general decline in the prices of farm products that characterized most of the period. Depreciation of farm buildings usually exceeds expenditure on construction and repair during periods of agricultural depression. If an overstatement of the physical inventory has resulted from the method used, it is believed to be small.

linked with Warren and Pearson wholesale price indexes of metal and metal products and lumber.

4. Livestock and crop inventories: Each crop and class of livestock is multiplied by the average price per unit on (or near) January 1 of the years 1910–14 by the number of units in the inventory at the beginning of the census years 1870 to 1950.

d. *Cash working balances:* The total of currency and demand deposits divided by the BAE's index of prices paid, interest, taxes, and wage rates (1910–14 = 100).

The Tostlebe estimate in current prices is based essentially on values reported by the owners of capital—in effect, a balance sheet approach. There is another series of estimates for agriculture prepared by Raymond Goldsmith and published in *A Study of Savings in the United States*, Volume 3. The latter approach is that of accumulated gross annual capital expenditures adjusted for capital consumption. The two estimates, however, are not completely independent, despite the difference in approach. Both are based on data compiled by the Census of Agriculture and the BAE. And in many of the annual series of the latter the level is established by the census enumerations. The difference in approach, however, is sufficient to justify a comparison of the two estimates (see Tables 1 and 2).

For the beginning of this century the two totals of reproducible tangible assets including land in current prices differ by less than 8 per cent and for 1945, the last year the two can be compared, by slightly more than 8 per cent—the Tostlebe estimate being smaller at both benchmarks. The largest difference among the four benchmark estimates was 12 per cent for 1930, with the Tostlebe estimate being the larger one. As one might expect, the differences are far larger—as much as one-third—in some of the components and neither estimate is consistently higher or lower. It may be inferred from this that at least there has been no accumulation of systematic bias.

Expressing the estimates in 1929 prices increases the difference in the case of farm real estate and crop inventories but sharply reduces the differences of the livestock estimates. It also substantially reduces the differences of total reproducible tangible assets.[3] One would characterize the rate of growth in real farm capital over the present century in much the same terms whether one used Tostlebe's estimate

[3] It is pointless to make this comparison for producers' durable goods used in agriculture since I deflated Goldsmith's estimate of this component in current prices by the implicit price index used by Tostlebe for this component. The justification for this is my failure to find this estimate in Goldsmith's volume—it would be rash to say that it is not there—and the evidence that both used the same BAE indexes beginning with 1910 and the extension to earlier years was based on similar but not identical indexes.

TABLE 1

Ratio of Wealth Estimates for Agriculture Prepared by Tostlebe (T) to those Prepared by Goldsmith (G), by Type of Assets, 1900-45

	Farm Structure T/G	Land T/G	Farm Real Estate T/G	Producers' Durables T/G	Livestock T/G	Crop Inventories T/G	Total Reproducible Tangible Assets T/G	Total Reproducible Assets Excluding Producers Durables T/G
	BASED ON ESTIMATES IN CURRENT PRICES							
1900	1.090	.898	.933	.641	.966	.978	.926	.941
1910	1.199	.964	1.000		.931	.966		.989
1920	.752	1.096	1.015		1.329	1.285		1.057
1925	.941	1.017	.998		.932	1.043		.995
1930	1.172	1.094	1.114	.853	1.337	1.282	1.122	1.143
1935	1.137	.950	1.000		.669	.973		.956
1940	1.080	.971	1.003	.872	.961	.921	.983	.993
1945	.968	.885	.907	.990	.921	.931	.916	.910
	BASED ON ESTIMATES IN 1929 PRICES							
1900			1.117		.989	1.012	1.073	1.092
1910			1.003		1.009	.841		.994
1920			.970		1.047	.740		.964
1925			.991		1.058	.863		.992
1930			1.009		1.014	1.038	1.001	1.011
1935			1.064		1.032	.572		1.033
1940			1.106		1.013	.910	1.069	1.082
1945			1.051		1.059	.939	1.040	1.044

Source: Tostlebe's estimates in current prices from Table 7 and in 1929 prices from Appendix Table G-1 in his monograph, *Capital in Agriculture* (Princeton University Press, 1957).

Goldsmith's estimates in current prices from Table W-1 and in 1929 prices from Table W-3 in Volume III, *A Study of Savings in the United States* (Princeton University Press, 1954).

TABLE 2

Indexes of Wealth Estimates for Agriculture Prepared by Goldsmith and Tostlebe, 1900–45

(1900 = 100)

	Total Reproducible Tangible Assets		Total Reproducible Tangible Assets Excluding Producers' Durables	
	Goldsmith	Tostlebe	Goldsmith	Tostlebe
CURRENT PRICES				
1900	100.0	100.0	100.0	100.0
1910			190.1	200.0
1920			339.9	381.9
1925			261.1	276.1
1930	229.2	277.9	223.9	272.1
1935			179.0	182.0
1940	189.9	201.7	184.1	194.3
1945	348.2	344.7	338.4	327.5
1929 PRICES				
1900	100.0	100.0	100.0	100.0
1910			122.0	111.1
1920			136.8	120.7
1925			128.5	116.7
1930	131.7	122.9	128.6	119.1
1935			123.2	116.5
1940	122.7	122.3	120.5	119.4
1945	135.4	131.2	130.3	124.6

Source: See Table 1.

or Goldsmith's. For a shorter period, 1930–40 for example, the analyst must decide whether real capital was unchanged as Tostlebe's estimates disclose or declined modestly as Goldsmith's estimates indicate. If this difference is important to the analyst's problem, he must judge the relative accuracy of the two estimates by examining the notes on sources of data and methods of estimation, and by study of any circumstantial evidence. But perhaps the best advice the estimator can give the analyst is not to ask of capital estimates any questions that can be answered by small changes.

Wealth Estimates for Nonfarm Residential Real Estate

The basic elements of this estimate, in the form of annual estimates of capital formation, were prepared by David Blank and first published in "The Volume of Residential Construction, 1889-1950," *Technical Paper 9* (NBER, 1954). These estimates also form the empirical core of the NBER's monograph, *Capital Formation in Residential Real Estate* by Grebler, Blank, and Winnick (Princeton University Press, 1956). In Appendix D of this monograph cumulated annual estimates of net capital formation are presented as wealth estimates.

419

Period Covered: 1889 to 1953. However, the estimates that are original with the authors relate to the years 1889 to 1920 inclusive. Thereafter these newly developed estimates are linked in 1921 to the official estimates of the BLS-Commerce. (The revised official series first appeared in Department of Commerce, *Construction and Construction Material, Statistical Supplement,* May 1950.)

Definition of Residential Real Estate: The estimates relate to non-farm residential construction, meaning new private permanent house-keeping residential facilities and new private nonhousekeeping residential facilities. Additions and alterations to existing residential structures are included. Public housing and farm housing are excluded.

Definition of Capital: Expenditures for residential facilities include payments not only for the buildings proper but also for the nonstructural site improvements associated with residential building, to the extent that they are privately financed, such as grading and landscaping, connections with sanitary and storm sewers, driveways, streets, sidewalks, etc. The cost of the raw land under new structures is initially excluded, but it is separately estimated to facilitate comparisons with wealth estimates based on census-type data.

Also included in expenditure estimates are "types of immobile equipment which when installed become an integral part of the structure and are necessary to a general use of the structure. Plumbing, heating, air conditioning, and lighting equipment are examples. Construction does not include the procurement of special purpose equipment designed to prepare the structure for specific use. Examples of such equipment are refrigerators, ranges, or washing machines in homes." (Quoted in *Technical Paper 9* from *Construction and Building Materials, Statistical Supplement,* May 1951, p. 1.)

Estimates of Wealth Components:

a. Structures net of depreciation including value of demolished structures.

b. Land.

The underlying elements of the wealth estimates are annual estimates of capital formation and consumption. The following series are presented:

a. Expenditures for new private permanent nonfarm house-keeping dwelling units.

b. Expenditures for additions to and alterations of house-keeping dwelling units.

420

c. Expenditures for new private nonhousekeeping residential facilities.

d. Capital consumption of nonfarm housing distinguishing depreciation and demolition.

Price Valuation in Source: Current prices. That is, the annual estimates of capital formation are based on building permit data on which are entered the current cost.

Sources of Data and Method of Estimation:

a. Nonfarm housekeeping dwelling units:

This was further subdivided into urban and rural nonfarm. For the urban areas building permit data in sample cities were transscribed from local official records as part of a WPA project under sponsorship of the BLS. Special tabulations of these data were made by the NBER from summaries prepared by BLS. Permit data are the source of both number of dwelling unit starts and average value of dwelling. Number of sample starts is expanded to the universe on basis of relationship of population change in all cities and in sample cities. In the absence of building permit data for rural nonfarm areas, the urban series of starts was extrapolated by the decade ratios of rural nonfarm population growth to urban population growth after allowance was made for urban growth arising from the extension of the geographic boundaries of urban communities. The average value of a dwelling unit in rural nonfarm areas was taken as 66 per cent of the average value in urban areas, following the adjustment factor devised by Wickens.

Average value per dwelling unit from permit data was deemed to be understated by 18 per cent, again following Wickens. A further upward adjustment of 8 per cent was introduced to cover expenses not covered by permit data, such as architects' and engineers' fees, land development costs and operative builders' profit margins on construction operations. (However, excluded from this and the official series are the speculative profits of operative builders.)

The product of the number of dwelling unit starts and the average value of dwelling unit after all adjustments equals expenditures on nonfarm private housekeeping dwelling units. This is converted to work-put-in-place basis by carrying over into the following year 10 per cent of the construction costs of dwelling units started in any given year. No adjustment is made for lags, lapses, and underreporting of building permits except for lapses in New York City.

Nonfarm, nonhousekeeping dwelling units: The urban subcomponent was estimated as the urban subcomponent of expenditures for housekeeping dwelling units except a carry-over ratio of one-third

421

was used. The rural nonfarm subcomponent was estimated by applying annual per capita building rates for nonhousekeeping dwelling units derived from cities of less than 25,000 population to the decennial estimates of rural nonfarm population prepared for this study.

b. Alterations and additions to housekeeping dwelling units:

A rough estimate of expenditures on alterations and additions for the years 1889–1920 was derived by graphic extrapolation. The Department of Commerce estimates of additions and alterations for the years 1921–50 were plotted against the Commerce housekeeping expenditures series for these years and the relation between the two series observed. Additions and alterations seem to follow the movement in housekeeping construction expenditures but have a smaller amplitude. These observed relationships were used as a guide for graphing expenditures for additions and alterations back to 1889 in relation to the new estimates on housekeeping expenditures.

c. Capital consumption:

An annual depreciation rate of 2 per cent was applied to the cumulated value of residential structures at the end of the preceding year, and a half year's depreciation was charged against the current year's construction. A ratio was derived of annual demolitions (taken as one-tenth of the total in each decade) to the average annual size of the inventory (taken as the average of the opening and closing inventories of each decade). These ratios, derived in terms of dwelling units, were then converted to value ratios by a one-third reduction.

d. Value of land:

Conceptually, what needs to be estimated is the site value free from those elements of capital formation, such as grading, landscaping, and paving. However, the paucity of data precludes this, and use was made of the ratio of the value of land under improved residential real estate to the total value of existing residential real estate based on FHA appraisal data and tax assessment data from a number of cities which permit the separation of residential from other real estate. For the period 1890–1953 the land ratio of existing residential real estate is estimated as having declined from 40 to 17 per cent, with the move to the suburbs accounting for most of this trend.

Goldsmith also made use of the ratio of the value of land to total value of residential real estate. However, his ratios show a much smaller decline, from 25 per cent in 1896 to 20 per cent in 1949 (*A Study of Savings in the United States, op. cit.*, Vol. II, Table B-50). In the accompanying notes, Goldsmith states that the ratios for 1896–1928 are "roughly estimated on the basis of data for later

422

years." From the respective descriptions, I conclude that the estimated ratios of Grebler-Blank-Winnick have a firmer empirical base than those of Goldsmith.

e. Estimation of the stock of capital in 1889:

This is based on the mortgage census of 1890 which gives the average value of owner-occupied mortgaged houses. Similar data for 1940 indicate that the ratio of the average value of a dwelling unit to the average value of an owner-occupied and mortgaged one-to-four family house was about 63 per cent. For 1890 this was assumed to be 55 per cent of an owner-occupied mortgaged home. The resulting average multiplied by the number of nonfarm dwelling units equals the total nonfarm residential wealth on June 1, 1890. This was extrapolated to January 1, 1889.

Adjustments for Price Changes:

a. Reference base: 1929 prices.

b. Components shown in constant prices are:
wealth estimates, i.e., structures and
annual estimates of capital formation and consumption which include structures, additions and alterations, depreciation, and demolitions.

The adjustments were for 1915–50, from the Boeckh residential construction cost index, as given in Department of Commerce, *Construction and Building Materials, Statistical Supplement*, May 1951, p. 40, converted to a 1929 base and for 1910–14 from the value for 1915 extrapolated by Boeckh indexes of residential construction cost, as given in Bureau of the Census, *Historical Statistics*, p. 172.

For 1890–1909, they were derived from the value for 1910 extrapolated by weighted average of an index of wage rates in the building trades and an index of building materials prices.

In appendix D of their monograph, the authors compare their wealth estimates of nonfarm private residential dwellings, based on the cumulation of annual estimates of net capital formation, with independent benchmark estimates based on census-type data. One set of estimates is based upon real estate assessment data collected by government agencies. Another set is based upon values and rents of nonfarm housing reported by the census in 1930, 1940, and 1950.

The authors point out some of the limitations of these comparisons for checking purposes. These limitations stem from differences in coverage as well as differences in the margins of the reporting and estimating errors in assessment and census-type data. The following are deemed to be the more serious differences:

423

1. Differences in coverage:

a. Grebler-Blank-Winnick estimates (G-B-W) exclude expenditures on public housing while they are included in residential wealth estimates based on housing census data.

b. G-B-W estimates include nonresidential space, such as stores or offices which may form part of a new residential structure. Those census data which report value on a dwelling unit rather than a structure basis exclude those nonresidential components; whether the residential wealth estimates based on assessment data include the nonresidential portions of residential real estate is not known.

c. The transfer between two benchmark dates of farmhouses into the nonfarm category, because of change in definition or actual change in use, will be reflected in a census estimate but not in cumulated estimates (G-B-W) since no capital formation has taken place. Conversely, when a residential structure is converted to nonresidential use, the transfer is not recorded in the G-B-W estimates since there has been no capital consumption. The census-type wealth estimates will probably register this wealth decrement.

2. Differences in method of valuation and in estimating and reporting errors:

a. G-B-W estimates, valued on the basis of a construction cost index, are essentially depreciated replacement costs. The census-type estimates are intended to approximate market values. Even if each estimate is free of errors, substantial differences in wealth estimates may be apparent at any benchmark year since year-to-year movements in the prices of housing inputs and in prices of existing houses have been far from equal.

b. Owners' estimates of market price probably have a tendency to lag behind actual market price and may well include separable household equipment such as screens, porch furniture, refrigerators, etc.

c. The conversion of reported rents for tenant-occupied units into market values by the use of a gross rent multiplier is fraught with its own estimating errors.

d. The wealth estimates obtained from assessment data and revalued to a market basis depend on the accuracy of the equalization ratio used. The derivation of a reliable country-wide ratio, in the view of these authors, requires a major statistical effort beyond the scope of the past attempts in this direction.

In Table 3 we reproduce the comparison made by the authors with one exception. We have omitted the comparisons with census-based

TABLE 3

Comparison of Cumulated and Benchmark Residential Wealth Estimates, Various
Dates, 1890–1950
(billions of current dollars)

Date	Cumulated Wealth Estimate of Structures and Land (G-B-W) (1)	Date	Benchmark Wealth Estimates of Structures and Land (2)	Net Difference (1−2) (3)	Net Difference as Percentage of Benchmark Wealth Estimates (3÷2) (4)
June 1890	15.0	June 1890	14.4[a]	+0.6	4.2
December 1900	22.9	June 1900	20.0[a]	+2.9	14.5
December 1912	40.1	June 1912	39.2[a]	+0.9	2.3
December 1922	71.3	n.a. 1922	65.0[b]	+6.3	9.7
December 1929	108.5	n.a. 1930	107.7	+0.8	0.7
December 1938	96.8	n.a. 1938	92.0[b]	+4.8	5.2
December 1939	99.2	April 1940	87.4[c]	+11.8	13.5
December 1949	212.5	April 1950	260.0[d]	−47.5	−18.3

[a] Simon Kuznets, *National Product Since 1890* (NBER, 1946), pp. 201–7.

[b] Robert R. Doane, *The Anatomy of Wealth* (Harper, 1940), pp. 213, 224, and 251.

[c] Housing—Special Reports, Bureau of the Census, Series H-1943, No. 1, September 11, 1943.

[d] *Census of Housing 1950*, Preliminary Reports, Series HC-5, No. 1. See footnote g to Table D-3, cited in source note for derivation.

Source: Columns 1 and 2, Grebler, Blank, and Winnick, *op. cit.*, Table D-3, Appendix D, p. 370.

estimates for 1930 since there is considerable confusion in the inter-pretation of census data on the value of owner-occupied dwellings.

The cumulated estimates exceeded the benchmark wealth estimates in all years except the last. When the comparison is with wealth benchmarks based on tax assessment data, the excess has varied from 2 to 10 per cent. These differences are within the range of the 10 per cent estimating error placed by the authors on their own estimates. The fact that the differences do not cumulate into ever larger totals suggest that there is no systematic bias in the G-B-W estimates.

The differences between the cumulative estimates and the census-based estimates for 1940 and 1950 are much larger; first higher by 13.5 per cent and then lower by 18 per cent.

The authors claim, however, that the exclusion of dwelling units covered by the census but not by the authors' estimate, such as public dwelling units, seasonal dwellings and shifts from farm to nonfarm status, reduces the difference to the order of 10 per cent. Margaret Reid, on the other hand, contends that the difference is much larger if the base of the value of tenant-occupied dwellings is free market rent and not rentals still substantially affected by rent control as used

425

by the authors. Only the former concept is consistent with the value concept implicit in cumulated wealth estimates.

The larger negative difference in 1950 reflects the now acknowledged understatement in the BLS-Commerce estimates of dwelling unit starts for the decade of the 1940's. These official estimates of housing starts are incorporated in the G-B-W estimates after 1920. Incidentally, the results of the 1956 housing census suggests that the downward bias in the official estimates of housing starts has persisted in the 1950's.

There is little to be gained in using Goldsmith's estimates of non-farm residential construction as a check since the approach is the same—cumulation of annual estimates of net capital formation. The data also are much the same except for the period 1896 to 1920, and Goldsmith introduces a correction factor to adjust his estimates to the level of the census benchmark estimates. (See note to Table R-3, columns 4, 5, and 6 in *A Study of Savings in the U.S., op. cit.*, Vol. I, p. 584.)

At the outset we noted that a judgment on the reasonableness of the inferences from the estimates is another form of appraisal. The authors using their own wealth estimates conclude, *inter alia*, that there has been a decline in real capital investment per dwelling unit. This result seemed "unreasonable" to Margaret Reid and prompted her to undertake an extended investigation of the authors' estimates. Her investigations lead her to conclude that the trend movement has been in the opposite direction. (Margaret G. Reid, "Capital Formation in Residential Real Estate," *The Journal of Political Economy*, April 1958, pp. 131–53.) Miss Reid's conclusion is based on the following alleged biases in G-B-W estimates:

1. Failure to include value added by unpaid labor.
2. Underestimate of the expenditures for additions and alterations.
3. Underestimate for most of the decades of the number of new dwellings added to the stock.
4. Overestimate for all decades except the Forties of the average value of new dwellings.
5. Overestimate of the upward trend in the real price of housing.

In reply the authors conclude that "Miss Reid's criticism is well taken in regard to [the second] item [and indeed the authors in their monograph had argued in favor of an upward revision of the official estimates of additions and alterations] but unwarranted in regard to the other four items."[4]

---

[4] From the typescript of the reply by Grebler, Blank, and Winnick. Mr. Blank was good enough to make a copy available in advance of publication.

The evidence and argument are too lengthy for review here. However, for whatever it may be worth, I venture the judgment that the estimates of Grebler, Blank, and Winnick do pass the test of reasonableness and there is no need to revise the major conclusions of their monograph because of Miss Reid's criticism.

Wealth Estimates for the Regulated Industries: Transportation, Communication, and Electric and Gas Utilities

These sector estimates were prepared for the NBER by Melville J. Ulmer. The notes that follow were taken from his manuscript (Mimeograph version of May 1957) before final editing for the printer. His monograph will be issued under the title, *Capital in Transportation, Communication, and Public Utilities: Its Formation and Financing.* Part II of this monograph is a series of appendixes describing the derivation of the estimates and the tests to which some of the estimates have been put.

For estimating purposes the regulated industries are subdivided into six branches: Steam railroads, electric light and power, telephones, street and electric railways, local bus lines, all other.

1. STEAM RAILROADS

Period Covered: 1870 to 1951. Annual estimates are provided. Nine-year moving averages centered on January 1st of the mid-year are presented for 1874–1946. The latter are recommended as more reliable by the author for trend analysis, i.e., for a period exceeding the length of a business cycle.

Definition of Capital: Value of road and structures and equipment. It includes all reproducible physical property, except inventories, used directly or indirectly for transportation. Excluded is a small amount of physical property, such as hotels, not used for transportation. The value of land, which, of course, is not reproducible, is also excluded.

Wealth Components Estimated: Road and equipment. Value of land is not given as a series but sufficient data are provided for its derivation in current prices.

Price Valuation in Source: Current prices.

Sources of Basic Data and Method of Estimation:

a. 1912 to 1951: Data on gross capital expenditures, including land, were obtained directly from annual reports of the ICC for Class I and II roads. These figures were raised to the level of all railroads by the ratio of book values of road and equipment of Class I and II roads to the book value of all classes as reported by ICC.

427

b. 1870 to 1911: Based on the financial statements of individual companies contained in a sample of annual reports of state railroad commissioners in benchmark years separated by an average interval of four years. Sample expenditures raised to level of all railroads by relationship of book value of road and structures of sample railroads to book value of road and structures of all railroads. The latter was derived from ICC reports beginning with 1890 and extrapolated to 1870 essentially by the compilation of balance sheets in Poor's. Annual figures between benchmarks were obtained by interpolating by changes in miles of tracks operated, weighted by an index of railroad construction costs. The former is an ICC series beginning with 1890 extrapolated to 1869 by a compilation reported by Poor's. For the index of construction cost see Poor's annotation for adjustments for price changes.

These estimates of annual gross capital expenditures were reduced to a net basis by subtracting estimates of capital consumption defined as capital "used up" either through depreciation or obsolescence. The series presented in this study is based primarily upon estimates of true composite depreciation rates prepared especially for this purpose by the Bureau of Valuation, ICC.

The stock of capital to which the annual net capital expenditures can be applied to derive the wealth estimates is based on an unpublished ICC estimate of the reproduction cost less depreciation of road and equipment of Class I railroads on January 1, 1937, expressed in 1910–14 dollars. This estimate was raised to the level of all railroads and expressed in 1929 prices.

Adjustments for Price Changes:

a. Reference base: 1929.

b. Components shown in constant prices are
wealth estimates, i.e., road and equipment and
annual estimates of capital formation and consumption, i.e., gross capital expenditures on road and equipment, capital consumption, and net capital expenditures on road and equipment.

The adjustments were derived for 1915–51 from the ICC railroad construction cost index after appropriate shift in base. For the earlier years, the 1915 index was extrapolated by a composite index comprised of W. H. Shaw's index of the cost of construction materials, his index of the cost of locomotives and railroad cars, the indexes of lumber and building materials and of metals and implements, excluding pocket knives, from Aldrich report. Weights were derived from an analysis of the composition of railroad expenditures in selected periods.

2. ELECTRIC LIGHT AND POWER UTILITIES

Period Covered: 1881 to 1951. Annual estimates are presented. Nine-year moving averages centered on January 1 of the midyear are presented for 1885–1946. The latter are recommended as more reliable by the author for trend analysis, i.e., for a period exceeding the length of a business cycle.

Definition of Industry: The estimates entering into the total of regulated industries are restricted to privately owned electric light and power utilities. Publicly owned power facilities as well as owner-user facilities are excluded from this total, although wealth estimates and their derivations are also provided for each of these two segments. The annotations that follow are limited to the privately owned light and power utilities.

Definition of Capital: Value of plant and equipment excluding land.

Wealth Components Estimated: Value of plant and equipment. Value of land is not given as a series but sufficient data are provided for its derivation in current prices.

Price Valuation in Source: Current prices.

Sources of Basic Data and Method of Estimation: Annual estimates of net capital formation are cumulated from the beginning of the industry in 1881 to derive annual wealth estimates. The method of estimation has varied over the seventy-year period depending on the data. The notes start with the most recent subperiod, for which the errors of estimate are the smallest. In each subperiod net capital formation is derived from gross capital expenditures reduced by capital consumption.

a. 1937–51: Annual gross additions to electric plants including land were taken from unpublished data of the Federal Power Commission. Value of land excluded by applying the ratio of the value of land to total value of plant for facilities placed in service during the respective years, from unpublished data furnished by the Federal Power Commission.

b. 1921 to 1937: Annual gross capital expenditures from the *Statistical Bulletins* of the Edison Electrical Institute. Land excluded as in (a) but with ratios that are less firmly based since the ratios were interpolated for two-thirds of the years.

c. 1881 to 1920: Benchmark estimates of value of plant and equipment gross of depreciation are available for 1898, 1902, 1907, 1912, 1917, and 1922 from the various official censuses of the electrical industries. The value existing at the end of 1902 adjusted for

429

retirements, is redistributed in the form of annual gross capital expenditures beginning in 1881 by a composite index consisting of the number of plants, index of increase in size per station and a construction cost index. The 1907 and 1912 benchmark estimates adjusted for retirements were redistributed annually by another composite index combining increases in generating capacity (derived by fitting a modified exponential trend to benchmark figures from the Censuses) and the construction cost index. The remaining two benchmarks, 1917 and 1922, are redistributed by the increase in fixed capital in the electric and power industry of four states as reported to state public service commissions.

Retirements are estimated on the bases of generating capacity at the end of each census period and the generating capacity remaining in 1946–48 by date of installation as reported by the Federal Power Commission.

Capital consumption is estimated by applying the average length of life of plant and equipment to the annual gross capital expenditures excluding land. An average life of seventeen years was assumed for plant and equipment installed 1881–1900 and average life of thirty-seven years for plant and equipment installed in 1920 and later years; average life for other years was derived by linear interpolation between the figures for 1900 and 1920. No evidence or source is provided for these assumptions.

Adjustments for Price Changes:
  a. Reference base: 1929.
  b. Components shown in constant prices are
     wealth estimates, i.e., plant and equipment, excluding land and
     annual estimates of capital formation and consumption, i.e.,
gross capital expenditures on plant and equipment, excluding land, capital consumption, and net capital expenditures.

For the period 1911–51 the adjustments were derived from an average of five regional indexes known as the Handy Index of Public Utility Construction Costs issued semi-annually by Whitman, Requart and Associates, Baltimore, Maryland. The weights for combining the regional indexes were derived from data on the distribution of generating capacity by region in 1902 and 1937 shown in the Census of Electrical Industries. For the years before 1911, the 1911 index is extrapolated by a composite index incorporating indexes of electrical equipment (from W. H. Shaw, *op. cit.*, and Aldrich report), construction materials (same sources) and wages in building trades (from BLS series and Aldrich report). The weights are 5, 3, and 2, respectively.

3. TELEPHONE INDUSTRY

Period Covered: 1880 to 1951. Annual estimates are presented. Nine-year moving averages centered on January 1 of the midyear are presented for 1885–1946. The latter are recommended by the author as more reliable for trend analysis, i.e., for a period exceeding the length of a business cycle.

Definition of Capital: Value of plant and equipment, excluding land.

Wealth Components Estimated: Value of plant and equipment, excluding land.

Price Valuation in Source: Current prices.

Sources of Basic Data and Method of Estimation: Annual estimates of net capital formation are cumulated starting with a wealth estimate for 1880. Estimates of net capital formation are derived from estimates of gross capital expenditures reduced by estimates of capital consumption. For estimating purposes the period is divided into two subperiods.

a. 1913–51: Gross capital expenditures were supplied by the American Telephone and Telegraph Company, covering all telephone companies.

b. 1881–1913: Changes in book value of plant and equipment, adjusted for retirements are taken as equal to gross capital expenditures.

Book value of plant and equipment available for Bell System annually from 1885 to 1913 from a Federal Communications Commission Exhibit; values for the years between 1880–85 were interpolated after the "write-up" in the 1880 figure had been eliminated. Until 1894 the Bell System was coextensive with the telephone industry; thereafter the figure for the Bell System raised to the level of the industry by the ratio of values for the Bell System to totals for telephone industry, reported by Censuses of Electrical Industries. The ratio was interpolated for intercensal years. The value of land was excluded from these book values by using an FCC ratio of plant and equipment excluding land to the total including land for the Bell System in 1913-14.

Retirements, the difference between the change in book values of plant and equipment and gross capital expenditures, were estimated at 40 per cent of depreciation for the period 1913–17 from A. T. and T. data. By applying this ratio to estimated depreciation 1881–1913 estimates of retirements were obtained which, when added to the annual changes in book values, resulted in annual estimates of gross capital expenditures.

431

The depreciation rate is based on information provided by A. T. and T. Its records indicate that in 1884 the comptroller of the American Bell Telephone Company had suggested that a depreciation rate of 10 per cent was applicable to the original cost of plant and equipment. This rate was used for 1880. The FCC prescribed rates for ten companies in 1950 that averaged 3.5995 per cent of plant and equipment, excluding land. The rates for the intervening years were obtained by linear interpolation. Gross capital expenditures, excluding land, multiplied by the depreciation rate, yields the estimate of capital consumption which, when subtracted from gross capital expenditures, equals net capital formation. The value of plant and equipment in 1880, to which annual estimates of net capital formation are added, is derived from asset figures reported in the 1880 census. The latter are adjusted for the "write-up" of American Bell Telephone Co. assets on the basis of FCC investigation of the value of plant and equipment of the Bell Telephone System as of 1881.

Adjustments for Price Changes:
   a. Reference base: 1929.
   b. Components shown in constant prices are
      wealth estimates, i.e., plant and equipment and
      annual estimates of capital formation and consumption, i.e.,
gross capital expenditures on plant and equipment, excluding land, capital consumption, and net capital expenditures.

For the period 1915–51 the adjustments were derived from a composite weighted construction cost index prepared from indexes of telephone apparatus. (These were compiled by Western Electric until 1936 and then continued by A. T. & T.) Commercial buildings (compiled by George A. Fuller Co.), telephone poles in place (compiled by ICC), and wages in building trades (from BLS reports) were also used. For the period 1880–1914, the index for 1915 was extrapolated by the composite index developed for deflating capital expenditures in the electric light and power industry for these years.

4. STREET AND ELECTRIC RAILWAYS AND LOCAL BUS LINES

The estimates here are extremely weak despite the exercise of much ingenuity by the author. Benchmark data are available only for electric railways (from Census of Electrical Industries). They are virtually non-existent for street railways and local bus lines. The amount of processing is extensive and complex, resulting in circuitous and devious routes to the final estimates. The only saving grace is that there is evidence, aside from these estimates, that these two branches are a relatively small component of all regulated industries. Based on the author's nine-year moving averages of the value of plant and

432

equipment, these values in street and electric railways and local bus lines amounted to 3 per cent of the total value of plant and equipment of railroads, electric light and power utilities, and telephone systems in 1885, 14 per cent in 1920 and 4 per cent in 1947. Even so, would it not represent the better part of discretion not to have gone through the *pro forma* motions of making annual estimates when the data are so woefully deficient?

5. ALL OTHER REGULATED INDUSTRIES

This catch-all group is comprised of gas, pipelines, and telegraph; motor transportation other than local bus systems; and pullman and express, water transportation, air transportation, water supply companies, irrigation and radio broadcasting. Gross capital expenditures of the last group were equal to about 3 per cent of those for the first two industries above in the period 1912–48, according to the author's estimate.

The same general procedure was followed. Annual estimates of gross capital expenditures were reduced by annual estimates of capital consumption to obtain annual estimates of net capital formation, which were then cumulated. For most of these industries, acceptable estimates of gross capital expenditures are available beginning with 1919 from George Terborgh, "Estimated Expenditures for New Durable Goods, 1919–38," *Federal Reserve Bulletins*, September 1939, February 1949, and February 1942, from Simon Kuznets, *Commodity Flow and Capital Formation* (NBER, 1938) and from official Department of Commerce—SEC series on capital expenditures. For the earlier years, changes between benchmark years in book values were interpolated by the gross capital expenditures total of the major industries studied in detail.

Capital consumption estimates were also dependent on applying the ratio of book values of industries studied in detail to the book value of the "all other" group for benchmark years to the capital consumption of the former to obtain capital consumption estimates for the residual group at benchmark years. These benchmarks were linearly interpolated to obtain annual estimates.

The construction cost indexes implicit in the current and constant price estimates for the industries studied in detail were used to express estimates for the residual group in 1929 prices.

There are no independent wealth estimates to compare with those prepared by Melville J. Ulmer. A series based on balance sheet data is precluded since virtually all branches of the regulated industries indulged in substantial fictitious revaluation of assets before regulation became sufficiently strict to prohibit these write-ups or, at least, to keep them within more reasonable bounds. Moreover, as these notes indicate, balance sheet data (with some attempt to remove the write-ups) have been used to set benchmark levels, particularly in the earlier years of the span covered by these estimates, and to arrive at other relationships that formed intermediate steps in the estimating process. Estimates based on balance sheets, therefore, even if they could be prepared, would not be truly independent.

Ulmer, accordingly, has restricted his testing to the interpolating or extrapolating indexes. His procedure is to prepare annual estimates of gross capital expenditures based on these indexes for the years when gross capital expenditures are directly reported. The relative differences between the two estimates are used to suggest the range of error in the estimates that are based solely on the interpolating indexes. Such comparisons are made for the three major branches, railroads, electric light and power, and telephones. When both the estimated and reported figures are compared in terms of five- or nine-year moving averages, the maximum difference is about 12 per cent, the average difference, excluding benchmark years, is about 5 per cent, and turning points and direction of movement show virtually perfect coincidence. As the author realizes, this type of comparison has at best only suggestive value for indicating the range of error in the untested portion of the series.

Mining

The wealth estimates for mining were prepared by Israel Borenstein and first appeared in "Capital and Output Trends in Mining Industries, 1870–1948," *Occasional Paper 45* (NBER, 1954). The same estimates, extended to 1953, have been incorporated into an NBER monograph, *Capital in Manufacturing and Mining: Its Formation and Financing*, scheduled for publication in 1960. These estimates based on census and balance sheet data relate to benchmark years.

Period Covered: Benchmark years 1870, 1880, 1890, 1909, 1919, 1929, 1940, 1948, and 1953. With the exception of 1919 these are years of high level activity in mining.

Definition of Industry: The census definition of mining is used. The census classifies establishments engaged in mineral extraction on an industry basis. That is, they are classified according to the main mineral extracted. Although earlier censuses were not quite consistent in drawing a line between mining and manufacturing operations, these inconsistencies are not of a kind to impair seriously the comparability of the data, and beginning with the 1919 census duplication became negligible. The census definition of mining includes generally

434

all activities up to the point at which a marketable product is obtained. Thus the figures include those preparation activities which are frequently carried on at the mine or quarry site and in which the preparation plants are operated in conjunction with the mines and quarries, but do not include those preparation activities which are more frequently carried on at the manufacturing plants.

Definition of Capital: The depreciated net value of structures and equipment is designated as "plant" and the sum of inventories, cash, and receivables as "working capital." The net value of surface land and mineral resources owned by the mining establishment, excluding leased land, is designated "land." The sum of plant and working capital is called "capital," and the sum of capital and land, "total capital."

Wealth Components Estimated: Total capital, capital, plant, and working capital for all mining and each of five subdivisions—metals, anthracite coal, bituminous coal, petroleum and natural gas, and other nonmetals.

Price Valuation in Source: Either undepreciated value in current prices as in the earlier census reports or book values net of depreciation reflecting essentially original costs.

Sources of Basic Data and Method of Estimation: The value of capital including owned land in reported values was taken from census reports for the benchmark years 1870 through 1919. The reported figures for 1880 and 1890 required adjustment to exclude value of leased land. When the value of leased land was not given separately, the adjustment was obtained by applying the ratio of leased land to total acreage or value in the next available year to the value of total land in the given year.

The estimates for the remaining benchmark years were obtained by applying the ratio of the sum of cash, notes and accounts receivable, inventories, and net capital assets including land to the sum of gross sales and gross receipts reported in *Statistics of Income* (or the *Source Book*) to the product figures consistent with census reports.

Adjustments for Price Changes:

    a. Reference base: 1929 prices.

    b. Components shown in constant prices: capital (excluding land), plant, and working capital for all mining and each of the five subdivisions.

The correction for price changes was done separately for equipment and improvements, and working capital, after deduction of the estimated value of land owned by the establishment. These breakdowns were not available in the sources for all benchmark years.

Their derivation depends essentially on the use of appropriate ratios from the nearest available year.

For the price correction itself the following price indexes were applied to the book values:

1. Equipment. Price index implicit in Goldsmith's estimates of the value of producers' durable equipment at original cost and in 1929 prices (from "A Perpetual Inventory of National Wealth," *Studies in Income and Wealth*, Vol. 14 (NBER, 1951), extrapolated by the price index for this group estimated by Simon Kuznets (from *National Product Since 1869*, NBER, 1946).

2. Improvements. Goldsmith's implicit index for underground mining structures and nonfarm nonresidential structures combined with equal weights and extrapolated by Kuznets' index for all construction.

3. Working capital. BLS index of wholesale prices converted from a 1926 to a 1929 base.

Borenstein devotes an appendix to the statistical reliability of the major findings. He was unable, however, to compare his estimates with an independent set of estimates simply because none seem to exist. Borenstein distinguishes two types of deficiencies—those arising from differences in definition, coverage, classification, etc., and those arising from the fact that the capital data are based on accounting records and are therefore affected by changes in accounting practices, such as in the treatment of capitalization, depletion, and depreciation. The first type of deficiencies is not considered serious and does not impart a systematic bias to the estimates. The second type is probably somewhat more serious and results in a downward bias in the estimates, at least in the years before the inception of the corporate excise tax in 1909.

Orris Herfindahl has expressed a different set of judgments. (See his review of *Occasional Paper 45* in the *Journal of the American Statistical Association*, March 1957, pp. 119-22.) In Herfindahl's view there is an upward bias in the earlier estimates based on census data because he "suspects radical under-reporting of capital in the early censuses with fuller reporting as time went on. . . ." His evidence, however, is restricted to statements of the census officials. These officials made similar statements about the capital data in the censuses of manufacturers and these fears can be shown to have been greatly exaggerated. [See Appendix B, *Occasional Paper 41* (NBER, 1954).] It may well be appropriate to apply a similar discount to the official, alleged undercoverage of the censuses of mines.

Herfindahl stresses also that the changes in classification associated with the shift from census data to balance sheet data from *Statistics of Income* causes a discontinuity in the capital estimates, resulting in their being too low. The discontinuity arises because the extraction activities of manufacturing companies would be classified in manufacturing in *Statistics of Income*. This argument applies with special force to the petroleum and natural gas branch of mining. For these years Borenstein's estimates of capital were obtained by applying the capital-output ratio derived from *Statistics of Income* to output comparable to census definitions. For this procedure to lead to distortion, it is necessary to establish that the capital-output ratio of the extraction activities of companies classified in manufactures differs significantly from the capital-output ratio of establishments classified in mining. Herfindahl acknowledges that there are no data for such a determination in the petroleum industry. On a priori grounds I would not look for any significant differences.

Herfindahl seems to be on firmer ground when he points out that contract well-drilling, which is not classified as mining, has become increasingly important. Such a structural change in the organization of the industry would result in the lowering of the capital estimates if Borenstein's estimating procedures are followed. However, if similar structural changes have not occurred in other branches of mining, which I suspect is the case, this one instance could not cause serious understatement of capital devoted to mining.

Manufactures

The capital estimates for manufactures were prepared by me with the assistance of Martin Bernstein. They first appeared in "Capital and Output Trends in Manufacturing, 1880–1948," *Occasional Paper 41* (NBER, 1954). Extended to later years they will appear in the NBER monograph, *Capital in Manufactures and Mining: Its Formation and Financing*. These estimates are based on the *Censuses of Manufacturers* and balance sheet data from *Statistics of Income*. They relate only to benchmark years.

Period Covered: Benchmark years 1880, 1890, 1900, 1904, 1909, 1914, 1919, 1929, 1937, 1948, and 1953. With the exceptions of 1904 and 1914, these are years of high level activity.

Definition of Industry: The census definition of manufactures is followed, except that for the years 1900 and earlier the artisan and craft classifications are excluded. (They were not included in the census canvasses after 1900.) It was necessary to establish comparability among the various *censuses* and the annual compilations of the "Source Book" of *Statistics of Income*, as well as between the

437

census classifications and *Statistics of Income.* Over the 1880-1948 period, forty-one comparable industries classified into fifteen major groups were established. The estimates for 1953 were prepared only for eighteen major groups.

Definition of Capital: Total capital in the Census enumerations is the sum of fixed capital (land, buildings, machinery, and equipment) and working capital (cash, inventories, and accounts receivable). This definition of capital can be closely matched with the balance sheet data reported in *Statistics of Income.* The essentially equivalent definition is total assets minus investments in government and other securities. That there is continuity in the figures on invested capital from the two sources is suggested by the closeness of the reconciliation of the data on capital from the *1919 Census of Manufactures* and from *Statistics of Income* for the same year.

Wealth Components Estimated: Total capital for all benchmark years and fixed capital (and working capital by subtraction) for 1890, 1900, 1904, 1929, 1937, 1948, and 1953. These estimates are available for all manufactures, forty-one sub-branches for the period 1880–1948, and for eighteen major groupings for 1948–53.

Price Valuation in Source: Book values net of depreciation reflecting essentially original cost.

Sources of Basic Data and Method of Estimation: Censuses of Manufactures was the source of reported capital for the benchmark years between 1880 and 1919. For the benchmark years following 1919, the data were taken from the "Source Book" of *Statistics of Income,* Part 2, the compilation of corporate income-tax returns prepared by the Internal Revenue Service (formerly Bureau of Internal Revenue) of the United States Treasury. Aside from the combining of minor industries in order to establish comparable industry classifications over the years, no adjustments were applied to the Census based estimates. The balance sheet data from the "Source Book" required several adjustments after industry comparability was achieved.

1. Adjustment for deconsolidation: *Statistics of Income 1934* carried tabulations from profit and loss statements on both a consolidated and deconsolidated basis. The ratio of gross sales on a deconsolidated basis to gross sales on a consolidated basis in 1934 was used to adjust capital reported on a consolidated basis in 1929. Although this is a rough adjustment, the entire adjustment for all manufactures is slight as it is for most industry sub-branches except metals and metal products.

438

2. Adjustment for unincorporated firms: *Statistics of Income* data relate to corporations submitting balance sheets, which in most years for manufactures include all except 1 or 2 per cent of all corporations. The ratio of gross sales of all corporations to that of corporations submitting balance sheets by industry sub-branches was used to raise totals for corporations submitting balance sheets to the level for all corporations. A comparable ratio of all establishments to corporate establishments from the *Censuses of Manufactures*, 1929, 1937, and 1947 was applied to the corporate totals to obtain capital totals for all enterprises (corporate and noncorporate).

3. Adjustment for accelerated depreciation: during the emergency period 1940–45 and again during the Korean war and the years of rearmament that followed, corporations were permitted to amortize capital assets certified as necessary for the national defense over an abnormally low period of five years. Normal straight-line depreciation was substituted for accelerated amortization.

4. Adjustment of fixed capital for intangible assets: intangible assets (patents, copyrights, good will, etc.) were included with fixed capital in the 1948 and 1953 compilations of *Statistics of Income*. In other benchmark years, intangible assets were classified in "other assets" which were included with working capital. *Statistics of Income* reported intangible assets in 1954 after not listing them separately since 1939. The value of intangibles by major industry groups in 1948 and 1953 was obtained by straight-line interpolation between the 1939 and 1954 values. These estimates of intangible assets were deducted from fixed capital as reported in 1948 and 1953.

Adjustments for Price Changes:

    a. Reference base: 1929 prices.

    b. Components shown in constant prices.

Total capital for all benchmark years and fixed capital (and working capital by subtraction) for 1890, 1900, 1904, 1929, 1937, 1948, and 1953. The industry detail is as indicated above.

The method consists in deriving a series of composite indexes, one for each of fifteen major industry groups, from (1) an index of prices of machinery and equipment differently weighted in each major group according to the length of life typical of the industry; (2) an index of building costs based on a fifty-year life, which is identical for all industries; and (3) an index of wholesale prices of output of each major industry group as a deflator of working capital. The composite index for deflating total capital was obtained by calculating a weighted harmonic mean of the three indexes. The weights used for the benchmark years from 1880 to 1937 inclusive were the average relative importance of the three components in 1890, 1900, and 1904 as shown by Census data. Limited evidence indicates that there was little change in the relative importance of these three asset components from 1880 to 1937. By 1948, however, there were significant changes in their relative importance and new weights were used based on balance-sheet data reported in *Statistics of Income*, 1948 and 1953, Part 2. The composite index for a given major industry is applied to all minor industries classified under the given major industry.

A similarly derived composite of indexes (1) and (2) was obtained as a deflator of fixed capital.

For a price series of machinery and equipment several series were linked: (a) Shaw's price index (*Value of Commodity Output Since 1869*, NBER, 1947) before 1915; (b) Chawner's price index (*Survey of Current Business*, March 1941) for 1915 to 1939; and (c) Department of Commerce's implicit price index for producers' durable equipment ("National Income Supplement," *Survey of Current Business*). The same sources also provide data on the annual capital expenditures in constant prices which figure in the derivation of weights.

The average length of life also used in deriving the weights is based on *Income Tax, Depreciation and Obsolescence, Estimated Useful Lives* and *Depreciation Rates* (Bulletin F, revised January 1942, Bureau of Internal Revenue).

For structures the volume (expenditures in constant prices) and construction cost indexes were taken from unpublished worksheets of Simon Kuznets for 1879–1919, from an unpublished table prepared by Raymond W. Goldsmith for 1919, 1929, and 1937, and from *Construction Volume and Costs, 1915–1954*, Statistical Supplement to *Construction Review* (Turner Construction Co. construction cost index) for 1948 and 1953.

The principal sources for the wholesale prices used to deflate working capital are the Aldrich report, Shaw's *Value of Commodity Output Since 1869, op. cit.*, and the Bureau of Labor Statistics series on wholesale prices.

There are independent estimates of annual gross and net capital expenditures on structures and equipment (fixed capital). These may be cumulated to obtain estimates of the stock of fixed capital owned by manufacturing establishments and the cumulated totals can be compared with the estimates of the stock of fixed capital derived from balance sheet data. This comparison can be made for the period beginning with 1919.[5] Owing to data differences over time, as to scope and detail, it is necessary to use one basis of reconciliation for the

[5] The material that follows will appear as Appendix I in *Capital in Manufactures and Mining: Its Formation and Financing* (Princeton University Press, 1960).

period 1919 to 1929, and other bases for the subsequent benchmark comparisons.

The comparison of relative change between 1919 and 1929 was carried out in the following manner:

		1919	1929
		(absolute values in millions of dollars)	
A.	Total capital from *Census of Manufacturing*	41,433	
B.	Estimated fixed capital including land	20,716	
C.	Estimated fixed capital based on *Statistics of Income*		27,410
D.	Fixed capital 1929 relative to 1919 (C÷B)		132.3
E.	Estimated value of building and equipment	20,411	
F.	Estimate of new capital expenditures, 1920–29		21,327
G.	Estimate of depreciation, 1920–29		14,889
H.	Net capital formation, 1920–29		6,438
I.	Value of building and equipment in 1929 (E+H)		26,849
J.	Value of building and equipment, 1929 relative to 1919 (I÷E)		131.5

Sources:

A. NBER Worksheets.

B. Fixed capital as per cent of total capital minus investment in securities equalled 49.1 in 1904 and 49.8 in 1930, both recession years; taken as 50 per cent in 1919, also a recession year.

C. See Appendix Table B.

E. Paul Douglas, *Theory of Wages* (Macmillan, 1934), p. 116.

F. Lowell Chawner, *Survey of Current Business*, March 1941, p. 10.

G. Solomon Fabricant, *Capital Consumption and Adjustment*, NBER, 1938, p. 32.

The absolute levels and relative changes on both bases are virtually identical.

For the next benchmarks, 1929 and 1937, the comparison entailing the least number of adjustments is the one based on net fixed capital excluding land.

		Dollar Amounts in Millions
A.	Net fixed capital excluding land, 1929, *Statistics of Income*	24,144
B.	Expenditures for structure and equipment minus capital outlays charged to current expenses, 1930–37	8,987
C.	Cumulative depreciation of structure and equipment	10,897
D.	Net fixed capital excluding land, 1937 (A+B−C)	22,234
E.	Net fixed capital excluding land, 1937, *Statistics of Income*	21,466
F.	Net fixed capital based on balance sheet data relative to net fixed capital based on capital expenditures (E÷D)	.965

Sources:

A, E. NBER Worksheets.

B. Wooden and Wasson, "Manufacturing Investment Since 1929," *Survey of Current Business* (November 1956), Table 1, p. 9. Estimate of capital outlays charged to current expenses supplied by letter by Mr. Wasson.

C. Wooden and Wasson, *op. cit.*, Table 2, p. 11 and letter.

For this period, the reconciliation is reasonably close and the difference is in the expected direction since one would look for a downward revaluation of balance sheet assets in a period of a slow recovery from a deep depression.

Gross fixed capital excluding land is the concept used for the remainder of the comparisons. Its use avoids many arbitrary assumptions in estimating depreciation and accelerated amortization.

		Dollar Amounts in Millions
A.	Gross fixed capital including intangible assets but excluding land, 1937, *Statistics of Income*	42,396
B.	Expenditures for structures and equipment, 1938-48	35,863
C.	Gross fixed capital excluding land, 1949 (A+B)	78,259
D.	Gross fixed capital including intangible assets but excluding land, 1948, *Statistics of Income*	77,094
E.	Gross fixed capital based on balance sheet data relative to gross fixed capital based on capital expenditures (D÷C)	.985
F.	Expenditures for structures and equipment, 1949–53	35,271
G.	Gross fixed capital excluding land, 1953, variant I (C+F)	113,530
H.	Gross fixed capital excluding land, 1953, variant II (D+F)	112,365
I.	Gross fixed capital including intangible assets but excluding land, 1953, *Statistics of Income*	113,794
	Gross fixed capital based on balance sheet data relative to gross fixed capital based on capital expenditures.	
J.	Variant I (I÷G)	1.002
K.	Variant II (I÷H)	1.013

Sources:

A, D, I. *Statistics of Income*, Part 2, raised to level of all firms.
B, F. Wooden and Wasson, *op. cit.*

For these periods also the two methods of estimation yield virtually identical estimates.

Summary

The annotations of the five sector estimates of wealth indicate that all possible routes are followed in arriving at the estimates. Censuses or balance sheet data were used to obtain the estimates for agriculture, mining, and manufactures; cumulation of annual expenditures for nonfarm residential construction estimates and a combination of cumulation of annual capital expenditures and balance sheet or census data for the estimates of regulated industries. The possibilities of testing the estimates by comparison with other estimates based on independent data and different estimating procedures are narrowly limited but run the full gamut from a completely independent estimate (all manufactures) to the complete absence of an alternative estimate (mining). Between these extremes is the alternative estimate for the agricultural sector based on a somewhat different methodology but involving much the same data that has gone into Tostlebe's estimates. The alternative estimate for nonfarm residential construction comes closer to being independently based but here, too, revisions for recent years of annual expenditures use census data to correct the level. In the case of the regulated industries only some of the intermediate steps of the estimating procedures are subject to this comparative test—and this only for the more important branches.

These notes also suggest that there are variants of the sector estimates that can be added together to obtain a larger aggregate. The highest common denominator is fixed capital (equipment and structures, excluding land), net of depreciation and valued in 1929 prices. The possibility of aggregating the sector estimates creates the opportunity of an indirect test of the aggregate of the sector estimates. The test, adapted from the one carried out by Simon Kuznets, consists in comparing the change in value of buildings and equipment derived from the sector estimates with the cumulation of net construction and net producers' durables, all in 1929 prices, of all private, profit-making sectors of the national economy, by decade intervals 1880–1948.[6] The latter estimates were prepared by Kuznets (Table 4). There is considerable independence in the estimation of the

TABLE 4

Net Construction and Equipment, 1929 Prices, Sector Totals and Commodity Flow Totals Compared, 1880–1948
(billions of dollars)

	6/1/1880 to 6/1/1890	6/1/1890 to 6/1/1900	6/1/1900 to 12/31/12	12/31/12 to 12/31/22	12/31/22 to 4/1/30	4/1/30 to 4/1/40	4/1/40 to 12/31/48
1. Total, five sectors	20.8	22.8	41.2	20.5	37.2	−8.6	24.6
2. Total private economy, excluding nonprofit institutions	21.3	31.0	53.5	20.5	44.8	−6.6	29.8
3. Difference: (2)–(1)	0.5	8.2	12.3	0	7.6	2.0	5.2

Source: Simon Kuznets, *Capital in the American Economy: Its Formation and Financing*, Appendix Table 35 (NBER, mimeographed).

two totals, more independence for the years preceding 1922 and less after 1922. Included in the total private, profit-making sectors and excluded from the total of the five sectors is the change in value of structures and equipment used in the construction industry, trade, finance, and services.

[6] I am indebted to Professor Kuznets for permission to use his material before he has published it. The data and observations are adapted from Appendix D of his summary volume on *Capital in the American Economy: its Formation and Financing* (mimeographed version).

The total of the five sector estimates should, therefore, be smaller than the total derived from flow of construction materials (or volume of construction) and producers' durables in private profit-making, industry, except for periods, if any, when net durable capital formation in the residual sectors can be assumed to be negative.

It is this modest test that the five-sector estimates pass since in no subperiod does the five-sector total exceed the total for the private, profit-making economy, although in one period, 1912–22, the difference is zero. This and the large difference in rate of change between the first and second decades for the sectors and the total suggest that the wealth estimates on either basis are more reliable for showing changes over the long term than over the short term.

COMMENT

RAYMOND W. GOLDSMITH, New York University and National Bureau of Economic Research

Creamer has produced so careful and circumspect a paper, systematically describing the estimates made for five main sectors of the national economy in connection with the National Bureau's study of capital formation and financing that not much remains for a discussant to say. I shall therefore limit myself to two comments, one referring to Creamer's paper and the other loosely connected with it, though prompted by it.

In the last few pages of his paper Creamer compares the total of the five separate estimates of sectoral capital stocks with an estimate of the capital stock of the entire private economy derived by Kuznets by accumulating, deflating, and depreciating total private gross capital expenditures. I suggest that Creamer is just a little too optimistic when comparing the two sets of figures. True, if the comparison is limited to the aggregate capital stock at the end of the years 1900 and 1948, the rate of increase seems to be about the same for the aggregate of the five sectors and for the entire private economy. The relation, however, is not nearly as satisfactory for decadal changes. Turning to the absolute level of the two estimates, it appears that Kuznets' totals for the entire private economy are fully one-fifth higher than the aggregate of the five sectors if the period from 1880 to 1948 is taken as a whole. This relationship seems reasonable, and that is all we can say because our knowledge about the smaller sectors outside the five big ones is so fragmentary. The picture, however, is again much less satisfactory for shorter periods. In some decades the difference between the two series is zero, or very close to it, leaving no net capital formation for some important branches of the economy—

444

including trade, services, and construction—which are not included among the five main sectors. Clearly, if decadal figures are wanted, either some of the sectoral figures have substantial shortcomings or the total is in error to a far from negligible extent.

What lesson does this hold for the future? It seems to me that one can conclude from the material marshalled by Creamer and from a consideration of the problems and potentialities of the two methods compared, that our best hope for the future is the systematic development of the perpetual inventory method of measuring the stock of capital, i.e., the cumulation of price-adjusted and properly depreciated figures for gross capital expenditures, sectorally classified and broken down by main types of expenditures, distinguishing at the very least structures, equipment, and inventories.

The indispensable basic material for the perpetual inventory method, the gross capital expenditure figures, are available since World War II by sectors separately for structures and equipment. Similar, though less reliable, figures can be developed for one or two decades preceding the war. Three obstacles, however, must be overcome before we can transform these gross capital expenditure figures —which themselves can stand a good deal of improvement—into estimates of gross and net capital stock. First, we must develop better price indexes for capital goods, irrespective of the relative weight we want to give prices in the secondhand market and reproduction costs. Second, we must make a considerable effort to develop more realistic figures for length of life, scrap value and loss of use-value of different types of capital assets. We know so little about appropriate rates of depreciation that all of the estimates we now have of capital consumption are of only very limited value. Third, we need at least one benchmark estimate of capital stock in the postwar period as we otherwise have no way of controlling the figures obtained by the perpetual inventory method. None of these tasks is more difficult than many statistical problems that we have solved. But all three are beyond individual research workers and even beyond the resources of the usual institutional research project in this field. This situation clearly presents a challenge to the federal government.

What is needed is a census of national wealth, not limited to any one approach, but exploring and utilizing all main avenues. The fact that the federal government abandoned its efforts to estimate national wealth with the attempt made for 1922, and apparently did so on the advice of a committee set up by the American Economic Association, should not be regarded as a precedent. We now know much more about the conceptual and practical problems of measuring national wealth than we did in the 1920's when national accounting was in its

445

infancy. We have many more and better primary data. Further, and possibly most important, we know that such a task can be successfully accomplished for many sectors and types of wealth on the basis of samples rather than requiring a comprehensive census type enumeration for every constituent of national wealth. Finally, a census of national wealth by the federal government now would not be an expedition into uncharted seas. Methods have been developed over the last decade, both inside and outside the federal government, that give considerable confidence that the work can be done if an effort of sufficient magnitude is made, and it would not be an effort of unreasonable size in comparison with other present-day statistical projects.

ZVI GRILICHES, University of Chicago

As I understand it, we are interested in "productivity" because we are interested in understanding the changes in output in the hope of uncovering the sources of our economic growth. We are interested in the forces that affect "output" because we hope, ultimately, to be able to affect them for the better. We approach this task first by trying to take into account the "obvious" factors: changes in labor and capital (and other materials if our output measures are gross). We measure these factors as best as we can, aggregate them using some sensible weighting procedure and get a "total input" index. We compare this index with our output index and call any discrepancy "productivity." Crudely speaking then, the "productivity" indexes measure those changes in output that have not been accounted for by the analyst's input measures. It is a measure of our ignorance, of the unknown, and of the magnitude of the task that is still ahead of us.

The task is to open this box, whose dimensions we now know, and see what is inside of it. Is it return to scale, the size of the market, changing market structure, changing quality of inputs, "pure" technological change, or something else besides all that? Therefore, I welcome attempts to measure quality changes in the labor and/or capital inputs and it does not worry me if this will drive the productivity index to unity. I would interpret that as a real gain in our knowledge of productivity.

Of course, one must beware of measuring quality tautologically and assuming away the answer. What we want are independent measures of quality. These are not easy to get and I am afraid that the threat of wiping out "productivity" completely via quality adjustments is not yet very great. There are too many other things that affect it. An attempt to do this for U.S. farm labor, 1940–56, will be

446

reported elsewhere.[1] I will only mention here that the increase in "quality" due to a higher level of education was just about counterbalanced by the increased proportion of women in the farm labor force. Measurement of quality is not easy, but it is not something that we should disregard.

Turning now to capital measures and Creamer's paper, I would like to sound an additional discordant note. As is often the case, the fact that several independent investigators come out at approximately the same place does not necessarily imply that they are close to the truth. They may be following the same blind alley.

The trouble with most capital estimates is that they are usually based on data that are a by-product of other calculations. The U.S. agriculture capital estimates, for example, are a by-product of the U.S. net farm income estimates. To get at net income the investigators needed depreciation figures, and to get at depreciation they needed a stock of capital figure. But what is good enough for net income calculations and for the income tax people, may be very far from what is wanted for productivity calculations. I would like therefore to illustrate, with the help of the U.S. farm data on motor vehicles and other farm machinery, the very real difference between alternative measures of capital. The difference is real because we do not have the information which would allow us to choose among all the alternative ways of measuring the "stock of capital."

That there is a difference can be quickly shown by comparing the Department of Agriculture (Tostlebe) estimate of the value of the stock of tractors on farms in 1940 (1935–39 dollars) of $509 million with the Goldsmith estimate of "cumulated net savings in tractors" in 1940 (1935–39 prices) of $891 million. Goldsmith's estimates are almost twice as large as those of the USDA, even though he is using the same data, the same conceptual procedure, the same deflators, and the same estimates of service life. The only difference between the two estimates is that Goldsmith uses a straight line depreciation scheme and the USDA uses a declining balance scheme. And that makes all the difference.

It can be easily shown that the USDA depreciation rates are much too high. Nevertheless, these are the estimates that underlie most of the farm productivity measures. The USDA, for example, uses currently an 18.5 per cent declining balance rate to depreciate tractors and has used higher rates in the past. This implies that a four-year-old tractor has only one-half of the "capital" contained in a new

[1] See my "Measuring Inputs in Agriculture: A Critical Survey," paper delivered at the Annual Meeting of the American Farm Economic Association, Ames, Iowa, August 11, 1960, pp. 9–11.

tractor. There is, however, a pretty good market for used farm equipment and used tractor prices are available back to 1937. The market depreciation rate is not higher than 11 per cent for tractors and is also lower than the USDA rates for the other items.[2] The official farm capital estimates, therefore, significantly understate the true quantity of capital on farms.

The underestimate of the stock of capital for productivity comparisons may be even larger than is indicated by the comparison of USDA depreciation rates with used machinery market data. Market value depreciation is affected by the physical deterioration in the services of a machine, by changes in the expected life of the machine, and by the expected rate of obsolescence. Only the first type of "depreciation" is relevant for productivity comparisons. The little data that we have seem to indicate that the rate of deterioration in the physical services of machines is substantially below their market value depreciation rates. For productivity measures, the one-horse-shay assumption may not be all that bad.

Table 1 summarizes five different measures of the stock of motor vehicles and farm machinery on farms. They are all based on the same

TABLE 1

The Stock of Farm Machinery, Tractors, Trucks, and 40 per cent of the Automobiles on Farms: Different Measures

Measures	1940 Value in 1935–39 Dollars (millions)	Indexes (1940=100) 1950	1956	1956 Value in 1935–39 Dollars (millions)
USDA[a]	2,456	215	267	6,565
Griliches[b]				
1. D.b.: 12 per cent	4,010	179	231	9,254
2. Net stock: 15–20 yr. str. line	3,823	205	306	11,699
3. Gross stock: 15–20 yr.	7,150	145	236	16,900
4. Logistic, depreciation	7,355	154	217	15,996

[a] Based on unpublished USDA data underlying the official depreciation estimates. Declining balance depreciation using (in recent years) 18.5 per cent for tractors, 22.0 per cent for automobiles, 21 per cent for trucks, and 14 per cent for other farm machinery. Average rate used is around 17 per cent (using 1950 stock values as weights).

[b] All the following estimates are based on the same USDA data but make different assumptions about depreciation.

1. Declining balance but only 12 per cent. Consistent with "market" depreciation figures.

2. Net stock—depreciated value of stock using straight line depreciation. Fifteen years length of life before 1940, twenty years since 1940. Comparable to Goldsmith estimates.

3. Gross stock—undepreciated moving fifteen year (twenty after 1940) total of past gross capital expenditures. Assumes that the flow of services is constant with age. "One horse-shay" assumption.

---

[2] *Ibid.*, Tables 4 and 5.

4. Logistic depreciation—based on "survival" information for tractors and grain binders (Tractor "survival tables" from A. P. Brodell and A. R. Kendall, "Life of Farm Tractors " (Washington, 1950), and A. P. Brodell and R. A. Pike, "Farm Tractors: Type, Size, Age, and Life " (Washington, 1942). "Survival" Table for grain binders from E. L. Butz and O. G. Lloyd, "The Cost of Using Farm Machinery in Indiana" (Purdue University, Agricultural Experiment Station, Bulletin No. 437, May 1939).) It is assumed that an investment depreciates to 10 per cent of its original value in twenty-five years and is scrapped after that. The pattern of depreciation is as follows: .990, .985, .975, .97, .96, .95, .93, .91, .88, .85, .81, .77, .71, .65, .59, .52, .45, .38, .31, .26, .21, .17, .13, .10.

As is seen from the figures in Table 1, the different measures of capital do not imply very different percentage changes, but they do imply substantial differences in the absolute amount of capital on farms. The "low depreciation" assumption results in somewhat smaller percentage increases, but in much larger absolute figures.

underlying data, using the same deflators, but differ in their assumptions about the rate and form of depreciation. Given the range of not unreasonable assumptions we can generate estimates of "capital" differing by a factor of three. I do not think that we have yet the knowledge which would enable us to choose among these estimates one "best" estimate. I do believe, however, that data are available or could be collected, both on used machinery prices and on physical deterioration with age, that would facilitate this choice. It may turn out, however, that we shall need very different measures of capital for different purposes. For an explanation of changes in the purchases of new machines we may need one measure of the existing stock of machinery; for an explanation of the changes in real output of the particular industry we may need rather different measures of the stock of capital. The relevant concept of capital depends on our question, and one concept will not answer all the questions that we may wish to ask.[3]

ROBERT W. BURGESS, Director, Bureau of the Census

Raymond Goldsmith and others suggest that a new census of wealth would be very desirable, and that such a census would, for instance, provide a benchmark or inventory that would thereafter be readily brought up to date and would be the foundation for standard ratios and distributions, facilitating detailed current wealth statistics.

While I agree that various censuses contribute helpful building blocks for an inventory of physical wealth, I am familiar with a number of cases in which there are unsolved, if not insoluble, problems when we try to express items of physical wealth in dollar terms in any reasonably uniform way. Just as illustrations:

[3] Some of the points raised in this comment are pursued further in my "Measuring Inputs in Agriculture," and "The Demand for a Durable Input: U.S. Farm Tractors, 1920–57," in A. C. Harberger, ed., *The Demand for Durable Goods*, University of Chicago Press, 1960.

1. While the 1957 Census of Governments derived a large number of ratios of sales values to assessed values for many kinds of real estate, actual free market transactions in the case of large industrial properties are so infrequent and so scattered over the country that the ratios in that field are not sound indications of exchange value.

2. There is no effective and comprehensive market price determination for used factory machinery and equipment. The theoretical principle of valuing such machinery on the basis of series of discounted present worths of net annual contributions of such machines to production has seldom been applied because the engineers do not feel that they have much foundation for guessing how the machine will be used over the next span of even ten or twenty years.

3. The value of minerals in the ground is highly conjectural and often controversial. The related concept of "discovery value" provides business for the tax courts.

I suggest, therefore, that the Census Bureau can make the greatest feasible contribution toward an ultimate census of wealth by contributing the results now provided by the various censuses and making some relatively modest changes and supplementary studies that will make these results more useful in the field of wealth. After more material of this general type has been accumulated, and more helpful conceptual analyses have been made, the Bureau might be in a position to cooperate effectively in conducting a single, comprehensive census of wealth.

Factor Substitution
and the Composition of Input

ERIC SCHIFF

MACHINERY AND ALLIED PRODUCTS INSTITUTE

NOTE: Grateful acknowledgment is due to John W. Kendrick, Charles L. Schultze, and Francis L. Hauser, who read an earlier draft of this paper and made valuable suggestions. Needless to say, the author alone is responsible for all shortcomings of the essay.

Scope of the Paper

THE introduction of a new method in the production of commodities or services regularly involves substitutions between input factors, including such "factors" as general business organization, technique of financing, etc. In the last few centuries the development of industrialism has been largely dominated by the substitution of durable producers' goods for human labor. The main stimulus for the absolute and relative intensification of investment in real capital was supplied by technological innovation. Substitution of real capital for labor in response to innovations which made the increased use of machinery and equipment technically feasible and economically profitable is even today the main instrument for actualizing productivity gains which the preceding change in the "production function" has made potentially available. However, even without change in technology, the rate of capital investment may be affected by changes in certain economic variables. This paper discusses some questions connected with the impact, upon the rate of mechanization and capital investment within a *given* technology, of exogenous changes in either of the following two variables:

1. The price of labor, by upward pressure on money wages. This is a chapter in the economics of factor substitution in response to a change in relative factor costs. The discussion on the following pages will be focused on the problem of evaluating the quantitative importance of this substitution effect, compared with other determinants of the relative intensity of capital investment. A few remarks will be added on the question of whether, and under what special assumptions, the stimulating effect of increased wage rates on mechanization and real capital investment may be welcomed as indirectly promoting general progress in industry.

451

2. The rate of the income tax imposed on industrial producers. While this variable is not itself a factor cost, it affects the (rational) choice between productive factors involving different degrees of capitalization. The mechanism by which, and the direction in which, this effect operates, will be made the subject of a brief analysis. Questions regarding the comparative quantitative importance of this variable, as well as questions of value judgment, will be left outside the discussion. But a brief glance will be cast at the probable connection of this mechanism with the development of capital coefficients in American industry during the last few decades.

The " Ricardo Effect" and the Development of Labor Productivity

It is rarely questioned that an upward pressure on money wages exercised by powerful unions may under certain conditions spur the adoption of more capital-intensive methods in industry. But as to the importance of this stimulus, compared with other incentives to increased investment in real capital, contemporary expert opinion is far from united. In a recent article "What Makes Productivity Grow?" Karl Borch of the European Productivity Agency, without definitely committing himself, inclines to the extreme view that the pressure for higher wages by organized labor, occasionally backed by legislation, is the main prime mover behind the steady increase in industrial productivity. (Borch seems to think primarily of labor productivity while management plays a more or less passive role.)[1] He says that little statistical evidence seems to be available to support any other hypothesis.[2] American union officials, trying to bring out the merits of an aggressive wage policy, have repeatedly reasoned along similar lines.[3] For a recent statement propounding the opposite view we may refer to Marvin Frankel's contention that the effect of upward wage pressures on the rate of investment in additional equipment can be no more than marginal by comparison with the

[1] *Productivity Measurement Review*, No. 14, August 1958, p. 28.

[2] *Ibid.*, p. 29.

[3] In a symposium based on talks given at the 1956 Pennsylvania State University Automation seminar (*Labor and Management, How They Look at Automation*), T. F. Silvey, of the National AFL-CIO Department of Education, epitomized this argument in favor of an aggressive union wage policy in the sweeping antithesis that employers were willing to use cheap labor as long as it was cheap, but turned to their engineers and ordered machines and equipment to take the place of men as soon as trade unions made labor expensive. (*Ibid.*, p. 74.) Cf. also S. Barkin, "Trade-Union Attitudes and Their Effect on Productivity," in *Industrial Productivity*, ed., Industrial Relations Research Association, 1951, p. 122.

really basic determinants of this rate.[4] The fact that so sharply divergent views have been advocated quite recently seems to justify taking another look at the matter.[5]

At the outset it will be useful to distinguish between two questions. For one thing, it has been asserted that an upward pressure on money wages stimulates discovery and invention by making the search for new labor-saving procedures even more imperative than it would otherwise be. Factual evidence on the quantitative significance of this tendency is scanty and inconclusive.[6] One leading authority has assured us some time ago, in fairly definite words but without going into corroborating empirical details, that collective bargaining does tend to accelerate technological discovery, and that this is one of its most useful effects.[7] On the other hand, a study of 1951 (which seems to be the only available empirical investigation) concludes that the effective rate of research and discovery in industry has little or no relation to either the level or the movement of wage rates.[8] Until substantial evidence to the contrary becomes available, the latter view must be regarded as the probable state of the matter, at least in this country.

The second question turns on the proposition that an upward trend in the price of labor accelerates the rate at which industrial management adopts labor-saving devices already known. The proposition defines a process of substituting capital for labor in response to the latter having become relatively more expensive, the assumption being that before the change in the cost ratio the various labor and nonlabor resources were used approximately in what was then the optimal (least-cost) combination. Of course, the incentive to substitute machinery for manpower becomes blunted to the extent that the upward push of wages raises the cost of machines, too. But it would probably be too mechanical to assume, as is sometimes done,[9] that machine prices always rise *proportionately* when wages go up.

[4] M. Frankel, *British and American Manufacturing Productivity*, University of Illinois Bulletin No. 81, 1957, p. 12, Footnote 5.

[5] For an earlier discussion, see Bloom and Northrup, *Economics of Labor and Industrial Relations*, 1950, Chapter 19.

[6] See the recent summarizing survey by G. H. Hildebrand, "The Economic Effects of Unionism," in *A Decade of Industrial Relations Research, 1946–1956*, Industrial Relations Research Association, Publication No. 19, 1958, p. 133.

[7] S. H. Slichter, *The Challenge of Industrial Relations*, 1947, pp. 90–1.

[8] G. F. Bloom, "Union Wage Pressure and Technological Discovery," *American Economic Review*, September 1951, p. 606 f. Cf. also J. Shister, "Trade Unionism, Collective Bargaining, and Economic Growth," *American Economic Review, Papers and Proceedings*, March 1954, p. 220.

[9] Cf. Friedrich and Vera Lutz, *The Theory of Investment of the Business Firm*, 1951, p. 137, and the literature quoted there.

Besides, it normally takes time for the effects of rising wages to work themselves through the price system. Sometimes, e.g., in the first postwar decade in this country, the rise in machinery prices has lagged the upward movement of wage costs quite markedly.

As Ricardo was one of the first to discuss this substitution,[10] it is today frequently referred to as the "Ricardo effect."[11] Under what conditions may this effect be expected to come into play, and how frequently are these conditions present in industrial practice? Let us first ask what light is shed on this question by the traditional text-book theory of the demand for productive inputs, that is, by the marginalist models which describe the connection between relative factor costs and the proportions in which the factors should be used to make net revenue a maximum.

One important qualification of the contention that a relative rise in the cost of labor is bound to stimulate capital investment is suggested by the marginalist approach itself, which postulates that any change in the relative costs of two productive factors generates not only a "substitution effect" but a "scale effect" as well.[12] The combined net impact of the two effects on the demand for each of the factors is quite different according to whether a change in the price ratio between the two factors is caused by a decline in the price of one factor or by a rise in the price of the other (or by a combination of both movements). Suppose that the cost of L (labor) relative to the cost of C (capital) goes up 5 per cent. Let us assume for the moment that the conventional capital/labor surface is a suitable analytical tool. This may have come about by a 5 per cent rise in the cost of L, the cost of C remaining unchanged, or by a 4.762 per cent decline in the cost of C, the cost of L remaining as before. In the latter case, the impact of the scale effect on capital investment is in the same direction as that of the substitution effect; they both stimulate it. Production as a whole becomes cheaper, total output of the final product, assuming an unchanged (downward) slope of the demand and marginal revenue curves, expands, and the demand for both C and L

[10] D. Ricardo, *The Principles of Political Economy and Taxation*, Chapter I, Sec. 5, Everyman's Library, No. 590, p. 25.

[11] The term was coined almost two decades ago by F. A. Hayek (*Profits, Interest, and Investment*, London, 1939, p. 8), who attempted to make this "effect" the cornerstone of a theoretical explanation of the upper and lower turning points of the business cycle. In this theorem, which we are not planning to go into, the term "Ricardo effect" refers, not to an exogenous wage increase originating in union action (the case we are concerned with) but rather to endogenous changes in real wages due to price level shifts as the economic system moves from one cyclical phase to another.

[12] See, for instance, K. Boulding, *Economic Analysis*, 3rd ed., 1955, pp. 764 ff.; P. A. Samuelson, *Economics*, 3rd ed. 1955, p. 482–3; R. G. D. Allen, *Mathematical Analysis for Economists*, 1947, p. 374.

rises (although the latter at a smaller rate). In the other case, only the substitution effect makes for enlarged investment; the scale effect acts in the opposite direction. A rise in the price of one factor while the price of the other remains constant is bound to exercise some upward pressure on the supply price of the product, even when factor substitution is possible in some degree. For the producing agency, the substitution of C for L is here, in contradistinction to the first case, always a "lesser evil" measure. While it reduces total cost below what it would be without the substitution at the new wage level, it cannot entirely prevent total cost from rising above what it was at the old wage level. Again assuming an unchanged downward slope of demand and marginal revenue curves for the product, this means that some depressing effect on the rate of the salable output is bound to remain despite the intervening substitution. In the net impact on the demand for C, the scale effect may in many situations outweigh the substitution effect. In other words, production may have to be curtailed to such an extent that even the demand for C, while rising relative to the demand for L, will decline absolutely, or at least in relation to what it would be had the price of L remained unchanged. In any event, the asymmetry in the manner the two effects combine in the two cases suggests one of the few safe generalizations about our question: Other things equal, a rise in labor costs (capital costs unchanged) should not be expected to stimulate real investment to nearly the same degree that an equiproportional decline in the cost of capital equipment (labor costs unchanged) would do.

The actual relative weights of the substitution effect and the scale effect in the case of a rise in wage costs depend on several variables, and the interrelations are, in part, rather complex. Thus, when the demand for the product is highly inelastic and the producer is therefore able to pass much of the wage increase on to consumers, the scale effect will not be much in evidence; but then the incentive to substitute will not be very strong either. Or, consider another variable, the relative importance of the wage bill in the expenditure budget of the producer. It has been emphasized that an addition to a wage bill which had already bulked large will make entrepreneurs more alert to substitution possibilities than a comparable addition to a relatively smaller wage bill would do.[13] However, in the former case there is greater likelihood that, after all substitution possibilities have been exhausted, the new wage bill will yet be too high to justify continuing the production on the former scale. Still another important variable is the size of the wage increase itself. Here again, a large increase will produce a relatively large substitution effect and a relatively large

13 Bloom and Northrup, *ibid.*, pp. 471 ff.

counteracting scale effect as well. In all these instances it seems hazardous to generalize about the net impact on the demand for capital.

For the rest, the net impact depends primarily on the extent to which substitutions of the kind here called for are possible in given situations. Thinking in terms of what has long been the basic analytical tool in the theory of the business firm, the neoclassical production function—with its gently sloping curves suggesting unbroken factor substitutability over wide ranges—one might be tempted to conjecture that opportunities for substitutions between labor and capital in response to even minor shifts in relative costs would turn up at every corner. Here, however, certain limitations of the conventional model in explaining the decision-making of individual producing units come into the picture. It may be useful at this point to recall some of these limitations before casting a brief glance at the empirical evidence.

In all commodity or service production, factor substitution is incidental to process substitution. Primarily and directly, it is processes, not factors, that are being substituted for one another. By the strict definition which activity analysis has adopted, and which is specifically tailored to reflect the economics of industrial decision-making, a process is a productive event (or a series of such events) in which inputs of specified quality (or input composites of specified qualitative and quantitative mix) are combined in specified proportions to produce output that is likewise specified as to qualitative composition. Two productive events that differ only in over-all scale of production are instances of the same process, although at different levels. Otherwise—when the qualitative input or output mix is altered, or when the internal ratios of qualitatively unchanged input or output elements are varied—the two productive events are instances of different processes.[14] Obviously, the technology available to a firm at any given "state of the arts" consists of what may be called a family of processes whose members are technologically substitutable for one another.

Let us now recall the basic marginalist model, the production function for a single output. In the two-factor case it is represented by a contour map on which technological possibilities of factor combinations for assumed output levels are pictured by a family of downward-sloping isoquant curves. Total factor cost at these levels is represented by a family of declining straight isocost lines, and the optimum level

[14] Cf. R. Dorfman, *Application of Linear Programming to the Theory of the Firm* 1951, p. 14.

456

of use of the two factors at any assumed rate of output is determined by the familiar tangency condition, the point of tangency shifting as the angle of the cost line (representing the ratio of factor prices) changes. Calling the two factors measured along the two axes "labor" and "capital," the question arises whether the substitution possibilities between labor and nonlabor inputs in industrial practice are as near-ubiquitous and as direct as this representation suggests.

They would be if all the families of processes covered by this representation were what we might call *input homogeneous*. Whenever, in producing some output, homogeneous labor can be combined in various proportions with individual capital goods, or with "kits" of capital goods whose aggregate size varies but whose internal composition remains constant as we change processes, we have an input homogeneous family of processes. In agriculture one can find some instances of this type: given quantities of practically homogeneous labor applied to larger or smaller areas of qualitatively equal land; homogeneous compounds of capital, consisting, e.g., of some more or less standardized combination of seed, fertilizer, manure, etc., applied in varying "doses" to given areas of land in cooperation with labor of unchanged quantity and quality. Here it is sometimes possible to vary, over relatively wide ranges, the quantities of individual capital goods or even of fairly complex composites of capital goods without altering the other specifications of the productive process such as quantity of labor used, general organization of work, etc. The relatively frequent occurrence of this invariance in agriculture is largely due to the fact that in this field there are changes of processes which do not involve any substitutions *between* capital goods.

In nonagricultural industry, where a change of processes usually does necessitate intracapital substitution, this invariance is rare.[15] It is present in certain special cases; if—to use an example given by Solow[16]—the intracapital substitution does not involve anything else than the use of aluminum fixtures in lieu of steel fixtures, the quantity of labor required is not altered, and the same is true of the other arrangements on the input side. Despite the technical difference in the two capital inputs, the two processes are here input homogeneous in our sense, and, for purposes of factor proportion analysis, representation of the two equipments as two different quantities of capital-in-general is operationally meaningful. In the great majority of cases,

[15] Friedrich and Vera Lutz, *op. cit.*, p. 7, emphasize that in the case of substitution between durable capital goods and labor the type of durable capital goods usually changes as the substitution proceeds. They hold that this fact makes the apparatus of constant product curves "clearly inapplicable."

[16] Robert M. Solow, "The Production Function and the Theory of Capital," *The Review of Economic Studies*, 1955, p. 103.

457

however, process variation by merely changing "doses" of individual input elements is precluded by fairly strict technological complementarity constraints. Most of the intracapital substitutions which in nonagricultural industry are normally associated with redesigns of processes affect quite a number of other input factors. They often call for far-reaching reallocations and reassignments among human as well as material input elements. Different machines require different numbers of machine attendants, etc.[17] In fact, given the present degree of technical specialization in industry, the family of processes making up the technology available at any given time to a productive unit in nonagricultural industry is predominantly input heterogeneous, its "members" being more or less sharply demarcated against one another by qualitatively and quantitatively specified sets of input factors (including such "factors" as organization, work outlay, etc.).

To be sure, this is not the whole story. It is sometimes possible to use several very different members of a family of processes side by side in various proportions (e.g., to move materials partly by hand, partly by processes involving various degrees of mechanization). Then something equivalent to substitution between labor and capital-in-general over sizable ranges may result in an indirect manner. In one particular field of industrial activity, materials handling, such possibilities are fairly common, and this may help to explain why, in this field, empirical research was able to trace stimulating effects of wage pressures upon the rate of mechanization with greater certainty than elsewhere. But even here, the decision to alter a combination of processes in response to some exogenous change normally affects a number of distinct inputs simultaneously. Hence, if one complicated combination is "least cost" at given prices of the various inputs, it may take a rather drastic change in the price of one single input to deprive the combination of its least-cost character. At more moderate price changes, the economic advantage of the existing combination will remain inframarginal, and no substitution of processes or factors will take place.

All this points to the conclusion that, at least in nonagricultural

[17] Solow, *ibid.*, p. 103, points out that even in the case of so closely similar capital goods as one-ton trucks and two-ton trucks the possibility of intracapital substitution is not invariant against changes in the factor labor, since this possibility depends technically on the number of drivers available. Solow uses the invariance criterion for deciding whether it is meaningful to sum up the various capital inputs in a single index figure defining a quantity of capital-in-general (scil. for the specific purposes of a production function—nobody doubts, of course, that for numerous other purposes it is perfectly legitimate to sum up one-ton trucks and two-ton trucks in an index representing "trucks-in-general"). We are using the same criterion to get a preliminary "feel" for the frequency or infrequency, in industrial practice, of direct interfactor substitution in the marginalist sense.

industry, marginal improvements—new machines or processes for whose profitable introduction a rise in the price of one input such as labor makes the decisive difference[18]—are less frequent than is suggested by the conventional smooth two-factor surface on which one factor is a generalized something called (physical) capital.[19]

Without attempting a systematic review of the empirical evidence on the Ricardo effect,[20] let us add a few observations on certain aspects which empirical research has brought to light. In this field one must guard carefully against *post hoc ergo propter hoc* inferences. In quite a few instances there is some indication of investment decisions having been influenced by an upward pressure of wages, but no safe conclusions can be drawn because of the difficulty of disentangling the effects of the changed factor price ratio from those of simultaneously developing technological invention, or economies of scale, or better capacity utilization, or several of these factors.[21] This difficulty reduces the value of attempts to trace the "Ricardo effect" in such indirect statistical indicators as the slower rise of labor costs compared with wage rates in individual firms or industries.[22] Attempts have been made to circumvent this difficulty by questionnaire investigations into the response of business firms to autonomous wage rises, but these have often produced answers difficult to reconcile with each other. It suffices to recall the discussion, which was conducted in the course of the "marginalism controversy" of the late 1940's, about the results of a questionnaire inquiry reported by Lester.[23] Of questioned firms from various industries, all of them having plants both in the North and in the South, the great majority denied that lower wages in the South caused the company "to use production techniques or methods in its Southern plants that require more labor and less machinery than the proportions of labor to

[18] Cf. Bloom and Northrup, *op. cit.*, p. 462.

[19] Indeed, in many instances even labor is so process-specific that it cannot be properly thought of as a homogeneous "factor" whose use in various processes is differentiated only by quantity.

[20] For further empirical material, see especially Bloom and Northrup, *ibid.*, Chapter 19.

[21] Cf. *Cost Behavior and Price Policy* (NBER, 1943), pp. 129 ff. The dearth of empirical material on redistribution of factors purely in response to increases or decreases in wage rates was emphasized by R. A. Lester, "Shortcomings of Marginal Analysis for Wage-Employment Problems," *American Economic Review*, XXXVI, I, March 1946. The statement by Joel Dean, *Managerial Economics* (1951, p. 254), that "much is known about the way in which they [high wages] alter the pattern of adoption of existing technology, hence the depth of capital" may well refer to theoretical rather than empirical knowledge.

[22] For a discussion of earlier attempts in this direction, cf. *Cost Behavior and Price Policy*, *op. cit.*, pp. 131–2.

[23] *Op. cit.*, pp. 74 and 78.

machinery used in its Northern plants," and stated that "the most efficient equipment available" was being used regardless of relative wage levels. On the other hand, when asked what adjustments in the South were most probable should a sharp narrowing of the North-South wage differential occur, many firms gave a higher probability rating to "introduction of labor-saving machinery" than to five other types of possible adjustment.[24] Somewhat more definite evidence was given not long ago by Brinker in a study analyzing the effects of the increase in the Federal statutory minimum wage rate (from $0.75 to $1.00 an hour) on March 1, 1956.[25] The study covered 136 medium-sized firms belonging to fifteen different low-wage industries in Oklahoma. Twenty-six of these firms paid all their employees more than $1.00 even before March 1, 1956. The remaining 110 firms had before that date employed some workers at less than $1.00. One among several classes of adaptive steps listed and tabulated by the author was "adding new machinery." Of the 110 firms which had to raise wages, thirty-four introduced new machinery in 1956, whereas none of the firms in the other group did so. Applying the conventional test for sampling reliability, Brinker's result is statistically significant well below the 1 per cent level. But the sample is obviously too local and sectional to support any far-reaching conclusions.

As mentioned above, materials handling is one field of industrial activity in which the operation of the Ricardo effect could sometimes be traced with a relatively great degree of certainty, one of the reasons being, probably, that marginal-improvement situations occur here relatively often. While even in this field the alternatives may be narrowed to either continuing entirely with the old procedure or switching completely to a new one (as was the case with some continuous-flow processes, whose introduction was, characteristically, quite independent of any change in wages), it is frequently possible, probably more frequently than in fabrication proper, to use little mechanized and more highly mechanized processes simultaneously in proportions which can be altered gradually as factor costs change. One major instance in which a differential effect of differential wage developments on the rate of mechanization and capital investment could be ascertained with some confidence was the gradual adoption of mechanical loading by American bituminous coal mining since the late 1920's. Regional differences in the rate at which mechanical

[24] On the difficulty of reconciling these answers, and the general difficulty of basing conclusions on questionnaire material of this kind, cf. F. Machlup, "Marginal Analysis and Empirical Research," *American Economic Review*, September 1946, p. 553 and *passim*.

[25] Paul L. Brinker, "The $1 Minimum Wage Impact in 15 Oklahoma Industries," *Monthly Labor Review*, September 1957, p. 1092 f. Cf. K. Borch, *op. cit.*, p. 29 f.

loading was substituted for hand loading were here for some time so definitely associated with regional differences in wages (caused mainly by differences in the extent of unionization) that little doubt remains about the causal connection.[26] It was even possible in this field to show the Ricardo effect operating in reverse—a rare feature which deserves a word in passing. Conventional marginalism portrays the factor substitutions induced by changing relative factor prices as perfectly reversible. In practice, substitutions in the direction of intensified mechanization are, if not completely irreversible, at least strongly unidirectional. In part, this may be due to a general "mechanization preference" which goes beyond the strictly economically rational: we are more reluctant, *ceteris paribus*, to abandon an already achieved degree of technical perfection than we are to introduce it as something new. Apart from this, however, the economic advantage of a more mechanized over a less mechanized method, even when only marginal at the time of the substitution, usually soon outgrows the marginal zone, owing to cheaper and better machine models becoming available soon afterwards, gradual improvement in handling the new method organizationally, etc. So the economic optimum life of the machines installed in the process of switching over to the more mechanized method normally outlasts the time during which the relative advantage of this method remains marginal. Hence, while wage increases do sometimes stimulate mechanization, subsequent wage reductions, although they may slow up the reinvestment turnover of the machines,[27] do not normally lead to outright demechanization (switchback from machine operation to hand operation). Loading in coal mines is one of the rare instances where this seems to have happened in some regions for a brief period during the early 1930's, thanks to the relatively long time during which in

---

[26] Cf. Hotchkiss, *et al.*, *Mechanization, Employment, and Output per Man in Bituminous Coal Mining*, WPA-Nat. Res. Project, Vol. I, pp. 136–7 (1939); Vol. II, pp. 209–10, 300, 333, 345; Ch. M. James, *Measuring Productivity in Coal Mining*, 1952, p. 68.

[27] If the outlays incurred by the upkeep of a machine rise as a result of rising unit maintenance costs, e.g., rising repair wages, the (optimum) service life of the machine will be shortened, i.o.w., the rate of reinvestment turnover will be accelerated. Declining unit repair costs will have the opposite effect. To the extent that unit repair costs depend on repair wages, we have here a case of true substitution between labor and capital. This relationship should not be confused with another one that operates in exactly the reverse direction. If maintenance outlays rise as a result not of rising unit repair costs but of a managerial decision to spend more on maintenance, the service life of the machine, to the extent that it is determined by wear and tear rather than by obsolescence, will be extended. There exists, obviously, a (limited) range within which it is optional for management either to make durable assets last longer by spending more on their upkeep or to cut maintenance costs by accepting a quicker reinvestment turnover. For a tentative empirical verification, see Solomon Fabricant, *Capital Consumption and Adjustment*, NBER, New York, 1938, pp. 103-4.

461

this case the economic advantage/disadvantage comparison between the hand process and the machine process stayed in the marginal zone.[28] Today, of course, this phase is long passed. During the late thirties, the economic superiority of mechanical loading gradually outgrew the marginal region, and today it is so far from this region that no practicable wage cut could induce mines where loading has long been mechanized to switch back to the hand process.

A more recent example was furnished by Melman's investigation of increased mechanization in British automotive industries between 1938 and 1950.[29] Characteristically, the clearest results were obtained for materials handling, where the switch to new methods consisted mainly of increased use of mechanized trucks and conveyors of various designs. Melman traced a fairly unambiguous pattern of decision-making at the firm level, leading from an increased labor/machine cost ratio as the motivation, to increased mechanization as the response. He emphasized that the process redesigns completed or under way in 1950 were technically possible in 1938 as well, but were not then introduced even by firms that were affiliated with American automobile producers and thereby had special knowledge of the more highly labor-productive methods used in the United States.[30] So the difficulty of disentangling the effects of changing ratios of factor costs from those of simultaneous changes in the known production function (technology) itself, could be kept out in this case.

It would seem that the statistical findings so far available are either too uncertain or too sectional and fragmentary to answer the question of the general importance of the Ricardo effect compared with other influences on the development of capital investment and labor productivity. While Borch may be right in saying that there is little statistical evidence to support any view which does not hold that wage movements are of paramount importance, neither is such a more conservative view clearly *refuted* by the available statistical record. All one can probably do at present is to fall back on the over-all impressions conveyed by broad historical development. And these impressions definitely confirm what is suggested by the theoretical considerations outlined above: the marginal improvement is not a much more frequent phenomenon than the marginal invention.[31] It is certainly

[28] Hotchkiss, *et al., op. cit.,* Vol. II, pp. 287, 290, 306; Ch. M. James, *op. cit.,* pp. 32, 62, 64.

[29] S. Melman, *Dynamic Factors in Industrial Productivity,* 1956, especially Part I. See also his article "What Does Productivity Measure? The Pulp and Paper Industry of the United States," *Productivity Measurement Review,* No. 6, August 1956, p. 5 f.

[30] Melman, *Dynamic Factors in Industrial Productivity,* p. 59.

[31] Cf. Bloom and Northrup, *op. cit.,* p. 462.

infrequent by comparison with redesigns of industrial processes independent of any change in labor costs. The great mass of these redesigns has always been, and probably will always be, the result of invention and discovery rather than of shifts in factor price ratios within a given technology. The economic advantages of the really path-breaking innovations have in most cases been inframarginal soon after their invention. No wage movement was therefore required to secure their prompt introduction, nor could acceptance of wage cuts have delayed their introduction appreciably. In this respect, the experience of 1923–29, a period of sharply rising production and productivity, goes a long way toward settling the question. During those years, while labor remained "cheap," entrepreneurs nevertheless did "turn to their engineers,"[32] and on an unprecedented scale.

There remains, of course, a further question which would require separate discussion: To the extent that a rise in labor cost does stimulate mechanization and capital investment, should one infer with some labor economists and other observers that this is one of the beneficial effects of an aggressive wage policy, one that goes a long way toward justifying such a policy even in the face of objections which otherwise would be serious? Suppose that an upward pressure on wages is about to push their level above what is in line with the currently prevailing level of productivity. Assume (for the sake of argument, without going into the pros and cons of this hotly debated question) that in a society insisting on unconditional maintenance of full employment the direct impact of such a pressure is inflationary. Is there something to be said for the idea that such increase in mechanization and labor productivity as may be indirectly induced by the pressure will neutralize some or all of the inflationary impact? The sketchy survey attempted in this paper does not provide the basis for a final answer, but it does provide at least one preliminary warning: If capital is substituted for labor in response to rising labor costs rather than to declining costs of capital equipment, then the effect on *total* productivity (output per unit of total input) is negative, despite the rise in *labor* productivity. This is an obvious corollary of the "scale effect" discussed earlier. Based as it is on an essentially static theory of production, this reasoning may not be the final answer in view of possible dynamic long-run repercussions. But it is certainly inadequate to discuss the question exclusively with an eye on what happens to man-hour productivity.

[32] Cf. Footnote 3.

Income Tax, Real Investment, and Capital Coefficients

This section analyzes, on the basis of a simplified model, the way in which the rate of income tax affects the choice between two durable producers' goods, one of which requires a higher capital investment but is superior in what we might call *productivity on current account*, meaning that it yields higher (time-adjusted) annual earnings. ("Earnings" are defined for this purpose as the excess of the revenue generated by the asset over the operating costs—before depreciation—incurred by it.) To simplify our model as far as possible, let us assume that the acquisition of either of two machines competing for installation is financed entirely by equity capital[33] and that neither of them has any salvage value at the end of its service life. Under these assumptions, the value of either machine at the time of installation equals the aggregate present worth of all future net (after-tax) earnings "stored" in it, discounting these earnings back to installation time at the prevailing rate of capitalization. Returns at that rate represent, in a sense, a cost element (the "opportunity cost" of investing in this particular activity), with the implication that a particular investment breaks even if it yields no more than a net return at just this rate. The cost price of the asset may or may not equal the aggregate present worth of the prospective net earnings. The stipulation that it does defines either a theoretical competitive equilibrium of all input and output values or, with respect to fluctuating real-world developments, a condition which the cost price must satisfy in a given situation to make the investment a break-even proposition. If the cost price of the investment equals its initial value as defined, the investment project is just at the borderline of eligibility.

Suppose now that we have the choice, for installation in some productive service, between machine A, having a specified schedule of prospective annual earnings, and machine B, which is more expensive but gives the prospect of a superior contour of annual earnings. Then we may study the development of the substitutability of B for A in response to changing variables by asking how the break-even capital costs of the two machines are related to each other at various income tax rates, or rates of capitalization, or other variables. For example, at any given tax rate, the break-even cost price—the maximum cost permissible if the machine is not to be a loss project—will normally be higher for the machine having greater current productivity. If the tax rate goes up, the break-even capital cost of either machine will be reduced—either will have to be cheaper to represent

[33] Under existing tax laws, the assumption that the investment is partially financed by borrowed capital would complicate the model because the tax status of interest paid on debt capital differs from that of return on equity capital.

464

a paying investment project. But in what relative proportion? Will the increase of the tax impinge upon the eligibility of the two in the same degree?

The first element we need for building up our model is the contour of annual before-tax earnings of the two machines. Empirically to ascertain the earnings imputable to individual machines is normally impossible, since the revenue generated by an individual productive asset operating in combination with many others is generally unknown and unknowable.[34] But if we assume the depreciation method used for tax purposes, and if we specify empirically plausible model values for a few variables characterizing the asset economically (initial capital value, service life, tax rate, and rate of discount), then we can deduce for our model the series of annual before-tax earnings (revenue minus cash operating costs) implied in these values, provided we make certain general assumptions as to the shape of the earnings series. Our first and most general assumption is that the earning power of a productive asset is normally highest at the time of its installation[35] and declines gradually as the asset ages, due to accumulating performance deterioration, rising maintenance and repair costs, and accruing obsolescence. For an asset with no salvage value, the point at which its earnings have dwindled to zero under the erosive impact of these forces, which marks also the running out of the after-tax earnings,[36] obviously defines the optimum economic service life of the asset. Finally, we need an assumption as to the most probable specific pattern of the declining before-tax earnings. While various assumptions are possible, a decline at a uniform (absolute) annual rate is the simplest of all, and since in the absence of special information this assumption is at least as plausible as any other, we shall use it here. Under this assumption, diagrammatical representation of the before-tax earnings as a function of time would show their contour to be a declining straight line, forming the hypotenuse of a rectangular triangle whose sides are the x-axis from the origin to the

[34] The way our accounting systems are organized, it is only for the enterprise as a whole, or at most for major divisions, that *both* earnings and cost data are obtainable from records. For the individual productive assets in a firm with diversified plant and equipment the books yield, at best, cost figures. No accounting record enables us to tell what fraction of the firm's gross earnings should be imputed to the contribution of this or that individual piece of equipment, nor is there any other basis for venturing such an imputation.

[35] Allowing, in some cases, for a brief initial break-in period, but this qualification does not alter the general picture.

[36] Assuming as we do that the tax-deductible depreciation charges end with the last service year, which is economically defined by the running out of the before-tax earnings, it is easily demonstrable that there are after-tax earnings so long as, but only so long as, there are before-tax earnings. See the model schedule on p. 476.

end of the service life and the y-axis from the origin to the level of the initial earnings.

The setting up of our model is now a simple matter. Let us use the following symbols:

V = initial capital value of the machine (equal to the aggregate present worth of all after-tax earnings) in dollars.

n = service life of the machine in years.

g = annual decline of the before-tax earnings in dollars.

i = rate (in decimals) of capitalization (discount) to be used in deriving V from the after-tax earnings.

v = the present-worth factor for i for one year, equaling $1/(1+i)$.

b = rate (in decimals) of income tax.

The first step is to develop the series of after-tax earnings. Since under our assumptions the annual depreciation allowance as charged for tax purposes is the only tax-allowable deduction from the annual before-tax earnings, we have, for each individual year,

After-tax earnings = before-tax earnings$-b \cdot$(before-tax earnings $-$depreciation allowance), or

After-tax earnings = $(1-b) \cdot$ before-tax earnings$+b \cdot$ depreciation allowance.

The series of before-tax earnings for successive years 1, 2, 3... $n-1$, n, is clearly: ng; $(n-1)g$; $(n-2)g$; ... $2g$; g. The series of annual depreciation allowances depends, of course, on the tax depreciation method. Let us first assume that straight-line depreciation is used. In this case the depreciation allowance remains constant from year to year at the level V/n.

We have thus the following series or schedule of after-tax earnings:

Year	After-Tax Earnings
1	$(1-b)ng \quad + \quad \dfrac{bV}{n}$
2	$(1-b)(n-1)g \quad + \quad \dfrac{bV}{n}$
3	$(1-b)(n-2)g \quad + \quad \dfrac{bV}{n}$

· · · · · · · · · · · · · · · · · · ·

$$n-1 \qquad (1-b)[n-(n-2)g] \quad + \quad \frac{bV}{n}$$

$$n \qquad (1-b)[n-(n-1)g] \quad + \quad \frac{bV}{n}$$

Assuming that the rate of capitalization remains constant during the service life, and treating the annual after-tax earnings as year-end magnitudes, we have for their aggregate present worth,

$$V = (1-b)ngv \qquad\qquad + \quad \frac{bV}{n}v$$

$$+(1-b)(n-1)gv^2 \quad + \quad \frac{bV}{n}v^2$$

$$+(1-b)(n-2)gv^3 \quad + \quad \frac{bV}{n}v^3$$

. . . .

$$+(1-b)[n-(n-2)]gv^{n-1} +\cdot \quad \frac{bV}{n}v^{n-1}$$

$$+(1-b)[n-(n-1)]gv^n + \quad \frac{bV}{n}v^n$$

for which we may write

$$V = \left[(1-b)ng+\frac{bV}{n}\right](v+v^2+\ldots+v^n)$$
$$-(1-b)g[v^2+2v^3+\ldots+(n-1)v^n].$$

For the two serial expressions in this equation, non-serial equivalents can be worked out. Doing this, and simplifying as far as possible, we finally obtain

$$V = \frac{gn(1-b)(in+v^n-1)}{i[in-b(1-v^n)]} \qquad (1)$$

or, if we take g as the dependent variable,

$$g = \frac{iV[in-b(1-v^n)]}{n(1-b)(in+v^n-1)}. \qquad (2)$$

The next step is to select for our representative standard model machine A absolute values of the variables whose proportions somehow reflect real-life conditions. Let us assume a cost price of around $10,000, a service life of fifteen years,[37] an income tax rate of 50 per

---

[37] This is close to what was obtained in the study by G. Terborgh, *Realistic Depreciation Policy* (Washington, 1954, p. 83), as the weighted average "life expectancy" of machinery and equipment in this country in 1953.

cent (for the reference model; later we are going to vary this rate)[38] and a rate of capitalization of 10 per cent per annum.[39] Then, assuming that the cost price of the machine represents its break-even cost value, and that the before-tax earnings imputable to the machine have a "triangular" contour, the series of these before-tax earnings is determined by equation (2). If V is exactly $10,000, we obtain $g = \$201.92$. For the purposes of our analysis it will be more convenient to construct the model the other way around, assigning a fully rounded figure to g and deducing the implied V, which in this case will be a nonrounded figure. Setting $g = \$200$, which means that the annual before-tax earnings start at $3,000 in the first year and decline to zero in the fifteenth year with an annual run-off of $200, equation (1) yields $9,905.06 for the break-even capital cost satisfying the stipulations of the model. Table 4 (page 476) makes explicit the development of all relevant annual values during the service life of this machine. It will be seen that the before-tax earnings each year just cover (1) the stipulated tax liability, (2) annual capital consumption in such amount that 10 per cent interest on the capital value still outstanding at the beginning of each year can also be covered, and (3) the 10 per cent interest on the unrecovered capital.

Suppose now that we are given the choice between installing this machine and installing a machine B of superior design whose before-tax earnings exceed those of machine A by $600 each year, owing to lower annual labor or nonlabor costs connected with its use, but maybe also to higher annual gross revenue due to better performance. As for the forces which gradually squeeze down the earnings as the asset ages—service deterioration, increase in certain operating costs, obsolescence—let us assume that they affect B with equal strength as they do A. Then the before-tax earnings of B start at $3,600 (20 per cent above those of A), decline by $200 annually, and run out in the eighteenth year. The breakeven capital cost of B is found by equation (1) to be $12,689.45. If the actual cost prices of the two machines are as indicated, there is economic indifference between the two alternative investments.

Let us now see how these breakeven capital costs change when we vary the rate of income tax over the full possible range from $b=0$ to $b=1$ (zero to 100 per cent tax). The technique of deriving the breakeven V's by equation (1) needs no further elaboration. Table 1 gives the results, and Chart 1 portrays them diagrammatically.

[38] The rate of 50 per cent approximates the present general rate of corporate tax (52 per cent).

[39] What rate of discount should be assumed as the "minimum attractive rate of return" for investment in plant and equipment, depends on various circumstances. Five per cent to 15 per cent may be a plausible range.

TABLE 1

Rate of Income Tax (per cent)	Capital Costs at Breakeven Level Machine A (Dollars) (1)	Machine B (Dollars) (2)	Excess of Col. (2) Over Col. (1) (Dollars) (3)
0	14,788	19,597	4,809
10	14,020	18,479	4,459
20	13,166	17,250	4,084
30	12,208	15,890	3,682
40	11,130	14,379	3,249
50	9,905	12,689	2,784
60	8,502	10,788	2,286
70	6,877	8,632	1,755
80	4,976	6,167	1,191
90	2,720	3,322	602
100	0	0	0

CHART 1

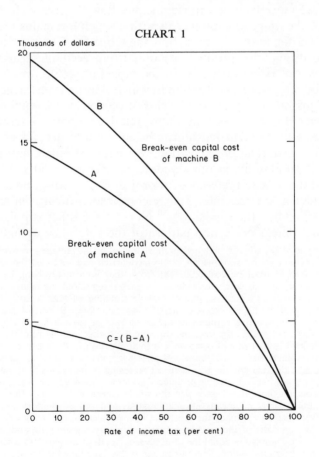

469

As expected, the breakeven capital cost of each machine is a monotonically declining function of the rate of tax. It is equally obvious why curve *B* remains above curve *A* at any tax rate short of 100 per cent, at which limit, for either machine, no cost price is small enough to make the investment break even. The main result of the analysis is the convergence of the two curves as we go up with the tax. Over the whole range of conceivable tax rates, any rise of the rate brings the breakeven capital cost of machine *B* closer to that of machine *A*.

The interpretation of this result for the problem of input substitution here analyzed is clear. The area between the curves *A* and *B* defines a zone of economic preference for the more capital-intensive project *B*. If the actual capital cost of *B* is within this area, rational decision-making will favor machine *B*; if it is outside the area (that is, above curve *B*), machine *A* will be preferred. The narrowing of the area as we move from left to right shows how the rise of the tax rate cuts into the range of capital costs within which *B* remains preferable to *A*. It shows, in other words, how the scope for *B* to give economic effect to its superior productivity on current account shrinks under the impact of rising tax rates. In the model as set up, this has been shown by reference to a situation in which *A* as an investment project is itself just at the breakeven level. But obviously, the finding about the impact of varying tax rates on the relative economic attractiveness of projects of different (current) efficiency is not dependent on this particular technique of exposition. We could stipulate any positive degree of profitability as our standard of reference, and would again find that the zone of preference for project *B* is narrower under a high than under a low tax rate. The reference to a breakeven situation merely simplified the exposition.[40] Nor are the other stipulations of the model (linear projection pattern of the before-tax earnings, etc.)

[40] It permitted us—this is perhaps its most important advantage—to avoid a controversial preliminary question which would have arisen had we based the analysis on the assumption of machine costs different from, that is normally lying below, their breakeven levels. In this case, we could not say anything about the relative economic attractiveness of the two assets without first determining whether a firm prefers the machine showing the higher excess of its true aggregate present worth (as derived by discounting its prospective earnings at the going rate of capitalization) over its cost price, or whether it prefers the machine showing the higher internal rate of net return, this rate defined as that rate of discount whose application to the prospective earnings equates their total present worth to the cost price. Demonstrably, it is only under certain conditions that the two criteria give identical preference rankings—a fact, incidentally, which shows that whenever durable producers' goods are involved, the basic assumption of "net profit maximization" on which the whole marginalist theory of the firm was originally built, is by no means as unambiguous and self-explanatory as was long believed. But when we approach the substitutability problem by analyzing what happens to the breakeven costs of the machines, that preliminary question does not arise. For when the cost is assumed to equal the total present worth of the earnings discounted at the going rate of capitalization, then this rate *is* at the same time the internal rate of net return as defined above.

vital for the general result[41] which may be summarized by saying that, other things equal, the "terms of trade" between a (currently) more efficient but relatively capital-requiring factor and a less efficient but relatively capital-saving one change more and more in favor of the latter as the rate of income tax is raised.

Since 1954, accelerated methods of depreciation for tax purposes have been authorized in this country, and American business, which until then had used straight-line write-off almost exclusively, has partially switched to the new methods. It might therefore be of some interest to ask how far the results of our analysis are modified if we use, say, sum-of-digits write-off, the most accelerated of the new methods authorized. In this case the annual depreciation charge varies with the age of the asset, being

$$\frac{2(n-t+1)}{n(n+1)} \cdot V$$

in the t'^{th} service year. For the rest, the buildup of the model completely parallels that outlined above for straight-line depreciation. Using the same symbols as before, we now obtain

$$V = \frac{gn(n+1)(1-b)(in+v^n-1)}{i^2n(n+1)-2b(in+v^n-1)} \tag{3}$$

and

$$g = \frac{i^2n(n+1)-2b(in+v^n-1)}{n(n+1)(1-b)(in+v^n-1)} \cdot V \tag{4}$$

Again setting $g=\$200$, $n=15$ years for machine A and 18 years for machine B, $i=0.10$ (10 per cent p.a.), Table 2 shows, and Chart 2 portrays graphically, the breakeven capital costs and their inter-relations:

TABLE 2

Rate of Income Tax (per cent)	Capital Costs at Breakeven Level		Excess of Col. (2) Over Col. (1) (Dollars) (3)
	Machine A (Dollars) (1)	Machine B (Dollars) (2)	
0	14,788	19,597	4,809
10	14,183	18,710	4,527
20	13,493	17,707	4,214
30	12,698	16,566	3,868
40	11,774	15,255	3,481
50	10,686	13,733	3,047
60	9,384	11,946	2,562
70	7,801	9,817	2,016
80	5,832	7,237	1,405
90	3,319	4,047	728
100	0	0	0

[41] On the degree to which the result depends on the assumption that straight-line depreciation is used for tax purposes, see the next few paragraphs.

471

For zero tax and 100 per cent tax, the figures of Col. (1) and Col. (2) are, of course, the same as in Table 1. In these two limiting cases the tax depreciation method makes no difference. Between, the permissible capital cost of either project is now a little higher, for any assumed tax rate, than under straight-line tax depreciation. Accordingly, the downward concavity of curve *A* as well as curve *B* is slightly more marked in Chart 2 than in Chart 1. This, of course, is

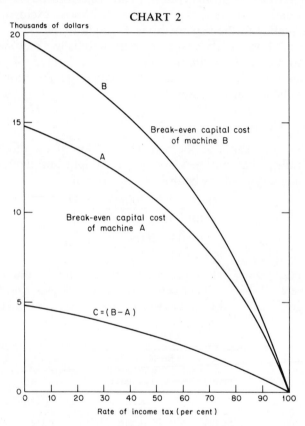

CHART 2

one of the facts in which the economic advantage of the accelerated write-off for the taxpayer finds expression. As the following comparison (Table 3) shows, the absolute advantage reaches its maximum around a tax rate of 70 per cent and tapers off on both sides of this value, whereas the relative advantage continues its increase.

But the excess of the breakeven capital costs of machine *B* over machine *A*—see Col. (3) in Table 2 and curve *C* on Chart 2—differs for any given tax rate only moderately from what it is under straight-line tax depreciation. Whatever the merits of the accelerated writeoff

TABLE 3

EXCESS OF THE BREAKEVEN CAPITAL COST UNDER SUM-OF-DIGITS TAX
DEPRECIATION OVER THE CORRESPONDING COST UNDER STRAIGHT-LINE
TAX DEPRECIATION

Rate of Income Tax (Per cent)	Machine A		Machine B	
	Absolute (Dollars) (1)	Relative (per cent) (2)	Absolute (Dollars) (3)	Relative (per cent) (4)
0	0	0	0	0
10	163	1.1	231	1.3
20	327	2.5	457	2.6
30	490	4.0	676	4.3
40	644	5.8	876	6.1
50	781	7.9	1,044	8.2
60	882	10.4	1,158	10.7
70	924	13.4	1,185	13.7
80	856	17.2	1,070	17.4
90	599	22.0	725	21.8
100	0	(28.4 lim.)	0	(27.5 lim.)

may be in other respects, it does not appreciably alter the impact of varying tax rates on the *comparative* attractiveness of (currently) more efficient but more capital-requiring durable inputs and less efficient but less capital-requiring ones. The level of the tax rate remains the more strategic variable.

Certain behavior properties of the capital coefficient—defined in most cases as the ratio of net real capital to current output—in American industry during the last few decades have recently attracted widespread attention. For an extended period before the 1920's, some investigations (Creamer, Fellner)[42] indicate a moderately rising trend of the coefficient in most industrial lines. Other studies (Goldsmith)[43] suggest that in this early period the trend of the coefficient was more or less horizontal. But all students are agreed that since the end of the great depression the over-all ratio of the net capital stock to output has been distinctly below its predepression level, notwithstanding a resumption of the upward movement around 1948.

[42] Daniel Creamer, *Capital and Output Trends in Manufacturing Industries, 1880–1948*, Occasional Paper 41, NBER, 1956; also "Postwar Trends in the Relation of Capital to Output in Manufacturing," paper presented at the annual meeting of the American Economic Association, Philadelphia, 1957 (*American Economic Review, Papers and Proceedings*, May 1958, p. 239 f.); William Fellner, "Long-Term Tendencies in Private Capital Formation," *Long-Range Economic Projection*, Studies in Income and Wealth, Vol. 16, NBER, 1954, esp. p. 306 f.

[43] See the tabulation of Average National Capital Coefficients 1897–1950 (based on structures and producers' equipment) in Raymond W. Goldsmith, "The Growth of Reproducible Wealth of the United States from 1805 to 1950," *Income and Wealth, Series II*, 1952, p. 297.

Various explanations of this development have been offered. To say that in the earlier period technical progress in industry seems to have been predominantly labor-saving rather than capital-saving, and that this proportion appears to have been partially reversed in the later period, would hardly amount to more than a re-statement of the finding about the development of the capital coefficient, unless the contention were interpreted in some specified sense. Thus it might be interpreted to mean that the character of the technological innovations themselves has changed so as to produce a relative reduction in required capital intensity.[44] To lift this idea from a mere conjecture to a plausible hypothesis may well be difficult. The technological innovations harvested during any given period invariably add up to an enormously diversified crop. To prove, or even to make it appear probable, that in some period the crop was on balance more capital-saving (or more labor-saving) than in some preceding or subsequent period, much more would be required than "selective enumeration" of the kind that was popular in the stagnationist literature of the late thirties. One would have to try to draw up, for each period compared, a list of at least all major innovations, to rank each of them according to the degree in which it is relatively capital-saving or labor-saving, to weigh each of them by some indicator of its economic importance, and to construct for each period some sort of a weighted average degree of capital-saving (or labor-saving) tendency of technological innovation as a whole. Obviously, this is a fairly hopeless task.

But the contention about the changed relative importance of labor-saving and capital-saving investments may be interpreted in a different and more promising way. We may ask this: Assuming that technology at any period produces capital-saving and labor-saving innovations in varying and unascertainable relative proportions, and granting that business always strives to economize on all input factors, do we have reasons to suspect that in the later of the two periods business was comparatively *more interested* in economizing on the factor capital, and therefore more interested in the specifically capital-saving potentialities of innovations, than it had been in the earlier period? A look at curves A and B on Chart 1 above suggests such a reason. The relevant thing, in this connection, is not so much the convergence of the two curves as the rather rapid decline of each of them over the range of tax rates from the moderate levels of the twenties to the present 52 per cent rate of the corporate tax. The higher the tax, the lower, for a productive asset of given productivity on current account, must be its original capital cost if it is to be

[44] This seems to be Creamer's interpretation; cf. "Capital and Output Trends, etc.," *op. cit.*, p. 76; "Postwar Trends, etc.," *op. cit.*, p. 251.

eligible for installation, which means that its net capital value at any time point during its depreciation period, as well as the ratio of this value to the current output imputable to the asset, must likewise be lower. The relationship may also be stated the other way around: the higher the tax rate, the higher, for any given net capital value, must be the current operating capacity of the asset. In general terms: For any productive facility, the economically justifiable capital coefficient declines, all other things equal, with the rate of the tax. This indicates that, by comparison with the period 1880–1920, the higher level of tax rates in the postdepression period presumably had a depressing effect on the over-all capital coefficient in American industry. To be sure, this effect was only one of several causes, and detailed empirical study would probably be required to evaluate its relative importance. But there is reason to think that it was one of the contributing forces.

COMMENT

VERNON W. RUTTAN, Department of Agricultural Economics, Purdue University

Schiff's discussion of the impact on the rate of technological change of upward pressure on money wage rates by unions deals with three questions: (a) Does upward pressure on money wages through collective bargaining stimulate discovery and invention in industry by making the search for new labor-saving procedures even more imperative than it would otherwise be? (b) Does an upward trend in wages accelerate the rate at which industrial management adopts labor-saving devices already known? (c) What is the effect of factor substitution induced by rising wage rates on total cost?

No attempt is made to deal exhaustively with the first question. He does, however, interpret the literature and Bloom's survey in particular to imply that "the effective rate of research and discovery in industry has little or no relation to either the level or movement of wage rates."

Any attempt to provide a convincing answer to this question will have to deal first explicitly with the question of whether collective bargaining has acted to raise wage rates above equilibrium levels. If, as Rees[1] and others[2] have argued, there has been no general tendency

[1] Albert Rees, "Wage Determination and Involuntary Unemployment," *Journal of Political Economy*, April 1951, pp. 143–53; "Postwar Wage Determination in the Basic Steel Industry," *American Economic Review*, June 1951, pp. 389-404. See also the comments by Lloyd Ulman, "The Union and Wages in Basic Steel: A Comment" and Albert Rees, "Reply," *loc. cit.*, pp. 408–33.

[2] H. M. Levinson, "Union Wage Trends and Income Distribution, 1914–47," *Michigan Business Studies*, Vol. X, 1951, No. 4; S. P. Sobotka, "Union Influence on Wages: The Construction Industry," *Journal of Political Economy*, Vol. LXI, 1953, pp. 137–43.

TABLE 4

Breakdown of Projected Earnings, Given the Stipulations Assumed for Machine A
(in dollars)

Year	Before-Tax Earnings (1)	Depreciation Allowance[a] (2)	Taxable Earnings[a] (3)	Income Tax[b] (4)	After-Tax Earnings (Service Values)[c] (5)	Capital Value Outstanding at Beginning of Year[d] (6)	Capital Consumption During Year[e] (7)	Interest on Capital Value Outstanding at Beginning of Year (10% p.a.) (8)	Col. (4)+ Col. (7)+ Col. (8)= Col. (1) (9)
1	3,000	661	2,339	1,170	1,830	9,905	839	991	3,000
2	2,800	660	2,140	1,070	1,730	9,066	824	907	2,801
3	2,600	660	1,940	970	1,630	8,242	806	824	2,600
4	2,400	661	1,739	870	1,530	7,436	787	744	2,401
5	2,200	660	1,540	770	1,430	6,649	765	665	2,200
6	2,000	660	1,340	670	1,330	5,884	742	588	2,000
7	1,800	661	1,139	570	1,230	5,142	716	514	1,800
8	1,600	660	940	470	1,130	4,426	687	443	1,600
9	1,400	660	740	370	1,030	3,739	656	374	1,400
10	1,200	661	539	270	930	3,083	622	308	1,200
11	1,000	660	340	170	830	2,461	584	246	1,000
12	800	661	139	70	730	1,877	543	188	801
13	600	660	−60	−30	630	1,334	497	133	600
14	400	660	−260	−130	530	837	446	84	400
15	200	660	−460	−230	430	391	391	39	200
		9,905					9,905		

a Col. (1) − Col. (2).
b 50 per cent of Col. (3).
c Col. (1) − Col. (4).
d Present worth, at beginning of year indicated, of Col. (5)—values still in prospect, discounted at 10 per cent p.a.
e First differences of Col. (6)—values.

for union pressures to push wage rates above equilibrium levels, one could hardly expect Bloom to find that such pressures have biased the general direction of innovation. As a minimum, it would seem necessary to identify specific instances in which wage rates have made substantial advances relative to the equilibrium level and then see if there was any response in either the level or the direction of research expenditures.

Schiff is willing to concede somewhat greater scope to the Ricardo effect—the effect of upward pressure of money wages on the adoption of known laborsaving devices—than on the rate of discovery of new labor-saving devices. He argues, however, that outside of agriculture and materials handling operations in industry, situations in which such substitution takes place are "certainly infrequent by comparison with developments which cause redesigns of industrial processes independent of any change in labor costs." In the very short run, which is the main focus of the controversy between Schiff and those who propose higher wages as a spur to increased labor productivity, one can hardly disagree that the opportunities for substantial direct factor substitution in modern industry are relatively limited. In the longer run, where the production function may resemble something closer to its classical form than do some of the models currently being employed, the possibilities for factor substitution may be considerably greater.

With respect to the effect of factor substitution induced by rising wage rates on total cost, Schiff correctly points out that, regardless of the effects on labor productivity, the effects on net returns or on total productivity must be negative.

The third section of Schiff's paper, the discussion of the impact of the corporate income tax on factor substitution, is the substantive contribution of the paper. His argument can be summarized as follows. Assume (a) an internal earning rate that is inflexible below a given level (10 per cent in the example presented), and (b) that capital acquisition is financed entirely by equity capital. In such a situation, a change in the corporate income tax has the same effect on factor substitution as a change in the required earnings rate. Thus, a rise in the corporate income tax, such as has occurred since the 1920's, encourages the substitution of processes that are relatively more labor intensive than would be employed in the absence of the higher rates. Within the set of assumptions imposed by Schiff, his analysis is formally correct.

Both of Schiff's assumptions are clearly essential to his conclusions. If, for example, we reverse the assumption of an inflexible internal earning rate by replacing it with the assumption that higher income

477

tax rates are completely absorbed by equity owners and are reflected entirely through reductions in the prevailing industry earnings rate, no convergence of the two break-even lines will occur. The same result can be achieved by assuming 100 per cent debt financing rather than 100 per cent equity financing. I do not want to become involved in any extended discussion of the incidence of the corporate income tax or of the feasibility of alternative debt-equity ratios. I do want to insist that empirically satisfactory answers to these questions must be found if the analysis presented by Schiff is to have more than formal validity.

It seems likely that the net effect of introducing more realistic assumptions with respect to tax incidence and the debt-equity ratio will be to produce a pair of break-even lines which, while not parallel, show only partial convergence. Any attempt to interpret the decline in the capital output ratio in terms of such partial convergence should also (a) provide some explanation of the factors which gave rise to a decline in the capital output ratio in a number of important industries before the corporate income tax rate became an important factor, and (b) evaluate the importance of the income tax hypotheses in relation to several other hypotheses which might be suggested to account for the observed decline in the capital-output ratio in broad segments of the economy during the last four decades.

I would like to present three alternative hypotheses. Two seek an answer in terms of limitations in the data. The third looks to a fundamental shift in the pattern of innovation itself.

First, one might hypothesize that the decline in the capital-output ratio represents but little more than the temporary impact of depression and war. Kuznets, writing in the introduction to Creamer's study of *Capital and Output Trends in Manufacturing Industries, 1880–1948*, points out that in the depression-dominated decade of the 1930's there would naturally be great pressure for economic use of capital and for a high ratio of replacement to gross capital formation with a consequent decline in the capital-output ratio. And "in the 1940's the extraordinary pressure, first of World War II and then of demand for peacetime goods during the postwar years, would make for a high and intensive rate of use of existing capital stock and hence, for a low capital-output ratio again in 1948."[3] Schiff has also emphasized this possibility.

There seems to be little doubt that the effect of depression and war has been to bias the data in such a manner as to overemphasize the extent of the shift in the capital-output ratio. As Kuznets points out,

[3] Simon Kuznets, "Introduction" to Daniel Creamer, *Capital and Output Trends in Manufacturing Industries, 1880–1948* (NBER, 1956), p. 8. (Occasional Paper 41.)

however, this argument fails to explain the very significant rise in the capital-output ratio that occurred in some manufacturing industries even before World War I and which occurred quite generally throughout private domestic economy between World War I and 1929.

A second hypothesis is that the measure of capital input employed fails to provide an adequate measure of capital inputs. In his paper on *Resource and Output Trends in the United States Since 1870*, Abramovitz points out that

"On the side of capital, there is a chronic underestimate of investment and accumulated stock because, for purposes of measurement, we identify capital formation with the net increase of land, structures, durable equipment, commodity stocks, and foreign claims. But underlying this conventional definition of investment is a more fundamental concept that is broader, namely, any use of resources which helps increase our output in future periods. And if we attempt to broaden the operational definition, then a number of additional categories of expenditures would have to be included, principally, those for health, education, training, and research."[4]

The Ruggleses, in their paper at this conference, have also stressed the inadequacy of capital-input measures, although on somewhat different grounds.

Again, one must grant considerable validity to this hypothesis. It seems unlikely, however, that improvements in measurement techniques would entirely destroy what appears to be evidence of a decline in the capital-output ratio during the last four decades. Creamer's experiments with alternative measures of capital input support the conclusion that a real decline in the capital-output ratio has occurred.

A third hypothesis suggested in a recent article by Henry Burton is that at the industry level the relative importance of labor- and capital-saving innovations is related to the stage of the industries' growth relative to advances in the basic scientific and technical fields on which the technology of the industry is based.[5] It is argued that the first applications of basic scientific or technical advances tend to be primarily labor-saving. After these basic advances have been translated into workable production processes and the technology

[4] Moses Abramovitz, *Resource and Output Trends in the United States Since 1870* (NBER, 1956), pp. 12, 13. (Occasional Paper 52.)

[5] Henry J. Burton, "Innovations and Equilibrium Growth," *The Economic Journal*, September 1956, pp. 465, 466. See also V. W. Ruttan, "Agricultural and Non-Agricultural Changes in Output Per Unit of Input," *Journal of Farm Economics*, December 1957, pp. 1566–76.

becomes widely disseminated, the industry's technology becomes subject to continuous experimentation and improvement. During this stage, increases in output per unit of capital input become an increasingly important component of the growth in output per unit of total input.

Burton's hypothesis does appear to be consistent with the history of at least three industries with which I am relatively familiar—the meatpacking, dairy, and fertilizer industries.[6]

This still leaves unexplained why capital-saving innovation should appear simultaneously in broad sectors of the national economy. An attempt might be made to bridge this gap by tying the above hypotheses with respect to the sequence of labor- and capital-saving innovation into the description of the sequence of innovation contained in the Schumpeterian theory of economic growth.[7] If Schumpeter's hypothesis with respect to long waves of inventive activity can be taken seriously, it seems likely that the first half of such a wave might well be characterized by a generally rising capital-output ratio and the second part by a generally declining capital-output ratio.

[6] Vernon W. Ruttan, *Technological Progress in the Meatpacking Industry, 1919–1947* (Washington: Govt. Print. Off., January 1954). (U.S. Department of Agriculture Marketing Research Report No. 59); C. E. French, and T. C. Walz, "Impacts of Technological Developments on the Supply and Utilization of Milk," *Journal of Farm Economics*, December 1957, pp. 1159–70.

[7] J. A. Schumpeter, "The Analyses of Economic Change," *Review of Economics and Statistics*, May 1935. Reprinted in American Economic Association, *Readings in Business Cycle Theory* (Philadelphia, 1944), pp. 1–19.

AUTHOR INDEX

481

SUBJECT INDEX

Agriculture: basic data, 152, 179–180; labor costs, 138; output indexes, 289; wealth estimates, 414–419
Amusement industry, production indexes, 298

Banking: basic data, 196; output measurement, 239; production indexes, 291–292
Broadcasting industry, basic data, 198
Business services, production indexes, 297

Canada, estimation of real product in, 10, 203-249
Capacity, measuring capital by, 402–403
Capital: capacity measurement and, 402–403; measurement of, 14, 16–17, 413–450; quantity of, as a concept for productivity measurement, 388–390; services of, 398–399
Capital formation: treatment in the national accounts, 17; valuation as a component of output, 399–402
Capital stocks and services, real: concepts of, 16, 387–411; existing measurements of, and their use, 391–398
Communications: basic data, 190, 191; production indexes, 294–295
Construction industry: basic data, 185–186; output indexes, 289, 290
Costs, see Factor costs; Labor cost; Unit costs

Depletion, economic effects of, 86–87, 89, 106-107
Diminishing returns, natural resources and, 79-86
Domestic service, measurement of output, 283–284, 296
"Double deflation," 4, 12

Employment: basic data, 159–161, 163; estimates of, 3, 6, 363–368; in natural resource industries, 109, 117–127, 143–147; per unit of output, 128–141
Extractive goods, relative prices of, 93–98

Fabricant-Geary output formula, 34
Factor costs, 214–217
Factor-saving shifts, 14
Factor substitution, input and, 19, 451-480
Financial institutions, measurement of output, 239, 291–292

Government enterprises, measurement of output, 282, 298

Hotels, production indexes, 296–297
Hours, basic data, 161, 163
Households, measurement of output, 282–283, 296

Income, national, 4; gross national by sectors, 287
Indexes: arbitrary nature of, 23; chain, 26n; classical theory, 24, 42; design of, 23–46; economic theory of, 23, 24, 42; free composition, 26n; historical, 23–24; sector price, 304–305; unit cost, 303–304; see also Price indexes; Productivity, labor, indexes of
Industry: estimates of real product by, 203–327; net output estimates in the U.S., 315–327; see also individual industries
Input: concepts of, difficulties in, 331–345; definitions of, 14; factor substitution and, 451–480; indexes, design of, 7, 23–46; labor, measurement of, 7, 14, 15, 347–386; measurement of, 3, 14, 331
Insurance: basic data, 196–197; measurement of, 237–238

Labor cost, in resource industries, 128–141
Labor input, measurement of, 7, 14, 15, 347–386
Legal services, production indexes, 298

Manufacturing: basic data, 153–155, 169–179; capital estimates for, 437–442; output indexes, 289, 290–291

483

STUDIES IN INCOME AND WEALTH

Volumes 1–25

Author and Title Indexes

AUTHOR INDEX
Volumes 1-25

(c = Comment; T.S. = Technical Supplement to Vol. 18)

Budd, Edward C., *22*: 231–274, 320–322 (c), 351–363; *24*: 365–398, 403–406 (c)
Burgess, Robert W., *25*: 449–450 (c)
Burroughs, Roy J., *12*: 159–163 (c), 190–218
Bye, R. T., *2*: 62–64 (c), 120–121 (c)

Caplan, Benjamin, *17*: 43–44 (c)
Carson, Daniel, *11*: 46–134, 144–150 (c)
Carter, Anne P., *19*: 287–310
Cavin, James P., *16*: 107–130
Cherin, G., *18* (T.S., Ch. 9): 3–34
Christ, Carl F., *18*: 137–169; *25*: 41–46 (c)
Christy, F. T., Jr., *25*: 109–141
Clark, J. M., *1*: 228–229 (c)
Clyman, Bernard, *10*: 133–159
Cobren, George M., *12*: 380–408
Cohen, Morris, *22*: 187–209
Colm, Gerhard, *1*: 175–227, 240–248 (c); *2*: 65–72 (c); *3*: 294–295 (c), 450–452 (c); *10*: 85–93, 124–217 (c); *16*: 38–40 (c); *18*: 315–317 (c); *20*: 113–133, 213–216 (c)
Cooper, W. W. *17*: 352–359 (c)
Copeland, Morris A., *1*: 3–34, 48–63 (c), 157–159 (c); *2*: 72–76 (c), 85–119, 130–135 (c), 167–172 (c), 240–243 (c); *3*: 295–300 (c), 390–391 (c); *6*: 37–42 (c), 91–92 (c), 136 (c); *10*: 61–63 (c), 120–123 (c), 133–159; *11*: 266–271 (c), 361–365 (c); *12* (Intro.): 1–17, 106–136; *14*: 250–251 (c); *16*: 373–375 (c); *18*: 285–288 (c); *19*: 280–281 (c); *20*: 19–95; *22*: 338–350, 375–379 (c); *25*: 69–74 (c)
Cornfield, Jerome, *10*: 321–324 (c)
Corry, Ormond C., *21*: 396–399 (c)
Cranmer, H. Jerome, *24*: 547–564
Crawford, Richard H., *5* (Pt. II, Ch. 3): 1–45; Ch. 16., 1–81
Creamer, Daniel, *18*: 362–366 (c); *25*: 413–444
Crum, W. L., *3*: 141–142 (c); *5* (Pt. II, Ch. 1): 1–58
Currie, Lauchlin, *2*: 267–291, 306–313 (c)

Daly, D. J., *21*: 33–34 (c)
Daly, James P., *19*: 57–89
Daly, Rex F., *16*: 131–189
Danhof, Clarence H., *24*: 312–315 (c)
Daugherty, Wayne, *5* (Pt. II, Ch. 14): 1–14
Deane, Phyllis, *8*: 147–174
Delaney, Marie M., *23*: 169–178, 352 (c)
Denison, Edward F., *10*: 3–22, 70–78 (c); *13*: 180–183 (c); *19*: 215–261, 281–284 (c); *21*: 161–179 (c), 366 (c); *24*: 399–403 (c); *25*: 347–372, 409–411 (c)

489

Reid, Margaret G., *10*: 311–317 (c); *11*: 179–206 (c); *13*: 125–179, 183–185 (c); *15*: 133–174; *21*: 267–270 (c), 314–315 (c)
Renne, R. R., *5* (Pt. II, Ch. 6): 1–28
Reuss, Lawrence A., *12*: 220–233
Rezneck, Samuel, *24*: 212–216 (c)
Richman, Raymond L., *25*: 74–76 (c)
Ritz, Philip M., *18*: 174–182 (c); *18* (T.S.): v–vii; Ch. 3, 3–93; Ch. 8, 3–75
Rosenblatt, David, *8*: 281–290; *18*: 29–31 (c)
Ross, Kenneth D., *22*: 275–300
Rothenberg, Jerome, *10*: 65–68 (c)
Ruggles, Nancy, *25*: 387–403
Ruggles, Richard, *16* (Intro.): 3–5; *20*: 101–104 (c); *25*: 387–403
Ruttan, Vernon W., *25*: 475–480 (c)

Salant, Walter, *3*: 217–293, 305–315 (c); *20*: 293–300 (c)
Sammons, Robert L., *12*: 550–567
Sands, Alfred, *23*: 207–236
Sapir, Michael, *11*: 275–351
Sauerlender, Owen H., *17*: 261–351
Schelling, T. C., *22*: 325–333
Schiff, Eric, *19*: 261–271 (c); *22*: 431–439; *25*: 451–475
Schultze, Charles L., *25*: 302–313 (c)
Schwartz, Anna J., *24*: 407–445
Schwartz, Charles F., *23*: 271–273 (c)
Schweiger, Irving, *13*: 483–554; *17*: 455–483; *23*: 281–284 (c)
Scitovsky, Tibor, *25*: 270–273 (c)
Segal, Harvey H., *24*: 565–570 (c)
Shoup, Carl, *1*: 251–281, 300–301 (c)
Shryock, Henry S., Jr., *21*: 377–391
Siegel, Irving H., *11*: 134–137 (c); *25*: 23–41
Sigel, Stanley J., *18*: 253–285, 288–289 (c)
Simon, Matthew, *24*: 629–711
Simon, H. A., *17*: 352–359 (c)
Simons, H. C., *2*: 255–259 (c)
Sirken, Monroe G., *23*: 127–168
Siskind, D. I., *18* (T.S., Ch. 4): 3–40
Smelker, Mary W., *16*: 333–364, 371–373 (c)
Smithies, Arthur, *8*: 49–72; *16*: 365–371 (c)
Snyder, Eleanor M., *11*: 259–266 (c); *23*: 321–344
Solow, Robert M., *25*: 64–69 (c)
Spencer, Vivian E., *25*: 141–147 (c)
Staehle, Hans, *11*: 223-251
Stallings, Carlyle P., *21*: 195–265
Steiner, Peter O., *23*: 347–350 (c)
Stewart, Charles, *3*: 97–128, 144–146 (c)
Stigler, George J., *25*: 47–63

494

495

TITLE INDEX

Volumes 1-25

(T.S. = Technical Supplement to Vol. 18)

499

Entrepreneurial Income (S. Lebergott), *22*: 470–486
Equivalent Levels of Living: Farm and City (M. Orshansky), *15*: 177–200
Estimated Income Distribution in Three Surveys of Consumer Requirements (C. Noyes and E. Hilgard), *8*: 265–277
Estimates of Real Product in the United States by Industrial Sector, 1947–1955 (J. Alterman and E. E. Jacobs), *25*: 275–313
Estimating Future Purchases of Capital Equipment for Replacement (R. N. Grosse and E. B. Berman), *19*: 389–417
Estimating the Number of Earners for Income Size Distribution Analysis (E. H. Welch), *13*: 561–571
Estimation of Real Domestic Product by Final Expenditure Categories and by Industry of Origin in Canada, The (V. R. Berlinguette and F. H. Leacy), *25*: 203–249
Extractive Industries (J. Lerner), *22*: 487–508

Factor Shares, 1850–1910 (E. C. Budd), *24*: 365–406
Factor Substitution and the Composition of Input (E. Schiff), *25*: 451–480
Family Income and the Income Tax Base (A. G. Hart and J. Lieblein), *8*: 237–262
Family Savings in Relation to Changes in the Level and Distribution of Income (D. S. Brady), *15*: 105–130
Farm and Urban Purchasing Power (N. Koffsky), *11*: 153–219
Farm Gross Product and Gross Investment in the Nineteenth Century (M. W. Towne, W. D. Rasmussen), *24*: 255–315
Feasibility of a Standard Comprehensive System of Social Accounts, The (M. A. Copeland), *20*: 19–111
Federal Statistics (W. L. Crum, C. L. Harriss, E. G. Keith), *5* (Pt. II, Ch. 1): 1–141
Field Surveys of Consumer Income: An Appraisal (R. Wasson, A. Hurwitz, I. Schweiger), *13*: 483–559
Final Demand Sectors (S. A. Jaffe), *18* (T.S., Ch. 1): 3–47
Financial Intermediaries (C. Warburton), *22*: 509–520
Financial Survey of Urban Housing, 1929–1933, The (D. L. Wickens), *5* (Pt. II, Ch. 15): 1–21
Financing of Capital Formation (D. H. Brill), *19*: 147–192
Fluctuations in the Saving-Income Ratio: A Problem in Economic Forecasting (F. Modigliani), *11*: 371–443
Forecasting Gross National Product and Employment during the Transition Period: An Example of the 'Nation's Budget' Method (E. E. Hagan), *10*: 94–130
Forecasting National Income and Related Measures (F. L. Thomsen and P. H. Bollinger), *6*: 169–204
Forecasts of Railway Traffic (Thor Hultgren), *17*: 363–380
Foreign Investment Aspects of Measuring National Wealth (R. L. Sammons), *12*: 550–578
Foreign Trade (M. Weitzman, P. M. Ritz), *18* (T.S., Ch. 3): 3–93

501

503

504

505